BAMBOOZLED
AT THE
REVOLUTION

BAMBOOZLED
AT THE
REVOLUTION

How Big Media Lost Billions
in the Battle for the Internet

JOHN MOTAVALLI

VIKING

VIKING
Published by the Penguin Group
Penguin Putnam Inc., 375 Hudson Street, New York, New York 10014, U.S.A.
Penguin Books Ltd, 80 Strand, London WC2R 0RL, England
Penguin Books Australia Ltd, 250 Camberwell Road, Camberwell, Victoria 3124, Australia
Penguin Books Canada Ltd, 10 Alcorn Avenue, Toronto, Ontario, Canada M4V 3B2
Penguin Books India (P) Ltd, 11 Community Centre, Panchsheel Park, New Delhi–110 017, India
Penguin Books, (N.Z.) Ltd, Cnr Rosedale and Airborne Roads, Albany, Auckland, New Zealand
Penguin Books (South Africa) (Pty) Ltd, 24 Sturdee Avenue, Rosebank, Johannesburg 2196, South Africa

Penguin Books Ltd, Registered Offices: Harmondsworth, Middlesex, England

First published in 2002 by Viking Penguin, a member of Penguin Putnam Inc.

10 9 8 7 6 5 4 3 2 1

LIBRARY OF CONGRESS CATALOGING-IN-PUBLICATION DATA
Motavalli, John.
    Bamboozled at the revolution : how big media lost billions in the battle for the internet / John Motavalli.
      p. cm.
    ISBN 0-670-89980-1 (alk. paper)
    1. Television broadcasting—United States.   2. Interactive television—United States.   3. Mass media—United States.   4. Internet industry—United States.   I. Title.
    HE8700.8 .M68 2002
    384.3'1—dc21   2002022969

This book is printed on acid-free paper. ∞

Printed in the United States of America
Set in Adobe Garamond
Designed by Nancy Resnick

To Nancy,

who recalls the brief interval

when I thought

I too was a dot-com millionaire

Boggle. Too much coming too fast to sort out. Too many named new things. Too much that needs explanation to even understand what it is, much less what it's for or what's remarkable about it. Too much that appears too consequential or inconsequential to take lightly figuring out which is which. And *it's all connected,* so any piece of confusion infects everything else. You don't know what to be impressed by. . . . The potential for being bamboozled is total.

—Stewart Brand, *The Media Lab*

ACKNOWLEDGMENTS

Susan Golumb, my agent, navigates the halls of publishing better than anyone I've ever met, and to her I owe a huge debt. Rick Kot made this sprawling manifesto into a book, and always shored up my flagging ego every time I lamented my lapses as a writer. I conducted well over 150 interviews for this book, losing count at some point during the process. Those who gave generously of their time, in no particular order, include Ted Leonsis, David Rheins, Kurt Sung, Melissa Blau, Mark Walsh, Jonathan Bulkeley, Walter Isaacson, Dan Okrent, Linda McCutcheon, Natalie Farsi, Tom Evans, Elizabeth DeMarse, Jeff Cunningham, Chan Suh, Andy Nibley, Jim Docherty, Richard Metzger, Craig Bromberg, Jim Moloshok, Jeff Weiner, Jim Banister, Scott Kurnit, Michael Mael, Pavia Rosati, Robert Levitan, Harry Motro, Jim Kinsella, Jake Winebaum, Errol Gerson, Jocelyn Greenky, Michael Wheeler, Eva Dillon, Dick Glover, Jeff Amorosana, Lee de Boer, Gene Quinn, Chuck Fletcher, Jane Weaver, Gerry Brown, Laura Berland, Evan Rudowski, Melanie Warner, Josh Grotstein, Martin Nissenholtz, Laura Brounstein, Larry Lux, Mitch Praver, Lisa Napoli, David Churbuck, Jim Spanfeller, Kevin Conroy, Dan Brewster, Jonathan Weber, Strauss Zelnick, Tom Wolzien, Tom Ryder, Kurt Andersen, Lee Masters, Whitney Goit, Andrew Rasiej, Bruce Judson, Oliver Knowlton, Stefanie Scheer, Alan DeBevoise, Andi Weiss, Harley Manning, Brian Hecht, Jeff Dearth, Alan Meckler, Curt Viebranz, Doug Greenlaw, Reg Brack, Chris Peacock, Mark Beneroff, Michael Rogers, Peter McGrath, Rick Smith, Jackie Leo, Tom Freston, Tom Phillips, Janice Page, Randy Coppersmith,

Betsy Richter, Dick Duncan, and many others too numerous to mention. Thanks to Michael Wolff, whose advice has been extremely valuable in this process. And I can't thank Tom Rogers enough for his generosity, friendship, and insight. Without all these people's help, this book could not have been written.

CONTENTS

I don't claim to be clairvoyant. When I started work on this book, I first saw it as a chapter in the ongoing history of what looked like a flourishing Internet business, a chapter in which the large-media moguls became hopelessly tangled and confused by the World Wide Web. In the seven-year period that began with the first hint of the arrival of the Web browser in 1993 and culminated in the AOL Time Warner merger at the beginning of 2000, there was enormous disruption of the media business as it was known then, a comfortable world comprising television, magazines, newspapers, and radio. The great media empires, consolidated into just a few big owners, as author Ben Bagdikian predicted in his seminal book *The Media Monopoly*, simply did not know how to deal with the Internet, which constituted a direct attack on the domination they had enjoyed for so long. I thought this made a fascinating case study of how business paradigms can be disrupted. But my initial vision quickly changed, as the story I had envisioned as part of an ongoing account suddenly had an abrupt end.

Starting in April 2000 but becoming definitive later that year, the Internet business I was writing about simply disappeared, leaving only a few battered survivors, including AOL Time Warner, Yahoo!, eBay, Priceline, and a few more. And of these, AOL Time Warner initially looked like the true success story, the one new-media company that appeared as if it would emerge from the business recession of 2001 with some of its once-lofty stature. AOL Time Warner had great assets, including the AOL subscription service, but most of its best holdings were "Old Economy": TV networks, a film studio, a record conglomerate, magazines, a powerful cable-TV operation. AOL's Steve Case, acting on advice from his top lieutenant, Time Warner veteran Bob Pittman, was the guy who had figured out that the old-media assets would endure, even if *Wired* magazine said they wouldn't. And Pittman had realized sooner than most that the majority of new-media companies lacked a solid "business model," some means to make money without continuing infusions of new cash. When he first started saying this in 1997 and 1998, it sounded like competitive AOL hype. Later he started to look less mercenary and more sanguine.

Ultimately Pittman and Case, who understood new media best, believed in the old assets more firmly than did Time Warner chairman Gerald ("Jerry") Levin, who, driven by fears that he would be left behind in the Internet revolution, chose to sell his company to AOL in January 2000, just as that revolution had peaked and begun its slow slide into nonexistence. A few months after the AOL Time Warner deal, the stock market crumbled, and Internet companies began to disappear. If Levin had waited a few more months, he could have picked up AOL for pennies on the dollar.

I was in a very good position to witness all this. I began work at a cable-TV trade magazine in 1985 in New York and worked for a variety of industry publications, including *Adweek*, seeing firsthand how a new-media form—especially cable—could disrupt and ultimately defeat much better entrenched rivals. In 1989, I became an editor at *Inside Media*, a magazine that covered television, magazines, and digital media, giving me a singular vantage point for the story I tell here. I left in 1995 to join MCI, in a doomed joint venture with Rupert Murdoch's News Corporation that was planned as a competitor to AOL. This massive dysfunctional partnership, profiled in this book, helped instill a sense of skepticism about technology that has stood me in good stead even as computers and the Internet became my central professional focus.

Later, as an Internet business consultant, I experienced the collision between new and old media, with all the industry's attendant dislocation, disruption, pain, and suffering that I detail in this account. I went back into covering the industry as the first Internet columnist at the *New York Post*, from 1996 to 1997, when many of these key events took place.

I later consulted for many major companies, including Primedia, Rodale, Hachette Filipacchi Magazines, Hearst New Media, BMG Entertainment, Bill Gates's Corbis Corp., Furniture.com (a November 2000 Internet casualty), InfrastructureWorld.com, and, most memorably, CMGI, which I joined in spring 1999. An "incubator" based in Andover, Massachusetts, that had dozens of Internet investments, CMGI had begun as a tiny, little-known company. By the year I joined, CEO David Wetherell had made the cover of *Business Week,* with an accompanying story implying he would quickly become a mogul on the order of Bill Gates. At that time, CMGI was an online behemoth that owned big stakes in AOL rivals AltaVista and Lycos, and saw itself as a direct competitor to AOL.

CMGI stock skyrocketed during this period. But starting in April 2000, the company suffered particularly harshly during the market's first correction, and now trades in the low single digits.

Wetherell went from being the toast of the town to just toast. Stock that was selling after a split at more than $150 plunged by the beginning of 2001 to $3. Venture capitalists started to refer to CMGI and other "incubators" as "incinerators." Internet business models suddenly stopped making sense. B-to-B (or business-to-business, companies that offered products to other businesses, not consumers) came to stand for "back-to-banking," and B-to-C (business-to-consumer) turned into "back-to-consulting."

For big media, which had belatedly, haplessly, and confusedly embraced the Internet, the sudden downturn caused massive headaches, with many of the public companies having to take charges in the hundreds of millions of dollars to pay for their Internet black holes. Disney was one of the hardest hit. But it was another media titan, Time Warner, that suffered the biggest meltdown. At Time Warner, what was involved wasn't a matter of writing off almost a billion dollars; it was about having agreed to trade tangible assets—its magazines, TV networks, books, and movies—for an intangible: AOL and whatever its future entailed. Time Warner was the only big-media company that didn't go back to business as usual in 2001—after the collapse of the Internet, and its bonding with AOL, it couldn't.

This book is about the ultimately quixotic effort by Time Warner and the other big-media companies to build Internet companies, a chimera that befuddled and bedeviled them, and ultimately produced fundamental shifts in the media business. One of the lessons that might have been learned from the cable revolution of the 1980s had been missed. During that era, most of the big success stories, including ESPN, CNN, TBS, the Discovery Channel, Lifetime, and USA Network, had been built initially by chance-taking entrepreneurs, while the big three TV networks—ABC, CBS, and NBC—had stood on the sidelines, spurning opportunities to invest in these companies even after it should have been obvious that they would make it. When big companies try to do things they're not geared up to do, they mostly mess up. It's like a Volkswagen assembly line suddenly being asked to start building Cadillacs. They simply don't have a clue, and all the machines are configured wrong. When the networks began dabbling in cable in the early 1980s, they came up with wacky ideas like pay channels offering live symphony broadcasts, an absurd idea that both CBS and NBC once championed. It took entrepreneurs to figure out that what people really wanted from cable was movies, sports, and news.

The story of big media's stumble with the Internet is similar, in that the antics and bumbling detailed here were almost painful to watch. It isn't pretty, but it was certainly an entertaining and wrenching debacle.

John Motavalli
April 2002

BAMBOOZLED
AT THE
REVOLUTION

The Chaos Engineer

Where else would you expect to encounter Carole Bayer Sager but in Beverly Hills? The fabulously rich Grammy-winning songwriter ("That's What Friends Are For"), former wife to both Burt Bacharach and Marvin Hamlisch, is the epitome of a particular type of show business success. One expects to find her shaking out her mane at the Jose Eber salon or lunching with other bejeweled matrons at Spago Beverly Hills. Indeed Sager's hair looks almost frosted in place, in a kind of spiky neo–Rod Stewart do that clearly requires a substantial investment. It is highly unlikely that there was anyone in September 2000 who looked less like a new-media executive.

But in September 2000 that is precisely where Sager was styling herself, and what is more, she had been selected as a featured speaker on a panel at an Internet conference. The venue for this gathering was the Beverly Hilton, on Wilshire Boulevard, an ungainly white building that goes off in several different directions simultaneously, in a manner typical of postwar California construction. The occasion was Digital Hollywood, an annual showcase for the myriad ways in which Hollywood, the entertainment community, the TV networks, and various show-business conglomerates had been attempting to start a big new revenue stream with CD-ROMs, Internet sites, or just about anything else "interactive." Carole Bayer Sager had just launched her very own web site, Tonos.com, a would-be music "portal" that she had founded with "Grammy-winning producer/composer David Foster and Grammy-winning singer-songwriter/producer Kenneth ('Babyface') Edmonds."

Sager had discovered the Internet, she told the assembled audience, partly because she liked to play backgammon at the MSN Zone web site. Name-dropping fearlessly, she added, "And Paul [Allen] likes to play chess online. And Warren [Buffett] finally went online to play bridge." She then explained that Tonos.com was already working out precisely as planned. The site had been established as a kind of music-oriented talent scout service. Only three days earlier, Sager had received a tape from a promising new singer/songwriter.

She paused a moment before breathlessly announcing: "*I have found an artist.*"

Of course, successful songwriters of pop tunes are always going to be inundated with tapes from aspiring "artists," whether they have a hugely expensive web site or not, but Sager didn't touch on that.

It's something of a truism that, in any gold rush, some people arrive very late to the field, either from the poorest strata of society, where information often fails to penetrate, or from the elite, which often doesn't pay much attention to trends until they're very well established or already in decline. This trade show, in fact, marked the culmination of an especially momentous period, one that suggested that such a decline might already be in the offing. Steven Spielberg, Jeffrey Katzenberg, and David Geffen, the high-profile trio that had founded DreamWorks, had just pulled the plug on their never-launched Pop.com, a ludicrous and hugely expensive attempt at an entertainment web site. A few months before, another big Hollywood Web effort, Digital Entertainment Network, had crashed to earth with rumors of its outrageous extravagance, sexual harassment by its principal, and the sheer stupidity of its operations. And only a week before, New York's Pseudo.com, a so-called online TV network, had announced a bankruptcy filing, laying off 175 employees and shutting down what had been touted as a future entertainment conglomerate.

Each of these companies had proclaimed with a huge amount of hubris and arrogance that it would take over the entertainment business, and watching them crash and burn had become a favorite spectator sport in resolutely analog Los Angeles and New York boardrooms.

"I took a couple of calls from Josh [Harris, the founder of Pseudo]," recalls Lee Masters, a former executive at Viacom's MTV, most recently the CEO of Liberty Digital, a large Los Angeles–based venture fund backed by entertainment/cable mogul John Malone. "The first time, he said to me, 'We're going to be bigger than Viacom.' All I could think of was, 'These guys are not for us.'"

Seated with Sager on the dais at Digital Hollywood was Neil Braun, a former president of the NBC network who had tried to launch another entertainment "portal" called iCast with the high-flying Internet "incubator" CMGI, only to clash with CMGI's David Wetherell over the direction of the company.

Braun was now suing Wetherell for tens of millions of dollars he was asserting was owed him under a contract he claimed Wetherell had breached. As a sign of how interbred this world had become, Sager's Tonos.com had some names associated with it that were familiar to Braun, including, as CEO, none other than Matt Farber, who happened to have been the chief operating officer at iCast and who, before that, had been in charge of MTV Networks Online for eight years, through all of its early incarnations. Farber had been hand-picked by Neil Braun to run day-to-day operations at iCast, which focused on music and movies, targeting teenagers and college kids.

A celebrated figure in the industry, Braun has the diminutive stature and slight build of Bob Balaban, the actor who played, coincidentally enough, the president of NBC on *Seinfeld*. Braun had parlayed his NBC experience into a big job at the hugely trendy CMGI, where expectations were so high that on the day Neil's hiring was announced in 1999, with the underlying theme that CMGI would now take on Yahoo!'s Broadcast.com, CMGI's "market cap" (the value of its outstanding stock) had increased by more than a billion dollars.

By the time of Digital Hollywood, however, Braun was no longer really a player; in fact, he was now running a small start-up in Astoria, Queens, called Vast Video, from which he was hoping to distribute 11,000 instructional and how-to videos on the Internet. With his corruscating lawsuit against Wetherell, Braun had not actually made much money out of the Internet boomlet of 1998 and 1999. Not surprisingly, despite the new video start-up, he had grown hugely cynical about the Internet and his role in it. Despite his presence on the panel that day, Neil Braun had become convinced that the online entertainment business was proving to be little more than a joke.

"I started iCast, and nine months into it I told David Wetherell that I'd built a business plan that I didn't believe in," Braun lamented to the panel's audience, sounding as rueful as anyone would who had discovered that his stock options, once valued at more than $100 million on paper, were now virtually worthless. "Content as the magnet for traffic on the Web is the wrong business model."

That line was coming to have more and more resonance. What Braun was saying was that media and entertainment companies sinking billions of dollars into the Internet and interactive media over the past seven years had been a wrongheaded move. Of course, he was also implying that the very premise of the conference he was addressing—which was, after all, about online entertainment and media—was misguided. After trying to reinvent himself as a dot-com guy, Braun admitted, "I concluded that I'm a card-carrying suit and I'm proud of it. There are only two ways that the entertainment business works. Either you attract enough eyeballs to sell advertising, or you make a product that is so compelling that people will pay for it. I don't see either one out there."

The Internet business was turning out to be the most mercurial, infuriating, fast-paced industry ever invented. As soon as a company managed to master the latest "business model" or newest "paradigm," it was being denounced in magazines like *Wired* or *The Industry Standard* as old news, ridiculously yesterday, a sign of cluelessness. It was hardly surprising that, in such a stampede, almost nothing the entertainment business put on the Web seemed to be working.

Yet many of the shell-shocked attendees at Digital Hollywood were nervously reassuring themselves that this, too, would pass. Have a little patience, they argued. After all, hadn't it taken Time Inc. ten years to make a profit on *Sports Illustrated*? But the magazine business hadn't changed significantly since Benjamin Franklin started his own effort in the 18th century. In the six years the Internet industry had existed in the United States, the nature of that industry had changed so many times and had gone through so many different incarnations that it might as well have been started anew with each one. It was hugely disrupting, upsetting, and infuriating for people like Neil Braun, a highly paid entertainment executive who was valued for his insider's knowledge, to fail so publicly in bringing entertainment to a promising new medium. He simply didn't want to believe it was his fault.

In spring 1992, eight years before Sager took the stage at Digital Hollywood, another interactive conference had taken place at the Beverly Hills Hotel. The HomeMedia Expo was the forerunner of Digital Hollywood. In 1992 there was no Internet, at least as far as Hollywood and the media business were aware. But the HomeMedia Expo did have CD-ROM magazines, video games, and interactive TV.

The HomeMedia Expo, later renamed Digital Hollywood, was founded in 1992 by New York–based Victor Harwood, an outspoken character who claims to have coined the expression the Digital Revolution. Harwood says he came up with that title because it was his revelation, way before a Web browser made its debut, that eventually people would want digital media products in their homes, and that Hollywood producers could capitalize on it. In 1992 this was a revelation. The conference was renamed Digital Hollywood for the 1994 event because it had become clear to Harwood that the movie business would get involved in a major way.

Harwood is a kind of conference and event machine, having developed and produced more than 100 conferences and events. Harwood says that his first new-media conference was called Hyper Expo, which he founded in 1987 and later renamed Multimedia Expo. In exploring the brand-new medium of hypertext in the late '80s, Harwood had stumbled upon its inventor, Theodor Holm ("Ted") Nelson, born in 1937. Nelson, who was studying for a master's in sociology at Harvard and was an acquaintance of LSD king Timothy Leary while Leary was still at Harvard, took a computer course and wrote as his term project a thesis on how text could be manipulated in a nonlinear format. In 1965 Nelson came up with the term "hypertext" to describe what he was after. The hypertext project evolved into something called Project Xanadu, which was supposed to be the first word-processing system, although it never was commercially released. Later, as Digital Hollywood evolved out of Home-Media, the connection with the more outrageous elements that dominated the early shows was phased out.

At the 1992 expo the top celebrity in attendance was Timothy Leary. Through Nelson, who later became a professor in Japan, Timothy Leary became a big part of Harwood's early conferences, when, many thought, it would be people on the fringe who would carry off a revolution in communications. Whippet-thin, dressed in a blue denim outfit, sporting a close-cropped white beard, Leary was an omnipresent force at the HomeMedia Expo of 1992, serving, if it was possible, as the closest thing to a guru the emerging new-media field could boast of. Leary and his entourage, which consisted then of various acid exponents, failed actors, and other Hollywood hangers-on, exemplified what passed in 1992 for cutting-edge thinking.

One panel at the 1992 HomeMedia Expo, which started characteristically 30 minutes late, was typical of the inauspicious signs as the new electronic Age of Aquarius dawned. Leary stumbled to a microphone and proclaimed, "My name is Timoth . . . ," only to be drowned in the electronic whine of howling feedback. "Technicians" were called in, the sound system was restored, and Leary began a diatribe. "We're groping through blue-sky media," he'd told the crowd, many of them sporting the hippie/Charles Manson look then favored by computer programmers. "We must be compassionate with each other because we don't know what we're talking about," he urged in an ironic premonition of Neil Braun's admission eight years later.

The acid avatar held up the April 6, 1992, issue of *Newsweek,* which heralded a cover story called "Computers to Go: The Next Electronic Revolution." "It's a little early in the morning"—in fact, it was 10:30—"to start a computer revolution, but we're doing it. It's particularly exciting for me, because we have some of the most avant-garde future pilots of the electronic business here." That was Leary's most lucid moment. Later, in response to a question, he began shouting, "I have to have control. I'm a chaos engineer. Control is the domain of Darwin and Newton." The audience went wild.

Leary wasn't the only participant at the HomeMedia Expo with visions of engineering his way to a bright technocratic future—Technocracy for a new generation of space cowboys. Speaker after speaker seemed to think that somehow, someway, technology would free the world from stifling big-media domination. New technology would usher in the kind of freedom that Leary and his acid-taking minions had once promised.

Yet dissenting, sober voices were already being raised. Many big-media observers were then convinced that new technology wasn't necessary, and that it would be too expensive to program competitively for audiences smaller than those served by cable TV. Betsy Frank, then an ad executive at Saatchi & Saatchi advertising, now the chief researcher at MTV Networks, posed a key question. "I'm not complacent about it, but right now the missing piece is going to be the software that is different enough to make the consumer invest in a new technology," she told *Inside Media,* a trade publication. The Internet never produced a compelling piece of entertainment software like *The Sopranos* or *Friends* because it wasn't designed to do that, and such stuff costs too much for a medium like the Web.

Frank could not have realized how prescient she was.

In the eight years that passed between these two Beverly Hills conferences, worlds collided, almost literally, with rockets glaring red and then sputtering out. The Internet industry, hyped as the future of all communications, had a dramatic birth and died in this brief period, leaving those who had participated in it and those who had just stood on the sidelines just as confused and bewildered when it was all over as Timothy Leary had been when he stood on that podium in 1992. An industry that promised the moon and ultimately delivered much less, an industry that was supposed to change the world, utterly failed to do so.

Between 1992 and 2000, all the major media companies took some steps toward integrating themselves into the "New Economy," but only one bet its future on technology, losing control of itself in the process. The sole exponent of big media to sell itself to a new-media company was Time Warner, and its ever-hopeful CEO Jerry Levin, who saw the road to that Nirvana technology "highway" as his future, whether delivered through cable systems or the Internet. The story of Time Warner's failed quest to master technology is central to the larger story of big media's hugely disruptive effort to conquer Internet content. Time Warner gambled far more than money on this fight; it gambled its independence and its survival as the company that Henry Luce had founded in 1923.

Bob Pittman, who became the co-COO of Time Warner after the AOL Time Warner merger, likes to say, with a large dose of irony, "The only business that looks easy is one that you don't know much about." If ever there was a phrase that summed up big media's Internet meltdown, it's that one.

At every media company, in the second half of the '90s, a beleaguered new-media division was assigned the thankless task of trying to make sense of the Internet. Almost universally, these groups were given small or virtually nonexistent budgets, an offshoot of the common proviso that all departments of a company had to make money. The only way such units could be profitable in this period was to hook up with AOL, Prodigy, or CompuServe, and that is what all of them did, to greater or lesser degrees. At Time Warner, however, the dream was more lofty. Time Warner, almost alone among media businesses, set out to dominate interactive media, because Levin was a true believer. In hindsight, it should have been clear that new media was never going to have it easy at the entrenched media companies, where the editors of magazines and newspapers and the top executives of TV networks regarded this pesky new rival as little more than a drain of resources and personnel from their profit centers. Chaos was going to ensue, and it did. And when it did, there was no chaos engineer to straighten it all out.

In hindsight, too, the parties involved could have recognized that they had actually participated in, or at least anxiously watched, a dress rehearsal for the Internet disaster. In the early 1990s, the telephone companies had promised they could deliver video on demand and other applications over their lines. All of these efforts failed, despite reams of rhetoric and press releases. Why? Because telephone companies might have wired your block, but they weren't programmers. You program your own phone with whatever you say into it. If you libel someone, that's your lookout. Phone companies, even if the fancy technology they promised had worked properly—which it didn't—were monumentally uncomfortable with the idea of being TV programmers and editors. Added to that, many of these companies were far more interested in the coming wave of big mergers, which yielded such giants as Verizon, than they were in delivering TV to the household.

Yet no one seemed to be paying close enough attention the second time around, and as it happened, the 2000 Digital Hollywood really was the beginning of the end. If they couldn't figure out how to program entertainment and news for the Internet, then they didn't want to play at all. By late 2000 and the first part of 2001, media companies massively retrenched their commitment to the Internet, all of them going through a massive round of layoffs. Again, the only member of the big media club that kept its eye on the Internet prize was Time Warner, and that was a consequence of its merger. Ironically, Levin's decision to sell out to AOL in January 2000 had been made at the very height of the Internet craze. Much of the Internet business on which he was fixated, which he sold his company to join, simply died after April 2000.

To be sure, it was a slow but inexorable decline. For much of 2000, the Internet business—and the Nasdaq as a whole—was like that often-cited frog in a pot of water placed over a flame. The frog doesn't notice the change in temperature as the heat gets turned up, but it's eventually boiled to death. Despite occasional rallies and hopes for a return to good times, it became clear as 2001 progressed that the halcyon days of dot-com good times were over for good.

During the go-go years of 1997 through early 1999, executives everywhere were shedding their ties and suit jackets as a sign of their embrace of the dot-com business. At the formal public announcement of the AOL Time Warner "merger" in January 2000, Steve Case wore a tie, while Jerry Levin had taken his off for the first time any staffers could remember. The message was clear: The two sides were diligently learning the cultures of their opposites. By late 2000, most executives had put their ties and jackets back on, convinced that the tried-and-true methods that had ruled their careers and lives until the recent dot-com blip were the soundest. In the end, it was almost as if the Internet culture had never existed.

To fully understand what happened at Time Warner and other media companies during the Internet craze, you have to go back a year or so before the World Wide Web became reality, when a powerful dream otherwise known as Time Warner's Full Service Network proposed to bring a limitless "information superhighway" to the TV of every American. Companies like General Electric had been promising a better future through technology since the 1950s and early 1960s, and Americans had eagerly bought into the idea of all-electric kitchens and atomic power as part of the progress that was our birthright and a panacea for all that ailed us. Thirty years later, a man named Levin believed he had seen an even richer technological future for all his countrymen. In 1993 he proclaimed it to the world.

CHAPTER 1

"I Stake My Career on the Full-Service Network"

On December 14, 1993, Time Warner CEO Gerald Levin stood on a stage in Orlando, Florida, and promised the future. It would be found, he explained, in an unassuming cable box produced by Silicon Graphics, the key to a futuristic cable system called the Full Service Network.

Five hundred invited journalists and a gaggle of top technology executives had gathered at the Sheraton Hotel to hear Levin introduce the interactive two-way cable system that would revolutionize communications. "Sooner isn't only better," Levin told the enthusiastic crowd. "Often it's everything. FSN will drive home this lesson with unforgiving velocity."

A somewhat ungainly man who then sported a cropped moustache, Levin was in his element. Uncomfortable in one-on-one encounters, he was a classic corporate creation, most at home in boardrooms and on the stages of big auditoriums, where his public pronouncements were carefully managed. He liked to make big proclamations, announcing he was transforming the world with a flick of a switch, convinced he could translate the dreams of his engineers into massive business success.

That day Levin stated, without fear of contradiction, that Time Warner would invest $5 billion in building FSN-style systems throughout the millions of homes served by Time Warner Cable. Within Time Warner, there was little challenge to Levin's vision, and that situation was institutional. With a compliant board and no strong executives challenging his rule, Levin was free to indulge his ideas with few checks and balances, despite the fact that the cost of developing the infrastructure needed to carry out Levin's promises was staggering. Levin and the CEO of Time Warner Cable, the burly Joe Collins, weren't underplaying that; in fact, they were celebrating it.

"FSN required more lines of computer code than was needed to put men on the moon," Collins boasted. Collins has a deep, rumbling voice and a demeanor so intimidating that reporters likened him to Lurch, the sepulchral butler on *The Addams Family.* But he was a Levin man, owing his promotions up through HBO to the top cable job solely to Levin. While he may have had private reservations about the FSN, they have never seen print.

In the 1993 Time Warner annual report, Levin was explicit about how much was riding on the FSN, noting that FSN venture partner US West was also fully committed. "In total, including US West's billion-dollar investment, we plan to spend $5 billion over the next five years on the FSN," he told shareholders. The FSN wasn't just a "cable strategy," he emphasized, but a complete, overarching event that would revolutionize operations at the media giant. "As we see it, the FSN is a uniquely powerful tool for achieving new levels of growth in all our businesses, enabling us to market and distribute our creative material in print, audio, video and film directly to consumers, on demand. Equally, it endows us with an unprecedented ability to meet the individual needs of consumers for information, entertainment, personal transactions and telecommunications."

In a Q&A-format interview included in the annual report, Levin was even more expansive. "You're spending billions of dollars to build Full Service Network systems," his unidentified questioner noted. "What convinces you this investment will generate a good return?"

"We're not just comfortable with this investment, we're excited about it," Levin replied. "Even if you're conservative in your assumptions, even if you simply look at existing dollars spent today by consumers and advertisers and you project only a modest shift of revenues to electronic delivery, this investment makes sense. Our assumptions aren't based on the creation of wholly new forms of expression or of consumer behavior—though we're convinced those will ultimately be very significant."

Levin noted that home catalog shopping brought in $51 billion in 1993, while local telephony generated $80 billion and home video $17 billion. The clear implication to shareholders was that, by encompassing all these businesses, the FSN would ultimately deliver similar numbers.

"Then consider that we will be able to add value, convenience and enjoyment for the consumer. We can cost-justify our investment strategy even if we capture only a small percentage of those revenue opportunities—and even if the pies weren't to grow significantly larger." Levin went on to speak of the "vision" that created Time Warner and firmly established FSN as being in line with that same vision. The FSN, he stressed, "is the ideal model for information superhighway convergence."

There's that pesky term, "information superhighway," the precursor of the World Wide Web and the dry run for the Internet. It was also, in fact, the first inkling that media companies had that they could scope out a future beyond the confines of their newspapers, magazines, cable systems, and TV networks. Most people have probably heard the expression hundreds of times without knowing exactly what it meant. When deployed in the early 1990s, the term had a certain *Rashomon* quality to it, into which media types and journalists tended to read whatever they wanted.

In 1995 the U.S. Department of Commerce attempted to define it this way: "The 'Information Superhighway' is an expression used to cover the global network of telecommunications and information technologies used by the international community to conduct commerce, educate, entertain, and inform its citizens." In other words, the idea referred to virtually any form of electronic communications, an amorphous mass that broadly promised amazing new applications that were themselves no easier to explain.

Like a lot of catchphrases, the "information superhighway" was really a marketing slogan, arising out of a planned merger between the so-called RBOCs (regional Bell operating companies) and cable. Until the early '90s, phone companies and the cable-TV industry didn't really work together much, seeing each other as eventual competitors. But cable's greatest visionary, John Malone, CEO of TeleCommunications, Inc., had a different concept. In Malone's grand vision, cable's programming services would combine with the superior switching power and universal network power of the RBOCs to create a mammoth, high-speed pipe into every American home. This vision was, for Malone, primarily a way of pumping TCI stock with promises of future revenue from interactive services. Like Levin, Malone was well aware that promising stock analysts expansive new revenue from interactive services was good business. Unlike Levin, Malone never committed much R&D and actual development costs, because, as a trained engineer, he knew much of what he was promising wasn't economically feasible.

In the early '90s, TCI tested Video on Demand, the supposed killer app of broadband services. The test actually used young people on roller skates feeding a huge well of video tapes into a bank of VCRs. If someone requested a movie, a TCI minion would skate over to the tape library, fetch the appropriate tape, and feed it into a VCR. What the test found was that customers would buy three or four movies a month priced at $3 or $4 each. This proved that VOD wouldn't bring in much more than, say, HBO, which was priced to consumers at about $10 per month and was much cheaper to deliver. After this test, Malone and his top lieutenant, John Sie, decided to compete with pay channels HBO and Showtime with their own pay movie channels, Encore and Starz. But they still paid lots of lip service to the information superhighway.

In the late 1980s, TCI, with its complicated financial structure and tendency to hold back investing in physical plant, was not an exciting company for many analysts, who believed that the days of fast growth for cable were over. Now that cable had become fully "penetrated" and most Americans could subscribe if they wanted to, how could TCI hope to get the financial community to become fully engaged with the stock again? For Malone, the answer lay in a union of cable and telco, a union that wasn't a proven entity but one that nevertheless had huge promise.

Malone's argument did seem sound: Cable on its own is not really an interactive medium. While you can use it to change the channel, when it comes time to order from the Home Shopping Network, you have to dial an 800 number to do it. You can't, in other words, talk back to your TV set, even with a digital box. In TV-industry jargon, that would require "two-way capability," the ability for cable lines to carry a signal a consumer generates back to the headquarters or "head-end" of the cable system for processing. If your system were capable of doing that, it could generate revenue that would be much greater than the $75 or so an individual customer paid for a complete package.

In the late '80s and early '90s, phone companies began to claim that they could offer precisely this kind of interactive power to the cable-TV world. Bell Atlantic (later Verizon), for example, among the largest RBOCs and the one that served the Northeast, announced that it had developed a technology called Stargazer that would enable consumers to view any movie they wanted, simply by pressing a button on a keypad and accessing a menu featuring thousands of films. While this was the same kind of capability cable operators were promising, the telcos claimed they could accomplish this by using ordinary copper "twisted pair" telephone lines, which were already delivering phone service into more than 100 million households, and a new "box" that sat on top of a TV set and could process these complex two-way signals.

If this was really possible as claimed, the telcos could instantly make cable seem outdated. The Stargazer technology was showcased at the industry's

Western Cable Show in Anaheim in 1992, although the movie being shown broke up and froze halfway through the demonstration.

Movies were hardly the only service promised. The phone companies, mindful of their own stock prices, were promising an entire array of services delivered through this new form of interactive television, ranging from home banking to travel and restaurant reservations and home shopping. Everything that is accessible today via the Internet—through services like Amazon.com, eBay, or AOL—was announced as immediately available in the early '90s by the RBOCs, made possible by an alphabet-soup array of new technologies like ADSL and ISDN. Each of these fast-paced technologies promised to deliver only the TV images and information that a given consumer would want. In this way, an information superhighway could be conceived in which information went two ways, not just one. This is a classic cornerstone of the consumer marketplace: that choice is always best. True happiness is always just a purchase away. That halcyon promise of two-way technology was enough to inspire floods of flowery prose about "empowering" the consumer, and publications like Time Inc.'s *Fortune* devoted breathless cover stories to the oncoming revolution in the once-stodgy world of telecommunications. The real goal was to get the consumer to buy more things and use more services over a two-way cable device.

The key to this plan was getting consumers to transfer a lot of their offline purchasing to their cable boxes. To this end, early efforts in interactive TV, such as GTE's experimental shopping service Main Street, had nomenclature that heralded a revolution that would eliminate the need for giant shopping malls. Just as the mall had once eclipsed America's Main Streets, interactive TV would now eclipse the mall.

Not surprisingly, such brave promises by the likes of Ray Smith, CEO of Bell Atlantic in the early '90s, caused a brief panic among cable operators, who worried that telephone companies could simply "overbuild" or bypass their cable systems, which had cost billions of dollars to construct. If their stocks weren't going to be demolished, they had to come up with an alternative plan, and quickly. When the hugely hyped merger between Bell Atlantic and TCI (then the biggest corporate merger in history) fell through and a series of similar alliances also failed to materialize, the cable industry had to think fast to protect its interests. Cable had to deliver what the telcos had promised, and do it in a big way.

Its solution was to duplicate the very same hype regarding expanded services that the RBOCs had started, and to insist that it could do it better. For Jerry Levin, presiding over the second-largest cable company (Time Warner Cable), it became almost an article of faith that his engineers, working with New Economy companies like Silicon Graphics and Microsoft, could actually deliver on the promises made by the telcos.

To understand why Levin placed so much faith in cable-delivered interactive television, you also have to delve into his psyche a bit, a task made somewhat harder by Levin's unwillingness to subject himself to close scrutiny. Few journalists have gotten close to this stiff, formal man, who scrupulously avoids one-on-one interview situations in which his views and vision would be questioned by an informed interrogator, and who is known for feeling the burden, as one wag put it, of always being the smartest person in the room. "If he wants your opinion, he'll give it to you," quips Curt Viebranz, a former new-media executive at Time Inc.

Levin's belief in the power of new technologies as a panacea has been strongly shaped by his own history in moving Time Inc. away from its sole reliance on print into television, helping the cable industry to explode, and changing the way Americans entertain themselves. This was a time when the concept of putting a TV signal on a satellite transponder, for distribution through cable wires, had never occurred to the big-three networks (ABC, CBS, and NBC), which relied on broadcasting their signals to TV antennas. It was cable mavericks like Levin and Ted Turner who realized it could and should happen.

Significantly, Levin never worked at any of the company's print properties and always had a decidedly video-centric view of media. A 1960 graduate of Haverford College, a small institution that would play a significant role in his life (he would later recruit several key executives who had attended the school), Levin got his law degree from the University of Pennsylvania in 1963. During the only part of his life that he actually practiced law, from graduation until 1967 Levin worked as a lawyer for a Manhattan firm, Simpson Thacher, and Bartlett. From 1967 until 1971, he worked at the Development and Resources Corp., ending up as general manager and chief operating officer of the investing and management company. When that company was acquired by International Basic Economy Corp. in 1971, Levin served as IBEC's representative in the Shah's Iran for a year.

When he joined Time Inc. in 1972, it was as vice president of programming at the still-gestating HBO. He had no experience in programming anything, but in 1972 his willingness to take on this tricky assignment and his belief in the premium TV concept were probably enough to recommend him. The pay-TV service had been the brainchild of Charles F. ("Chuck") Dolan, who dubbed it initially the Green Channel, but then sold the fledgling concept to Time Inc. in 1972, going off to start his Cablevision Systems cable operation the following year. Levin rose quickly at HBO and was named president and CEO of the service in March 1973. In an important decision that few around him have been allowed to forget, Levin came up with the idea of distributing HBO by satellite in 1975, effectively setting in motion what became the cable programming industry.

Bob Pittman explained the phenomenal success of cable quite well in a 1998 interview with *Upside* magazine: "The three broadcast networks looked at the cable business and chose not to start a cable network because they didn't want to ding their earnings to build a new business," he noted. "They said, 'If it ever gets big, then we'll come in.' But by the time they got in, Ted Turner had news, ESPN had sports, MTV had music, Nickelodeon had kids, and there was no opportunity. So if you don't ding [your earnings], you lose the opportunity."

Virtually all of Levin's later moves at Time Inc.—from merging with Warner Bros. in 1990, to buying Turner Broadcasting six years later, to the epochal AOL deal—involved some variation of showing how well he had learned that lesson. His efforts were geared toward expanding Time Inc., which was primarily a print company when he joined, into electronic media and filmed entertainment. From the start, Levin has been a huge believer in the idea that technology can transform society, as he had seen it do at HBO. The rise of HBO coincided almost exactly with the popularization of the big-screen entertainment center and the VCR: Together, these new forms of TV delivery promised a brave new world of choice and freedom. Viewers were no longer at the mercy of TV programmers, and they were suddenly free of commercials, able to watch better programming in a more movie-like environment.

Levin's ultimate vision was that of a cable-based wired world, one in which cable operators could deliver transformative images and entertainment directly into the home, using an ever-fatter data pipe to permit an expansive palette of offerings. In fact, he didn't waver from that vision until the end of 1994, by which point many other executives had realized that the modem-based PC could deliver such information more efficiently. This blind spot was to prove costly to Time Warner.

People around him agree that Levin is a technophile, that he enjoys arcane technological discussion and does his homework on the mechanics of technology. "I think Jerry understands technology very well; it's one of his strong suits," says Curt Viebranz. But he adds that Levin became "fixated" on the FSN technology, convinced that it was insanely great, to borrow a phrase from Steve Jobs. Essentially the FSN was designed as a digital computer-based system, which would process information much the same way computers do, although it used an upgraded cable box as its hardware. The cable box that was already sitting on Americans' TVs in 1993 was fundamentally a very simple machine costing the cable company only a few hundred dollars. Cable companies passed the cost of the box on to customers but did so in various sneaky ways so that virtually no subscribers realized they were paying for it. As Time Warner Cable was then the second-largest system operator, the company had millions of these little boxes deployed all around the country. If, by simply switching to upgraded boxes, Levin could coax unheard-of new revenue streams out of his customers, it would be a huge win for him.

But first, the technology not only had to work, it had to be cost-effective. That meant that the expense of the box had to be justified by the amount of revenue it would bring in. It was simple mathematics, but math that seemed to elude Levin, who jumped into the project with all the zeal of a convert. If he questioned his engineers closely on the economics of their fancy new systems, there's no evidence to support it. Levin has always had a bit of a stubborn streak, an unwillingness to deviate from his "vision" once he has outlined it, and at no time was this on display more starkly than in 1994. In many ways, the FSN was Jerry Levin's Genesis Project, the wayward *Star Trek* technology vision that was supposed to build a new world from scratch but went tragically awry.

Time Warner Cable's Joe Collins had announced that the FSN required more code than it took to put men on the moon. As it turned out, putting men on the moon was much easier. And while Levin's remark about unforgiving velocity did prove true, it was only in the sense of being a measure of how quickly the FSN was revealed to be a hugely expensive chimera.

For those who actually worked inside FSN, there was an incredible trajectory, from believing that they were destined to be the sole and vanguard gatekeepers of the information superhighway to realizing they were roadkill. The project certainly started promisingly enough.

In fall 1993, Hal Wolf III went house-hunting in the Orlando area. As the newly appointed vice president for programming and interactive development for the Full Service Network, he had a reason to be selective about where he would live—his new house had to be within the initial service area of the FSN, which was to be launched with service to 3,500 homes and 500 businesses in Seminole and Orange Counties in suburban Orlando. This sprawling, somewhat soulless city, home to Disney World and innumerable related businesses and theme parks, was chosen because it had a highly regarded Time Warner Cable team, and because it was a place where the spotlight tended to shine. The core of this digital, fiber-optic system—the cable box in the consumer's home—would end up being hugely expensive, almost $20,000 per unit. But Time Warner was convinced it would get that amount back and more with all the services it was going to offer the lucky few in Orlando.

Wolf is a pudgy, round-faced, enthusiastic kind of guy who looks like he'd be at home in the Midwest. People like Wolf were miles away in demeanor from the legions of overconfident, tie-less dot-com guys who would grab the spotlight in the late '90s. The cable industry was and is a pretty meat-and-potatoes kind of business. In the mid-'80s, cable trade reporters would take bets at industry conventions as to how many "Full Clevelands" (white tie, white shoes, polyester pants) they would spot on the floor of the show. While Wolf was a few steps up from that kind of sartorial splendor, favoring dark business suits, his general demeanor was a kind of open-faced guilelessness reflecting a belief in technology's ability to deliver the goods and a sincere desire to spread the message to the media.

In his quest for the right home, Wolf drove around the area in search of "for sale" signs. He finally found a likely-looking house that he thought would be included in the test of the Time Warner Cable system. The real-estate agent who met him at the house confided without prompting that the place was the bargain of a lifetime because it had a secret bonus: It was directly in the middle of what was soon to be the most futuristic cable system in the country. "Oh yeah?" asked Wolf. "What's the cable system here?"

"It's Storer/TCI," the agent enthused.

"I thought this futuristic cable system was being built by Time Warner Cable," Wolf prodded, playing dumb.

"Oh no," the agent chided, "[Storer/TCI] is building one, too."

In fact, it was only Time Warner that was investing hundreds of millions of dollars on what was intended as a showcase for the most futuristic, interactive two-way cable system that money could buy. TCI, which did offer service to other parts of the Orlando area, was more interested in selling out to a telephone company (after the trial run with Bell Atlantic, it finally concluded a deal with AT&T) than actually investing significant money in interactive cable.

By November 1993, Wolf and his boss, FSN president Tom Feige, were out-lining the vision they had for the system to a couple of visitors from New York. The pair worked out of a glass-walled office building in a bland-looking office park in suburban Orlando. Visitors to FSN, expecting headquarters that re-flected the cutting-edge nature of the business, were bound to be disappointed. The window of Feige's first-floor office looked out on a small patch of palm trees and a parking lot. It wasn't glamorous by any stretch of the imagination, and it certainly didn't look like the center of an interactive revolution. Nor did Feige and Wolf look like revolutionaries. They looked, indeed, like what they were: cable executives, representing the one utility Americans like most to hate. Feige and Wolf were straight-talking, technically adept bureaucrats, and they were trying very hard to implement a strategy that had been handed down from New York: Build us interactive television.

The pair had no intention of starting small and working their way up to more ambitious offerings. From the onset, the FSN was promising viewers that it would be able to deliver any National Football League game planned any-where in the country. "We've kicked around with the NFL ways their product can be maximized with the interactive environment," Wolf explained. And he was echoed by Neil Austrian, the president of the NFL, who told a reporter, "One [FSN] option you might test would be all out-of-market games. Another might be to digitize the whole NFL library, giving people a shot at watching whatever they want whenever they want it."

Expanding the parameters of series television was another possibility. In 1993, Warner Bros.' sitcom *Full House* was a major hit show. "Within a half-hour, or as soon as the show ends on broadcast, I would love to be able to make it available for someone to pull up and watch anytime," Wolf enthused in Or-lando. "Stop me if I get too scary."

"Why do we have commercials?" Wolf continued. "The answer is to pay for programming. So if you make more money because someone's watching *Full House* and they're willing to pay an extra twelve-and-a-half cents [for the show without commercials], can you imagine how much money a show could make? Television was born from ad agencies, which said, 'I need a place to sell prod-uct so I'm going to create an entertainment venue that will hold people's at-tention. That way I can sell my goods and make money.' Now we're saying to the producers of programming, 'Hey, you guys right now are selling your prod-uct to the ad agencies who then get you distribution on network.' That basi-cally is what it works around to. But if the programming is good enough to stand on its own and the issues are that people don't want to see the commercials, then we need to have that option."

Such effusions were, understandably, hardly popular with the ad agencies that actually did make programs like *Full House* possible in 1993, and still do.

Network TV shows without commercials constituted only part of the vision. With the first two-way boxes due to arrive in Orlando in April 1994, Time Warner Cable began promising a service from *Money* magazine, its sister institution, that would allow the 3,500 test subscriber homes to do all their banking through the system. "We can create a venue where you literally walk into a bank and there are a number of tellers, and above each teller is a different bank logo," Wolf explained. "So you just walk up to the teller you want to do business with, and then that takes you into their venue." All of this would happen onscreen.

Video on demand would allow users to choose from about 70 early-release films for $3 apiece, while older movies would cost 95 cents. Instead of watching a single newscast, viewers could choose to watch news about a single subject—say, the Middle East—from a variety of newscasts, for a fee. Sports, including important games owned by Time Warner, would also be offered up on demand, with interactive sponsors, companies producing ads on the unique FSN platform. "Instead of Sports Illustrated on Demand, it's Procter & Gamble's Charmin Sports on Demand," Feige offered. Also on the programming menu were health services, such as "ask a nurse," health tapes, advice on how to cure illnesses at home, long-distance medical diagnostics, and long-distance medical imaging.

Of course, many of these forms of interactive content would, in one form or another, become part of the Internet dream only a few years later. But for interactive TV, the vision was predicated on the notion that consumers could be convinced to pay more and more money for services they had once obtained elsewhere and would now be willing to get through Time Warner. The problem actually kept Feige and Wolf up late.

"It's a sensitive subject, obviously," Wolf noted. "We're talking about it quite a bit internally."

Feige added, "You're not going to get one bill for all these services. We're going to be breaking this up in various ways. For example, since Spiegel will be the ones who will be sending you that shirt, because they're fulfilling it, they will be the ones billing you or charging your credit card. So the company that fulfills, bills. We don't want people to think, 'Gee, my cable bill just went from

30 bucks to 300 bucks a month' because they ordered all this stuff from L.L. Bean."

Even though the bills would be coming from a plethora of sources, Time Warner would still have been collecting a fee from all the participating companies, such as Spiegel or Chrysler, but the consumer wouldn't see that part of it. Feige's "he who fulfills, bills," was a diktat meant to minimize the impression left with the consumer that suddenly the cable bill had skyrocketed. Still, Time Warner had to collect a lot more than it had been from each household. How else was Time Warner going to pay for all this hugely expensive equipment?

"I remember that period extremely well, because I'd just gone over to work for American Express," recalls Dan Brewster, who eventually became CEO of the magazine company Gruner + Jahr, in which Bertelsmann was majority owner. Most of Brewster's previous career had been spent at Time Inc. In March 1993, Time Inc. had signed an agreement to jointly operate *Travel & Leisure* and *Food & Wine* magazines with American Express. Brewster was appointed to head the unit in April 1993.

Brewster retains the trim good looks viewers of CNN got used to in the '80s, when he was an on-air Washington correspondent. Despite the salt-and-pepper hair and the professorial glasses he sometimes sports, Brewster still manages to evoke youth. He arrived at Time Inc. from CNN in 1985, working his way up on the business side. A classic Time Inc. product—polished, smart, and smooth—he's a little more open than other business executives at the company, maybe because he eventually left, but also perhaps because of his background as a journalist. The story he tells of his time there is a pretty vivid account of a dysfunctional operation. What he mainly remembers about the FSN and its corporate bosses in New York is a lot of profligate spending:

"They created the illusion of a fully interactive television studio, in a room in the Time & Life Building [in New York] that was set up to look like an ultra-high-tech room. You'd enter and there was this kind of master control area with lots of cool gadgetry. And there was this kind of theater seating with two rows of seats. A large screen, and lots of multiple small screens and a tremendous sound system. It was the Wow Room. You would bring someone in and sit them down, and you would show them how one minute you're watching a dramatic program about something, and moments later up would come a retail screen that would allow you to select clothing that had been worn by the people on the program. And you could buy the clothing. Or we would create a custom tape for the client. Of course, it was all illusory, because none of it was in fact accurate."

In other words, Time was showing potential advertisers capabilities it didn't really know how to deploy in the real world. It's one thing for an academic outfit like the M.I.T. Media Lab to demonstrate a prototype of cool technologies of the future and quite another for a big ad-supported corporation like Time Warner to flash a hand it isn't really holding. In poker, that is called bluffing. Big companies aren't supposed to bluff.

As the in-house liaison with American Express, Brewster was asked shortly after his appointment to put together an interactive FSN presentation to wow the top executives at AmEx. He remembers the presentation tape, which featured a large spinning image of the globe. Operating through touch-screen technology, the kind of thing they love at Disney World, "the world would come up and begin to spin. You could then touch the screen at, say, Egypt, and Egypt would come forward. And you touch Cairo, and Cairo comes forward. And then you'd have a menu that would include restaurant bookings, hotel bookings, flight insurance, and an application for an American Express card. You could do all these things electronically, and then a blue AmEx button would come up, and you'd push that button and everything would be booked on your cards. That was the fantasy."

Time went all-out for the AmEx presentation, eventually showcasing the tape in the Wow Room for John Linen, the vice chairman of American Express. The meeting was redolent of tradition—Linen's father had been the CEO of Time Inc., and the relationship between the two companies was a close one. Linen made suitably appreciative noises, but American Express, much to its eventual relief, did nothing about the FSN. Tom Ryder, then a top American Express executive running the company's international business, later CEO of Reader's Digest Association, says the idea of working with the FSN never moved up the food chain at AmEx, and that if it had been taken seriously, it would have. "I never heard a word about it," Ryder recalls. "I can't imagine it went beyond John Linen."

It was only later that Time executives like Brewster would realize that the "fantasy" they were selling was precisely that: based on an overly optimistic belief in the power of technology to deliver products of astounding complexity simply because it should work theoretically. In the world they did know, Time Warner would try to avoid that sort of behavior, never paying a music act a $1 million advance when they knew the group would sell only 10,000 CDs. But there was no comparable set of controls in the world of technology, in a company that was far more clueless about high-tech issues than it thought it was.

"The problem was that they didn't have the hardware or the software that would allow any of this to work," Brewster recalls. "It was dreaming." Anyone who has seen David Mamet's classic play *Glengarry Glen Ross* knows that a central axiom of salesmanship, voiced in the movie version by Al Pacino, is that you don't open your mouth until you really know the play. Time Warner was making just that mistake.

When it came to marketing the FSN, the print guys didn't really know anything about what they were selling to their advertisers. They were simply taking the word of the company's cable engineers that they could deliver on their promises.

Time Warner desperately needed big advertisers to take the FSN seriously for, even with only 3,500 homes in the trial, the company was depending on ads to pay for the considerable start-up and operating expenses. Advertisers always paid the freight at Time, and the company saw no reason to change tack with the FSN. The ad team was led by a former Warner Bros. executive named Karl Kuechenmeister, newly installed as vice president of ad sales for Time Warner Interactive, a sandy-haired hard-charger who exuded confidence, at least at first. But he struggled with a huge problem, the fact that nobody at Time Inc. or anywhere else knew how to deal with interactive ads.

In 1993 ad agencies faced a fundamental problem, in that they had no idea how to price interactive media. Ads are generally bought on TV and in print with a formula called cost per thousand, or CPM. Advertisers pay a set amount for each thousand viewers or readers delivered. A low CPM is, say, $5; a high one might be as much as $100. Fair enough. How could this formula be adjusted to account for the fact that there were only a few thousand users in the test?

An FSN memo from late in that year reveals the extent to which the company was making things up as it went along. One client was told in the document that to participate in the interactive test, it had to make an upfront commitment of $200,000. For that huge total, which could have bought an ad on *Seinfeld* reaching tens of millions of viewers, the client would get "30 minutes [of run time] or 550,000 gigabytes of video server time/space." A gigabyte is a billion bytes, a concept that was difficult to deal with at a time when all computers came with hard drives capable of storage only in megabytes. What would Chrysler or Ford do with trillions of bytes of video, even if the pricing made sense?

At that cost, even if Time Warner actually delivered all of the 3,500 viewers it was promising, and even if all of those viewers actually used the ads, the pricing worked out to close to a $50,000 CPM, certainly the highest amount ever demanded for an advertisement in any medium.

Time Warner, declaring that the $200,000 cost was "non-negotiable," restricted this marvelous opportunity to companies in the "automotive, pharmaceutical, financial, beauty, and fast food" categories, according to the above-quoted memo. The high cost was justified, Time Warner argued, because the companies involved would learn so much, and besides, the FSN would be reaching 14 million homes by 1998. By that time, the early advertisers would be old hands at the interactive ad game and would be miles ahead of their competitors.

Part of the initial fee, $50,000, would go into an "incentive fund," the memo stated, co-op money earmarked for coming up with ways to encourage Orlando subscribers to actually use the interactive ads. The incentive that was proposed was that users who spent a lot of time with the ads would actually see their cable bills reduced, a scheme much like one that some Internet businesses would propose five or six years later. Advertisers would also get access to research from the 18-month test and would be enrolled at two digital-video training centers that proposed to show the agencies how to create effective interactive video ads.

Surprisingly, perhaps as a measure of how confused the interactive media landscape was in 1992 and 1993, some big clients went for the pitch. These included the catalog company Spiegel, General Motors, represented by the formidable Phil Guarascio, general manager of marketing and advertising for GM's North American operations at the time, and Chrysler, then repped by ad agency Bozell Inc.

Joel Kushins, senior vice president and media director at Bozell, commented that the pricing issue was "so abstract at this point. It's very difficult to put a benchmark on it. Depending on the results the experiment will demonstrate, we could spend twice that per gigabyte, and we could be right, wrong, or indifferent." Ad people, trained to be careful with client money, loathe this kind of uncertainty.

FSN proposed to place the auto advertisers' hugely expensive ads in what it was calling the Auto Mall. A video presentation that the network used to sell the Auto Mall featured a viewer shopping for a Jeep Cherokee via an FSN remote-control device. The viewer used his remote to view a Jeep Cherokee ad, at the end of which a prompt asked the viewer if he wanted additional information or, perhaps, a test drive. If the viewer opted for the test drive, the FSN would send a signal promptly to the local participating Jeep dealer, and a shiny new Cherokee would be outside the viewer's house in minutes.

By March 1994, a month before the scheduled, much-hyped April launch of the FSN, things were a bit more problematic. By that time, Toyota, Mazda, BMW, and Nissan/Infiniti had also signed up for the $200,000 trial, though Ford had now pulled back. Larry Dale, marketing specialist at Ford's North American Automotive Marketing and Sales Operations, was one of the first auto representatives to voice concern over the test. A number of factors were at play, he cautioned. "The overwhelming one, as with all new media, is when is it really viable in the marketplace?" he asked. "Does Ford need to move fast in '94 to be involved in this?"

Dale was showing unusual prescience when he posed those questions. The projected 3,500-home test bed of the FSN had by now shrunk incredibly, as Time Warner had managed to wire only 45 homes in Orlando, and FSN's damage-control team was madly backtracking to explain that because of technical problems in building the Silicon Graphics–powered FSN cable box, the 3,500 homes would not be wired until the end of 1994. And even that goal was quickly abandoned. "They kept giving people dates that were supposed to be certain for the rollout, and then missing one after the other," Dan Brewster recalls with chagrin.

By August 1994, Time Warner was admitting that the only homes they had wired so far belonged to Time Warner employees. Even the Post Office was questioning the FSN. Rod DeVar, manager of interactive projects at the USPS, noted plaintively, "The credibility is starting to wear pretty thin. We're about at a point where we're going to have to challenge them on it, say, 'Get specific, what's the date?' "

Most of the advertisers in the test had already stopped payments on whatever checks were in the pipeline, and the FSN's Karl Kuechenmeister had already jumped ship, leaving in July. As it turned out, the few advertisers who signed on ended up with a ludicrously high CPM, a travesty resulting from the fact that Time Warner didn't actually deliver 3,500 users, more like 400.

With the FSN apparently falling apart, Kuechenmeister wasn't immediately replaced, partly because no senior executive at Time Warner wanted to go near the job. Ad agencies were already angry with the fledgling interactive media industry because of its many slights and inappropriate remarks. Bell Atlantic, in a 1994 northern Virginia test of the fledgling ADSL system, which offered video through copper telephone wires, had made the questionable decision to bypass ad agencies and solicit big clients directly. Bob Townsend, the president of Bell Atlantic Video Services justified that decision in August 1994 by arguing that ad agencies just didn't understand the media future.

Ad agencies "aren't risk takers," Townsend lamented. "They need to justify what they do. And when you say [to ad agencies], 'You have to learn for the future,' that sounds good intellectually, but when you get down to the real business, the day-to-day stuff, it's not meaningful to them. Whereas the advertiser has a far more strategic orientation." This may have been true, but it was a sentiment a seasoned media executive would have known not to voice, especially an executive trying to attract clients' advertising dollars.

Other interactive video tests were going on at the same time as the FSN, including one planned by Viacom International in Castro Valley, California. In late '92, an ad agency employee was stunned when told that Viacom was also asking $200,000 for a tiny test-bed audience. "How can you justify that?" the employee asked Viacom. "That's what Time Warner is getting" was the answer.

Around the same time Bob Townsend was approaching clients on his own, a man named Chris Whittle was doing the same thing, and his Whittle Communications, based on "out-of-home media," such as television in doctors' offices and the Channel One school TV network, would have just as big a crash as would Bell Atlantic Video Services. Advertisers got the final revenge, proving the wisdom of not trifling with agencies that control billions of dollars of client spending.

The FSN debacle occurred against a backdrop of considerable disruption and change in the telecommunications industry. It was in late 1993 that the Bell Atlantic/TCI merger was announced, and that December Bell Atlantic chairman and CEO Ray Smith had wowed a crowd with a powerful presentation at the Western Cable Show, an annual event that is the largest cable convention. Given the success of powerhouses like Bell Atlantic, which at that time had an annual revenue stream that rivaled that of the entire cable industry, many observers believed the telcos would be the real hotbed of innovation. In the end, though, Bell Atlantic's experience in many ways mirrored that of the FSN.

A big advantage the telcos had at the time was that journalists are not technology experts and lack the background to be able to question any of what they were being handed in telco press releases. When the Bell Atlantic/TCI merger failed in early 1994, many in the cable industry saw the debacle as more a product of John Malone's demanding nature than any inherent technical or organizational difficulty. It was still widely assumed that cable and telco businesses would merge (as they eventually would do, but not until 1998, when AT&T bought TCI).

Mitch Praver, a former vice president of programming at Lifetime, the women's network, had been lured to Reston, Virginia, by Bell Atlantic Video Services CEO Art Bushkin. Praver is a trim, preternaturally youthful-looking fellow with the dark hair and arched eyebrows of a Persian prince. He's had a unique career, often right at the cusp of change in the telco, cable, and publishing industries, and in the early '90s he had a ringside seat as the telcos tried to go into programming and compete with cable networks.

As he interviewed for the job in 1994, Praver had been impressed with the fact that BAVS had no titles, and an organization chart that looked positively futuristic. A few months after his arrival in early 1994, Praver was even more impressed by the number of top TV executives making the trek to Reston, then a Virginia backwater. John Malone, Barry Diller, Gerry Laybourne, and Michael Eisner, the top talents in television, were among those convinced that ADSL and BAVS had a future.

"I had been in conversations with ABC," Praver remembers. He had given two ABC executives a guided tour of the promise of BAVS's ADSL facilities. When the network asked for a follow-up meeting, however, "I said, 'We don't have the time to keep doing incremental meetings. If you want to do another one, why don't you bring down the whole shooting match, because I really want to talk to you, but we have to get this thing up in nine months and don't have time for multiple meetings.'

"We schedule the meeting and down comes, from New York, Tom Murphy, Bob Iger, David Westin, Herb Granath, Steve Weisswasser, Bruce Magin," Praver says, still sounding incredulous almost seven years later. For all intents and purposes, this was the entire brain trust of the ABC network, when the company was still owned by Capital Cities. Murphy was the chairman of Capital Cities.

"I remember Tom Murphy walking over to me, after he saw the ADSL demonstration, and saying, 'Some day I'd like to work here. Do you think there is any room for me?'" Praver says. The incongruity of that remark is with him still.

Some of the most potentially damaging results of the FSN's misadventures in the advertising world were its ramifications for the corporation as a whole. Time Warner is a huge player in the ad world. On its own, Time Inc., the magazine arm, scoops up more than 20 percent of all print advertising. Advertising managers at Time magazines like *Fortune* and *Sports Illustrated* started to hear from their clients, who were all angry with the FSN, and immediately a split started to develop that would help insure that new media would never be easily integrated at the traditional media companies. Ad executives, as well as magazine publishers, are paid big bonuses based on profitability and what's called in the business "revenue per page." If major advertisers like Ford and GM weren't happy with Time Warner, it was easy to understand why the publishers weren't as well.

In April 1994, Time Inc. CEO Reg Brack had just announced that the earnings from his division had jumped 25 percent over the previous year, earning $70 million on revenue of $751 million. Nobody at Time wanted to see those numbers jeopardized, and if angry advertisers were on the phone, Time Inc. didn't want to be part of it at all.

Brack, then pushing retirement age, is a thin-lipped, dour, bottom-line-oriented executive. In his days at Time Inc., he favored somber, dark business suits and gave off an aura of earned privilege, occasionally hosting staff parties at his gated estate in Greenwich, Connecticut, that made the visitors feel like interlopers. Not exactly loved by his subordinates, partly because he often called on the consulting firm McKinsey & Company to second-guess their decisions, Brack never seemed to get a lot of joie de vivre out of his job. The joke around Time was that the only way to get Reg to smile was to turn him upside down.

In early 1993, Time Inc. had done what it always had done when it encountered something it didn't understand: It created a task force, this time to deal with new media. Former magazine division CEO Kelso Sutton was appointed by Levin to head the group, which included an enthusiastic former Boston Consulting Group consultant named Bruce Judson.

Judson had been brought into the company as a technical whiz, having pioneered an advertising method called selective binding. In the process, magazine subscribers could be addressed directly through direct mail, with marketing material using their names in personalized pitches. Selective binding used a technique called inkjet printing, which filled in a blank space on a magazine page with dot-matrix messages, separate from the regular press run, that were customized for individual subscribers.

Judson and Sutton, with a few others on the task force, had recommended that the committee mutate into a small division of the company, mostly to oversee content development with the Full Service Network. This cadre coalesced around a programming venture called the News Exchange, also known as News on Demand. The idea was to carry out on the ground some of the high-minded ideas being kicked around Orlando by Hal Wolf and to offer viewers any news that they might care to see, instantly. If a viewer wanted to see news from the Middle East, a customized menu would offer a range of stories from that region, from a variety of video news sources. The idea was to offer an interactive service with a subscription fee, much like that of HBO.

The executives who were assigned to this division included the bespectacled Paul Sagan, who had been recruited from Time Warner's New York cable channel, NY1, and was reputed to have once been the youngest news editor ever at CBS News; Walter Isaacson, a corporate infighting genius recruited from the back-of-the-book section of *Time* magazine, who was then moonlighting by writing a biography of Henry Kissinger; Curt Viebranz, who had come from running Time Inc.'s European book and magazine business; and Oliver Knowlton, a general factotum and *Sports Illustrated* veteran who was supposed to work with the techies to figure out how it all worked. Judson was named general manager of the division, which came to be called Time Inc. New Media. Part of his job was to be the liaison with some of the angry FSN advertisers who had heard Karl Kuechenmeister's spiel.

The actual product that the group was trying to create for the News Exchange was very ahead of its time—or perhaps of any time. To accept the viability of the concept, you had to first believe that there existed a potentially huge audience of news junkies, and that these people would pay for access to their drug of choice.

Oliver Knowlton, still holding a job at *Sports Illustrated* in 2001, explains that the product was highly conceptual: "It was news on demand. You had an anchor person who read you the news, and the overlay underneath her had eight icons—sports, weather, national news, those kinds of things—and you could select one with your remote at any point. You could move on to the next subject and could pick an individual story to watch. So you could program it to watch weather, sports, national news, local news, and it worked. But the problem was that when they started they knew how to put videos on a big SGI [Silicon Graphics, Inc.] server and get that to work. They couldn't figure out how to change those assets beneath the anchor as the news broke."

In layman's terms, that meant that the grand vision of the News Exchange was way ahead of the existing technology. Compared to computer files, video files are huge, unwieldy behemoths, and a large menu of such files could consume terrabytes (trillions of bytes). Few servers then could even store files of this size, much less a large group of them accessible by multiple users.

To appreciate the limitations of the News Exchange format, try to imagine viewers watching the News Exchange during the election disaster of 2000. The last thing people needed was another dysfunctional form of television making the mass confusion even more incomprehensible. Adding to the News Exchange's built-in problems was the fact that network news divisions, which had annual budgets of $150 million or so at the time, were already losing money by putting on a 22-minute canned newscast every night. Examine in that context the complexity of what the News Exchange was trying to accomplish, helmed by people who weren't even TV professionals, for the most part. It was hubris on a scale that only Time Warner could muster.

Levin had stubbornly clung to the FSN after many others in the company had given up on it, but once it became clear, late in 1994, that the costs would be prohibitive, a high-level transition team was put in place. Almost overnight, executives began to promote a new piece of technology that had caught the company's eye, a hopefully cheaper technology that seemed to promise much of what the FSN had been touting and that for the beleaguered staff of Time Inc. was as welcome as the cavalry coming to the rescue. That vision for the company's future was none other than the Internet, which was in its infancy in 1994, but at least looked promising. Almost overnight, company public relations people began to tout the Internet and Time Inc.'s predominant place in it as if the FSN had never existed.

After the huge buildup the previous year, the FSN was barely mentioned in the company's 1994 annual report, and when it was, the context had completely shifted. Levin's only acknowledgment of the FSN in his "Chairman's Message" was to say that it had been introduced in Orlando "and successfully demonstrated its capability to deliver movies on demand, video games and home shopping services." This bizarre statement ignored the fact that Levin had never really touted the FSN as an experiment at all but had promised results and profits from it. And when they failed to materialize, there was no one to call him on it, least of all Time Warner's eternally complacent board.

The annual report also described the FSN as "a real-world laboratory for the digital age, providing Time Warner and its partners with invaluable insights into the capabilities of the technology and consumer needs and preferences." A $5 billion laboratory? Less was being spent trying to find a cure for cancer. Still, it was a clever strategy, the old military tactic of what to do when faced with a defeat: Simply declare victory and withdraw.

"The thing about Jerry is that he gets on a horse and if the horse starts to fail, he gets off and gets on another one. The guy is amazingly resilient, personally resilient," says Dan Okrent, who served as editor of Time Inc. New Media in the late '90s. A thoughtful, energetic man with a salt-and-pepper goatee, Okrent has been at the center of much of the Internet activity at Time Inc. in the '90s, either participating in it or writing about it for *Time* magazine.

Everything that the budding technologists at Time Inc. had been hearing about the Internet confirmed their belief that they could dominate this new medium, as they had predecessor technologies like cable. As Bob Pittman has noted, a central truism that has to be understood about big conglomerates like Time Warner is that they never, ever see the possibilities inherent in revolutionary new technologies or companies until they've grown big enough to take seriously. By which point, of course, they're much more expensive to acquire. That conservatism is fundamental to the mind-set of large, established companies. If you were lucky or talented enough or simply sufficiently blue-blooded to have gotten a job at Time Warner in the early 1990s, you felt you had arrived. The company was utterly self-confident that it stood at the absolute center of virtually every important media development. It was, therefore, almost axiomatic that it would look at the emerging Internet as just another medium in which it would vanquish any rivals.

In fact, the World Wide Web, as it came to be known, had first emerged back in the 1980s, but in a format that not even the most advanced engineers at Time Warner Cable were even aware of, much less prepared to deal with.

The Internet arose out of a need for the exchange of research by scientists involved in defense industries and other advanced studies. It had absolutely nothing to do with the media as we know it, and the only people familiar with it then were the nerdiest sort of nerds. Even Bill Gates and Paul Allen later passed up numerous opportunities for early and significant investments in AOL and other online services because they didn't see any significant upside.

Some observers trace the origins of the Internet to August 1962, when J.C.R. Licklider of M.I.T. wrote a series of memos discussing a concept called the Galactic Network. Largely forgotten today, even in official histories of the Internet, Licklider proposed a group of interconnected computers sharing information. He was also the first person to use the term "online" in this context, as his report at M.I.T. was called "On-Line Man Computer Communication."

Three years later, two computers, one at M.I.T.'s Lincoln Lab and another one at Systems Development Corp. in Santa Monica, were directly linked for the first time, using a dedicated 1,200-bps telephone line. In 1966, Lawrence G. Roberts at M.I.T. pioneered a study called "Towards a Cooperative Network of Time-Shared Computers," later suggesting the formation of the network that became ARPANET. This was the first actual network of computers, pioneered by people like Vint Cerf, later a key executive at MCI. Usenet, the network of bulletin board systems (BBSs) still in use today, was set up in 1979, by computer pioneers at Duke and the University of North Carolina.

All of these developments were completely under the radar of the popular media. Even if you had been paying attention in the late 1970s, the few reports that were available would have been densely technical and not in a form any editor at a consumer magazine or newspaper could have deciphered. This is true of most new inventions—a piece that Thomas Edison wrote for *American Review* magazine in the 1870s about his invention of the phonograph, for example, is a dry monograph about sound reproduction that never mentions a practical use like recorded music at all. Scientists are not great at the applications business, which is usually left to marketers and businessmen.

Gradually, however, developments in computer networking assured that some consumers might notice. The first dot-com address was registered in 1985, the zippy Symbolics.com. While this might be considered typical of the kind of thing computer nerds cared about, that same year the WELL was established, and that did attract some attention in information-gathering centers.

The Whole Earth 'Lectronic Link was set up by Stewart Brand (the founder of the *Whole Earth Catalog*) and Larry Brilliant as an electronic dialogue between the readers and editors of the *Whole Earth Review*, a periodical that grew out of the *Catalog*. It was an online BBS, but it differed from previous such services because it fostered conversation about ideas and politics rather than just tech issues, and as such it attracted some genuine intellectuals and freethinkers.

Indeed, many New York–based media pioneers like to boast that they were on the WELL in the 1980s. It's the kind of credential that used to mean something, for even if users were exchanging ideas at only 1,200 bauds or less, they were doing so before anyone else. Users of the WELL were simply using modems to talk to one another, and it wasn't until 1990 that the first commercial company to provide Internet access, The World, became operational, and it was tiny.

The Internet was still a confusing set of warring protocols and technology.

In 1991, three separate protocols were announced: the World Wide Web, developed by Tim Berners-Lee, WAIS, and Gopher. Each was equally promising, according to the few users who were actually aware they existed. For those who worked in visual media, such as television and print, the Internet was boring and irrelevant, whatever the entry point. It lacked pictures, sound, and motion. It wasn't media, in other words, as it was understood at the time. Moreover, most major media figures were baby boomers, who had come of age in the 1960s and 1970s. They tended to dismiss anyone who cared about computers as the classic four-eyes who wore glasses, sported pocket protectors, and couldn't get a date on Friday nights. It was not a glamour field.

In 1993, and 1994, Marc Andreessen's Mosaic browser, developed as a college project, started popping up in a few media offices. Mosaic, which later became Netscape, supplied a graphics interface for the formerly ASCII–dominated Internet, offering the possibility of a world of pictures and colors. It was akin to the moment radio became TV, and almost as dramatic.

Andreessen, whether he knew it or not, created an interface into a medium that big media would want to deal with, that could be easily molded into a recognizable media property. But Andreessen was a techie at heart, not a programming person. To media executives aware of what he had come up with, it appeared in 1993 and 1994 that Andreessen's breakthrough was in simply coming up with a medium that the adults in the room (big media) could exploit for big profits.

America Online's one-time president Ted Leonsis remembers this moment clearly. Everything about Ted Leonsis is bigger than life; he's such an outlandish character in some ways that it's easy not to take him seriously enough. A large man with a tightly trimmed beard, Leonsis is both carefully controlled and wildly improvisational. He has always given the impression of saying exactly what he thinks, annoying many other media executives in the process.

A good number of the pronouncements Leonsis has made at AOL sounded like just that, empty pronouncements, when he made them, and he was widely derided in the mid-'90s as a company hack who would be swept aside in the Internet tide. Yet most of what he said turned out to be right, and his understanding of the nexus between media and the Internet has been extraordinary, far more astute than that of other executives who emerged from big media itself.

"The metaphor that the Internet developed upon *sounded* like it was about publishing," Leonsis observes, interviewed in his expansive Dulles office in early 2001. Leonsis, now worth hundreds of millions of dollars, depending on how the stock market is doing, has pulled back from his former duties as president of the AOL service, but he's still involved in running some of the entrepreneurial divisions. In his career, he's had myriad dealings with media executives, observing them as something of an informed and bemused outsider. "Page views, browser, there was this manifest destiny that 'we' get it. The thought was that they wouldn't have called it a page view if it wasn't about publishing. Instead the Internet was really creating this new life form that wasn't about the traditional relationship between a reader and a publisher, or an advertiser and a reader. It was something new altogether."

Newsweek's Michael Rogers, echoing that thought, argues that media people simply projected the elements of their own businesses onto the Internet. "I used to call it 'dial a metaphor.' When you went to the early new-media conferences, people would get up and say, 'It's really like the recording industry' or, 'We're going to use the movie studio model.' Or, 'We're going to use the book publishing model.' And then the next level of sophistication would be, 'It's a combination of these two businesses.'"

That's pretty much what happened at Time Inc., still reeling from the FSN fiasco. The Web looked made to order for the company, a malleable medium that could be quickly dominated by the experienced sophisticates in the Time-Life Building. This tiny elite felt that they already had a leg up over the media competition because the FSN had at least got them thinking about technology, and it wouldn't require a giant leap simply to transport the whole operation over to the Web. In fact, with the group put together for Time Warner's News Exchange, the cast was assembled that would be most responsible for building Pathfinder, the Time Warner web site that in many ways would prove even more dysfunctional than the FSN.

Pathfinder was named after a James Fenimore Cooper character who led early Americans through the forests of upstate New York near the Canadian border. "I rather pride myself in finding my way where there is no path, than in finding it where there is," Cooper has the Pathfinder saying in the novel of that name. While Time Warner was certainly heading down an untraveled road, Pathfinder the Web operation ultimately lived up to its namesake in one way only—it showed Time Warner the way to a new-media future at a crucial juncture in the company's history, a time when new media seemed all important. If it eventually led to failure, well, don't blame James Fenimore Cooper.

CHAPTER 2

Print Discovers the Internet

March 22, 1993, was Jonathan Bulkeley's first day as the brand-new media manager at America Online. Or at least he thought it was.

That morning, when Bulkeley entered the nondescript red-brick building at 8619 Westwood Center Drive in Vienna, Virginia, the heart of the AOL revolution, he could be forgiven for having believed that in leaving *Money* magazine and joining AOL he'd just made the biggest mistake of his life.

To fully appreciate that assessment and what Bulkeley faced when he reported to work in Vienna, you have to consider just how ridiculously makeshift and tiny AOL was at that point in its history, compared to *Money* and its corporate parent, the Time Inc. division of Time Warner. It had barely 300,000 subscribers and was dwarfed by its far better known rival CompuServe, which had a base of nearly 1 million members. *Money* itself was larger than AOL.

AOL's headquarters might have been mistaken for the regional office of a small insurance outfit—the antithesis of the big magazine Bulkeley had just left. Time Inc. was, and still is, the ultimate in powerful media entities, publisher of leading magazines like *Time, Fortune, Money, Sports Illustrated,* and, most significantly, *People,* its cash cow. The chaos he encountered almost immediately at AOL was many, many corporate paradigms away from the ordered calm and patrician demeanor of the Time-Life Building.

And the chaos only seemed to increase when Bulkeley entered Steve Case's office for their initial meeting that day. "You're hired, but you can't tell anyone you're an employee," the khaki-clad Case instructed him. "Tell anyone who asks you're a consultant until we figure out what your job is." At that stage,

Case had just emerged, with shaky underpinnings, as the new CEO of AOL, and he seemed tentative to Bulkeley.

By any measure of what was right and proper in the media business of 1993, 31-year-old Jonathan Bulkeley should not have quit his job as director of franchise development and marketing at *Money* to join AOL. Everything in Bulkeley's life had prepared him for the kind of white-shoe company Time Inc. was in those days. "I didn't have casual clothes. At every school I had been to in my life I had worn a coat and tie. I went to Hotchkiss, and then Yale, like Henry Luce, and even at grade school before that I had had to wear a tie."

Jonathan Bulkeley's roots in the American establishment run very deep. He lives today mainly in Manhattan, but his summer house is a large Victorian stone and clapboard "cottage," in the Newport style, in the well-guarded enclave of Fenwick, Connecticut, part of Old Saybrook. Though only about 30 miles or so across Long Island Sound from the fashionable Hamptons, Fenwick is old money, a world away in style from the Lizzie Grubmans of this world. Its quiet downtown has none of the nouveau-riche gaudiness of East Hampton and Southampton, and most of its inhabitants are WASPs of the old school, for whom wealth is supposed to be understated.

Fenwick is where the Bulkeleys have lived for generations. At the beginning of the last century, Jonathan's great-grandfather, the Honorable Morgan G. Bulkeley, a handsome fellow with a big white moustache, was "probably the best-known man in Connecticut," according to *An Illustrated Popular Biography of Connecticut,* published in 1901. Morgan Bulkeley, born in 1837, became the president of Aetna Life, the mayor of Hartford, and the governor of Connecticut. A Victorian character of the best sort, he built the Fenwick house as a getaway from the workaday world of Hartford, where Aetna and many large insurance companies were established.

While Jonathan Bulkeley, who was prematurely bald, lacked the full head of sandy hair that seems so ubiquitous among Time Inc. executives, everything else about him fit the corporate environment of Time Inc. like a glove, and he quickly rose through the ranks during his eight years there. Were it not for the fact that the job he held led inexorably in the early 1990s to the fledgling world of online services, Bulkeley would today probably be a publisher or president of one of the organization's biggest magazines.

In 1993 Bulkeley's home base was the Time & Life Building on Manhattan's Sixth Avenue, an elegant skyscraper with abstract paintings in the lobby, planted in the middle of corporate row. McGraw-Hill, News Corp., Simon &

Schuster, and Time-Life are all within a few blocks of one another, close to Radio City and other tourist attractions. Many of the other big-media companies— Viacom, Hachette Filipacchi, Hearst, Condé Nast, Disney/ABC, and the New York Times—have headquarters nearby.

Time Inc. executives have comfortable offices, a subsidized store where any employee can buy a huge range of products at discount prices, a large subsidized cafeteria, and an executive dining room where important clients and contacts are entertained. Lunches are long and leisurely, at Cité on the ground floor of the building or, if the lunch is important enough, at Palio or the Four Seasons. Most Time Inc. employees take it for granted that their company represents the pinnacle of success in the print world, and it's not unusual to hear executives casually mention they've been at the company for more than two decades. Time Inc. is a big cocoon that many are loath to leave.

Bulkeley landed there in 1985, where he got an entry-level sales job at *Discover,* the firm's struggling science magazine. It probably helped that Reg Brack also worked at *Discover,* an important element in Bulkeley's rise through the organization's clubby ranks. "Reg Brack was the man during my tenure," Bulkeley quips, doing a dead-on imitation of Brack's stern expression. In keeping with well-established Time tradition, which emphasizes moving "our kind" of executives around different properties, rather than hiring from outside, Bulkeley next worked as publisher of Time's college magazine, *Student Life.*

"Along the way at Time I started getting into new products, what they called in the late '80s 'franchise development,'" Bulkeley recalls. "The magazine subscription boom was over, and the ad business was bad in that time period, 1987–1988, after the markets had gotten slammed in '87. So magazines were looking at how the brands could make more money. I ended up in late '89 going to *Money* as the director of franchise development, which meant doing other stuff besides print. *Money* was doing well; it had come back after the market crash. The franchise was pretty strong; there was no real competition. *SmartMoney* wasn't out yet. So my job was to create new products using the *Money* logo and resources." In pursuit of that goal, Bulkeley in 1990 became the first Time Inc. executive to investigate the world of software and what was then called online services.

At that point in time, modems were few and far between, and those that were available probably ran at 300 bps, a glacial speed that is almost inconceivable today. People who had computers tended to use them for organizing financial portfolios, with products like Quicken already on the market. *Money* magazine saw potential in that area, and Bulkeley was deputized to create a rival proprietary financial software package for personal investors that would enable them to manage their portfolios. Software updates were to be offered online through the newfangled modems.

Working with a company called Reality Technologies, based in Philadelphia, Bulkeley created a software package called WealthBuilder, and also completed the first deal to put *Money* magazine mutual fund information online with the leading service at the time, CompuServe. The only other top magazine on CompuServe then was *U.S. News & World Report,* in a pioneering deal overseen by publisher Tom Evans.

WealthBuilder did not overtake Quicken, but it did manage to establish an interesting paradigm for the company in that Bulkeley recognized that financial information, including stock quotes, has to be constantly replenished if it is to have any real value. To feed the latest stock quotes, WealthBuilder accordingly set up a proprietary online service for its users to download data. The system, which ran on Sun Solaris servers based at Reality in Philadelphia, was designed to work on the new 1,200-baud modems just coming onto the market. Though not exactly speedy, they were definitely an improvement.

Being Time Inc.'s only online executive was habit-forming, Bulkeley found: "I started getting hooked on CompuServe, and I was spending a lot more time online than I was doing anything else. I started to get a little bit of a bug. My wife and I decided it was time to leave New York. We had had our first baby and were ready to do something else. I started thinking about leaving Time Inc. I had had a great career there. I'm sure I would have gone far if I didn't blow up, but there was something about the plodding corporate culture, especially compared to the job that I was in, which involved creating new products, taking risks with a new brand and building the franchise. They [Time Inc.'s management] weren't getting it very quickly."

The solution, Bulkeley decided, was to work for Reality Technologies, which seemed to be at the epicenter of where he wanted to be. Bulkeley and his wife went down to Philadelphia several times in early 1993, looking at houses and negotiating his contract at Reality. But when negotiations dragged on, and the company was hesitant in granting the concessions he wanted, he began to get frustrated.

"I had dinner with my friend Phil Harris, who went on to run Intuit; at that time he was running ChipSoft," Bulkeley remembers. "I said, 'What do you think, should I do this or not?' He said, 'I don't know about Reality, but I know AOL is looking for some people. You might give them a call.'"

At this stage, AOL was about eight years old, but it had really been a serious company for only a very brief period. AOL was founded in May 1985, incorporated in Delaware under the title Quantum Computer Services, with a starting focus on video games. It didn't go online until November of that year, when it established a rudimentary, modem-delivered service, called Q-Link, for the fledgling Commodore computer platform. Steve Case, a co-founder, was the force behind the online strategy from the beginning. The America Online name was coined four years later, in 1989, when the company launched a new online service for the Macintosh and Apple II platforms only; a DOS version wasn't available until 1991. When Bulkeley first encountered AOL in 1993, it had just launched its first version for Windows and had gone public the previous year.

As it happened, Bulkeley knew someone highly placed at AOL. The only problem was that his contact, Christopher Meigher III, was a board member who had been a high-ranking Time Inc. executive and until fairly recently the person to whom Bulkeley's boss reported.

Chris Meigher exemplified the Time Inc. executive of the late '80s and early '90s, and his ultimate fall is one of the more poignant stories in media. A product of Albany Academy and Dartmouth, Meigher joined Time Inc. in 1968 and did the usual string of apprenticeships—sales positions at *Time, Fortune, Sports Illustrated,* and *People,* where he became one of the first publishers, eventually landing on the 34th floor, where all the important decisions used to be made at the Time-Life Building.

As Carl Swanson noted in a devastating portrait of Meigher that ran in *New York* magazine July 24, 2000, Time Publishing Ventures, which became Meigher's operation in 1988, was the apex of his career. The company's entrepreneurial arm, Time Publishing Ventures had been set up to allow start-ups to function outside the rigid Time Inc. culture. The unit went on a spree during Meigher's leadership, launching *Parenting, Cooking Light,* and *Emerge,* and buying *Sunset.* It was Meigher who gave Martha Stewart entrée to the company, and he initially oversaw the launch of her hugely successful *Martha Stewart Living.* By early 1992, many people, including Meigher himself, were predicting that he would succeed Brack as president of Time Inc. But Brack knew when he was being undermined, and in a devastating move, Meigher was summarily fired.

Though he balked at calling Meigher directly, Bulkeley was acquainted with another board member, Douglas Peabody, a friend of Meigher's who had worked on various magazine deals with Meigher. Peabody was a venture capitalist who had put up some of the early seed money for AOL and had been hugely influential there. It was Peabody who had recruited Meigher to the

AOL board, and together they formed a media-savvy phalanx at the tiny start-up. The two men eventually went on to launch Meigher's ill-fated luxury-oriented magazine company, Meigher Communications, which ultimately lost investors more than $20 million. Not impressed with former AOL marketing director Steve Case's savoir faire, the two formed a faction on the board that was resistant to the elevation of Case to the CEO position. This faction lost out, and the two were later forced off the board, selling their stock for a fraction of what it would be worth just a few years later. But they were both still with AOL when Bulkeley started thinking about taking a job there.

In early February, Bulkeley called Peabody, who, over lunch in Manhattan, was immediately encouraging. "He said, 'Yes, you have to go to AOL. I'll hook you up with Steve,'" Bulkeley recalled. When Reality called that same day to negotiate final points in his employment package, Bulkeley informed them everything was on hold. "Steve came into town two days later, and I flew down to Virginia the next week, and met with five different people, including CFO Len Leader and Jean Villaneuva," later to be Steve Case's wife and at that time head of public relations.

There were, however, a few problems. For one thing, the AOL job came with a 45 percent reduction in salary from what *Money* was paying. For another, as Bulkeley recalls, "They didn't tell me what the job would be. They just said 'come work here.' I said, 'Okay.'"

Bulkeley returned to the Time-Life Building, strode into the office of his boss, *Money* publisher Bill Myers, and told him he was leaving the company. The situation was made all the more dramatic by the fact that Lindsay Valk, the general manager of the magazine, had quit just a few minutes earlier. When the news of Bulkeley's departure made the rounds, the overwhelming consensus at Time Inc.'s offices was that commitment papers should be drawn up for him as soon as possible. Avoiding the disapproval of his peers, Bulkeley took the wife and kids and flew off on vacation for a month.

Bulkeley went to America Online to be in on the ground floor of software and online development, but few would have depicted Steve Case or his company as ready to set the world on fire. At this stage in his corporate development, Case was described by many who worked with him as an improviser, a man who was making up the business as he went along. This was a fairly necessary stance in 1993—no one really understood where the world of online services was going anyway. "He was pretty loose," Bulkeley recalls, "it wasn't very structured." Despite the lack of direction, Bulkeley knew precisely what he wanted to do from the beginning—forge partnerships with media companies, starting with Time Inc. In early 1993 AOL had relationships with only a handful of fairly minor media players, including the *Chicago Tribune,* the *San Jose Mercury–News* (a tech-heavy daily that covers Silicon Valley), and one or two computer magazines.

AOL desperately needed "content" to distinguish itself from its competition. In the early '90s, there were no Web operations like MSNBC.com or ESPN.com. If you wanted news content, you might approach the *New York Times* or *Time* magazine. They had brand names and content that could be used to market an online service. More important, they had millions of subscribers, which meant that AOL could tap into their databases, the lists of subscribers who could be tapped to try an online service. Bulkeley knew that Time Inc. and other media companies would consent to market AOL to their large number of subscribers because they wouldn't initially see an online service as a threat. The whole operation was so alien to the way print companies operated that they would not initially see themselves as being in the same business.

The most ambitious deal AOL had with a media concern at this stage was its partnership with the Chicago-based Tribune, which later bought Times Mirror's stable of newspapers, including the *Los Angeles Times,* and which is a major TV station operator. The Tribune Company was never in lock step with the more myopic Manhattan-based media conglomerates. The AOL relationship included a 10 percent stake in the pre-public AOL, purchased for $6 million in October 1991. That investment had been championed by now-retired chairman and CEO Charles Brumbach.

As former Tribune executive Gene Quinn, now semi-retired and living in suburban Westport, Connecticut, recalls, Brumbach viewed an investment in an online service early on from the perspective of his background as an accountant. "Charlie had this vision. He saw the computer world as a giant cost-containment vehicle to use technology to increase productivity. He thought that computers would dramatically reduce the overhead of all companies, including media companies."

AOL first came to Tribune's attention through investment banker Alex. Brown, as AOL was looking for a mezzanine round of investment so that they could move the company's marketing up in dramatic fashion. Indeed, the $6 million Tribune invested was earmarked exclusively for marketing purposes.

Quinn notes that newspapers recognized the promise and threat of the online world earlier than magazines and TV because it clearly impacted them more directly. The idea of networked computing, Quinn recalls, alarmed Tribune. "We didn't know what the business model was going to be. We were scared that it was going to undo traditional profitable models like classified advertising. We were fearful that the RBOCs [regional Bell operating companies], which had been recently created out of the AT&T breakup, would transition their yellow-page businesses to create daily classified-style businesses. So Charlie decided to ask the board at Tribune for some investment capital. At first it was just a few million dollars to take investments in new-media businesses." Borrowing from Wayne Gretzky, Quinn remarks that "it's always about skating to where the puck was going to be, not about trying to wind up and take a shot where the puck had been."

Initially Tribune had approached Prodigy in 1990, but the number-one online service, which had launched in 1984 with an uncomfortable melange of owners in CBS, IBM, and Sears, wasn't looking for a partner. CBS exited Prodigy two years later.

Quinn continues, "AOL, at the time we made the investment, was the fifth-largest online service behind CompuServe, Prodigy, Delphi [later to be purchased by Rupert Murdoch], and GENIE [owned by General Electric]. We were transitioning from being a publishing business and a broadcasting business into an investment business around new technologies and new distribution channels for information."

A burly, bearded Philadelphia native who favors baseball caps, shorts, and sports metaphors, Quinn was a longtime sportswriter at papers like the *Philadelphia Daily News* and the *Wilmington News Journal,* and he had become associate managing editor of the *Chicago Tribune* when Brumbach tapped him to manage the AOL relationship. The MBA he'd gotten in 1990 at Kellogg, in an effort to move up to the executive ranks, helped cement the appointment. Part of his responsibility was overseeing the exclusive pact that gave Tribune the right to control AOL's local content in the cities where the company had newspapers and TV stations, which included vital hubs like New York, Chicago, Denver, Atlanta, and New Orleans.

Tribune and AOL launched their first local content areas in beta in March 1992, and by that May the entire text and classified sections of the *Chicago Tribune* were available in a service called Chicago Online. The *Tribune* was the first newspaper to go up on an online service, a year before the *San Jose Mercury–News* launched its Mercury Center on AOL.

For the Tribune Company, this was less than the immediate triumph it might have been. A faction of editors at the powerful *Chicago Tribune,* for example, were very resistant to the notion of simply giving the paper away online. In fact, newspaper editors in general were concerned about the implications of such decisions for their jobs and their products. As Ted Leonsis recalls of his dealings with one newspaper partner: "They wouldn't put chat or message boards up. When I asked them why, they said the quality of the posts or the questions or the chat would be below our editorial standards. And I said, 'Let me get this straight: You think your customers are stupid.' That's essentially what they were saying."

And there were still other reasons why newspapers were ambivalent about going online. A central dilemma for newspaper companies in dealing with the online marketplace is that the Internet is a terrible, disaggregating thing for them, and they have to make it look as if it isn't.

The admirably straightforward Kenneth W. Lowe, the president and CEO of the major newspaper player the E. W. Scripps Company, puts it this way: "It's the same reason magazines have always had trouble doing television shows. Because the editor of the magazine says, 'If you're going to take my brand and put it on television, I want to be involved.' But that person is great at producing a magazine; they're not necessarily good at producing television. So there's always been that kind of conflict when dealing with an editorial staff. It's complicated by guilds, by unions at the papers, by rights issues. Those kinds of things—we'll all work them out. Those are short-term problems. But they are very real. And it gets down to the content you are developing for a particular audience, who the end user ultimately is, what the platform ultimately is, and the credibility of that content. Sometimes the editor of a newspaper is older and is not a person who remotely comes close to what the Internet user is all about."

In fact, one newspaper did discover a form of electronic publishing early on. Evan Rudowski, who later became one of the first executives at the Excite portal, was a cub reporter at *Newsday* in Melville, Long Island, in 1986 when the idea of creating an electronic bulletin board service (BBS) first surfaced. By then, Rudowski had graduated to the enviable task of writing the headlines for the "news zipper," the electronic public news display that the paper had established in Times Square in 1986. In that year, this was about as close to electronic journalism as you could get. But the BBS concept was already being discussed in the trade journal *Editor & Publisher,* and *Newsday* thought they would give it a shot.

The paper consequently formed a group around the BBS in 1987 and called it Electronic Information Services; it was one of the first new-media units at a media company. The BBS, which operated at 300 bps, used an $8 shareware package, and its hardware consisted of one PC server and a modem. It attracted "several hundred" users throughout Long Island, Rudowski says, "people who were geeky enough or farsighted enough to have a modem. Our big upgrade was when we upgraded to 1,200 baud, and from one phone line to two."

In 1993 *Newsday* decided it was time to expand beyond its own BBS. The paper first talked to AOL, but eventually a decision was made by Times Mirror, *Newsday*'s parent, to partner with Prodigy, which at the time had a bigger audience.

AOL's relationships with newspapers, including its investor companies, were never smooth. "Gene Quinn and I became friends," Leonsis recalls. "We'd be in meetings. I would say, 'Gene, you're way complicating this. Are you a friend or are you a foe? You have to approach this [in a certain way because] you have a big investment in AOL. And we're going to do things together. Yes, we might transform a lot of these industries that you're in, but it's better that you're a part of it than not. I had to say that, of the newspaper companies, they were the most aggressive, and they're the best managed."

Leonsis believes that newspapers were then and are now out of touch with their readers. "For the most part, media companies are run by fifty-five-year-old white men. Newspapers are edited by fifty-five-year-old white men. But you look at the population, and it's more women than men, more young people than older, more people of color. You look at the *Washington Post,* and there's this huge college community in Washington, and it's like they don't exist for the *Washington Post.*"

That's the way it looked to Ted Leonsis, but he never owned a major newspaper. Newspapers are franchises that have lots of tradition behind them. Families like the Sulzbergers, who control the *New York Times,* or the Chandlers, who built the *Los Angeles Times,* had spent generations building their newspapers into the cash cows they had become. By the 1990s, most of the competition, especially afternoon newspapers, had been vanquished. And now suddenly a new competitor was looming, one that threatened to be able to deliver both news for a fraction of what it cost newspaper chains and a national network of classified advertising that would directly compete with newsprint. The major newspaper companies believed that giving their content to AOL could be suicidal, that it would facilitate AOL becoming the place people went to for local news. Digital City looked like a Trojan horse, and they wanted to try something else.

On April 24, 1994, a group of newspaper representatives met secretly at San Francisco's Fairmont Hotel, a follow-up to an initial gathering held in February of that year in Palm Springs. The driving force behind the conclave was to educate their fellow newspapermen about the threat posed by the online services, and the tone was alarmist. Newspapers were in imminent peril, they warned. The group presented a confidential paper called the "Newspaper Consortium Project Report." The document called for $10 million in funding for the establishment of a new company, or "newco," that would launch "successful local on-line services in their 30 top newspaper markets and achieve a combined subscriber base of 2 million users within 5 years." The report also urged the creation of a national classified business.

Reading this document today, it's hard not to marvel at the naivete of those who had written it. They simply had no idea what they were up against. "Early national service providers such as Prodigy, America Online, and CompuServe have exceeded or are fast approaching the 1 million user level for their individual services and are experiencing growth of more than 50,000 new subscribers a month," the report warned. "In recent months, Ziff, Microsoft, AT&T and Apple have each announced the launch of an ambitious national online service targeted at the home computer market. Based on a market of 20 million subscribers in 1999, and assuming some industry consolidation, it is possible that several of the national online services will capture active subscriber bases in excess of 5 million within 5 years."

If someone had told the newspaper group in 1994 that AOL alone would have more than 30 million subscribers within a little more than six years, they probably would have all accepted their eventual defeat outright. But as it was, the group eventually launched its newco, New Century Network, in June 1996. Although NCN was headed by a remarkably clearheaded former HBO executive named Lee DeBoer, infighting and confusion doomed the project from the start. "They fundamentally disagreed on what the nature of the partnership was," DeBoer says. The nine daily newspaper partners "didn't want to work together," he concludes.

While the nine papers—which included such names as Times Mirror and Knight Ridder—had already banded together to form a jobs classified site called CareerPath.com, they could never agree on what they were creating. Was it a for-profit entity that could stand on its own, or a support group for newspapers that would be funded by them? And even the original goal of the enterprise—to attract national advertising to newspapers at a time when daily papers were getting only 3 percent of such ads—proved elusive.

While newspapers were failing to find any unity of purpose, AOL had plans to grab some of their thunder. Mark Walsh, who joined AOL as senior vice president of branded Internet services in April 1995, after a short stint as CEO of General Electric's GENIE, recalls an ambitious effort within the company to dominate newspapers' prime territory, classifieds. Between 1995 and 1996, among other assignments, Walsh headed a secret consortium within the online industry to form a big web site that would consolidate classifieds from Prodigy, CompuServe, News Corp.'s Delphi, GENIE, and others. "It would have been a common spot on the Web, with one macro site," Walsh explains.

Throughout late 1995 and early 1996, representatives of the major online services had regular meetings on the project. Walsh had consulted a battery of lawyers from across the industry, who assured him that the consortium would be legal. "We made a lot of progress," he remembers. But just as its parameters were being established, the *New York Times* found out about it and was suitably "outraged," as Walsh recalls it. The *Times* and its then-online executive, Henry Scott, had stayed out of NCN. Always a feisty entity, the *Times* thought it could go its own way online and that it could stop AOL from poaching its turf.

The *Times*'s three-year contract with AOL was up for renewal in early 1996, and the paper made it clear that AOL would have to choose between continuing to get its content and backing the consortium. The *Times* had signed a deal with AOL in 1993 that provided marquee-quality daily news and features, and AOL needed well-known content providers at this stage of its development.

Always a powerful adversary, the *Times* could have made life very difficult in Washington for the fledgling online services. Considering the extent to which government policy favored keeping newspapers alive, with the federally sanctioned Joint Operating Agreements propping up many otherwise failing papers, influential organizations like the *New York Times* and the *Washington Post* were likely to get a sympathetic hearing. It was Steve Case himself who ultimately made the final decision on the problem. "Steve said, 'Kill it, because I want to re-sign the *New York Times*,'" Walsh explains. "He said we could revisit the consortium later."

In 1996 AOL was still tentative enough that when faced with pressure from big-media companies, it would sometimes back down. After 1997, however, when AOL had gained the definitive upper hand over media content, that equation changed and acceding to media demands was no longer an option. Today, if AOL wanted to revisit the classified business, it wouldn't need a consortium to do so, for it has a much larger circulation than the handful of top newspapers in the country combined.

Even though newspapers managed to defeat the online classified consortium, they were discovering that the online world was hardly a hospitable place for even their editorial content. When papers first went online, they believed they could charge consumers a fee for that content. A comparison between two New York–area papers is instructive.

The New York Times Company first went online with a product called @Times, available through AOL, which was then charging a $3.50 hourly fee to its customers, while *Newsday* offered its *Newsday* Direct through Prodigy. The @Times service came with a regular AOL subscription, and the *Times* split the revenue from its users with AOL, as did other content providers. The @Times service was initially popular and attracted about 500,000 visitors a month. *Newsday* Direct had a separate subscription model—$4.95 a month for Prodigy subscribers, and $6.95 without a Prodigy subscription but still using Prodigy's software.

Like most newspapers at the time, *Newsday* simply assumed that the subscribers to their print edition would loyally build their online habit around the brand they preferred. A *Newsday* promotion from November 1994 makes amusing reading today. "Your first 30 days on *Newsday* Direct are free," the paper announced. "Then, *Newsday* Direct costs just $6.95 a month." The hodgepodge pricing plan was enough to confuse the most dedicated customer. "Direct Plus Prodigy—free for 30 days. With this option, you get the *Newsday* Direct access described above, the 5 free hours on *Newsday* Direct Bulletin Boards PLUS 10 FREE HOURS ON PRODIGY (Also a $2.95 an hour value.)" Searching back issues of *Newsday* cost another "introductory rate" of $6 an hour, while using the bulletin boards cost 4.9 cents a minute, or another $2.95 an hour. Only the most loyal of readers would bother to decipher what all that might add up to, much less rush to subscribe.

Seizing an opportunity, the *New York Times* quickly moved in to explain its competitor's baroque pricing scheme that same month, explaining in a release that "in a comparison of moderate users of either service, defined herein as people who go online for up to five hours per month, *Newsday* Direct users will end up paying about $15 to $20 per month or more, depending on the surcharges they hit. On the other hand, a great number of @Times users will pay the simple flat fee of $9.95 per month—and nothing more. One of the advantages of America Online is that AOL's pricing is simple and easier to understand, and manage, than Prodigy's."

To targeted subscribers, these policies all sounded confusing and unappealing. For the newspapers, the potential subscription money looked promising at first, but the revenue that was being generated soon dipped alarmingly as flat monthly pricing became the norm for online services. A more fundamental concern was that the usage numbers weren't increasing as had been predicted.

When Tribune's Gene Quinn and others examined usage reports from AOL, they found that, essentially, "people were not reading the newspaper online." While AOL was growing rapidly from the tiny entity it had been when Tribune invested, the company was receiving statistics indicating that 85 percent of the 500,000 Chicago-area AOL subscribers never even looked at the news the *Tribune* was posting. While such figures were an effective tool for the online executives to use in arguing that AOL wasn't cannibalizing the paper's readership, they were an early harbinger of the terrible threat the Internet would later pose to newspapers, as an entire generation of readers stopped relying on print media to give them news at all. What younger users seemed to want was short headlines and very brief newswire-style summaries that services like AOL could easily get from Reuters or other wires. What they didn't seem to want was ruminative newspaper stories that went on for 1,000 words or so. Long stories didn't seem to work online. And that's what newspapers like the *New York Times* prided themselves on. They could either become like *USA Today* and offer short stories of a few paragraphs, thereby jeopardizing their own DNA, or they could risk becoming irrelevant to the new online paradigms.

In some markets today, the highest-circulation daily newspaper has the sixth or seventh most popular web site locally, with younger readers in particular getting their minimalist news primarily from AOL, ABCNews.com, and the web sites of MSNBC and CNN. The more perceptive newspaper executives might have foreseen that this shift would take place, but there were many unanswered questions in newspaper boardrooms in 1993. Fundamentally, newspaper executives weren't sure what to do. Should they go online and risk helping the trend away from paper, or should they sit the whole thing out and possibly lose out totally to new online competitors?

While newspapers were becoming increasingly unhappy with what the online world was offering them, magazines were struggling with their own online challenge. So when Jonathan Bulkeley arrived at AOL, bringing his special knowledge of the magazine world, he had his work cut out for him. Audrey Weil, AOL's vice president of corporate development, now at CompuServe, was in charge of the *Tribune* relationship and the other media deals but wasn't all that keen to hold on to the portfolio. By the end of his first week, Bulkeley had defined his job with Case as the top media executive at AOL and was on the way to building a staff of four for the brand-new media department, including such later-prominent AOL personalities as Bob Smith, Roger Neal (who went on to head a dot-com called Productopia that flamed out in spectacular fashion in November 2000), and John Coulson.

Bulkeley's insight was fairly straightforward: "I knew exactly what magazines were thinking, and I knew exactly how we could leverage it to get subscribers." He was aware that magazines wanted to figure out the online world, and he could make it simple enough for their executives to understand; he could form partnerships with them that could be the secret weapon that would enable AOL to leapfrog over Prodigy and CompuServe. With his background at Time Inc., he was also familiar with just how effective a magazine-style promotion for AOL might be, reaching millions of subscribers at a fairly low cost. Jan Brandt, who joined the company only a few weeks after Bulkeley, would go on to spearhead a huge blitz that saw an awesome 250 million AOL software disks go out to the public, many of which were distributed through magazine partners.

Magazines, like newspapers, needed a lot of help adjusting to the kind of interactivity the online world allows. Magazines, and media in general, whether they have a letters column or not, are essentially one-way communications tools. They publish a product, it's shipped to distributors, and they somehow manage to get paid circulation (also know as the rate base) up to an acceptable level to sell advertising. In no part of this model do readers really loom all that large, at least not in the Manhattan corporate towers maintained by Time Inc., Hearst, Hachette Filipacchi Magazines, and Condé Nast, the golden quartet that controls the consumer magazine industry.

The closest that magazines get to readers is through endless sessions with supposedly representative focus groups, usually held in some bland suburban setting. Contact with the actual audience is so rare that one magazine owned by S.I. ("Si") Newhouse, *Jane,* edited by Jane Pratt and part of the Fairchild division of Newhouse's Advance Publications, actually goes out of its way to emphasize that it does encourage interaction with its readers as a point of differentiation.

In the '80s, Pratt had launched a magazine, *Sassy,* which had enough of a vogue then to be featured in a recurring *Saturday Night Live* skit with the late Phil Hartman. "The reason *Sassy* was a big success in the '80s was because it was the first teen magazine to actually have a dialogue with its readers rather than a dictatorial tone," notes *Jane* publisher Eva Dillon. "Because Jane has such a peer-to-peer dialogue, readers actually see the editors as their friends, and they come to our building [*Jane* is housed separately from the Condé Nast publications, on West 34th Street] and ask to see Jane." At least once a week, Dillon says, readers are given tours of the offices and are taken in to meet Pratt. But this is very much the exception. "Can you imagine anyone thinking that they could just go and meet [*Vogue* editor] Anna Wintour?" Dillon asks.

Magazine editors really didn't want to go "interactive," preferring their clubby Manhattan universe. But interactivity was suddenly all the rage in the early '90s, and most editors had to at least pay lip service to the concept. Promoting interaction clearly meant going online, but in 1993 magazines really did not know how to do that, and the very prospect was terrifying. Magazine editors are paid big salaries because they're supposed to know how to communicate with and be in touch with readers. In the accepted ethos of the business, legendary editors like Helen Gurley Brown or Jann Wenner are believed to possess an almost mystical knowledge about what their readers want, even if their own lives have little in common with those readers.

Suddenly, however, a new way of communicating was at hand, and the magazine editorial staffs were virtually clueless. The last thing most magazine editors and publishers are is technologists. And to them, the demimonde of computers was an incredibly alien netherworld, full of arcane buzzwords like "server," "router," and "HTML." Given that they were typically in their forties or fifties, they were unlikely to be suddenly reborn as digital zealots anytime soon.

What was particularly troubling to them was that in their ignorance of this area, they risked looking ridiculous in a meeting. At every big magazine company, the following scenario was almost inevitable: A 23-year-old techie from the MIS department with a buzz cut and an earring in his earlobe would be drafted to address the subject of the Internet. The senior-level editor and publisher would sit there, growing increasingly uncomfortable as the guy rambled on about things digital.

One such techie tells a story of being summoned to brief a top editor on the ways of the Internet. Halfway into the discussion, the techie realized the man was about to become head of new media for the whole company, with no background whatsoever for the job. So he dutifully loaded ISP software onto the editor's computer and watched him gingerly hunt and peck. The very next day, the editor chaired a meeting on the company's online plans, during which he proclaimed to the assembled throng, "Now, I know some of you are new to the Internet and haven't been familiar with it as long as I and [the techie] have."

One New York–based online editor in 1993 and 1994 personally loaded AOL software on the desktops of four separate highly placed media executives, all of whom had responsibility for online developments at their companies (and were too embarrassed by their ignorance to ask company MIS people to help).

The first noncomputer magazine to go online had been the "thought leader" publication *The New Republic,* in 1993. Jeffrey Dearth, the head of the Washington-based weekly owned by the irascible Martin Peretz, had first conceived the idea of posting some articles from magazines on the Internet. A bit of an intellectual masquerading as a publisher, with an impressive head of graying hair, Dearth was not really an ad salesman.

Dearth called his creation the Electronic Newsstand. The problem was that when he came up with the idea, no commercial Web browsers were available. The first *New Republic* site consisted of text only and was posted on Gopher, a very early Internet protocol, at Gopher.enews.com. It switched to the World Wide Web in 1995 with the URL www.enews.com, after Netscape's Web browser became more widely distributed. The Electronic Newsstand had two roles. It posted some articles from various magazines, including *The New Republic,* but its primary purpose was to sell magazine subscriptions. Participating companies, including Hachette Filipacchi titles like *Elle* and *Car and Driver,* paid the Newsstand a bounty for the subscriptions it delivered.

Each magazine that participated posted two articles to the site per month (most were monthlies) and a table of contents. Enews.com would post a link to the e-mail of the magazine editors participating—an early form of interactivity—and there was a subscription form for the print editions of the magazines involved. Enews went on to introduce a number of innovations, including the first Web-oriented sweepstakes.

Electronic Newsstand was also the first magazine-oriented entity to go up on AOL. Dearth notes that in late 1994, he met with Steve Case and newly hired AOL president Ted Leonsis, with an agenda that had selling Enews to AOL at the top of the list. Dearth, based in the Washington, D.C., area, in common with AOL, could see the rise of the service even at this early stage and wanted to join forces. He envisioned a sale that would not only make him rich but give the service a powerful parent company to help it grow.

"Jonathan Bulkeley was the champion for it, because he was doing all the magazine deals," Dearth says. The meeting was going well from Dearth's point of view, until they got to Electronic Newsstand's revenue figures, which were then in the low six figures. "Even Redgate got to $7 million," Dearth recalls Leonsis exclaiming, in reference to his former company. The meeting went downhill from there.

Dearth left the company in early 1995 for MecklerMedia, another up-and-coming Internet media company. On the day he arrived at MecklerMedia, he got a call from a job recruiter, asking him if he wanted to interview for a job as CEO of a start-up directory/search site called Architext, based in the Silicon Valley. Not wanting to relocate to California for a shaky start-up, and already committed to Meckler, Dearth declined. But an executive at Times Mirror Magazines, George Bell, who had championed ancillary businesses at the company, was willing to talk to Architext. Bell was in place when Architext became Excite, soon to enjoy a spectacular run-up in its valuation. Around the same time, Ted Leonsis, the guy who had decided not to buy Enews, asked Dearth to join AOL in a senior-level position. "But AOL didn't excite me. It wasn't the Internet business," Dearth says. Bell went on to lead Excite through an explosive period of growth in the late '90s, leaving the company at just the right time and making tens of millions of dollars off Excite stock. Dearth tries not to think about that too much.

Brian Hecht, a later CEO of Electronic Newsstand, explains that Enews was seen as a "big deal" in 1993 "simply because there was nothing else out there. If you do a Lexis/Nexis search using the word Internet in 1993, a third or even half the articles mention Electronic Newsstand because it was the first time that people began to realize that there was a thing called the Internet and there was cool stuff on it. People said, 'You can get magazine articles!'" Because it also sold magazine subscriptions, Electronic Newsstand could be considered one of the earliest commerce sites on the Internet. A variety of magazine publishers, including Hachette Filipacchi and Time Warner, invested in it, because whatever its shortcomings, it successfully established the idea that magazines could get some buzz by going online.

This was the state of affairs when Jonathan Bulkeley and John Coulson began paying visits to Manhattan media circles in 1993 and 1994 to build up AOL's magazine portfolio. They were seen as people you could talk to, non-threatening, friendly guys who really understood media.

"Having Jonathan Bulkeley there certainly helped AOL with its dealings with us, no question," says Oliver Knowlton, a long-time Time Inc. executive, now at *Sports Illustrated*, who played a key role in building Time Inc.'s online assets. To the people making the relevant decisions at Time, AOL seemed to also offer a panacea for all those worrisome "community" features that had to be addressed, such as chat, e-mail, and message boards. No publisher in 1993 had a clue as to how to set any of that up. Bulkeley and Coulson did.

Tapping into his magazine training, Bulkeley consulted data from Simmons, the magazine research firm, to find out exactly which magazines best fit the AOL demographic. At the time, the users were primarily males who owned both a computer and a credit card. The top magazines to cater to that demographic were the now-defunct *Omni,* owned by Penthouse founder Bob Guccione, *Popular Photography* (a Hachette title), and *Scientific American.* While these may seem rather cerebral choices now, guys who owned computers and credit cards in 1993 tended to be eggheads.

Of the top 20 magazines in the Simmons runs, virtually all of them eventually signed up with AOL. Some of the negotiations were drawn-out affairs; the German-owned *Scientific American* didn't bend for six months. The deal was fairly straightforward. Since AOL was on an hourly fee–based structure then, the partners would get 15 percent of the hourly rate that AOL was collecting from consumers. In many cases, this amounted to only $2,000 or so a month because, like newspapers, magazines were not a big draw at AOL.

This didn't particularly worry AOL, which already recognized that magazines wouldn't be a huge traffic-builder. It was already obvious that most people spent 30 percent of their time online chatting and sending e-mail, and another 30 percent downloading software (downloads were very slow in those days). Magazine partners were important to AOL for two reasons. The first was brand-building; because the magazines were all established and respected brands, they would help legitimize AOL. The second was marketing clout. As part of their deal with Bulkeley's group, magazines had to agree to market AOL in their pages, through preprinted inserts that they had agreed to sell AOL at cost. AOL would supply the inserts, customized with the name of the specific magazine partner, which would offer some kind of sign-up promotion. In some cases, the magazines bound in AOL disks themselves.

This ended up being a lot cheaper than the other methods Jan Brandt was finding to circulate the millions of AOL disks that were going out, such as list rentals. The magazines would also receive a bounty for each AOL subscriber generated, which proved a highly effective incentive to get them as partners. By the end of 1993 and in early 1994, up to 30 percent of new AOL registrations were being generated by these magazine promotions, and they were coming in at an unheard-of rate of 50,000 a month. The reason the magazine campaign was so effective was that, through Simmons, AOL had managed to target the exact demographic most likely to buy an AOL subscription.

By summer 1994, AOL had signed an impressive 36 magazines to the service, including *Atlantic Monthly, Backpacker, Bicycling, Car & Driver, Compute, Consumer Reports, Disney Adventures, Elle, Entertainment Weekly, Flying, Home PC, Home Office Computing, Inside Media, MacHome Journal, MacWorld, Mobile Office, Multimedia World, National Geographic, The New Republic, Omni, PC Magazine, PC World, Popular Photography, Road & Track, Saturday Review, Scientific American, Smithsonian, Spin, Stereo Review, Time, Travel & Leisure, Windows, Wired, Woman's Day,* and *Worth.*

"After we got through the first twenty on the Simmons run, we started thinking okay, what do we do now?" Bulkeley remembers. "We started thinking about television, radio, newspapers, and professional publications in our space. We wanted [*Inside Media*] there because, if the media people use it, they're going to talk about it, and they're going to recommend it to their friends. It was great content." Cowles Business Media, the owner of *Inside Media,* recruited a former CBS correspondent, Gordon Joseloff, to do a daily media wire on AOL, and Prodigy quickly countered by signing rival *Advertising Age.*

To put AOL's achievement in perspective, consider what its competitors then featured. CompuServe, still much larger than AOL, had only eight magazines signed, and these were second-tier for the most part, although the list did include Time Inc.'s *People, Fortune,* and *Sports Illustrated.*

Prodigy, despite its large reach, likewise had only a handful of magazines, including *Kiplinger's Personal Finance* and the guide service *Total TV.* While *Newsweek* signed with Prodigy in 1994, it was mainly because *Time* was already committed to AOL. Rupert Murdoch's Delphi online service hosted only two Murdoch properties, *TV Guide* and the women's magazine *Mirabella.* By this point, only 30 percent of Americans even owned a computer, much less a modem, but it was already clear that the online revolution was unstoppable, and that AOL was beginning to lead it.

AOL may have been leading in the competition to sign magazines, but that doesn't mean that relations were that smooth between the online service and its erstwhile print partners. *Spin* magazine, the youth-oriented, rock-and-roll publication begun by Bob Guccione, Jr., had been one of the first magazines to go up on AOL in 1993. David Rheins, then president of *Spin,* recalls that AOL was barely able to work with media companies at that time. "AOL was a nightmare to deal with then. You could never get anyone. The producer was never available." A year into the relationship, *Spin* had gone through countless producers, and AOL was looking pretty shaky indeed.

"Every time you would go down there," Rheins continues, "they would march in, and say, 'We profusely apologize. We know we've neglected you. We know your value as a content provider. We've assigned new people, and this will be the new team and we'll streamline the process. You're generating huge profits.'"

Spin was then a mainstay of AOL's entertainment area, an important brand for attracting the teenage male market, a key demo at AOL and one that helped make another online innovation a success. "We were one of the first companies to sell ads on AOL," Rheins says. "It was a Calvin Klein Kate Moss fragrance ad for CK1, a semi-nude Kate Moss image file. Thousands of kids downloaded that file. It said to us that these kids were interested in the digital experience, the downloading. It took forty minutes to download at the slow baud rates then, and kids were paying several dollars [to do it]."

Calvin Klein was paying *Spin* about $10,000 a month to carry the download, not a huge sum, and *Spin* had to pay 15 percent of that to AOL. But Calvin Klein also bought a schedule in the magazine, which allowed *Spin* to run fragrance ads for the first time. Of course, those same kids who downloaded the Kate Moss ad could have bought a magazine for those same few dollars and gotten a better copy of the image, but as Rheins points out, this was as much about having fun with technology as it was about owning the image. *Spin* knew that, and AOL was coming to learn it.

By the end of 1994, it was clear that online ads were potentially hugely profitable, and that AOL was on to something. AOL Time Warner's Bob Pittman likes to say that he taught Steve Case everything he ever knew about advertising, a tongue-in-cheek exaggeration but not wholly untrue.

"I came to AOL from Century 21 real estate," Pittman noted in a 2001 speech. "I knew nothing about the real-estate business. It took me about ten minutes to figure out it's all about generating leads for agents. I called Steve Case, and said 'I want to be an advertiser.' He said, 'What's an advertiser?' I said 'It's someone who gives you a million dollars a year.' AOL was laughing all the way to the bank, but what they didn't know was that in the real-estate business, I was spending $30 million on direct response TV and got three thousand leads a day. And then I went online, for $1 million, and got sixteen thousand."

Rolling Stone founder Jann Wenner likewise recognized the value of this new medium, if somewhat belatedly. A key former *Rolling Stone* employee tells this story: "In 1994, Steve Case went to Jann and said, 'I want you to put *Rolling Stone* content on AOL.' Jann asked, 'Why should I do that?' Case replied, 'Otherwise you won't be hip!' And Jann just stared at him. Case continued, 'You have to start having your people do this to learn about the future.' And Jann replied, 'Why can't I let your people learn about the future, and I'll hire them away from you?'"

By 1994, *Spin* was making $100,000 a year from its AOL deal, proof to Wenner, however skeptical he was at first, that an online presence was a necessity. Soon *Rolling Stone* joined *Spin* in AOL's music area, but only after Wenner had failed to kick *Spin* off the service and sign an exclusive deal with AOL.

AOL's *Time* magazine agreement, which was concluded in September 1993, was in a class by itself. Former Time Inc. CEO Reg Brack, who ended up on the board of several Internet companies, describes receiving a call from Walter Isaacson, about the pending deal with AOL. Brack says he had heard something vague about the Internet at the Davos (Switzerland) economic summit in 1992, but this was the first time he had actually been forced to pay attention professionally to the online world. In that call, Isaacson informed Brack that he had Case, Bulkeley, and others on the premises, and asked him to join the group. "We went down to a little conference room," Brack recalls. "They hooked up a computer to AOL, such as it was at the time. It wasn't much. I wasn't impressed at all. But when they started throwing around the numbers, and the fact that they were willing to pay us a fee for content, I became very impressed and interested with what the potential—according to Steve Case—was. I just became very intrigued with the Internet, both as an opportunity and as a threat. I had no idea of the scale and scope it would ultimately take on, but I felt it was something we had to stay close to."

After that meeting, Brack subscribed to CompuServe, which he personally found easy to use, and he began doing his own personal banking online with Chemical Bank, which had a fledgling online effort. He believed the best policy was to "play CompuServe and AOL off against each other," which partially explains why some Time Inc. magazines signed with CompuServe, and others with AOL. But Brack was hardly thrilled with AOL's potential at that point. Were it not for Isaacson, it might have been several years more before Time Inc. paid much attention to the online world.

CHAPTER 3

Do You Know the World Wide Whatever?

I n November 1993, Walter Isaacson went on a cruise around Manhattan on
the *Highlander,* Malcolm Forbes's private yacht. The occasion was a party
for the newly launched *Forbes F.Y.I.,* a lively publication that celebrates the
wealthy lifestyle with just enough of a jaundiced eye to make it amusing. Edited
by the witty Chris Buckley, *F.Y.I.* is not read by the New York cognoscenti,
which doesn't seem to have affected Buckley's popularity among the Manhattan dinner party set.

The protocol was that all the leading executives in the company—Steve
Forbes (who hadn't yet run for President), Jeff Cunningham (the publisher),
Malcolm Forbes, Tim Forbes (little brother was running *American Heritage*)—
would take their place in a receiving line as they boarded at a pier on the west
side of Manhattan, serenaded by a kilted bagpiper. The whole scenario was repeated at the end of the cruise, when Forbes tchotchkes like umbrellas and
pens were handed out. During the night, another Forbes staple was in
progress—helicopter rides from the top deck of the *Highlander,* which was
strewn with Malcolm's motorcycles. Witnesses recall a thrilled Isaacson saying
it was the first time he'd been aboard a chopper.

Isaacson was on the guest list that evening because, in many ways, he was a
fast-rising star at Time Inc.—maybe *the* fastest. Internally, the managing editors of the magazines were called the "princes," and as managing editor of
Time, Isaacson was the prince who was already being viewed as heir apparent
to the top editorial-related position at the corporation. Born on May 20, 1952,
in New Orleans, he had followed a path typical of senior members of the company's editorial team.

At Harvard he had been a member of the *Lampoon,* a training ground for top media talent, and he had gone on to a Rhodes Scholarship. After college, Isaacson served as an apprentice at the *Sunday Times* of London, and as a reporter and city hall columnist at the *New Orleans Times–Picayune.*

He caught the attention of *Time* magazine editors who saw his resume as virtually the model for the type of Time organization man they were looking for. Besides the impressive academic credentials, he had married well; his wife was the daughter of a founder of MCI, a connection that would come in handy later. In 1986, he co-authored a book called *The Wise Men: Six Friends and the World They Made,* which was an early indication of his preoccupation with American power and how it is wielded. Isaacson's 1992 book *Kissinger: A Biography* also helped immeasurably in establishing the editor's bona fides as one of the more intellectually gifted members of *Time* magazine's staff, even if the book was somewhat overshadowed by Seymour Hersh's monumental *The Price of Power: Kissinger in the Nixon White House.* Isaacson's book was far more measured than Hersh's indictment, which enabled him to encounter the former secretary of state without embarrassment, a necessity on the haute monde Manhattan party circuit, where Kissinger and Isaacson were both fixtures throughout the late '80s and the '90s.

It's easy to see why Isaacson found Kissinger a conducive subject, as both men are born diplomats. A former Time Inc. executive who worked closely with Isaacson puts it this way: "When you're talking to Walter, you're thinking of Bill Clinton. He's incredibly infectious, a delight to be around, a very decent guy. But he's totally political. If there are an array of choices, he'll take the one that's politically expedient. But all the time, he's telling you he loves you. And it's probably true."

Isaacson revealed his political agility during his first crisis as managing editor of *Time.* A planned collaboration between the magazine and CNN turned into a disaster with its opening installment of a planned series on July 2, 1998, a factually incorrect report appearing in both venues about an alleged Operation Tailwind, in which the U.S. government was said by the two news organizations to have used nerve gas against American defectors during the Vietnam War. When government officials questioned CNN's reporting, reported on air by veteran Peter Arnett, the sources the reporting had been based on seemed to crumble. Isaacson quickly put out a correction in a press statement the same day the story ran on CNN.

"Like CNN, *Time* is retracting the story and apologizing for running it. Based on our own investigation and that conducted by CNN, we have concluded that the facts simply do not support the allegations that were made. A piece saying so will be in Monday's issue," Isaacson wrote. The timely response helped deflect the responsibility to CNN, where a few hapless producers were still attempting to defend the problematic story. The producers were eventually fired, while Isaacson escaped without any serious damage to his sterling career.

In November 1993, however, Isaacson had a different turf to protect. Newly appointed as editor in chief of Time Inc. New Media, he was still not sure what that title meant. At this juncture, Time Inc. New Media was a hodgepodge operation. On one hand, it was operated separately from Time Online, which was a unit set up largely by *Time* magazine executive editor Dick Duncan to oversee *Time*'s relationship with America Online. Originally established as a liaison with the Full Service Network, Time Inc. New Media also encompassed the News Exchange, the digital video news experiment that never worked properly and was run separately in a large studio in the basement of the Exxon Building in Manhattan. While the FSN itself hadn't tanked yet, it was a problematic enterprise for Isaacson from the start, for it involved TV, something that print editors across the board knew little about.

Since Benjamin Franklin first picked up his quill pen, American journalists basically have been asked only to get the story straight, whether their medium of choice was longhand, typewriters, or shared terminals. But Isaacson was among a small coterie of journalists asked to make sense of a confused series of technological developments that threatened to completely change the scope of what scribes actually do. When you've spent years honing a particular craft, it's always a bit unsettling to put all that by the wayside, and that's what Isaacson was struggling with by the time he took his cruise on the *Highlander*. Which is why he was really paying attention when he encountered on the yacht a dark-haired young man in his twenties named Craig Bromberg holding forth to a group of acquaintances about something called the World Wide Web.

As Bromberg recalls, "He started talking to me about electronic this and that, and I told him I was involved with Echo. 'What's that?' he asked. [Like the WELL, Echo was a popular bulletin board system, especially popular among New Yorkers.] Then he asked me, 'Do you know anything about this World Wide Whatever?' I said, 'You mean the World Wide Web?' He says, 'How do you go on it?' When I told him all you need is a slip connection, he said, 'Can I call you tomorrow?'"

To fully understand this exchange, you have to recall the state of the Internet in 1993. Today Isaacson himself prefers to gloss over this period, a necessary tactic and part of his razor-sharp instinct for corporate survival. In the office he maintained in the Time-Life Building, you were reminded, through prominently placed photographs, that as *Time*'s managing editor he was accustomed to dealing with world leaders and, through various memorabilia and books, that he was at work on a biography of Ben Franklin, but there are no obvious mementos from the period when he headed new media for Time Warner when, rightly or wrongly, he held what was seen as the future of the giant corporation in his hands.

In 1993 Netscape had not yet launched its main browser, and none of AOL's competitors, led by CompuServe and Prodigy, featured Internet access. While the struggling Delphi service, which had only 100,000 subscribers or so, did offer Web access, it was text-based and did not incorporate the newly emerging browser technology, and was thus far less appealing than the visually striking AOL. At this time, very few corporations had web sites, and the Web was still largely invisible in the mainstream media. Almost no media people used the Web, or even AOL.

Many in the media had just started hearing about AOL and Prodigy, and the very idea of the Web seemed to be a closely guarded secret. Rochelle Udell, the first new-media executive at the giant Condé Nast publishing empire, recalls the prosaic atmosphere that pervaded the magazine world when it came to new media. Udell told Condé Nast owner Si Newhouse in the 1980s that if he ever launched a new-media division, she'd like to be involved. Years later, he took her up on it, partly because she was one of the only people in the company who'd gone online and because she had taken a course in international business, which had a homework assignment involving going online.

Udell, the former editor of *Self* and a corporate art director for the company, was tapped to launch CondeNet in 1993 and 1994. She started with virtually no help or signposts and spent a lot of time going to conferences, because there was no one in the company who could help. Even then, it wasn't until Udell was preparing a Thanksgiving turkey dinner for 30 people in 1993 that the possibilities of the online world truly came alive in a sudden "epiphany." She had been sidetracked in preparing the meal and found herself with a huge bird and only a couple of hours to prepare it. How would she get it done in time? "I had become an AOL junkie," she recalls, "so I went online to the Talk Turkey Chat Room." There were 21 residents there, all had pertinent advice, and by 7:15 when the first guests arrived, the turkey was done to a turn and Udell had learned about the value of the online medium as a community.

She went on to conceive a food and gourmet web site that would focus on that community, to be named Epicurious, drawing from the company's *Gourmet* and *Bon Appetit* magazines.

Perhaps the earliest Internet evangelist to try to convert the big-media companies was Alan Meckler. A slender, balding fellow who exudes energy and has some of the aura of a prophet without honor in his own country, Meckler began his media career with a small newsletter dealing with electronic library science. He eventually transformed that tiny publication to the first Internet-oriented trade publication, which became *Internet World* in 1992, making Meckler the first media executive to try to make money off the Internet. And he also formed the first broad-based Internet convention, also called Internet World.

Based in suburban Westport, Connecticut, although he himself lived in Manhattan, Meckler's company stayed small in the early '90s, partly because nobody would give him money. "I was turned down by well over twenty different organizations," he recalls, listing Ziff-Davis, CMP, Cowles Business Media, the Hearst Corporation, and Time Warner. In 1992 even major computer magazine companies like CMP, chronicled so lovingly in Michael Wolff's book *Burn Rate: How I Survived the Gold Rush Years on the Internet,* were not very Web-savvy either. They made their money doling out information on how to use computers and how to get more people to use them. Internet companies weren't advertising then, and so at best they were a mere blip on CMP's radar screen.

Meckler offered CMP 50 percent equity in MecklerMedia, including the magazine and the trade show, for $500,000 and was rebuffed. Even Ziff-Davis, with its impressive array of computer-oriented magazines, looked askance in the early 1990s at the idea of an Internet magazine. But by the end of December 1994, with the Internet clearly taking off, Ziff CEO Eric Hippeau was to offer $35 million in cash for *Internet World* magazine alone, which Meckler declined despite a desperate need for the cash—he'd had to take out a second mortgage on his New York apartment to pay the company's bills. Meckler stuck to his visions of *Internet World* becoming another *PC Week,* and his conference becoming another Comdex, the huge annual computer convention in Las Vegas.

Meckler wanted to sell the whole company for about $80 million or not at all. "So Eric brought in a guy named Tom Thompson," as he recalls, "one of the financial analysts at ZD, and they did due diligence for about forty or fifty days, and I can distinctly remember Tom Thompson calling me up in late February, and telling me that they just didn't think the Internet would be that big, so they were going to pass."

Time Warner was one of the few big companies to take the Web seriously in the early 1990s. This was partly out of its need to fulfill Levin's interactive dreams, which were not an obsession of any other big-media chieftain at the time, and partly because Time liked to think of itself as tech-savvy and forward-thinking. By the end of 1993, there was a pervading sense at Time Inc. that the World Wide Web was coming, and you had to know something about it, especially if you were the editor of Time Inc. New Media. Walter Isaacson stepped into the breach with the level of confidence that only a trusted lieutenant at that company could muster.

Isaacson recalls his introduction to the online world as having taken place almost a year before he met Craig Bromberg. "I first got interested in the Internet at the end of 1992, when I was back-of-the-book editor at *Time* and the technology writers did a story called 'Cyberpunks' about people in online chat rooms and hypertext links.

"This was in an era before the Web was really big," Isaacson continues. "Netscape hadn't launched. A few people were downloading Mosaic from the University of Illinois, but the cyberworld was mainly confined to chat rooms and online services, Fetch and Gopher and FTP protocols. The Web was sort of nascent. In the fall of '92, *Wired* had not yet launched, but there was a great magazine called *Mondo 2000* that was the bible of the cybergeek. R.U. Sirius [an editor at *Mondo 2000*] was a great writer. The cyberpunk culture was starting to develop, and so I asked Philip Elmer DeWitt, who was the editor of the technology section at *Time,* to help get me online to start figuring it out."

The future president of Time Inc. New Media actually first went online on Christmas Eve 1992, after his family had gone to bed. Of course, it was not at the Web that Isaacson was looking, with DeWitt's help. "I went on the WELL, which was then the most popular chat room and online service. I watched people on the WELL talk about what they were doing on Christmas and became somewhat fascinated by it. Only a few months later, I met with Steve Case and others at AOL, which was then the fifth- or sixth-largest online service after Prodigy and CompuServe, Delphi and that Apple service [eWorld], and GENIE. We decided we should put *Time* online to find out what it was like."

In 1993, when Isaacson was discussing a deal with AOL, the service did not yet offer direct access to the World Wide Web, though its users could read the Usenet "newsgroups," which included a multiplicity of bulletin boards accessible through the Internet. This actually pleased Time Warner in some ways, because the newly emerging Web seemed impossibly anarchic, while the controlled world of AOL was the kind of environment in which *Time* could work.

Isaacson says *Time* "ended up going with AOL because they were the coolest, most user-friendly service, and the one that was the most likely to popularize it for people. I remember working with the other editors at *Time* to get that [deal] approved, but AOL was paying us money, and we were doing a marketing agreement. It was a few of us deciding to do it. There weren't a lot of meetings about it."

Indeed there couldn't have been many meetings because, in the vast expanse of the Time-Life Building, there was virtually no one who knew anything about the online world. The corporation was essentially without resources to deal with this new phenomenon. Sixth Avenue was a long way from Silicon Valley, where geekdom was already in flower, And Vienna, Virginia, where AOL had its first headquarters, might as well have been in Mongolia, given the level of scrutiny AOL had been getting from Time Warner and other media companies. This is what made someone like Craig Bromberg, a media insider who knew how to connect to the World Wide Web, such a valuable commodity.

Still Craig Bromberg was an unlikely person to bring the Web to the corporate behemoth Time Inc.—or, for that matter, to have a corporate job at all. At age 35 in 1993, he was an early convert to the online world. A native of Jamaica, Queens, he'd gone to the trendy Oberlin College, and compensated for not going Ivy League by getting an M.A. from the London School of Economics, in the history of political thought. He returned to the U.S. in 1980, and the next five years left a blank spot on his resume while he worked at being an artist. Bromberg turned eventually to writing and began publishing art, dance, and music criticism in publications like *Vanity Fair, New York,* and the *New York Times Magazine.*

As he became a favorite with editors like Tina Brown, Bromberg gained more visibility in 1989, with his book *The Wicked Ways of Malcolm MacLaren,* a biography of the redheaded British "impresario" who invented the seminal punk groups the Sex Pistols and Bow Wow Wow. Bromberg was a very early user of the pioneering message board service Echo, which debuted in 1989, three years before Isaacson logged onto the WELL. He had actually begun going online as early as 1980, when he attached a 300-baud modem to his Kaypro 2 to get access to fledgling dial-up services.

Because he was one of the few technology-savvy writers in the early 1990s outside of the hackery so prevalent in the computer trade publications, Bromberg got choice assignments from the major magazines, such as writing on John

Sculley for the *New York Times Magazine* in 1992 and another interview with Netscape/Mosaic pioneer Marc Andreessen in December 1993, also for the *Times Magazine*. A brief, disastrous stint as features editor at *Avenue* magazine also happened that year, followed by a brief period at *People*.

After their chance meeting aboard the *Highlander*, Isaacson and Bromberg kept in touch. "Every once in a while, I would look at my fiancée and say, 'Watch this, I'm going to call Walter Isaacson,'" Bromberg recalls. "She'd look at me like I was crazy. I had his direct line. Sure enough, Walter would get on the line and talk for an hour, half hour."

To Isaacson, Bromberg began to look like a fount of good judgment after a somewhat unfortunate flirtation at the consultant level with Michael Wolff, the *New York* magazine columnist and author of the coruscating Internet memoir *Burn Rate*. In 1993 Wolff was running his own company, Wolff New Media, which was then pioneering a series of books for Random House on on-line content.

Outspoken and fiercely intelligent, Wolff had attended several meetings of what was then known as the Online Steering Committee, at which Isaacson and others at Time Inc. groped for a way toward the Internet. Wolff describes his experiences there quite vividly in *Burn Rate*, basically making the combined brain trust at Time Inc. look like bumbling idiots, while still managing to be amusingly self-deprecating.

Isaacson was looking for inspiration from other sources when Bromberg and he had a phone conversation, soon after Bromberg got back from his interview with Marc Andreessen. This led to more discussion about what Andreessen was trying to accomplish with his fledgling Mosaic browser, and in turn prompted Isaacson to ask Bromberg to come down for an interview. Again, Bromberg impressed him, and Isaacson offered him the top editorial position under him in March 1994. As a sign of just how novel a venture new media was at Time Inc. then, Bromberg was given an office on the 40th floor of the Time-Life Building, the floor's only other occupant being Bruce Judson, the department's marketing head.

And when Bromberg met some of his new colleagues at *Time* Online, the experience was an unsettling one to say the least. *Time* Online was supposed to be the unit that headed new media at *Time* magazine only, but connections between it and the other magazines at the company were already under way.

Jim Kinsella, a former reporter for the *San Jose Mercury–News*, which had gone on AOL in 1993, had been brought in by Dick Duncan to run the operation. Kinsella and Duncan had a mutual acquaintance by the name of Joseph

Quinlan, an engaging, straight-talking TV news veteran who had been hired to work with the print staff on the News Exchange. Quinlan had told Duncan about Kinsella, who had launched a BBS company in Philadelphia in 1992, as well as one of the first commercial web sites that same year, before the Mosaic browser had even been launched. Something of a Web pioneer, Kinsella had gone to Haverford, the same college in Pennsylvania that Time Inc. editor in chief Norman Pearlstine and Jerry Levin had.

The meeting in November 1993 at which Duncan met Kinsella did not go well on the surface. When Duncan explained that *Time* Online was about to launch a daily *Time* news service on news-starved AOL, Kinsella scoffed at the notion; daily news was not *Time*'s core competency, and Duncan recalls Kinsella's reaction: "That's incredibly stupid. I can't imagine anyone using the Internet for daily news." But something about the brash Kinsella inspired Duncan. Somehow, he thought, "someone as hard-headed as [Kinsella] was just the guy we needed." There's a certain irony here, because Kinsella would go on in 1996 to join the start-up MSNBC's online effort, which pioneered the idea of an aggressive online newsroom that produced not just daily but hourly news. But as Kinsella had always argued, daily news couldn't be produced without resources, which is precisely what *Time* was trying to do.

Exactly where Bromberg's duties began and Kinsella's ended was unclear to both of them, and Kinsella took a somewhat direct approach to achieve dominant status. "The first day I started working, Jim Kinsella asked me if I wanted to have lunch with him," Bromberg recounts. "He took me to City Grill, and we were sitting there over our swordfish. He asked me what I thought my job was going to be. I said, 'We might do this, we might do that.'

"And he looked at me and asked, 'What do you mean "we"?' I said, 'Who knows what the thing is going to be called, 'Time Inc. Internet Project, Time Warner, who knows?' He sat there for thirty seconds and then announced, 'I've spent my entire life preparing for this. And you're not going to walk over me.' "

Bromberg responded with a mollifying line, which turned out to be a tactical mistake when dealing with the hugely ambitious Kinsella. "I said, 'I'm over my head, I'm the first one to tell you. Any way you get involved is fine with me.' " An uneasy truce was established, but the two were clearly uncomfortable with each other. (Kinsella doesn't deny this exchange took place, but he thinks it would have been out of character for him to be as rude as Bromberg recalls him as being.)

From then on, things only got worse. Soon after that lunch, Isaacson asked Bromberg to meet with Dick Duncan. While Bromberg sat in Isaacson's office,

"Walter called Dick and said, 'Dick, I want to introduce you to the guy who's going to run the editorial side of new media.'" Isaacson paused, apparently being given some pushback from Duncan on precisely who was going to be responsible for that job. Isaacson listened for a minute, and then told Duncan, "Well, don't worry about that. We'll sort it out."

Isaacson and Bromberg went down to Duncan's office, which reeked of cigar smoke. "Dick is sitting there, silver hair reflecting the light. And Jim Kinsella is sitting there, along with Bruce Judson. We start the meeting. I'm introduced as the guy who's going to head up the editorial side. And I see Kinsella's face turn bright white.

"He looks at Duncan. Duncan says, 'Well, Walter, don't you think this is a little premature?' Walter says, 'Don't worry. If there are any problems we'll worry about them later. This is Time Inc., you're *Time*,' meaning that the two entities, the magazine company and the magazine itself, could function with separate editorial staffs." The meeting ended abruptly and tensely and with no clear resolution. A battle for control of new media was clearly at hand.

Bromberg wasn't the only problem Kinsella had to deal with. Back in October 1993, shortly after Isaacson had been given the new-media position, Time Warner CEO Jerry Levin called a meeting that involved publishers from all the top Time Inc. magazines. It was to be held in the normally off-limits space on the 34th floor of the Time-Life Building, the executive suite where CEO and president have their offices, called the Map Room. *Time* had just signed with AOL, and publishers and other executives who had been summoned were now asked to describe what each was doing online. *Sports Illustrated for Kids,* for example, said it was affiliating with Prodigy because the service had the highest percentage of children among its users. *Time* magazine said it had gone with AOL because they had offered the best deal. One participant recalls that affiliation with an online service was simply assumed to be the paradigm of choice for most of its presenters.

But that was not the case when it came time for Chan Suh to speak. A 33-year-old Korean-born dropout from Sarah Lawrence, he was at that time the marketing director for the monthly *Vibe* magazine. *Vibe,* which celebrates hip-hop, was a joint venture between Time and African-American impresario Quincy Jones's investment arm. While it was nominally part of Time Inc., the magazine was housed in separate offices at 30th Street and Lexington Avenue, and was not really fully integrated into the Time Inc. ethos, especially since much of the "gangsta" world it celebrated was very alien to Time company style. Suh, a tall, burly Korean-American with a disarmingly straightforward manner, told the group, "'You know we're on this thing called the World Wide Web.' Everybody goes, 'What the hell is that?'"

Suh elaborated on "this thing called the Internet, which is not the same as CompuServe and AOL." He recalls "trying to explain this to a bunch of marketing types who have ten thousand other things to do rather than to handle this pesky little thing that doesn't make money."

After the meeting, Isaacson pulled Suh aside and began peppering him with questions. As Suh recalls, "Walter says to me, 'Who told you you could take editorial and put it up for public viewing?' I said, 'I don't know.' He said, 'Do you know if the writers and photographers have been compensated for this?' This was before any licensing agreements were in place. I told him, 'Walter, I really don't know. I took it and I put it up. All I can tell you is it's profitable from day one. It cost only about $400 a month for hosting. I'm getting subscriptions from it, and advertisers want to get into it, and they are paying me money so I will build little pages for them on our web site.'"

Suh, not lacking in *cojones* (he claims he didn't really care if he was fired or not), quickly attacked the whole premise of the meeting. "I was saying to Walter, I don't think you should give this stuff to AOL, because they have no content. I think you should get a piece of that company or something so that you have a vested interest. Right now they're paying you, but as soon as they leverage your content to get people they will be requiring you to pay them."

Looking back, Suh says, "I think I was unfettered by hubris, and I was an Internet user at that time before [most people were]. And Walter says, 'We have a great relationship with AOL.' Walter looks at it from the point of view of most people at Time Inc., that we're Time Inc. and they're not. Like that old line from *SNL*, 'I'm Chevy Chase and you're not.'"

Today best known as the CEO of an Internet consulting firm, Agency.com, Chan Suh has never really gotten credit for launching the first Time Inc. web site, one of the first web sites up for any media property. And he did so without any input or help from the company at all.

After his parents transplanted him from Korea to Paris and later to the United States—he arrived when he was 15—Chan Suh spent three years at Sarah Lawrence, intending to be a writer. That plan went awry, and Suh dropped out of the college without much idea of what he was going to do with his life. But a temp job at *New York* magazine in 1987 turned him around. The magazine (which ironically was a latecomer to the Web) was then investigating distributing Minitel, the French interactive telephone service. New York editor Ed Kosner, now at the *Daily News,* was also working on a dial-up bulletin board system for New Yorkers, an idea 10 years ahead of its time. Suh suggested that *New York* create a dial-up service using its "Cue" listings section. The idea would later be championed in the late '90s by Microsoft Sidewalk, which managed to waste tens of millions of dollars on it, but at the time the concept was full of promise, even if few people had modems in 1987. But Suh bought one for himself and quickly became addicted to Echo, the same BBS that had entranced Craig Bromberg.

"I was strangely attracted to this medium for cultural reasons," Suh explains. "There was no preconception on dial-up on the Internet. You can't tell if someone is Asian, well-educated, black, or well-dressed, or living anywhere. I found that appropriately freeing. I found it liberating to be able to talk without any assumptions, and to live and die by the quality of your communications. There were no graphics back then, you did modem-to-modem communications, and you would tap Enter twice to indicate you were done, kind of like a walkie-talkie."

Suh eventually landed a job at Time Inc.'s *Life* magazine working on sales development, research, and special advertising programs, and it was there he was introduced to John Rollins, the publisher of *Vibe.* The two were kindred spirits. Neither of them particularly like hip-hop, but they did understand enough about it to recognize that *Vibe* was a maverick operation, where they would have far more freedom to do whatever they wanted than at the typical Time Inc. operation:

"*Vibe* was a distant, barely tolerated cousin of the august *Time* magazine," Suh explains. "It was very much under the radar. I wasn't important at all. Even if I had thought there was a new-media infrastructure at Time Inc., I wouldn't have known where to go to get it. I had certain latitudes as the marketing director. I thought I could combine what I was doing six hours a day after 5 p.m. with what I was doing ten hours a day before 5 p.m. So I found the *Idiot's Guide to the Internet,* and I learned the basics of how it worked."

After an exhaustive search, Suh found "two guys in California" who had a pair of HP Internet servers and offered to host Vibe Online, with 20 megabytes of storage space, for only $400 a month.

"The whole thing is reversed now—it's 400 megs and $20 a month. I learned FTP, and I learned HTML. I would go up to editorial and say, 'Hey, can I have some of those pictures and text, the Quark files.' I learned Quark, and I stripped the files out, and all I needed was 72 dpi FPO pictures, I didn't need the original scans. I learned Photoshop and I put it together. Back then it was all gray background, and you couldn't move the pictures, you couldn't center it. Picture, text, picture, text, right. So I put that up as the first Time Warner web site."

As part of that effort, Suh also sold the first Time Warner online ads, including one for Timex that featured animated Timex watch faces that told the actual time. He still remembers the 1993 sales call on the company, perhaps the first time a major client was pitched what became known as a banner ad. "John and I went to Timex and told them, 'There's this thing called the Internet; a lot of college kids use it.' I asked for $30,000, which was a lot of money for *Vibe,* where an advertising page cost $25,000." The magazine eventually got $20,000 for the ad and made about $15,000 profit.

Being a Web pioneer did not really endear the brash Suh to Isaacson and others at Time Inc. New Media. "Nobody likes the kid who is right in the beginning," Suh exclaims. Not surprisingly, he quickly ran afoul of Jim Kinsella, for many of the same reasons as Craig Bromberg would. "Kinsella reminds me of that Richard Hatch guy on *Survivor.* Jim came in and thought he was the lord god and CEO of this whole thing. He and I used to have roaring fights."

Suh charges that Kinsella built a "funnel" around him "so he had to approve everything. This was at a time when the Web was exploding. It very quickly became not really about Time Inc.'s web site or the Web, but about Jim and Bruce. They weren't open to new ideas. I would see Jim on weekends, and he always had on this pressed white shirt. Buttoned down. Always in some kind of turmoil, because of Bruce."

Bruce Judson and Kinsella, in common with Chan Suh and Craig Bromberg, had clashed early, over an array of issues, although clearly the main battleground was simply a power play. In this crucial period, executives vied against each other to be the designated guy who "gets it" at major companies. To demonstrate that you were Web-savvy, it was often necessary to denigrate rivals, and this happened to a large degree at Time Inc.

Kinsella doesn't deny that what he was trying to create was ambitious. He wanted Time Warner to build immediately its own Internet-based ISP (Internet service provider), a dial-up "gateway" that would be a direct competitor of AOL. The scheme would later prove to be his undoing at the company.

Before Kinsella could fully deal with Judson, he still faced the obstacle of Craig Bromberg. For while they were co-existing uneasily, matters would soon have to come to a head, because the future clearly had a Time Inc./Time

Warner web site in it, and one of the two was going to be tapped to lead it. Given the editorial-oriented culture at Time Inc., the celebrated church/state dichotomy that tends to grant creatives more control than business people, the top editorial job at the Internet project would de facto be the top job overall, and Kinsella made no secret of his desire for that kind of power. To do it, he had to push out of the way both Judson, who came up through marketing, and Bromberg, as the rival editorial person.

"At this point, Isaacson knew there was so much tension between me and Kinsella that he says, 'I want both of you in my office,'" Bromberg recalls. Isaacson faced the two combatants and told them bluntly, "I don't know which of you will be the guy who runs this thing, but we have to figure it out. We have this thing called a bake-off. Let's see who comes up with a better idea for a web site."

"Who am I supposed to do this with?" an outgunned Bromberg asked. "I have no resources, Walter, I'm just a guy on the 40th floor." Kinsella had all the extensive resources of *Time* magazine behind him.

The bake-off lasted an agonizing couple of months. During it, Jim Kinsella proved that despite his beginnings as an ink-stained wretch, he had learned to play corporate politics like a seasoned master. Compared to the cerebral Bromberg, he proved himself to be in another league entirely.

Bromberg was always just a little later than Kinsella in getting to the finish line. In one meeting, Isaacson asked, "All right, which of you has a home page designed?" While Bromberg looked down at his shoes, Kinsella piped up and said he had it all but done and could bring it to the next meeting. Whether he actually had anything completed at that point, he did arrive with a finished product as promised, and ultimately that's what counted.

The two contestants also battled over the name, which came to be key to how the web site would be understood within the Time Warner hierarchy. Bromberg was proposing Calliope, symbolizing the concept that the 40 individual brands within the Time Warner fold could somehow sing together in harmony. Isaacson's name, also championed by Kinsella, was Pathfinder, which was truer to the spirit of the enterprise, the idea that Time's web site could guide you through the uncharted Internet as James Fenimore Cooper's eponymous character had led the way through the American wilderness. Only the literate Isaacson knew the true meaning of the term, but everyone agreed it had a ring to it.

Bromberg also lost ground because the name Calliope had already been claimed on the Internet by a CD-ROM manufacturer that didn't want to sell it to Time Inc.

Chan Suh remembers the Pathfinder name first being proposed at one of a series of endless meetings in the Map Room, where concepts for the Web operation were outlined. He didn't think he'd heard correctly. "I said, 'You mean like the pickup truck?' He says, 'No, as in the novel.'"

Isaacson's thinking on the name issue and on the underlying philosophy of a Time web site is clear in a September 6, 1994, memo he addressed to "Naming fans." "There is a sense that Time Warner, or Time Inc., should be part of the title in order to be more descriptive about what this is," he wrote. "Conceivably, we could have a name such as 'Time Warner's Gateway' (or whatever) and then eventually let the Time Warner branding recede and emphasize just the name ('Gateway' or whatever) when we market it a year or two from now." (Among the alternative names he suggested were: TimeLine, Time Warner's Cavalcade, Time Warner's Arena, Tempo, Time Warner's Roadrunner, which later was used for the cable modem service, and a ludicrous entry, The Time Machine: An Online Service from Time Warner.)

However much effort was being spent on it, the tentative nature of the project was clear—note the reference to "when we market it a year or two from now." Anyone proposing a time frame like that at a pure-play Internet company, where everything had to be done that very day, would have been fired. The Time group was compelled by none of the sense of urgency that was already routinely driving online services.

An earlier 16-page August 1, 1994, confidential document from Isaacson, entitled "Time Inc. Internet/Online Service: A Proposal for a Time Inc. Electronic Network and World Wide Web Site," shows the same hesitancy. On its first page, Isaacson states boldly, "The foundation of the system will probably be a set of Time Inc. servers connected to the World Wide Web, an organizing element of the Internet." That "probably" is key, for it reflects the dueling fiefdoms, the uncertainty, the lack of commitment, and the confusion that plagued the venture from the start.

Its lack of vision and definition did not mean, however, that the project wasn't embraced by Levin and the 34th floor of Time Inc. *Time*'s Dick Duncan recalls that Levin was consulted frequently during this period. "Walter was on the phone to Jerry three times a day," he says, and remembers attending web site meetings with both Levin and James Chiddix, the senior vice president at Time Warner Cable who had been largely responsible for selling Levin on the FSN.

Duncan believes that Levin was particularly eager to replace the failed FSN venture with another interactive dream—a role that Pathfinder filled perfectly. In his August 1 proposal, Isaacson went so far as to echo Levin's FSN vision about staying ahead of the curve.

"In targeting an audience," he wrote, "we will follow Russell Long's advice about shooting a duck: Aim ahead of the duck." He concluded, "Among the hallmarks of the digital world are that nothing is final and everything remains in our control. Creation becomes a process rather than an act. Which is why this endeavor will be so exciting."

Suh and others say that the mentality that would plague Pathfinder for the next two years was already in place. Because Time had been dealing with CompuServe and AOL as "walled gardens," the concept was simply extended to the Web.

"They thought they would start Pathfinder as the next-generation online service where people would come into it and they would never get out," Suh says. "So searching the Internet didn't make sense for them. Why would you want to search anything other than Time Warner content? Time Warner brings the world to you."

Indeed Isaacson's memo does not mention bringing in content from outside Time Warner, nor does it make any reference to the concept of offering a general guide to the Internet, a project on which Yahoo! was already at work. It was completely self-referential and had the salutary virtue, in Time Inc. eyes, of offering a paradigm under which "everything remains in our control." That was the all-important phrase in this document and in this vision of the digital future. The truth was that neither Time Inc. nor any one single company could control the Internet or the content available on it. But Time Inc. had always looked at itself as unique, dominant, superior. While virtually all media Web operations were guilty of this form of hubris, Time Inc.'s mistakes were greater simply because their hubris was more monumental and all-encompassing.

The top echelon at Time Inc. went to great lengths in later years to alter the past a bit, making the dysfunctional Pathfinder appear to be a more coherent concept than it actually was. In a startling claim, Time Inc.'s editor in chief Norm Pearlstine told *Adweek* in September 2000 that Pathfinder had been a "useful, legitimate, and appropriate investment" for the company. Pathfinder had been the "first portal," he told the trade magazine, and "we did understand that a search directory was something you'd want to do with it. We had lots of conversations about how content would be aggregated from sources outside Time Inc. and Time Warner."

This is history in retrospect, because Time did not aggressively seek an alliance with a viable Web search engine, offering instead a lame search capability branded Verity that even its own executives thought was inadequate. Time always looked inward to its own properties, not outward to the new world the Web was creating. Pathfinder was designed to feature Time content and never considered the Internet itself to be the ultimate destination. While services like Yahoo! and Excite used the Internet as a whole as their ruling paradigm, for Pathfinder the Web was an afterthought, and it provided links only to those web sites that were within the Time family. While Yahoo! was a directory, not a search engine, it always placed a licensed Web search icon (including AltaVista, Inktomi, and Google) front and center, because it always assumed that its users wanted to surf the Web, not just Yahoo! and its proprietary directory.

Another shortcoming of Pathfinder was that its design, hierarchy, and content and staffing structure were based on the magazine model, not the Internet paradigm. A glance at an undated staff list confirms that even years after Pathfinder's launch, when many thousands of web sites were online and Yahoo! had already achieved supremacy, Pathfinder was still clinging to a typical magazine hierarchy, with an editor of new media at its top (Isaacson), a Pathfinder editor (Kinsella), a deputy editor (Maria Wilhelm), an assistant deputy editor for entertainment (Bromberg), and an array of associate editors, assistant editors, and art directors.

What Bromberg had been pushing for was something closer in spirit to Salon.com, an online forum for ideas, the kind of thing he had done in his earlier career. While he wasn't advocating hiring a gaggle of online journalists, as Salon had done, he did argue for drawing from the wealth of Time Inc. content to create something like an online magazine.

Part of the difference between what Kinsella wanted and what Bromberg was advocating was fundamentally about synergies—Bromberg's concept had the web-site staff working with the magazines to produce a coherent whole, while Kinsella's was more focused on Pathfinder's dictating to the rest of the company how the Web worked. While that difference might seem petty or trivial on its surface, it was all-important internally, for it was a matter of style. In Kinsella's battle for supremacy, he was to win the battle against Bromberg but lose the battle for control of Time Warner's digital destiny.

Bromberg found out he'd lost to Kinsella in an almost casual manner. During this whole period, Kinsella was nominally in charge of the *Time* magazine Web operation, and Bromberg was supposed to be Isaacson's deputy, figuring out the online destiny of the magazine company as a whole. But in practice, it never worked like that, because Kinsella never confined his ambitions solely to *Time* magazine. And it quickly became clear that Kinsella knew how to play the corporate game far better than Bromberg. In a meeting that was almost proforma by this stage, considering how hard Kinsella was working for the title, Isaacson informed Bromberg that Kinsella would now have responsibility for the Time Inc. Internet project, now officially dubbed Pathfinder.

While Kinsella pushed for Bromberg to be fired immediately after this meeting, which took place in early summer 1994, getting rid of him wouldn't be that simple. Time Inc. has a somewhat paternalistic culture, and its complacent employees were fond of reciting, in the 1990s, just how difficult it was to get fired at the company. Whenever someone was shown the door, it had to be for fairly extraordinary reasons. So Bromberg wasn't dismissed outright, but he didn't really have a formal job afterward. Kinsella routinely did not invite Bromberg to meetings and often held long staff sessions in his office with the door closed. "He was trying to get me to quit, and I was not going," Bromberg says, with a hint of defiance still apparent years later. As preparations for the September 1994 launch of Pathfinder quickened, Kinsella quickly began moving in people above Bromberg, including an art director Bromberg particularly detested.

The process of creating Pathfinder was not organic. One participant recalls that not a single detail flowed smoothly or reflected how things were done online. The entire process had, in effect, become politicized. "Everything was a huge fight. Where would you put the names of people? Where would you put an ad? Every one of those things was a huge fight, politically, not artistically. We were reacting to ground that was being carved out by *Wired*, to a great degree."

Wired was a comparatively tiny magazine based in San Francisco, with the same big ego, Louis Rossetto, presiding over both it and its web site, HotWired.com, which appeared roughly contemporaneously with Pathfinder. When, in late 1995, Rossetto got wind that an upcoming feature in the magazine would be critical of IBM, a major advertising client, he canceled the feature. When challenged, he called a special meeting and told the staff that they were "crybabies" and demanded that they grow up. Such peremptory behavior just wasn't possible at Time Inc., where editors weren't supposed to act like publishers, where myriad turfs had to be protected, and where power was hugely decentralized. Ironically Rossetto himself, with a hipper-than-thou entourage in tow, visited Pathfinder as it was prepared to launch. Everyone from the Time Inc. side wore ties; everyone from *Wired* did not. Rossetto pontificated about the Internet for a couple hours and then left. No one later seemed to know what they could do together.

"We were meeting for the sake of meeting," recalls one of the attendees. Still, Rossetto had been highly influential in convincing Time Inc. to do a web site.

In hindsight, the *Wired* magazine of the 1990s proved a poor guide to what would happen in the cyberworld. It combined boundless optimism about the power of technology to transform society with a permanently curled upper lip toward anything that smacked of the old ways of doing things, media included.

Perhaps the nadir of this false prophecy was the July 1997 cover story by Peter Schwartz and Peter Leyden, which prophesied confidently that the good times brought on by technology would last practically forever. "We are watching the beginning of a global economic boom on a scale never experienced before," the two wrote. Historians "will look back on our era as an extraordinary moment. They will chronicle the 40-year period from 1980 to 2020 as the key years of a remarkable transformation. In the developed countries of the West, new technology will lead to big productivity increases that will cause high economic growth—actually, waves of technology will continue to roll out through the early part of the 21st century."

Wired's zealotry was almost akin to that of the Chinese during the Cultural Revolution, burning priceless antiques because they were part of the old society and weren't needed anymore. Indeed the magazine's editors believed they were launching a cultural as well as a technological revolution. Just what that culture valued, other than making money and feeling superior to the old elites in New York and Los Angeles, was hard to determine.

In the late '90s, it was almost a cliché to hear desperate old-media executives swear fealty to *Wired*, so eager were they to prove their technological bona fides. At Time Warner, a belief in that mind-set would have far-reaching consequences.

Kinsella ended up doing most of the heavy lifting for the actual launch of Pathfinder, while Isaacson conferred with Levin and attended corporate meetings. Kinsella was working harder on it than anything he'd ever done—and beginning to wonder if it was all worth it.

"I remember being up night after night after night," Kinsella says. "I slept in my office a lot." He ruefully harkens back to an incident during the start-up period when he asked a secretary to stay late with him. "She wasn't happy about it. She had said to somebody that I didn't get it, that it wasn't the Time Inc.

way. I remember thinking that this isn't going to work, that I should go out and do my own start-up."

The overall atmosphere at Pathfinder was gloomy from the start, partly because Levin, uncharacteristically, was somewhat tepid in his response to the actual product. Curt Viebranz, one of the executives who debuted the beta version of Pathfinder for the CEO, does not recall the experience fondly.

"Jerry saw Pathfinder for the first time in August 1994 in Walter's office," he says. "It was late in the day, about 6:15. Jerry was still riding the TV horse, not the PC. On seeing the demo, he was noncommittal and distracted." In fact, Levin's lack of enthusiasm—or knowledge—had been clear as early as the 1993 annual report, where his chairman's message contains not a single reference to the Web. (To be fair, his underwhelmed response is typical of TV executives who wanted the Web to be more like TV—with moving pictures, lots of flashy graphics, and a generally zippier approach.)

Levin's indifference, long after many, including Viebranz and Isaacson, had seen the possibilities inherent in the Internet, was the source of intense frustration to many at Time Inc.'s new-media group, but particularly Viebranz, who had made a belief in the Internet a cornerstone of what he hoped to accomplish at the company. There was a huge contradiction between Levin's supposed vision for interactive media and his actual involvement or granular knowledge of how it worked. After the demo, Viebranz became involved in several shouting matches with Levin on the subject, never a factor in guaranteeing longevity for Time Warner executives. Viebranz left for a job at HBO in October, the same month Pathfinder launched.

Pathfinder did not, of course, set the world on fire, but it would have been surprising if it had. Few people had Web browsers in October 1994, and fewer still could have been hugely excited by the hodgepodge of content that greeted the intrepid souls who dialed up Pathfinder that day: a few news stories from *Time* magazine, a Virtual Garden service that had been created by Time-Life executive Sean Callahan (a former editor of *Folio:* magazine), and the content from *Vibe* that Chan Suh had managed to put up. Unlike the huge press coverage that greeted 1990s Time Inc. magazine launches like *Entertainment Weekly,* Pathfinder made its debut with little attention. A lot more interesting information was available on CompuServe, Prodigy, and AOL.

The Pathfinder experience really created more questions than it answered. It was online, but it wasn't generating any real revenue. Should Time Inc. compete directly with AOL by offering dial-up service as well? Should it partner with a developing online power like the brand-new Netscape? What Isaacson would later call a "parade" of powerful high-tech forces began to call on Time during 1994, each of them arguing that Time should ally with them to create a joint venture that would generate far more than the amount it was generating from licensing its content to online services.

At this stage, Time had an online tabula rasa before it. The company was to fill that blank slate with what it knew best: stories and files from its magazines, and content that was based on the journalism that was its core competency. It insisted that it knew media best, and there were few doubts in the Time & Life Building that this was the best approach.

CHAPTER 4

Time Doesn't Need Any Help Online

On a hot August day in 1994, shortly before Pathfinder finally appeared, the then-current braintrust at AOL, Steve Case and Ted Leonsis, had breakfast in the executive dining room in the Time & Life Building in Manhattan with their counterparts at Time Inc., Walter Isaacson and Curt Viebranz. *Time* had just signed its carriage deal with America Online, a deal in every way presided over by Walter Isaacson. Viebranz was present as the business-side representative.

Leonsis, who is more effusive and socially comfortable than the more sober-sided Case, had just joined AOL as a result of that company's purchase of his Redgate Communications Corp., a Florida-based e-commerce company. Leonsis had been an author, as well as a publisher of computer magazines, and had become something of an expert at the list-management business. He had come to Steve Case's attention more through happenstance than by design.

Leonsis's colleague at Redgate, Randy Coppersmith, himself later an AOL executive, recalls how the two joined together. "Ted was raising money for Redgate, and he had me set up a meeting with Dan Case at Hambrecht and Quist. He took the meeting with us, and he was really kind. He said you guys are great—you could sell ice cream to eskimos. But Dan said he didn't invest in marketing companies. We were packing our bags, dejectedly, when he said, 'By the way, why don't you call my kid brother, he's got this little company in Tysons Corner.' So Ted called Steve and they fell instantly in love."

As president of the AOL Services Co., a position that involved supervision of the content-acquisition strategy, Leonsis had quickly identified Microsoft and its budding Microsoft Network as the principal enemy, not because he thought it would have superior technology, but because he knew that Microsoft could afford to pay more for content than AOL. (Indeed a multimillion-dollar deal that MSN would shortly sign with the Paramount studio for exclusive on-line rights to material from the *Star Trek* series would dwarf any payment AOL had ever made for content.)

AOL, therefore, needed to make a flanking bid to lock up Time Inc.'s all-important content before Microsoft got in the game. To do so, Leonsis had to come up with a business proposal that played to Isaacson's empire-building ambitions. Using the *Time* magazine deal as leverage, Leonsis set up the August meeting to make an extraordinary proposal to Time Inc., his first important appearance in his new position. The proposal was simple—and sweeping.

"We'd like to negotiate a blanket deal to put all of your magazines online," he told Isaacson and Viebranz. "And then we'd like to do a fifty-fifty joint venture that we'd both fund and both own, which would go after the organizing, cata-loging, and searching of the Internet space." In short, AOL and Time Inc. would join forces to create a joint venture offering Time's content and the front door or "front-end" of a dial-up Internet service using AOL's network. This is what AOL later became, so, in essence, this was a proposal for Time Warner to own a huge stake in the fledgling online service. "They would use our computer network back-end, and they would program the front-end, and together we would go after the Web business," is how Leonsis summarizes his offer. Users would sign on AOL and be greeted with a plethora of content provided by everything from *People* to *Time, Fortune,* and *Sports Illustrated.* It was nothing less than a full partnership between Time Inc. and AOL.

As part of the proposal, the two partners would together acquire a company called GNN, or Global Network Navigator, which owned the then-popular WebCrawler search engine. (It seems clear, in hindsight, that if Time Inc. had done this, it would have been years ahead of the other so-called portals, in-cluding Excite, Infoseek, Lycos, and AltaVista, or even Yahoo!, which did not offer Web access.)

The quartet stuck to generalities at first, but by the middle of the breakfast, Leonsis switched into high sales mode and tried hard to convince Isaacson and Viebranz of the potential of his proposal. It was a powerful combination: the search capability of WebCrawler, with the powerful Internet network main-tained by Advanced Network & Services, known as ANS, which AOL had ac-quired for $35 million in April 1994, and Time Warner's preeminent brands and content. AOL and Time Warner would sweep over the competition, par-

ticularly the just-emerging Yahoo! Equity in the still-struggling AOL was definitely on the table and was a further inducement.

The breakfast concluded with a pitch loaded with all the visionary fervor
that only Leonsis could muster, as he essentially presented the Internet business
as ripe for the plucking, but Isaacson was not convinced.

"We really admire what you guys have done," Isaacson told his guests.
"We're thrilled to be partners with you at *Time* magazine." But that's as far as
it was going to go. When it came to doing deals with other Time Inc. magazines, Isaacson said (somewhat disingenuously, given his corporate position at
Time Inc.) that he couldn't speak for them, and that Case and Leonsis were free
to deal with them on an individual basis. But Time Inc. couldn't or wouldn't
make a "corporate decision" on a joint venture with AOL.

In Leonsis's version of the meeting, Isaacson was quite dismissive: "And in
regards to doing a joint venture with you, Steve and Ted, we look at it and fundamentally we say, What are the core competencies that you have that we need
to get into the [Web] business? One, you get customers or subscribers, and certainly we know how to get subscribers. Two, you program, and certainly we
have more editorial experience and art direction and programming experience.
Three, you'll build the back-end, and now, we've learned enough about that,
we don't really think we need to partner with you. It's a big market and everything will be fine, and we'll meet in the marketplace."

Leonsis was a bit dumbfounded by Isaacson's demurral, because he was gen-
uinely convinced that he had just laid out the blueprint for the deal of the century. For his part, Case was somewhat miffed, because he had believed Leonsis
could deliver Isaacson and Time Inc., based on Leonsis's assurances. Case, ever
the diplomat, regarded Isaacson with a quizzical stare for a moment, and then
replied, "You know, you're probably right, Walter, you know how to get subscribers better than us, you know how to program better than us. But if the
AOL service fails, I'm going to kill Ted. But if whatever you do fails, you will
get the job as editor in chief of *Time* magazine." It was a prescient, if cutting,
remark—Case's way of asserting that AOL would work harder to achieve number-
one status online than Time would. In the end, of course, Case was absolutely
right. Isaacson did go on to become managing editor (the equivalent of editor
in chief) of *Time* magazine, proving that the online business really wasn't
halfway as important to Isaacson as it was to Case and Leonsis. On November
15, 2000, when Isaacson was interviewed by the *Washington Post* for an article
on his promotion, his second after landing the top editor job at *Time* maga-

zine, to editorial director at Time Inc., he dismissed all speculation that he had ever been interested in the online business, with what could be presumed was a straight face: "I know that I don't know anything [about the Internet], which is why it's going to be fun to learn." Astute student of history that he is, Isaacson takes it for a given, probably correctly, that there is no institutional memory in American corporate life.

Curt Viebranz puts yet another spin on that pivotal meeting. He recalls that he and Isaacson had, in fact, discussed the idea that they could probably get a better price for licensing the Time Inc. properties if they negotiated all the online licenses for them as a single deal, despite the fact that the magazines themselves wanted the freedom to work out their own agreements. Viebranz recognized, however, that the Time Inc. culture was so divided about new media that the prospects of a significant joint venture were little more than a pipe dream. "We hadn't even figured out how to rob the stagecoach, and these guys want to divide up the loot," is his colorful way of explaining the dysfunctional atmosphere of the company at that time. The rejection of the AOL proposal was more about Time Inc.'s difficult corporate culture than its arrogance, he concludes. (It was Viebranz who coined the phrase, later used by other Time Inc. New Media figures, that the job of trying to get the magazines to work cooperatively was "like herding cats.")

Viebranz reveals that Time also had discussions with CompuServe about a big overall online deal. Those talks had proceeded to the point of a term sheet being prepared, but the plan eventually fell apart because of Walter Isaacson's animosity to a key CompuServe executive. In a subsequent meeting with Leonsis, according to Dick Duncan, the AOL president offered Time a whopping $20 million outright for exclusive online rights to its content. Under the proposal that Duncan recalls, this would have been more of a simple licensing deal and less of a joint venture. But finding themselves so ardently pursued by the two online companies had the affect of making Time Inc. New Media wary of agreeing to *any* deal.

If you go to a flea market and offer a seller $100 for something he would have parted with for $10, he'll naturally grow suspicious and come to believe it's worth $1,000. In the end, he might not sell it at all. This is more or less what happened at Time Inc. Bruce Judson recalls a key meeting after the pivotal AOL breakfast: "I always remember being in Walter's office and the two of us saying, 'There's something going on here. We don't understand what it is.

These people do. If CompuServe and AOL are talking to us about wanting our content, before we go into a joint venture we should understand what it is.'"

Judson says the three Time Inc. New Media musketeers—himself, Isaacson, and Viebranz—had been inspired by a profile of Barry Diller by Ken Auletta that had run about a year earlier in *The New Yorker.* The article somewhat comically portrayed the volatile Diller, armed with a Macintosh PowerBook, on a fact-finding mission to understand what was happening in the computer world. Auletta portrayed the ailing Home Shopping Network and its rival, QVC, as promising new-media vehicles in Diller's hands. Diller, who would go on to try to build his own somewhat cobbled-together media empire, is an unlikely role model for new-media executives, but he was someone the three of them knew, and they soon embarked on a transcontinental fact-finding mission of their own.

In the ensuing year, through the remainder of 1994 and early 1995, "We went out and traveled across the country," Judson recalls, "trying to figure out how all this new-media stuff was working out. We met with anyone who was significant in the Internet." Isaacson and Judson met with WAIS (an early Internet protocol), Cisco, Spry (an early browser company later acquired by CompuServe), and Yahoo! (represented by CEO Tim Koogle). In common with most discussions between Time Inc. and outside companies, all these discussions would prove frustrating and inconclusive, as shoe-horning magazine company ambitions into the imperatives of high-tech outfits proved difficult.

Even companies that had been founded with the idea of partnering with media companies had trouble doing business with Time Inc. The magazine company's encounter with the fledgling Netscape Communications Corp., of Mountain View, California, was extremely frustrating. Some former Pathfinder/ Time Inc. New Media executives blame Bruce Judson for having given the thumbs-down to an investment proposal by Netscape founder Dr. James H. Clark, who had introduced the world's first commercial browser product in April 1994, in partnership with Marc Andreessen, the creator of the Mosaic research prototype for one of the first Internet browsers. (Andreessen and co-worker Eric Bina had developed Mosaic at the National Center for Supercomputing Applications at the University of Illinois. It debuted in March 1993.)

Netscape, represented by Morgan Stanley & Co., was looking for a round of funding from publishing companies in 1994 and 1995. Clark, together with the fresh-faced recent college graduate Andreessen, made the pilgrimage to the Time-Life Building, meeting with a group that included Kinsella, Isaacson, Duncan, and Judson. Judson explains that Clark was already known to Time

Warner, because he had been CEO of Silicon Graphics, Inc., the company that built the ill-fated Orlando cable boxes.

"So when he left SGI, he came in and met with us repeatedly," Judson notes. "They were going to build a super publishing platform for the Internet, which became the Netscape Navigator. He was looking for us to invest, and they would be our infrastructure provider."

Netscape's product was the first browser to appear after the noncommercial Mosaic product, the entity that gave rise to Netscape Communications, and ultimately served as the default home page for millions of users' Web experience. Since most people then and now don't know how to change their default home page, they were automatically directed by the software to www.netscape.com when they signed on to the Web. As a pure software company, Netscape had no experience in the content business, nor did it have ambitions to get into it, as AOL eventually did. As a result, for several key years Netscape had some of the highest traffic of any web site, but the actual content of its home page consisted of boring press releases and download instructions. If Time Inc. had recognized the potential with Netscape and had jumped at the chance at investing and collaborating with the company, it would have instantly transformed Pathfinder into the most popular web site, and the powerful Time Inc./Netscape combination could have easily become an adversary that would have severely hampered AOL's ability to grow. It's hard not to see this as the biggest lost opportunity the Web has yet presented. In turn, if Netscape had had a powerful partner like Time Warner in the mid-'90s, it might not have had to sell out to AOL.

Judson recalls that Viebranz did offer to take a proposal to Levin that Time Inc. invest in Netscape, but only under certain conditions. "We didn't have a pool of money for investments, as an operating division. I do believe that Curt negotiated with Clark and said we could come in if you give us a significant piece of the company. Curt was ready to go with Time Warner's investment arm and to push it up to Levin, if it was going to be a significant piece of the business. [But] Jim Clark wanted a variety of investors, and when Time Inc. invested in something, it was always with the right to buy it outright. We don't invest for investment's sake. What does an investment get you? It gets you financial returns, and that wasn't our business."

Viebranz himself says that Clark's investment proposal was that Time buy 1 percent of the company, based on a $100 million early valuation. It would have been a negligible amount for Time but, as Viebranz stressed, investing was not part of the makeup of the company—it was foolish to gamble on investments when you believed you had the best minds in America working for you, minds that regularly came up with hit media properties like HBO and *Entertainment Weekly.*

Netscape decided it didn't need Time's help, and on April 7, 1995, it announced that it had concluded a private placement of Series C preferred stock, representing an 11 percent stake in the company, with five big businesses from the publishing and technology worlds, including Adobe Systems Inc., the Hearst Corporation, Knight Ridder, TCI Technology Ventures, and the Times Mirror Company. The investment was fairly small, about $20 million, which represented a valuation of about $140 million for Netscape as a whole. The announcement riveted the media world, which was then assuming that it would be bedrock builders of the Internet content business to come.

The diversity of partners and the minority stake each of them held insured that the new ownership consortium wouldn't have much influence at Netscape, or that any kind of media culture would become persuasive in the Mountain View, California, Netscape headquarters. Still, the partnership featured an interesting provision in that it had stipulated an advertising component. In the early days of the company, the home page sported ads from AT&T, EDS, General Motors, MasterCard, Adobe Systems, and Netcom. Advertisers paid $40,000 each for their banner positions, which was very competitive during this period. Had the company worked more closely with its media partners, however, it could have become a much larger ad powerhouse.

When the Netscape consortium was announced, Time Inc. was glaringly absent. Jim Kinsella blames Judson, while Time Inc.'s culture, which deemphasized partnership on a major scale, was clearly equally at play. "Bruce Judson had a friend, a guy he went to business school at Yale with, and that guy was at a company called Open Market," Kinsella says. "I was in the pitch session with Clark, and it was really obvious that Judson wanted to do a deal with his guy at Open Market, not with Netscape."

Kinsella says this with some degree of animosity—he's definitely not a fan of Judson's, but he doesn't quite have his facts right about Judson's ties to Open Market founder Shikhar Ghosh. Open Market, a Boston-area company that debuted in 1994, was a less visionary route onto the Web than the more promising venue Netscape was offering. The company was essentially a big server farm and provided fledgling web sites with proprietary software that enabled them to do transactions.

Judson doesn't deny that personal ties to Open Market cemented the deal. "We decided to go with Open Market as an infrastructure provider for a variety of reasons," he says. "I had personal experience working with Shikhar. I had been a partner at the Boston Consulting Group, where he had come from, and he had gone to school with Curt, so we had a rapport. We were a nontechnology company dependent on technology. Jim Clark was clearly going to be, from the beginning, huge and significant. Our leverage with Netscape would be zero. I could see that.

"We were [Open Market's] biggest client. I said, 'Shikhar, if we go down, you go down too.' From the whole perspective of leverage, relationships, and because they were on the East Coast, we went with Open Market. We thought that, as our technology provider, it made more sense. At that moment, we were very convinced of the future. We saw it as there being a group of technology masters—AOL, CompuServe, Prodigy. They licensed access from GTE, AT&T, or Sprint. They then went out and licensed content. We felt that they would all disaggregate, and that access wouldn't be difficult, and that content would be paid for. The only thing that wouldn't be a commodity would be content."

As part of its Open Market deal, Time Inc. New Media invested $500,000 in the company and received in return 500,000 warrants to buy Open Market stock at a low pre-IPO price, and Judson also took a seat on the Open Market board. (Later, when Time Inc. exercised the warrants, the company cleared about $7 million after taxes, far less than it would have made if it had taken a significant stake in Netscape.)

Early 1994 was a confusing, critical period for media companies. Take the terminology being tossed around. For more than a decade cable companies and cable networks, dominated by Time Warner and TeleCommunications Inc., had seen themselves as on the cutting edge, new media in every sense of the term. Cable was the industry that represented technical innovations, offered choice, and had the aura of newfangled technology.

By 1994 the cable programming industry was less than 15 years old. Time Warner's Jerry Levin had been one of the guys who had launched it. Executives like Levin had gotten accustomed to thinking of themselves as on the cutting edge of media, and suddenly their industry's most seasoned executives, men and women still in their thirties or forties for the most part, were being dismissed as representing old media. No one wants to be called old, but more problematically, few executives wanted to be part of an outmoded form of media. Cable network executives liked to laugh at the complacency and slow reaction time of broadcast executives at CBS, NBC, ABC, and Fox, but now suddenly they were the ones looking old-fashioned. This mind-set, the sense of being left behind, explains a lot about big media's rush to get into the Web in 1994. Nobody wanted to miss an emerging technology this time, as the TV networks had missed cable in the not-so-distant past.

This meant that Time Warner had a lot of meetings with companies it wanted to work with. The tragedy was that the company didn't know how to work with software companies and their representatives—people who didn't wear ties, had no titles, didn't have a rigid corporate hierarchy. It was as if they were talking two separate languages. It was hard to tell these businesses apart, with their whimsical names like Yahoo! and Excite, and it was almost impossible to gauge the relative value of what each of them was proposing. They all talked fast, used a lot of insider lingo, and displayed unflappable self-importance. Worse, they didn't bother to show the proper sense of deference when someone of the stature of Levin was present. Many couldn't even hide the fact that they considered companies like Time Warner to be dinosaurs, perhaps useful for a quick deal, but shark bait in the long run.

A typical example is the approach that Yahoo! made to Time Warner in 1995, which was characterized by mutual confusion and distrust. (Yahoo! was represented in the discussions by Sequoia Capital.) Time Inc. did not see a lot of value in Yahoo! as its content-based approach—simply offering a directory of the Internet—seemed antithetical to the goal Time Inc. had set for itself, which was to keep users within its orbit.

The two entrepreneurs who had formed Yahoo!, Jerry Yang and David Filo, had started the business in 1994 by keeping a list they called Dave and Jerry's Guide to the World Wide Web. The Yahoo! name was born late one night as a meaningless acronym. Or almost meaningless, it actually stands for Yet Another Hierarchically Officious Oracle. By the following year, however, Yahoo! was still a very small operation, with only 36,000 entries in its directory and about 200,000 users a day. In April 1995 Yang and Filo announced that they would take leaves of absence from Stanford, where both were Ph.D. candidates in electrical engineering, to work with Sequoia Capital to raise money for the service.

The failure of their mission at Time Inc. could easily have been predicted. Yang was then 26 and Filo 28; two graduate students, no matter how articulate, and no matter how much the grown-ups at Sequoia Capital pleaded their case, had little chance to make headway at blue-chip Time Inc., especially since it had already launched Pathfinder. Today, in fact, it's hard to find anyone who will admit to having been in the meeting with the boys, although several sources insist it took place.

At approximately the same time, Yang and Filo met with MCI and AOL. The two told MCI director Michael Mael during this time period that they had just been offered $1 million each in AOL stock to sell their company and were confused about what to do. In her book *aol.com,* Kara Swisher notes that Yahoo! had wanted just a little more from AOL. "And we probably would have taken it if the offer had been just a little bit higher," Yang has said. Ted Leonsis, who considers his lack of enthusiasm for buying Yahoo! one of his biggest mistakes, jokes that every time he sees Yang he tells him, "You could be a vice president of AOL by now."

As it had with Netscape, Time Inc. quickly passed on the opportunity to work with Yahoo! and its young entrepreneurs. Yang and Filo would have sold a big chunk of their company to Time Warner for very little money but couldn't find anyone to take it seriously. The talks sputtered out quickly.

Isaacson sums up all this furious and epochal activity by admitting that it all began to blur after a while. "There was a parade of people, whether it was Yahoo! or the six other portals that were being developed, and whether it was Netscape or CompuServe or any other online service, everybody paraded into Time Inc. and said we will give you 20 percent for large sums of money," he recalls. "And obviously we would have been incredibly successful if we had picked the right three out of the fifty deals that came to us and pumped $100 million into each one, and if we had been an investment bank we could have pumped a couple million into a whole lot of things."

Seeming to forget that he did serve as president of Time Inc. New Media for part of his tenure there, Isaacson adds, "My own perspective was that I was on the editorial side, I thought we should just produce really cool stuff. If the people on the business side wanted to play investment banker and bank on Yahoo! or Excite or Lycos or AltaVista or any of those, we could have made some strategic investments that would have been smart." This version of events, certainly, underplays his own role considerably. It was Isaacson who represented Time Inc. in numerous business meetings. Dick Duncan recalls Isaacson getting incredibly excited during a trip to AOL in 1995 that featured a lengthy session with Walter at the white board, mapping out the possibilities. In the end, according to Leonsis, it was Isaacson who turned down the joint venture offer.

True to its ego-driven heritage, true to the then-dominant belief that it alone could best figure out its destiny, Time Inc. decided to forgo a partnership with a high-tech company in 1995. This was entirely consistent with Time Warner's history, and the advent of a technological revolution wasn't about to change that. At least, not yet.

CHAPTER 5

Dialing for Dollars

Time Warner's quixotic efforts to find a big technology partner in 1995 took place against a backdrop of a serious onslaught by the telephone industry into areas traditionally reserved for media, most especially cable TV, Jerry Levin's own turf. The top executives of the largest telephone companies—Bell Atlantic and AT&T, among others—had always thought that their extensive networks could be redeployed to deliver video, and 1995 was the year that it seemed to be about to happen.

During 1995 there was still a pervasive feeling among many top media companies that it was the giant telephone industry that held the key to the new-media future. AT&T had started its own Internet service provider, Worldnet, which was widely believed to have the potential to overtake AOL. Long-distance companies like MCI had in fact pioneered many elements of new media, including rudimentary e-mail, and MCI provided the backbone that drove much Internet traffic. Although MCI would eventually become key to what a lot of big-media companies did, or tried to do, during this crucial period, its own involvement in the Internet had been gradual, and grudging. Its Net business had basically been a by-product of other company interests, and had never been a central focus of MCI activity. It took the efforts of two key executives, Scott Kurnit and Michael Mael, to bring a higher profile to the company's Internet efforts in 1995.

A former entrepreneur, Mael, a tall man who sports a moustache and glasses, began at MCI in 1992 in corporate finance and later transferred to the data services department as a director. It was the data services group that had brought in Vint Cerf, a key player in the early development of the Internet, as senior vice president in charge of architecture. "Vint went out and hired every Internet engineer he could find," Mael recalls, harkening back to the spring of 1994, when Cerf's recruiting began.

Groups were soon put in charge of developing a national Internet business, including a business suite called NetworkMCI Business, consisting of an upgraded version of a hoary e-mail product dating back to the 1980s called MCI-Mail, and an e-commerce destination with proprietary dial-up software called MarketplaceMCI. None of these amounted to much, but they seemed to form a basis for the launch of a competitive online service, if MCI ever wanted to go that route.

For MCI, these Internet projects were primarily a way of appearing technologically up to date, an important consideration in getting the stock price up. Its executives would contemplate an announcement about an Internet-related venture, and say, "This sounds like a good press release," rather than judging whether it represented a good deal. Many of the arrangements outlined in these press announcements weren't real, substantial agreements, but they sounded impressive. The company also wanted a good front man for its half-hearted efforts, which it found in Scott Kurnit, a former number-two executive at Prodigy, who had also been president of Viewer's Choice, Viacom's pay-per-view network.

"Scott was very unhappy at Prodigy," says Michael Mael. "Being in the middle of a joint venture with two companies [IBM and Sears] at Prodigy that didn't speak the same language was very unpleasant, and Scott swore he would never do it again. Most people at MCI had no idea who he was. I knew him because Prodigy had bought services from MCI, and I had spent a fair amount of time with him. I was excited about him because he understood the business. He understood what we were trying to do, and he could drive it in a way that no one inside the telco industry could do."

Kurnit is fond of practical jokes and irreverent humor. He had enjoyed a long career in the television industry and might have stayed there but for the fact that he kept getting excited about the possibilities of interactive media. His father, Shep Kurnit, was a legendary ad man in New York, co-founder of a firm called DKG, but Scott had followed a slightly different path, taking a position in the late '70s with a tiny PBS station in Springfield, Massachusetts, called WGBY–TV, a sister station to the much better known WGBH in Boston. WGBY was the equivalent of that little 5,000-watt radio station Ted Knight was always talking about on *The Mary Tyler Moore Show,* an operation in which everybody did everything and as a result couldn't help but learn the business in granular fashion. At 24, Scott became one of the youngest program directors ever at a professional TV station. He still had a full head of hair then, as well as a beard, a feature that would figure later when he interviewed at Prodigy.

At WGBY, the maverick Kurnit was determined to do things differently from the usual PBS formula. The station managed to achieve the fourth-highest rating for a public-broadcasting outlet in the country at the time by programming something other than the usual fare of classical concerts and BBC dramas. "We ran shows like *Mary Hartman, Mary Hartman,* which we picked up from syndication and which other PBS stations weren't running," Kurnit says, "running it up against the eleven o'clock news at the other stations. We were business- and ratings-conscious even back then."

Perhaps because of his willingness to break the TV mold, Kurnit was recruited in June 1979 from WGBY to a much more offbeat operation, Qube, the late Warner Communications chairman Steve Ross's idealistic effort to introduce interactive television to the Midwest. Little remembered outside the business, the so-called Qube experiment was based in, of all places, Columbus, Ohio. Kurnit recalls, "It was the time in my career when I expected to go to New York, but I ended up going from Springfield to Columbus, Ohio, on my way to New York, because Qube was so interesting. I went out there on a lark."

Qube, operated by the cable partnership of Warner Communications and American Express, was technically much less sophisticated than the FSN, but it boasted 30 channels of programming, unheard of in an era when most cable systems were "classic" or 12-channel, with primitive cable boxes that had to be manually manipulated. The system did boast a rudimentary "two-way" capability: Customers had five response buttons and a message light, allowing for basic communications, such as taking part in contests and local game shows.

The Qube system also allowed the operator one-to-one communications, and indeed Scott's going-away party was beamed into a single home, his own. Some of the first pay-per-view programming was also tried in Columbus, with Ohio State football games. And more than 15 years before the cable modem was born, Qube offered a fledgling online service called CompuServe to Columbus customers in 1979, with the first high-speed online access.

For the next year and a half, Kurnit functioned as Qube's interactive programming genius. Whether or not the system really delivered anything substantial to customers, it had enough *Jetsons*-style whiz-bang features to impress franchise holders, which was Warner-Amex's real goal with the experiment. In 1981, Kurnit was transferred to New York, where he was made vice president of programming at Warner-Amex and succeeded in duplicating the Qube format in six other markets across the country, including Cincinnati, Dallas, and Chicago. "Warner got the plum franchises because it had something nobody else had," Kurnit believes.

"At the time, Cox Cable [then headed by the young Bob Wright, later CEO of NBC] was also enamored with [interactivity]. Once you get this stuff in your blood, it doesn't leave very easily, because the opportunity to engage users, and to make money from that, is very compelling. You've seen, at NBC, Bob do things based on his early vision for interactivity, such as the [doomed] Olympics pay-per-view 'Triplecast.' NBC was very early into the Internet. Qube was in many ways the early Internet." Among the other top executives overseeing Warner-Amex at the time were Lou Gerstner, later CEO of IBM, Jim Robinson of American Express, and Tim Price, later the president of MCI, whom Kurnit clashed with later.

Qube was ultimately a failure, which Kurnit blames on the Atari crisis. Warner had invested heavily in the fledgling gaming company, which became a huge debacle. Drew Lewis, the secretary of transportation in the Reagan administration, who had garnered headlines by firing striking air controllers, was brought in as the CEO of Warner-Amex, and slashed the Qube experiment down to nothing. Kurnit managed to survive the housecleaning as the result of a memo he wrote to Lewis urging the use of satellites to run pay-per-view programming, chiefly movies. This 1985 document gave rise to a Warner-Amex and Viacom joint venture called Viewer's Choice, with Kurnit appointed as CEO.

Viewer's Choice was another example of the possibilities for interactivity, but it was mostly a negative one. In the pay-per-view model, cable operators program movies or events like wrestling matches at a certain time, and customers call up their local cable company to order the feature. In order to receive the feature, a customer must have a so-called "addressable" cable box. This device is not two-way, but only one-way addressable, which basically means the cable operator can program your box from a remote location. Despite the fact that Qube had proved the feasibility of allowing cable customers to interact with operators, it had few successors, and virtually all boxes remained one-way throughout the '80s and up until the mid-'90s. Pay-per-view faced a further setback during that time from video rentals, which grew in popularity partly because operators never allowed customers the convenience of movie and event ordering directly from the cable box. A Warner executive named Ed Bleier crisscrossed the country in the late '80s, endlessly repeating the mantra that viewers would buy movies "on impulse" if they were offered two-way capability from their cable boxes, but few were listening. Cable operators like the all-powerful John Malone of TeleCommunications Inc. were far more interested in selling their operations to a telephone company than in upgrading their systems with expensive two-way gadgets.

By 1993 Kurnit had been basically treading water for a long eight years at Viewer's Choice, which had by then been rolled into Showtime to become Showtime Event Television, also a joint Warner/Viacom operation. SET also sponsored pay-per-view events, and Kurnit tells an amusing story about his relationship with fight promoter Don King. For a Mike Tyson heavyweight match, Showtime had worked out a deal with King, his manager, whereby the fight would be broadcast on pay-per-view, and a tape of it would be shown the next day free on Showtime itself. Concerned that if TV viewers knew that the fight would be on Showtime they might not buy the pay-per-view event, SET ordered a minion to keep the listing out of *TV Guide*. Somehow, it appeared there anyway, and Kurnit recalls being in a hotel room in Atlantic City when an underling showed King a copy of the magazine. King advanced toward Kurnit with murder in his eyes, and the two men had to be pulled apart. Kurnit decided that packaging pay-per-view events was not a great career.

When a Prodigy recruiter called in 1993, Kurnit was definitely ready for a change, although his eventual hiring there was more the result of happenstance than of design. "By accident, I had shaved my beard off, which I had had for twenty years. I had just come back from Mexico, working twenty-four hours a day. And literally, my beard trimmer didn't have the right attachment on it, so I mistakenly removed part of my beard. I have to believe, based on what I learned about Prodigy after I'd been there, that if I had walked into Prodigy with a beard, I never would have been hired.

"Prodigy was the most conservative, the most by-the-book, bureaucratic company I had ever seen. I went there the year after the *Wall Street Journal* wrote that AOL was the real Prodigy, and the week after that *Fortune* had on its cover the three dinosaurs of American business, circa 1993. They were GM, and Prodigy's two parents, IBM and Sears. I still have that cover. People thought I was crazy to go there." But by now Kurnit didn't have that much to lose, since he had become resigned to the fact that he wasn't going to be named CEO of Showtime or MTV anytime soon, and Viacom wasn't offering him any other CEO jobs.

Prodigy began in 1984 as a joint venture among IBM, TRINTEX, Sears, and CBS. The service had been built using a quickly outdated pre-HTML graphics code, the North American Presentation Level Protocol System, or NAPLPS, which was extremely clunky to work with, recalls Harley Manning, its former creative director. By 1993 it was much bigger than AOL, and despite its difficult corporate ownership, it did sometimes manage to innovate. Kurnit, who was hired as an executive vice president with 200 people working for him, was not CEO, and he chafed under management dictates. But he can lay claim to having launched World Wide Web access six months before AOL, and to turning Prodigy profitable.

With partners like IBM and Sears, neither of which knew anything about the content business, Prodigy had difficulty deciding whether it was about news, entertainment, information, or e-mail. In the Kurnit era, Prodigy was more news-oriented, a focus that did not survive in the later regime of Ed Bennett, a former MTV Networks executive who, not surprisingly, was more interested in developing it as an entertainment center. When it did deal with news and editorial issues, Prodigy's growing pains were obvious. Prodigy's former editorial director, Mark Beneroff, who had been recruited from his Atlanta-based job as a CNN producer, is an incredibly animated, outspoken character who went on to careers at Sony and Priceline. Beneroff's predecessor had been an old newspaperman, Jim Bellows, who had been brought in to run the journalists in White Plains, and under his guidance Prodigy was the first online service to consciously use a newspaper newsroom as its model for content creation. Beneroff recalls that IBM's corporate "Open Door" policy, which allowed managers to challenge the decision of their superiors, was in place at Prodigy in the early '90s and helped it deal with completely unfamiliar editorial issues. It was Open Door, Beneroff says, that was the basis for a noteworthy stand for free speech at Prodigy at a critical moment in its history, shortly before Kurnit arrived.

By 1992 Prodigy had 1.5 million households subscribing, and it was a dominant force in the online world. Its bulletin boards, with 2 million postings a day, were ahead of their time, being coded in TPF (Transactional Processing Facility), the same software airlines and Amtrak use. Prodigy's task was hardly easy. Not only was it in totally uncharted territory, but neither partner had any experience navigating the very difficult terrain involved in trying to reconcile freedom of speech with the apparent need to monitor offensive material. TV, radio, magazines, and newspapers had had many decades to hone what was acceptable to their audiences. But how could Prodigy do that? What was acceptable to the online audience? Truthfully, the top brass at Prodigy didn't have a clue. Beneroff had built screening software that was designed to prevent the use of words like "shit" on the boards, but it had the unintended result of also forbidding words like Matsushita, the Japanese conglomerate that owned Panasonic. A more serious problem arose on a popular bulletin board called Books: Nonfiction, which quickly became an open forum on many diverse topics. One of those was "Holocaust Revisionists/Zionists," featuring discussions of books that various pseudo-historians had published claiming the Holocaust was a myth.

Prodigy had received complaints from the Simon Wiesenthal Center objecting to the board, but a reply explaining its free speech policy had smoothed things over. But then the Anti-Defamation League, which monitors anti-Semitism, "decided to make Prodigy its fund-raising topic for the year [1992]," as Beneroff recalls. When an ADL letter-writing campaign led to a flood of letters canceling Discover Cards, Sears demanded that Prodigy close the Holocaust board. But IBM, on the strength of the Open Door policy, decided to fight the ADL.

Beneroff and a delegation from Prodigy paid a visit to the ADL's Manhattan headquarters, to meet with its longtime head, Abraham Foxman. Gifted with great eyesight, Beneroff noticed some papers the ADL representatives had gathered on their side of the very long conference table and realized that some of the messages that the ADL had accused Prodigy of allowing to be posted on the discussion board—such as one saying that Hitler had been right—were actually e-mails that had been exchanged privately between individuals, and thus had never been "published" by Prodigy. "The ADL didn't understand the difference between public [postings] and private mail," Beneroff explained.

After the meeting, Beneroff and his colleagues pored through the bulletin board TPF files, hundreds of thousands of messages, to prove that the offending messages were never posted on Prodigy, while Prodigy's corporate overseers brought in public relations giant Burson-Marsteller to do damage control. Beneroff asked everyone he knew at CNN, including talkshow host Sonya Friedman, to take a stand in support of free speech. Despite a credible appearance by a Prodigy spokesperson on *Sonya Live* defending its position against an ADL representative, Sears capitulated to the ADL and agreed to take down the offending board. A press release announcing the decision was about to be put out on the wire when Beneroff actually grabbed the offending document and ripped it in half, well aware that this would probably be his last defiant act at the service. Just before he was escorted out of the building, the ADL's Foxman called, offering a compromise.

"He knew they had lost the argument," Beneroff said. The next day, the *New York Times* published an editorial in favor of Prodigy, and free speech was saved at the service, even though Beneroff departed fairly soon afterward.

Although the Constitution had been successfully upheld, there were a lot of things that still didn't work at Prodigy when Kurnit arrived. Among them was the e-mail system, which used meaningless strings of letters and numbers when assigning screen names instead of words chosen by users. Kurnit quickly angered many of his fellow executives by telling them that if they wanted to e-mail him, they should use his Kurnit@aol.com address rather than the utterly arbitrary PMMK78A@Prodigy.com. In fact, the e-mail system was so unwieldy that Prodigy didn't use it to communicate internally, resorting instead to an IBM product called PROPS. Prodigy's e-mail was also not Internet-based, as was AOL's, and Prodigy was years behind AOL in real-time chat because of company concerns about bad language.

An increasingly frustrated Kurnit soon became openly defiant. A die-hard Mac user, he would walk into Prodigy board meetings clutching his Duo laptop and take a seat next to the executive running the IBM PC division, which did not endear him to IBM management.

After two years at Prodigy, Kurnit had few misgivings about leaving when MCI CEO Bert Roberts came calling in 1995, offering a CEO title at an as-yet unnamed joint venture with Rupert Murdoch's News Corp. At that point the partnership was little more than a press release, and the real job of building a working relationship was left to the incoming chief executive to figure out. There was still even a little wiggle room to partner with another big-media company, if a better offer should arise.

Bert Roberts had been persuaded to put together the $1 billion joint venture by no less than the disgraced former junk bond king Michael Milken, on behalf of his client Rupert Murdoch. Milken had argued that it would be content that would be the cornerstone for the future of communications, not the kind of infrastructure play MCI represented. Milken's ideas were ultimately responsible for the drafting of an MCI internal document, commonly known as the "90-degree-turn" manifesto, that suggested the MCI could, in fact, successfully move into content. Kurnit was the guru who could see the project through.

The press release announcing the venture is a masterpiece of obfuscation and hyperbole. Released on May 10, 1995, it reads in part, "MCI Communications Corporation and the News Corporation Limited, two companies that have radically changed the telecommunications and media industries, today joined forces to create and distribute electronic information, education and entertainment services to businesses and consumers worldwide. . . .

"The companies said they will create a worldwide joint venture that they will own equally, leveraging the vast broadcast, satellite, programming and publishing resources of News Corp.; and the marketing prowess, customer base and intelligent networks of MCI and its global partner BT [British Telecom]. To solidify the long-term strategic relationship, the companies announced that MCI will invest up to $2 billion for an equity stake in News Corp., which would make MCI the largest outside shareholder. An initial investment of $1 billion of preferred stock and warrants will be made at the closing of the agreement, expected in a few months."

The venture partners made it clear they were creating an online service that was directly targeting AOL, and Prodigy. "Until today," thundered Rupert Murdoch, "no one has put together the right building blocks—programming, network intelligence, distribution and merchandising—to offer new media services on a global scale. MCI's strengths are terrifically synergistic with News Corp.'s."

On paper, as summarized in an internal document, it all sounded quite impressive. MCI had $13.3 billion in sales the previous year (1994). It was the world's third-largest carrier of international calls and, more important, the leading carrier of Internet traffic over its network, with more than 40 percent of U.S. volume. It was America's eighth-largest advertiser, with 8 billion ad impressions per month in 10 languages, and it also had the dubious distinction of being America's largest telemarketing operation: 6,000 consumer sales reps and 1,400 business sales reps called literally millions of "targeted prospects" every week.

For its part, News Corp. was contributing content from properties including Star TV, BSkyB, U.S. and overseas newspapers and magazines, Harper-Collins book publishers, Fox TV, Fox Films, CBS/FOX video, and every other division that made it a hard-charging media conglomerate.

The "premise" of the venture, a 1995 MCI document claimed, was to "marry the 'stuff' everyone wants (entertainment), with the services everyone needs (communications.)" It would "act as a catalyst for creative thought between the two companies [and] create MCI and News Corp. channel opportunities to accelerate acquisition and reduce churn." And it would likewise "capitalize on MCI and News Corp. distribution, marketing and database strengths."

A big attraction of the partnership for MCI was access to News Corp. products as premiums for its long-distance customers. Initially, the company proposed such "only at MCI" customer "rewards" as private, free preview screenings of Fox movies for big customers, a sports pager with sports scores from Fox, and premium giveaways of HarperCollins books, Fox Videos, and television and movie merchandise. MCI's web site would feature online chats from "Fox stars." All of this must have sounded sexy to MCI initially, although the sports pager was the only one of them that actually happened.

The initial stages of the joint venture seemed promising. Kurnit got along well with MCI's Roberts and Rupert Murdoch. "The first meeting I had with Rupert, we surfed the Web for about an hour," Kurnit remembers. Also present was *TV Guide* editor Anthea Disney, who was Murdoch's point person for editorial in the venture. This surf summit took place in summer 1995 in the conference room at the Manhattan headquarters of the joint venture, an elegant 19th-century building that housed the formerly housed the Siegel-Cooper department store on West 18th Street, between Fifth and Sixth Avenues.

"Rupert understood that the Internet was a wide-open publishing system, that anyone could get on, that it didn't have the strategic distribution barriers that you have in a broadcast or cable environment, where you have to look for a cable operator to carry your wares. He understood it was a more open meeting, and I think Rupert really understood that when we surfed onto some sex sites, where you realize that anything goes in this medium."

Despite the apparent harmonic convergence between the companies, a significant obstacle to the success of the union was already in place. News Corp. had already bought, for $50 million, the Boston-based Delphi Internet online service, perhaps the most dysfunctional of the various online properties operating then.

Delphi had hundreds of employees in Boston, and Murdoch's son James had briefly held a supervisory position there, although insiders claimed he would often simply disappear for days at a time into Boston music clubs. Delphi was in even worse shape than Prodigy, with only slightly more than 100,000 subscribers, most of whom were tech geeks. While it offered Internet access, it had no graphic interface and did not support available browsers. Users simply made do with a text interface of the Internet, as they had since the 1980s.

Murdoch had appointed his brother-in-law, Jaan Torv, to jointly run the service with a former IBM executive named Alan Baratz. Baratz had had visions of Murdoch's appointing him the interactive guru of News Corp. and so viewed Kurnit's advent as a major calamity. Through much of early 1995, Kurnit was locked in conference rooms with Baratz, the two yelling at each other in a struggle to define the new joint venture hierarchy.

The venture was only conceptual when Kurnit joined MCI as president of a new interactive division. What Kurnit inherited at Delphi was the usual fuzzy outline of an ill-planned concept. Somehow News Corp.'s news operation would join forces with MCI's Internet expertise. But the operation wasn't run like a news venture. It was too confused for that.

While all of the details of its MCI partnership were being sorted out, News Corp. was thinking big about its own future. In September 1995, the company's thinly staffed News Technology Group held an Online Symposium, strictly for internal purposes. Outside speakers included Gene DeRose, president of Jupiter Communications; Emily Green, a senior analyst at Forrester Group; Myer Berlow of America Online; and a high-level delegation from McKinsey & Company.

The summary document that was circulated after the gathering is very instructive in revealing how big-media companies viewed the Internet in 1995. As Alan Baratz summed it up in a memo to Rupert Murdoch and other top executives: "We heard that the online medium is an entirely new medium, unlike any other that currently exists. Moreover, the success and sustainability of this new industry will depend on the extent to which there is an emergence of a new media genre that fully exploits the new medium and provides subscriber value beyond that available through any other existing medium. Specifically repurposing existing or traditional content is not a viable approach to building a sustainable online business."

Baratz made an appeal to the bottom-line sensibilities of the News Corp. group by predicting that a revenue stream they were confident they understood—advertising—would "likely" be the "primary revenue-producing opportunity for pure content providers." He went on to suggest that "the integration of communications with content may be the key to the new media genre that will fuel the growth of the online industry."

AOL's Berlow, then busily engaged in setting up AOL's first advertising unit, was probably the most prescient speaker. He told the group, which included Murdoch and high executives of MCI, "Content is not king, the experience is king. Context is important in online." At that time, AOL was still relatively small, with 3.5 million customers. Berlow's message should have been a wake-up call, but of course it went unheeded. The $2 billion that MCI had pledged to invest in News Corp. was predicated on the belief that content, if not quite king, was at least one of the key elements of the new-media future. If the context of the online experience—the chat, e-mail, instant messaging, and other services that defined what AOL was doing—turned out to be more important than content, why enter into the joint venture at all?*

Scott Kurnit, always the practical joker, had been given to pulling up personal information on his Mac from the vast MCI database. At the symposium, while he had the floor, he booted up this database and joked, "I can tell you that one person in this room has a mortgage of more than $10 million." Everyone knew that only one of the attendees could possibly have had a mortgage that big, and Rupert Murdoch looked abashed to hear so personal a detail blurted out in front of the senior executives of his company. MCI may have had a great database, but embarrassing Rupert Murdoch may not have been politic.

During his talk, Kurnit noted, "The Internet is a gold mine. The question as to whether the [joint venture] should make money finding the gold or making the pans still needs to be determined." This was an articulation of a view, later expressed ad infinitum by Jeff Bezos, that in order to reap profits on the Internet, you had to be willing to lose money first. It was never a philosophy that either MCI or News Corp. was comfortable with, as neither company was accustomed to accepting the necessity of negative growth.

If the News Corp. symposium was a barometer of just how confused the online marketplace was in 1995, on the ground, at the joint venture headquarters on West 18th Street, the situation wasn't much clearer. Kurnit had been impressed with the examples set by two companies, the financial information business Bloomberg and the West Coast–based Chiat/Day ad agency (which had served as the model for the ad agency on the TV series *thirtysomething*), both of which had eliminated some of the long-standard ways of doing business, favoring open office plans and deemphasizing titles. Jay Chiat, Chiat/Day's co-founder and a hugely influential figure in the media world, called this arrangement the "virtual office." In the early 1990s, before it became common at Internet companies, Bloomberg's Park Avenue headquarters featured a large common area festooned with huge and incredibly expensive fish tanks and a large array of snack foods and fruit. (The rationale was that, instead of em-

---

* Five years later, in a postmortem report dated July 5, 2000, called "Content Failures Doomed by Scope," Jupiter Communications concluded that "online content ventures must develop ancillary revenues such as commerce fees, access revenue sharing, paid content and licensing and syndication fees, and should aim to draw 10 percent to 30 percent of total revenues from each stream." That was clear in 2000, but not in 1995, when most media companies were focused primarily on advertising.

ployees having to leave the building for a snack or coffee, they could get them
for free in the communal area.)

On December 21, 1995, joint venture COO Ken Cirillo issued a memo to
all employees that included a tentative "org chart": "You'll notice that something is missing from these boxes: old-fashioned titles. From now on, JV managers and staff will be identified by their area and their function," Cirillo wrote.
"It's all part of the flat, nimble organization that we are building to be competitive in our business. As Scott said not long ago, we want this to be a place
where the value of your contributions matters, not the size of your cubicle;
where your ideas count, not your title."

The joint venture also saw other attempts to emulate digital culture. Ties
and jackets disappeared, which was an uncomfortable adjustment for many
long-time executives. Kurnit informed his direct reports that they could, if they
wished, all become "virtual executives." It wasn't important if they were in the
office, or even in the state. If they wanted to do their jobs from home in their
bathrobe, fine, as long as they got their jobs done. Every week, his reports
would connect in a virtual executive meeting, held via an MCI conference call.
No one was asked where he or she was.

The adoption of these novel ideas didn't change the corporate cultures of either party to the venture but merely papered over the fundamental differences
between them. To set an example, Kurnit himself took a small, cramped office
at the West 18th Street location, in the middle of a sea of similar offices. Anthea
Disney, however, owed far more to Rupert Murdoch than to Jay Chiat or
Michael Bloomberg. She took a big corner space for herself and began acting
with the authority that it inexorably conveyed. Every morning, she would hold
an "old-fashioned" editorial meeting, complete with a video conference (courtesy of an MCI satellite link) with the Fox people on the West Coast, insuring
that she positioned herself much more closely to the West Coast nerve center
of News Corp. than did Kurnit. The press, including the snide Suck.com, was
soon running stories claiming that Disney and Kurnit didn't get along.

The only person in the joint-venture hierarchy with major news experience
was Anthea Disney. She struggled with making some sense out of the initial
business plan, which called for an international news operation. She had experienced firsthand the gulf between MCI and News Corp. at the start of the venture when she, Rupert Murdoch, and Bert Roberts had gone on a retreat
together. Roberts had leaned over to Disney at one point and asked, "So,
Anthea, what exactly does an editor do, anyway?" She also clashed with Jonathan
Miller, the witty, British-born executive who initially headed the news opera-

tion. Miller, an outspoken former columnist at the *Times,* Murdoch's newspaper in London, styled himself as a digital Oscar Wilde, full of dot-com epigrams and cutting retorts. He wrote a memo to News Corp. executives criticizing Disney's leadership, which was promptly forwarded to her, and the resulting profane fireworks could be heard throughout the entire office. After Miller's departure, with no clear sense of how to rescue the news operation, she switched to a directory approach, spearheaded by a former editor at the *Village Voice,* Betsy Richter. Richter had been quietly toiling on a side project called iGuide, which offered reviews of thousands of web sites. With no alternative presenting itself, iGuide suddenly became the operating paradigm, and the venture was renamed, albeit briefly, iGuide.

Initially iGuide generated some positive buzz. Anthea Disney landed on the cover of *Fortune* in 1995 wearing a black leather jacket, as one of a new breed of Web visionaries. But shortly afterward, she attended a meeting with a number of content people at MCI. The group of managers and directors, who had been appointed to study content "categories," reeled off statistics that all too clearly indicated they had no organic knowledge of the subject matter whatsoever. For a trained Fleet Street journalist like Disney, the session was torture, especially when an MCI functionary named Ann Shack made the case for a Women's Channel. For Disney, who had edited *Self* magazine for Condé Nast, it was an almost surreal experience to be lectured about women's interests by a woman wearing unfashionable clothing whose previous job had been selling long-distance phone service. Disney left convinced that the venture would be extremely difficult to make work. "Who were those people?" she asked, incredulity at the forefront.

While the venture's executives were experiencing culture shock, among the troops on the ground things were hardly more focused. One of the first joint-venture employees in New York was an attractive 24-year-old with long, wavy brown hair named Pavia Rosati, a former assistant to Grace Mirabella at her eponymous magazine, who had later migrated to the *Village Voice* with *Mirabella* editor Karen Durbin. At the *Voice,* Rosati was introduced to Echo, the early New York–based online bulletin board popular with many media people who, Rosati remembers, "liked to see their words appear immediately." As did so many people in the mid-'90s, Rosati stumbled upon the Internet when a friend asked her to do an article for *World Art* magazine on Web-based art. Rosati had never seen a Web browser before and had to borrow a friend's computer to do her research.

In the heady days of 1995, merely to have written this article, as obscure as it was, qualified Rosati as an Internet expert. Meg Siesfeld, an assistant to Anthea Disney at *TV Guide* and the joint venture, knew Rosati, and she was recruited to the venture. "They offered me so much money, more than double my salary at the *Voice*," Rosati recalls. "The project had so many names I can't even remember them all. There were eight of us at the beginning. I was hired to do features. These were the days when it seemed that the Web was going to save journalism, and all the constraints of journalism were going to disappear. I didn't know what the constraints of journalism really were, but everything that was bad about the types of publications I had come from would go away."

Being an online reporter required a good deal of scrappiness, as Rosati recalls. "A reporter would take a digital camera to the field. She would come back, and HTML her story and press a button and publish it. And sure enough that is what I did. The first week I was there, Jerry Garcia died, a crowd had gathered in Central Park, and I was assigned to cover it. I was barely a journalist, certainly not a reporter by any stretch of the imagination. Jonathan Miller put a digital camera in one hand, and a DAT recorder in the other, which I couldn't even use, and we headed up to Central Park to report on the action. Of course, the one cultural force of the '90s I totally loathed was the Grateful Dead. It was nuts."

The next day, Rosati wrote the story, downloaded the pictures, picked the ones she wanted, cropped them, entered some supporting audio, created a tie-dyed background, put the bold tags where they needed to be, pressed a button, and the story was live. "That was the tone of work in that place for the six months I was there," she says.

It was improvisational, in that no one really knew what he or she was doing, and it was anarchic—two characteristics that big companies generally hate. And even worse, it was costing a huge amount of money. Months before the site was scheduled to go live, Delphi executives had hired online "columnists" at huge salaries. As with Rosati, the assumption was that top dollar was necessary to attract Web-enabled talent. One of these writers, Lisa Robinson, who covered rock music, was being paid $20,000 a month for a column she hadn't even started writing yet. Even by the standards of the Internet business, this was considered excessive. Lisa Napoli, later a reporter for the *New York Times* and an on-air reporter for MSNBC, was assigned to be music editor of the joint venture and nominally oversaw Robinson. Her protests about Robinson's compensation quickly produced tension with News Corp., where the music maven was a long-time star.

A former CNN producer, the dark-haired, diminutive Napoli had arrived at the joint venture in 1995 after a brief stint at the fledgling, cutting-edge cable home-shopping channel Q2, a New York–based division of QVC, where she worked for Candace Carpenter, the prickly, ambitious manager who would later go on to found iVillage. In some respects Q2 served as something of a dry run for the Internet business for many New Yorkers. Like the average Silicon Alley Web operation a few years later, Q2 tried to do things differently. Napoli remembers, for example, that none of the people in the set-dressing department had any experience with constructing sets; they were all hired simply because they were young and quirky. Q2 was "tumultuous" and wacky, and never could get adequate distribution. It closed shortly after Napoli left. In television, running a quirky, badly managed, money-losing operation was a one-way ticket to Palookaville. In a few years, in the Internet business, it would make you a millionaire many times over.

Napoli arrived at the joint venture in 1995 to find almost complete chaos. She had been hired by the ubiquitous former Prodigy editor Mark Beneroff, who worked briefly for the organization. Brought in with the title of director of original programming, Napoli was told to hire people as fast as she could. She quickly complied. "We were paying twice as much as television," she says. "I hired a production assistant, who would have been paid $25,000 in television, for $45,000. These people were kids. When Anthea got there, she was shocked at what we were paying people." MCI executives, with their rigid salary scales and meritocracy system, were also shocked and highly offended by this kind of profligacy. They didn't understand the sometimes out-of-control pay demands of media "stars" like Robinson, and they questioned why such accommodations were necessary.

Napoli quickly clashed with Anthea Disney, who "couldn't stand me," Napoli says. Quickly stripped of all her producing assignments, Napoli was reassigned as a kind of all-purpose talent scout, holding endless—and ultimately futile—meetings with people who wanted to work for the joint venture. "I'd always tell them we'd get back to them. Of course, we never did," Napoli laughs.

Napoli was in a meeting with e-mail guru Seth Godin at his Westchester headquarters in Irvington, New York, when she got an urgent page to return to the office. When she got back, she was promptly fired by an Anthea Disney underling. She later became a tech evangelist at the *New York Times* and at MSNBC.

Given his edgy relationship with Alan Baratz, and the confusion and many contradictions at News Corp., it's not surprising that Scott Kurnit would have started looking for a more compatible partner. He thought he had found one in Time Inc.

"Back then, everyone was trying to figure out what the relationship was between access dial-tone, browser, screen, and content," Kurnit remembers, referring to a series of discussions held between Time Inc. and MCI during the summer of 1995. Although the News Corp. venture had already been announced, it wasn't set in stone, and Kurnit believed he could find a better partner for MCI. With vague authorization from Roberts and the rest of the company's hierarchy, he began having exploratory conversations with Walter Isaacson, whose wife's personal connections gave impetus to the talks.

"The meetings I was in were in New York," Kurnit recalls. "I have great respect for Walter [Isaacson] in those early days. He did understand, but they had conflicting corporate objectives which became overwhelming. One of the reasons the large companies are failing on the Internet, versus pure Internet plays, is that they can't move at even half the speed of an Internet company. And this was a time where the interactive world was kind of a blank slate.

"Walter and I exchanged a lot of e-mail, about issues and things. The one piece that you can fault them for is that they probably weren't as inclined to understand community and user participation. In the traditional world, you publish and it gets read. It's a one-way endeavor. The concept of listening and including the voices of the user-interactor was conceptually foreign. But I give Time Warner tremendous credit for bringing Pathfinder forward way ahead of the other media companies. In hindsight, perhaps the error was in not giving the juice to Pathfinder, and having the conflicts from around the empire. The assumption was that because they owned magazines like *People* and *Fortune,* they would have what they needed. The reality was that Pathfinder needed to be created separately, and to run at Net speed, like Yahoo! The problem wasn't at the top. Jerry Levin, for a senior executive, understood it. The problem happens in the troops. You get into the world of interdepartmental politics."

The Time/MCI meetings culminated in an "executive briefing"—essentially an MCI technology presentation—held at MCI's Washington headquarters. A formal luncheon there followed, after which Isaacson, Bruce Judson, and top MCI executive Jerry Taylor spent quality time. Bert Roberts had championed a News Corp. pairing, at the advice of Michael Milken, but there were other executives at MCI who favored a different path, Taylor and Tim Price among them. These forces arrayed around Kurnit coalesced with a plan to meld MCI's Internet backbone with Pathfinder, creating a rival to AOL and, ultimately, News Corp. and its Delphi service.

The behind-the-scenes machinations reflect two realities—MCI's willingness to completely deep-six its budding relationship with Rupert Murdoch if it thought Time Warner had more to offer, and the major uncertainty that gripped executives like Bert Roberts when they were forced to deal with media partners. The telephone business is different in so many ways from that of media companies that it was like a meeting at the United Nations while the translators are on strike. There were no familiar reference points for MCI to gauge the differences between companies like Time Warner and News Corp. That forced Roberts and his underlings to rely on newcomers like Kurnit, whom they never fully trusted and didn't fully understand either. It made for a treacherous brew.

The Washington summit was so successful that a follow-up was called for in August, at Time Inc.'s Sixth Avenue headquarters, at which a plan would be finalized for the two companies to form a joint venture. The depth of strength on the MCI team planned for this gathering gives an indication of how seriously the venture with Time Inc. was taken in Washington: Michael Mael and director Mort Aronson arrived in New York, and they were due to be joined in a phone conference by president Tim Price and Kurnit. Time Warner dispatched its own top financial talent, as well as Isaacson, Judson, and then Pathfinder CEO Paul Sagan. As the two sides faced each other across a long conference table, Mael told the group how eager MCI was to do a deal with them, and then dialed Kurnit in Washington.

Kurnit, however, had some unexpected news. "He said, 'You're there, we're here, you're on your own,'" Mael recalls. Kurnit told Mael that Rupert Murdoch was in Washington that very day and had cemented his deal with CEO Bert Roberts. There was nothing the would-be MCI insurgents could do now. "It was the most uncomfortable professional moment I've ever been through," Mael admits. When he hung up the phone and told the group what had happened, "Walter, who was a very kind, very decent person, proceeded to absolutely rip us to pieces. There wasn't a whole lot more to say." Isaacson did tell the group that he was "very disappointed," since the two sides had had a very good discussion in Washington, and that Time Warner CEO Jerry Levin was standing by to come over and "shake hands on this thing."

The deal with News Corp. was still not signed a few weeks later, however, and a follow-up meeting was held, at which MCI's Price and Taylor challenged Time to come up with a deal that was better than that offered by Murdoch. By that time, however, Isaacson had turned cynical about his would-be partner, and the conversation was frosty and unproductive. The News Corp. deal was finally signed in September, creating a joint venture that was always tentative.

One irritating factor was that News Corp.'s top executives had a lot of perks and made much higher salaries than did MCI officials. MCI was also stingy with titles. For example, a director, a minor title at News Corp., was a big gun at MCI, and the two sides had difficulty reconciling what level they were dealing with. MCI, of course, had its own share of interdepartmental politics, and Kurnit's rich contract—which Michael Mael says was of unprecedented scope for the MCI of 1995—caused some resentment among veteran telco executives.

"I don't say this in a negative way, but Scott is probably one of the best self-promoters I've met anywhere," Mael explains. "And I think the feeling at MCI was that he spent more time promoting himself than he did the company. That certainly rubbed [MCI President] Tim [Price] the wrong way. Scott never made much of an effort to curry favor with the executives at MCI. He was more focused on the News Corp. people and the outside community."

In September 1995, shortly after the News Corp. online symposium in New York, MCI held its annual sales and service meeting for its Business Markets division at the Marriott World Resort in Orlando. The huge division contained more than 8,000 salespeople, and Price was their guru. Three thousand people attended the event, which cost an astonishing $3 million. No detail was overlooked. Although the Marriott resort used AT&T pay phones, MCI took the trouble to print up dozens of removable paper labels to paste over its competitor's product. Each of the attendees was given an IBM Thinkpad.

Kurnit was introduced to the salespeople in dramatic fashion, stepping out of a puff of smoke, befitting the magic and pizzazz of the Internet. His subsequent remarks, which might have been suitable in the New York media scene he was raised in, or at a Dean Martin roast, were perhaps not chosen particularly wisely, given the context. Kurnit, who appeared after Price at the podium, began by lamenting what a tough act the legendary MCI marketer was to follow, "and you *have* to laugh at his jokes," Kurnit recalls quipping. It was a seemingly offhand remark, but one that would have deep repercussions throughout MCI, where the bond between the marketing troops and the motivationally driven Price was considered sacrosanct. "That was the nail in the coffin," Mael says. "You weren't even supposed to ad-lib, much less insult a major executive. It was not well received. Tim was very angry."

Even with the tremendous tension, mistrust, and culture clash between MCI and News Corp., and between MCI and its own hand-picked Ambassador to Media, Scott Kurnit, the venture did put together a rudimentary Web-based Internet dial-up service that could have been a serious challenge to AOL, had it been understood and properly marketed. It combined a Yahoo!-style

Web directory, readied at a time when Yahoo! was hardly an established brand, with a dial-up service. This was years ahead of its time. But that may have been one of its key problems; pioneers very often get ignored. The Frenchman who designed the bicycle died broke and unheralded.

Anthea Disney remained uncomfortable with the Internet process but still prevailed formidably over the divided editorial team, which consisted of seasoned News Corp. journalists and green MCI content people. While News Corp. offered content from its media properties, an MCI task force created one of the first online white and yellow pages services, called Source.411, spearheaded by a feisty MCI executive named Andrea ("Andi") Weiss. As Weiss described it in a company document in December 1995, "Source.411 is as comprehensive as having all the nation's phone books at a user's fingertips." For its yellow pages service, called Business.411, MCI purchased basic information on 10 million companies from Dun and Bradstreet. Weiss recalls that the project had 35 people working on it and cost $5 million. It was way ahead of its time—similar software was later used to launch highly lucrative Internet properties like Infospace and Switchboard—and could have been used by MCI to take the lead in the online directory business. But Weiss recalls a lot of confusion about their mission, with little commitment on the part of MCI that they were building properties that were worthy of distracting the company from its core long-distance phone service.

At the end of 1995, Kurnit, Anthea Disney, and other representatives of the joint venture flew down to Washington to showcase the new service, which was already bundled on disks. This was the first online service built entirely with a Web interface, years before similar services, like AT&T's WorldNet, were launched. The MCI executives watched the presentation impassively. Later, when many of them tried to load the software on their own PCs, the iGuide software clashed with the protocols of the Internet software used by the Washington office. Many assumed the software simply didn't work, despite Kurnit's protestations about software glitches in any early release, and doubts about the venture hardened in Washington.

Unbeknown to anyone in New York, however, Price and other MCI executives had quietly opened a back channel to Microsoft. The software giant had been talking to MCI about going into the online business together as early as 1993, before the creation of the Microsoft Network. These discussions, which involved Microsoft's Nathan Myhrvold, had coalesced into an ill-fated plan code-named Project Mars, in which the MCI Internet-access network would be linked to Microsoft software to create a business-based information services company to be headquartered in Denver. By January 1994 the two parties had co-drafted a letter of intent, which MCI had signed and Microsoft had not. Although the deal ultimately collapsed, Microsoft approached MCI's Tim Price and Jerry Taylor again in late 1995, this time offering a fairly rudimentary distribution deal, in which MCI would get a royalty of $5 for each copy of Microsoft's Explorer browser it shipped, and MCI would drop any plans to utilize the Netscape Navigator browser, which was the software of choice at iGuide. None of the MCI executives involved in the News Corp. joint venture, including Mael and Kurnit, were consulted, despite the fact that it would clearly spell the end of the partnership.

Just before Valentine's Day 1996, Kurnit was summoned to Washington and handed a press release by an MCI executive named Michael Rowney announcing the Microsoft joint venture. Kurnit protested to his stone-faced colleague about the hundreds of joint-venture staffers in New York who were expecting to launch an online service in a matter of weeks. "So what?" Rowney replied. A few days later, the iGuide staff was gathered at an emotional session at the West 18th Street headquarters and given the news. "This is the hardest thing I've ever had to do," Disney said to the stunned group. Kurnit told a few friends he was going to write a book about the experience, but he soon thought better of the idea.

In the weeks that followed, MCI simply shut down every online-related project it had going, whether or not it was directly part of the joint venture. Andi Weiss's Source.411 project was one casualty. "We were ready to launch on Valentine's Day 1996," Weiss says. "On February 7, we got word that News Corp. and MCI were going to split." With that, the $5 million division was simply abandoned, and Weiss's 16-year career at MCI was effectively over. She wasn't the only longtime MCI staffer whose career was forfeited simply because they'd worked with News Corp. Indeed virtually every executive at MCI who had been involved with the venture was terminated.

Kurnit was thus one of the first Internet business executives to discover that corporate support for Web operations that were barely understood at headquarters would always be tenuous. This was now the second time that Kurnit had presided over the failure of two large corporations to be able to mount a credible challenge to AOL and its dominance, and it was a source of terrific irritation to him. The implication that he, like his erstwhile partners, didn't fully understand the Web and its implications was anathema to Kurnit, who did get where the business was going and was determined to profit from it. Not just profit with a big salary, but profit in the kind of terms Gordon Gecko would relate to. That meant starting his own company, becoming an entrepreneur for the first time in his life, and gambling a little. He made plans for what he liked to call the "Human Internet," forming an organization originally called the Mining Co. Identifiable experts would guide the site's visitors to content they cared passionately about. It would hopefully be an antidote to the soulless corporate disasters he'd presided over for years.

There are those who think of John Malone as the ultimate soulless corporate power broker, but that's hardly the way Malone himself likes to see it. A pioneer and visionary, he was always among the first executives in the cable industry to recognize the possibilities inherent in new technologies like broadband, even though his investing strategy in such innovations was always conservative to a fault. As early as 1992, Malone had promised a "500-channel interactive universe," the so-called "information superhighway." The cable chieftain never really appreciated the Internet, and the many stops and starts of his various online ventures provide proof for this surprising assertion.

In a chapter of TCI's history that Malone would doubtless like to forget, TCI had bought out a Santa Monica–based CD-ROM production company called A.N.D. The company, run by Alan DeBevoise, was acquired for $18 million in 1994, renamed TCI Interactive, and redirected as an investment and development operation that was part of a larger unit called the Internet Services Group.

TCI Interactive, modeled after Liberty Media, the TCI unit that invested in cable programming, started out well. DeBevoise steered the company into investments in Netscape and the broadband service @Home. But TCI Interactive is more notable for what it didn't accomplish.

DeBevoise recalls, "TCI had an opportunity to take a stake in AOL. Steve Case really looked up to John Malone. Case had met with Malone in 1994, and Malone had suggested to Case that AOL 'get big fast.'" This was the period when Microsoft co-founder Paul Allen had made his run at buying AOL, which was rebuffed by AOL's board. "Allen wanted to sell his shares of AOL, and he offered them to TCI first, for a 20 to 25 percent stake." But there was a problem with that transaction: Microsoft's Bill Gates and Malone had become close during the mid-'90s, with lots of promises about collaboration on Microsoft-enabled cable boxes that would lead the way to a broadband future. When Gates heard that Malone was talking to Case, he got "nervous" about what the combination could mean.

As DeBevoise recalls the denouement, Gates stepped in and managed to convince Malone that his fledgling Microsoft Network service would be a better investment than AOL, even though it hadn't yet launched and was therefore completely unproven. So instead of buying 25 percent of AOL, which would be worth tens of billions of dollars today, TCI put up $125 million and purchased 25 percent of MSN. (To be fair to TCI, Microsoft's reputation in 1994 was that it was such a fearsome competitor that most observers believed it would streamroller over AOL, which was then highly vulnerable to serious competition.) The investment, announced on December 21, 1994, was made by TCI's Technology Ventures group, the investment arm of TCI Interactive. The new entity was awkwardly titled the Microsoft Online Services Partnership. Bruce Ravenel, senior vice president of TCI Technology Ventures, said at the time, "This partnership reflects TCI's confidence in the growth potential of online services. Online services are a key element for our customers, and this gives us the ability to offer current services and, as we build out broadband networks, offer the Microsoft Network as a high-speed, interactive online service."

This was typical rhetoric from cable executives, who wanted to simply transport the online experience through copper and fiber-optic cable lines. But the limits of technology in 1994, coupled with the fragmented nature of the cable industry, made such dreams hard to achieve. A full eight years later, they still are, and broadband applications reach only a minority of the cable customer base.

When MSN had been announced the previous month, Gates had described the service as primarily a way to offer e-mail and bulletin board communications for users of the Windows 95 operating system. In fact, MSN had already begun wooing a number of media companies in order to acquire content, and TCI clearly thought that if it invested in the company, it would provide a strong partner for the online sites developed by media operations such as CNN and the Discovery Channel, partly owned by TCI. In its announcement of the partnership, TCI noted that MSN "is based upon enabling richer, more compelling content by providing superior publishing tools and a business model that gives information providers the majority of revenues associated with their services."

Because "programming"—or "content," in online parlance—is what TCI knew best, TCI Interactive invested primarily in content-oriented Web operations like Sportsline USA, iVillage, InterZine (sports content), and American Cybercast, a Los Angeles company that pioneered The Spot, an online serial. These operations all had two things in common: high burn rates (the amount of cash they consumed) and cable-like content. But the companies didn't perform like cable networks, and TCI didn't see the measurable growth with them that it would typically get from a Liberty Media investment.

TCI had a lot of trouble understanding the freewheeling ways of Web content. The company, which based its business strategy on controlling the cable box and the programming that was made available through that box, always had trouble with search and directory concepts like those of Yahoo! It was antithetical to TCI to merely point to content it didn't own. And then there were other problems with Web content, in that some of it offended John Malone's conservative politics and mores. A.N.D. had spent more than $1 million supporting a fringe-oriented Web concept called Disinformation (www.disinfo.com), a cutting-edge site devoted to strange phenomena and conspiracy theories, not to mention left-wing politics, where radical thinkers like M.I.T.'s Noam Chomsky were treated with reverence. This was a web site that someone like Oliver Stone could best appreciate; John Malone was something else again. Although originally from suburban Milford, Connecticut, the Denver-based Malone often depicts himself as a typical Western conservative, and he often derides liberal elites in private conversations.

The Disinformation site was the brainchild of Richard Metzger, a waggish thirty-something. (He posed for the March 1998 cover of the industry magazine *Silicon Alley Reporter* wearing a devil outfit, complete with little red horns.) Working 16-hour days out of TCI's Los Angeles offices, Metzger was getting ready to launch Disinformation in September 1996, when TCI suddenly pulled the plug on TCI Interactive, fed up with the uncertainty of the new-media marketplace. The end came, appropriately, on Friday the 13th of September, Metzger remembers, with furniture being hauled away from TCI Interactive's spiffy new offices at the corner of Sunset and Delaney. (Appropriately enough, Metzger immediately began talks with Oliver Stone, the idea being that Stone would offer his name and imprimatur to Disinformation and that it could serve as a central clearinghouse for his own ideas, whatever they might be. But ultimately his people seemed to have concluded there were one too many articles about devil worshiper Aleister Crowley and way too many morally neutral interviews with Charles Manson for them to be comfortable.)

Disinformation launched anyway on the Monday the 16th of September, 1996, and, perhaps because of its attention-grabbing content, was quickly named the site of the day on MSN. Before the ax fell, TCI had signed a $150,000 check to Netscape to place Disinformation on the Netscape Net-Search page, which garnered a huge amount of traffic and publicity. Disinformation was written up in *USA Today,* the *Los Angeles Times,* and the *Atlantic Monthly,* and was featured on CNN. TCI suddenly realized that it still had a stake in Disinformation, even if it had shut down TCI Interactive.

A TCI executive named Grayson Hoberg, then vice president of accounting, administration, and business strategy at the Internet Services Group, was dispatched to check out the strange operation in Los Angeles. "TCI really didn't know how to evaluate this stuff," Metzger recalls. "Grayson looks at the home page, with its content on space aliens and JFK conspiracies. He says, 'This isn't my type of thing, but it seems like you're doing a great job.'"

As Metzger recalls it, Hoberg went back to Denver and conferred with his colleagues. A decision was made to allow Disinformation 90 days to prove itself. The following month, with Disinformation featured in both *Variety* and the trade publication *Interactive Week,* and with Metzger appearing on the *Ron Reagan Show* and on the CNET web site, the Disinformation czar got a call from Hoberg: It seemed that Malone had now actually seen the site. Word reached Metzger that Malone had been horrified. "What is this anarchist bullshit?" Malone supposedly shouted. "Get rid of it." (DeBevoise won't confirm whether Malone visited the site.)

Hoberg demanded that Metzger shut down the site immediately, but Metzger had some aces up his sleeve. "I don't have it in for you as a person," he told Hoberg, "but if you shut us down I will call the *Washington Post* and explain how $1.2 million of your money was spent on creating 'anarchist bullshit,' without your even seeing it!" This seemed to impress TCI. Metzger was later informed that he could keep the site and was also given a nice severance package. He moved to New York City the next day.

DeBevoise, who later launched a film-oriented B-to-B site called Creative Planet, says Disinformation was simply alien to TCI's basic makeup. He calls it "one of the disconnects. John [Malone] and TCI's culture was just too alien for TCI. Richard was a driven guy, very smart, very passionate about his topic. The disconnect is that that is just not Malone's style."

As TCI Interactive faded, the company focused on passive investments, such as iVillage. During an interview in November 1996, Hoberg admitted that TCI had cooled to the Web. "We're going to slow down a little bit here, and be a little more picky about which companies we want to be investing in," he noted. Asked, for example, if TCI wanted to take part in iVillage's then-current third round of financing, Hoberg put miles of road between the two companies: "That isn't on my radar screen yet," he deadpanned. TCI also turned down a chance to invest in Wired Ventures, which then included *Wired* magazine and its web site, HotWired.com. Another TCI executive, Liesl Pike, stated the company's position succinctly: "The days of any 'cool' company automatically getting funding are over."

In any event, by fall 1996, TCI was exiting the Internet business, just as the industry was headed for its epochal stock run-up, and had certainly come no closer to figuring out the Internet than any other media concern. In the mid-'90s, many observers had expected TCI to lead the way onto the information superhighway, but there were personal factors that prevented that from happening. DeBevoise notes that the demise of TCI Interactive coincides with a period when Malone seemed to have lost interest in the business. After the collapse of the planned merger between Bell Atlantic and TCI a few years earlier, a lot of the verve seemed to have gone out of Malone. "The real issue is that John had checked out of TCI," DeBevoise remembers. "He was semi-retired. The stock price was not performing well. It wasn't a good time for a move on the Internet. At that point, we all left, and much of the push toward interactive media at TCI went with us." If the image of the inventor of the information superhighway largely missing out on the Internet revolution is a stark one, it's also painfully true.

CHAPTER 6

Camelot and Web Collide

The World Wide Web was an equal-opportunity paradigm-shifter—it bamboozled sober businessmen, ambitious 18-year-olds, and, to their chagrin, lots of otherwise sane celebrities. Like everybody else, the well-born and the famous also had to figure out what the Web meant to them, and one of these unfortunate souls was John F. Kennedy, Jr., voted the sexiest man in the world repeatedly by *People*, one of the few so named who probably deserved the title. A charismatic, intensely handsome man, Kennedy had nonetheless wrestled publicly with his career choices, serving for a time as a junior-level prosecutor in New York City, even at one point flirting with acting. Ultimately he decided to stick with the family business—politics—but at an ironic remove, not fully committed the way his father had been. This resulted in his new position as editor in chief of a magazine called *George* (after George Washington), a somewhat awkward mix of celebrities and politics. It was the *People* of politics, whether this was a necessary part of our commonweal or not.

When it launched in 1995 with backing from the French-based Hachette Filipacchi Magazines group, the resulting press conference was a media event. The company announced that the debut issue would boast more ad pages than any other launch issue of a magazine in history, perhaps fueled by impressionable, young ad-agency media planners who hoped Kennedy would pay a visit to their corridors. The Web wasn't part of the launch, but soon enough it reared its ugly head, posing a conundrum for all involved. By the time the topic was fully addressed in 1996, it was problematic indeed. Although a basic AOL area for *George* had been cobbled together, solely consisting of articles from the magazine, a *George* web site was much more of an undertaking, and it was an undertaking that John himself found distasteful and unpleasant to deal with. When it came down to it, he really didn't know what *George* could be on the Web, and didn't have the patience, the interest, or the skills to articulate a vision for it. The endeavor necessitated endless meetings with a succession of underlings, as John himself was loath to deal with the subject, with each minion struggling to articulate just what it was that he might want online. The resulting web site, at Georgemag.com, was a mess; virtually everyone agreed on this, even the people who physically produced it. How could it be anything else? Staffers at *George* had provided virtually no material beyond magazine articles to the small Web production group at HFM, headed up by content editor Jocelyn Greenky. She and her staff were already beleaguered, producing web sites for a plethora of Hachette titles on an assembly-line basis. The vision thing was supposed to come from the magazine's editors, who mostly avoided it as one more distraction that, at worst, was taking the attention of readers away from the magazine itself.

George Online, as it was called, could not hope to compete with online political hubs like Salon.com and Slate, not to mention Web operations from the *Washington Post,* the *New York Times,* and CNN. A monthly political magazine itself is hard enough to make real, given the long lead time and the sudden shifts in the political winds. But when stale material like this was put up on the Web, trying to compete with daily filings from the online publications listed above, as scandals like Monica Lewinsky and Whitewater roiled the nation, it became downright ridiculous. The result was a typical stalemate—no one was happy with the product, and no one knew exactly what to do about it, least of all JFK, Jr.

In late 1996, Jim Docherty received a summons from David Pecker: "Come to my office. I want to see you *now.*"

Docherty, the president of Hachette Filipacchi New Media, had just been brought onto the job to take over the reins of new media at the sprawling magazine empire (which included such varied properties as *Elle, Car and Driver, Premiere, George,* and *Woman's Day*), replacing the flamboyant Paul DeBenedictis, who had defected to AOL and its Digital City local content project.

David Pecker, later a figure on national television when the Florida offices of his American Media became the epicenter of the 2001 anthrax epidemic, was the CEO of Hachette Filipacchi Magazines. He had worked his way up from the Bronx as an accountant, and at Hachette he'd been a key financial executive. He'd evolved into an autocratic CEO who nonetheless inspired great loyalty in some, including Docherty.

Like the heads of most magazines, Pecker had the reputation inside the company of not knowing how even to turn on a computer, but he did become interested in the online business early in its development, primarily as a new revenue source. In that respect, his approach was vastly different from that of Time Warner's Jerry Levin. While Levin was given to heartfelt flights of rhetoric about the brave new world of technology that first the FSN and then the Web would bring to consumers, Pecker tended to see everything through the prism of his accountant's training. He was shrewd enough to recognize that on-line content licensing could make a lot of money for Hachette, and he quickly began to explore the opportunity.

Like many other media CEOs, Pecker had a hard-and-fast rule that he used to run Hachette: If it's not about profit, it's a hobby. As he noted in a 2001 speech, "I'm from the old school. There are only two words that matter—making money." Other powers in the magazine world often derided Pecker for his philosophy, although they in truth operated with the same basic set of principles. In big media, it's considered axiomatic to dress up your efforts with some degree of lip service to the consumer. Pecker was simply focused on making money.

At Hachette in what may be termed the Pecker Era, when the CEO called everybody jumped, Docherty perhaps more quickly than most. The son of a former street cop in New York and Los Angeles, Docherty had grown up in Los Angeles watching his dad rise up in the ranks of the LAPD. In the late '60s, and early '70s, the elder Docherty was among a tight-knit group of department officers who moonlighted by writing scripts for low-budget movies and cop-beat TV series like Angie Dickinson's *Police Woman* and the lurid film *Vice Squad.* Because they weren't supposed to be involved in such extracurricular activities, young "Doc" was tapped to deliver the scripts to the studios, so his formative years were spent hanging out at Universal, Paramount, and Warner Bros.

Instead of pursuing a career in Hollywood, however, Doc, who found the movie business distasteful, became an ad salesman, working at Times Mirror and other magazine companies. He landed at Hachette in 1994 as director of advertising sales for the East Coast and was later given the new-media title. A big, powerful man with close-cropped sandy hair and a blond moustache, Docherty had inherited a little of his father's streetwise manner.

While that sort of affect might seem out of place in halls roamed by the fashion designers and chic editorial types at *Elle* and *George,* street smarts are, in fact, prized in the ad departments of major magazines, where a tough argot and demeanor are often considered a valuable part of the negotiating arsenal. (Ron

Galotti, the former president of *Talk,* and the model for "Mr. Big" in HBO's *Sex in the City,* is a typical example, an executive who often drops his "g's" in conversation and loves to talk about how his minions beat up on some big advertiser.) It's not unusual to hear Mafia terms thrown around with abandon in magazine ad sales circles. Ad salespeople aren't fired, they're "whacked"; behind their backs, advertisers are called names that would make Tony Soprano blush.

Doc owed much of his career to Pecker, as he himself was first to acknowledge. And it was, in fact, friendship that was the reason for the summons to Pecker's office that day—not Pecker's friendship with Docherty, but his tight bond with Bob Pittman, who was then running the Century 21 real estate company.

During his fairly brief tenure at Century 21, Pittman had worked with Pecker and HFM on a custom-publishing project. The idea had a brief vogue in the '90s, when companies like Sony wanted product catalogs that didn't look like catalogs. Sony is a large advertising client of Hachette through its home electronics magazines, and HFM produced a glossy quarterly, *Sony Style,* that looked like *Elle* but was in fact an elaborately produced Sony catalog. Many CEOs wanted equally glossy promotional literature on their own coffee tables after they saw *Sony Style.* One of those was Bob Pittman.

Custom publishing is not the glamorous part of the magazine world. Print companies like Forbes, Time Warner, and Hachette have convinced many corporate chieftains that they need a magazine to help establish their brands. It's a business fueled somewhat by corporate ego—many CEOs just like to see glossy magazines that are all about them—sort of like ultimate good public relations. Pittman was one such customer, and it wasn't hard to figure out that, while at Century 21, he missed the media world and the glamour of it all. Perhaps because of this exile, he appreciated the opportunity to dabble in media with a Century 21 magazine project and began to spend considerable time at Hachette on the idea.

It was during this relationship that Pecker and Pittman became friends. Throughout his tenure at Century 21 in 1995 and 1996, Pittman had been having discussions with AOL's Steve Case about eventually moving to Virginia and helping AOL become a marketing giant, which he eventually did in October 1996.

Docherty, of course, was aware of Pittman's friendship with Pecker and had often been in meetings with the two men. So he wasn't too surprised to hear Pecker suggest, during the meeting he had been summoned to, that he hire a young Amerasian woman named Veronique Choa as Hachette Filipacchi New Media's first designer/art director. Choa, as Docherty knew, was the recently divorced Pittman's new girlfriend. The beautiful, rail-thin product of a Hong Kong upbringing, Choa had met Pittman at a party in Salisbury, Connecticut, in the tony confines of Litchfield County, where Pittman had a home. Bob and his then wife, Sandy Hill Pittman, frequently socialized there with the actress Susan St. James and her husband, NBC sports guru Dick Ebersol. As something of a lark, the foursome conceived the idea of launching a hip FM station to serve leafy Litchfield County.

Pittman, in common with Steve Case, was in the midst of a somewhat messy divorce—in Pittman's case, from Sandy, the would-be mountain climber whose rich-girl prima-donna antics during a historic climb were to figure prominently in Jon Krakauer's bestseller *Into Thin Air.* In happier times Bob and Sandy had been a regular fixture on New York's social scene and had been named "Couple of the Minute" by *New York* magazine in 1990.

As Docherty recalls the meeting in which Choa was proposed, "We were asked to bring Veronique aboard because she wanted to get involved in the design side and because she was a very good designer. Pecker offered her up to the division. She became the art director, effectively, although her title was designer. She became the driving force behind the look of all our AOL sites. She was very, very good. A lovely woman."

The Choa connection, after Pittman jumped to AOL, was one of the factors that eventually led to HFMN's becoming AOL's largest content partner, with as many as 23 AOL areas based on Hachette magazines, and Hachette clearing as much as $5 million annually from its AOL partnership. The money was welcome, as well as the legitimization, because it had become increasingly important to Pecker and his French overseers that Hachette prove itself in the new-media space.

The American operations of Hachette Filipacchi Magazines are based at 50th and Broadway in Manhattan, in an imposing black-glass corporate tower called Paramount Plaza (no relation to the movie studio). The sprawling French conglomerate, with interests in everything from the Mirage jet fighter to *Elle* magazine, was the product of a union between the venerable French publisher Hachette, which dates to the beginnings of French book publishing, and Daniel Filipacchi, a driven roué and risk-taker who made a fortune with *Paris-Match,* the French version of *Life* magazine. Perhaps best known for its grainy photographs of European celebrities cavorting in the nude shipboard or on a supposedly private Greek island, *Paris-Match* practically invented paparazzi photojournalism.

The American-based Hachette Filipacchi Magazines unit is the result of many mergers and acquisitions, and includes magazines once owned by publishing world kingpin Bill Ziff and by the TV network CBS, as well as such all-American brands as *Road & Track* and *Home*. *George* lost the company a great deal of money but brought it enviable glitz, which was perhaps its main function. The Gallic touch is evident in the American versions of the French fashion magazine *Elle*, the largest worldwide fashion brand, and in *Premiere*, originally a French film enthusiasts' magazine. The American *Premiere*, which was launched in 1987 as a film buff title, has been altered under HFM to become more of a fanzine, with fawning, uncritical profiles of movie stars edging out serious writing about the cinema. HFM has long labored under a kind of corporate inferiority complex, overshadowed by the more upmarket Condé Nast (*Vogue, GQ, Vanity Fair, Glamour*), Hearst (*Harper's Bazaar, Redbook, Good Housekeeping, Esquire*), and Time Warner.

HFM was often stigmatized as the company that would cut its advertising rate card the greatest amount, a factor that would be most likely to make editorial subservient to commerce. These charges, which were often unfair and inappropriate, were usually fanned by jealous rivals, who watched as HFM made a major success out of *Elle*, which soared past *Harper's Bazaar* and was much bigger internationally than *Vogue*. Meanwhile, HFM's bedrock auto titles, *Car and Driver* and *Road & Track*, were not only the dominant buff magazines but had also forged a synergistic advertising relationship with Detroit and Japan that was the envy of the rest of the industry. *Woman's Day*, which appealed to the supermarket set with a very unsexy stew of recipes and household hints, was also a major profit center. If the rest of the magazines on its roster lost money or barely broke even, it didn't seem to present a huge problem for HFM's French owners, who were enjoying socializing with JFK, Jr., and attending Hollywood parties, to which they gained entrée via *Premiere*. And among these assets Hachette also had a secret weapon that contributed to its building a very close relationship with America Online, and to its arguably making more money from its AOL licenses than did any other media company.

In the early '90s, Hachette, like other print giants, began to investigate CD-ROM publishing. In 1994, it had hired a smart, somewhat ruthless former Prodigy executive named Paul DeBenedictis as CFO. Because of his background, DeBenedictis was tapped to get a "multimedia" division going in earnest, while still keeping his CFO title. Two previous new-media gurus, who had tried to move the company into various TV projects, had been quickly dispatched by the impatient Pecker.

Since Hachette's licensing division had made a lucrative deal with the *Road*

& Track name on an early auto-oriented video game, CD-ROMs seemed the logical direction to take. DeBenedictis arranged with a New York–based production company called Radical Media to produce a *Car and Driver* buyer's guide CD-ROM for the 1995 model year. But production delays, inexperience with multimedia, and other problems postponed the product until well into 1995, long after most new car buyers had made their purchases, and huge piles of the disks ended up littering HFM's offices. The project was a major failure, but DeBenedictis, a glib, expert corporate infighter, managed to keep his job, mainly because all the other magazine publishers, including Newsweek and Time Inc., ended up with failed CD-ROM projects as well.

DeBenedictis, who had first dabbled in the online world at Hachette with a text-oriented CompuServe deal, quickly rebounded with a major pact with AOL concluded in 1994, negotiated with AOL's e-commerce head Meyer Berlow. The agreement guaranteed Hachette an impressive $5 million a year for at least seven of its titles, initially. (The amount was later whittled down to $3.5 million, and then to a little less than $2 million.) This income allowed Hachette Filipacchi New Media to run at a profit, which Pecker had demanded for it to continue in existence. (In 2001, Pecker would quip, "I can remember getting checks from AOL. Now all you get are disks.")

What initially made Hachette attractive to AOL and Berlow was its close ties to the auto industry through *Car and Driver* and *Road & Track,* which were filled with ads from the car companies every month. David Pecker was often seen in the company of General Motors' ad director Phil Guarascio, who loved the dedicated car nuts who read Hachette's auto titles. The pioneering online advertisers were virtually all automobile companies: AOL's first advertiser was Oldsmobile, and Hachette's first online ad came from Nissan.

This was an era when New York–based Jupiter Communications, a kind of research company and online consultant that also held well-regarded conferences, was constantly making huge projections for ad spending online. If you believed Jupiter's analysts, ad spending would become huge within just a few years, and AOL wanted to be in the center of that growth. But AOL had very little institutional knowledge of the advertising business, traditionally based in New York. AOL wanted to acquire as much advertising expertise as it could from its media partners, especially Time Warner and Hachette, which had close relationships with key advertisers. To do this, it had turned to one former Time executive who did know his way around an ad agency.

/ / /

In 1995 and 1996 AOL was far from being an advertising powerhouse. Myer Berlow was actually the second ad maven at the company. The first was Jonathan Bulkeley, who had moved into the top ad position when AOL reorganized its divisions, breaking up the media content group and assigning licensing teams in various content areas, such as sports and news.

When Bulkeley started thinking about ad sales, in late 1994 and early 1995, AOL had only about 750,000 subscribers, about the same number as a middle-sized magazine. And it faced an ongoing problem in that, as Jim Docherty says, advertisers "hated working with AOL," because they had no creative already prepared in AOL's proprietary software language, Rainman. Bulkeley experienced this firsthand when he met with skeptical clients. "They couldn't build any creative [in Rainman.] And they had no tools to create creative. We went out to try to create a package. [To do an ad for AOL, it had to be produced in AOL's proprietary software, which advertisers didn't know how to use.] I knew it was a bit of a minefield, because it was so early in the process. We were also doing e-commerce. Internet ad banners hadn't started yet, they started in early '95. But when I went to sell Web links from AOL pages, I was told that we couldn't have banners on any AOL pages, any AOL content pages. Prodigy was doing that. They had ads on all their content pages."

Despite the difficulty of essentially starting an entire ad business from scratch, Bulkeley began to make headway. In 1995, he estimates, the company generated about $2 million in ad revenue, from clients like McDonald's, Zima, Hanes, Federal Express, American Express, Tower Records, Office Max, Hallmark, and Coke. The biggest client was Oldsmobile, which paid $700,000 for a separate Olds-sponsored site on AOL called the Oldsmobile Celebrity Circle, which featured chats with movie stars, in partnership with the talent agency ICM. AOL also built online stores for big retailers like 800-Flowers, Starbucks, and American Greetings.

The slow progress of this advertising caused a lot of media companies to question the wisdom of their alliance with AOL. "They were pissed off," Bulkeley says, "because it was the new-media person within the media organization [who was responsible for the ads]. The new-media person at media companies thought that that would be the new revenue stream for them. We had told them that they could go out and sell ads within [their own AOL areas], but you have to give us a cut. And we're also going to sell ads in our areas, the areas we control." When media companies quickly complained that AOL controlled the best, most highly trafficked areas, Bulkeley countered that they should make their areas competitive. When the media companies insisted that AOL didn't give them enough promotion, AOL replied that if the media areas were better, they'd get more promotion. It was a vicious circle, with pressure building quickly.

At the annual partners conference in February 1995 Bulkeley caused even greater dissent when he announced that AOL would start selling ads on its own, essentially competing with the media companies they'd partnered with. What this meant, in practical terms, was that if Time, for example, did a deal with Ford, and Ford created Rainman ads for the Time site on AOL, then it would be a simple matter for AOL's ad people to sweep in and offer more traffic for less money, essentially making Time's sales job redundant.

As Bruce Judson recounts, "Jonathan and I were friends, but I would say to him, 'Let me get this straight. I'm Time, I go out, and I bring Ford in. Ford content is put up within the Time area. I'm responsible for all the support for Ford, all the back and forth, and how do we bring you up [in Rainman], etc., etc. The second Ford turns on, every other magazine on AOL is going to link to them, off all the work I did. And if Time leaves AOL, Ford is still going to be there, so I've brought you an advertiser, and I'm the one that went to all the expense. I'm creating a business for you, were I to do this.' And he says, 'Can't say you're wrong.'"

"At the conference, people were freaking, and Steve freaked because everyone else was freaking," Bulkeley recalls. AOL partners, especially Time Inc., reacted strongly, with cries of "We don't know how you could do this to us" flying through the air. Ted Leonsis remembers: "It was really ugly. And then Jonathan said, 'All right, I will take the three or four guys who are really mad, and I'll spend the evening with them, I'll just take them out to dinner.' I remember coming back from something and seeing Jonathan at 11:45 [p.m.], and they were still at it! He says, 'I'm wearing 'em down. I'll get them on our side. I'm wearing 'em down.'"

Unlike the majority of the partners, *Spin*'s David Rheins thought the new policy was a canny move. "AOL was smart to bring the advertising in-house," he says. "Publishers weren't aggressively selling the online. They didn't know how to sell online. They didn't know how to price."

AOL didn't make any secret of its intentions regarding advertising. Within months, it was quietly distributing a rate card that offered "What's Hot" ad banners that would run in key areas such as Computing, Travel, and the Internet Connection. Prices ranged from $7,500 a month for 120,000 guaranteed impressions to $3,000 for 50,000 impressions. For a banner on AOL's Web home page, AOL.com, an advertiser would pay $20,000 a week. Those numbers would soon be dwarfed by much higher rates, as the AOL subscriber base grew.

"Jonathan was a riot," Judson adds. "Just like Leonsis, he would tell you exactly what AOL was planning. I do recall meeting with Ted Leonsis and hearing him say, 'We're paying you now, but some day you will pay us.' He said that because he was right. He was saying it because Ted was Ted, and Ted likes to talk. AOL was one of the prime examples of the network effect, what happens when you get a giant audience, and Ted had the foresight to see that." It's hard not to invoke the famous Lenin quote here, in which he stated that the capitalists would sell the Bolsheviks the rope with which they would later be hung.

At a second partners conference that June, Leonsis, who was then president of the newly created AOL Services Co., spelled out just how formidable a player AOL had become in the short time that had passed since the previous gathering. Paying homage to AOL's "hyper growth," Leonsis noted that the service had leaped from 1 million members at the end of 1994 to about 3 million members at the start of the summer. From $100 million in revenue in 1994, AOL had already more than tripled, to $350 million for 1995, and had grown from 350 employees at the end of the previous year to more than 2,000 by the time of the conference. AOL had added more than 100 new areas to its service and had added more than 50 new partners, including *Spin,* the Discovery Channel, Nickelodeon, *Business Week, Entertainment Weekly,* ABC, and MTV. Moreover, Leonsis had introduced the Greenhouse program, which had developed in-house content like the Motley Fool, the African-American oriented NetNoir, and the astrology-rich Astronet.

AOL members, he announced, were largely 18 to 44 in age and mostly male, and more than half had incomes over $50,000. While only 13 percent of the U.S. population had a college degree in 1995, 43 percent of AOL users were clutching a diploma.

Leonsis then presented a path to success online he called "The Five C's." These included:

- Content that is programmed, not aggregated
- Community that is endemic to the programming
- Commerce as part and parcel of the channel
- Companion web sites and CD-ROMs that are connected properties
- Context, and point of view.

AOL had concluded that its members wanted faster access, more personalization, more depth of content, more personal publishing, less-intrusive ads, fewer busy signals, and, in what should have been an ominous portent of what was to come, less "repurposed content." That, in essence, is what magazines and other media companies had been serving up. No media companies had actually hired the large, dedicated online staffs of the sort that AOL was assembling. The only one that got close was Time's Pathfinder.

One of the astonishing things about Leonsis's presentation at the conference was how many of his bold predictions came true. Leonsis projected that AOL would become the "industry's first billion-dollar interactive services company," that it would "launch and claim an Internet consumer service leadership position," that it would "bear hug" its "best partners with one-stop shopping services." All of this it accomplished, and more.

Essentially, Leonsis was warning media companies that they had to make their AOL areas into something *real,* just as Bulkeley had. He told the partners that AOL wanted "more commitment to the medium. . . . New services for the medium and more interactivity. Daily freshness, more exploitation of new tools, more photos and sound." AOL, he concluded, was looking for "clarity in the relationship." It wasn't getting it from media companies, who weren't about to change their corporate cultures to answer the needs of a bunch of software guys in Virginia.

Shortly after the AOL partners conference in October 1995, Pathfinder held its first anniversary party in the eighth-floor auditorium of the Time-Life Building. Recalls one attendee: "It wasn't the Black and White Ball [the famous Truman Capote extravaganza], but it was fairly expensive for an unprofitable Internet company that was really struggling with a lot of very fundamental problems. There were speeches by Levin, by Jim and Walter; it was a moment of self-congratulations."

But at least one of the participants, Time Inc. New Media's then ad director Linda McCutcheon, remembers a feeling of disquiet at the event: "What struck me was that it was all in-house. It wasn't customers; it was us saying, 'Gee, aren't we wonderful. We're so cool.' That's what got me. There was a feeling that there was no problem here. I was worried."

Like Time Warner, Hachette didn't follow any of Leonsis's dictates, but it still had the car magazines, and AOL was still going to want to keep those on its service in one form or another. The operating concept at Hachette Filipacchi

New Media had initially been "self-fund," but it soon shifted to "self-fund plus," as AOL's millions helped new media become a major profit center. By 1996, Hachette properties were generating almost 50 million page views a month on AOL, enough for major advertisers—and Hachette's magazine editors—to start paying more attention to online.

Or at least some of the editors. Like many new-media divisions of media companies, HFNM was kept totally separate from the traditional publishing side of the business, a situation that outsiders rarely understood. New-media minions like editorial head Jocelyn Greenky were forced to pry huge Quark files out of the hands of magazine editors who were reluctant to surrender them. Editors at Hachette magazines made little effort to acquire electronic rights to any of their articles, except for those that were staff-written. Because magazines like *George* were mostly written by freelancers, and the photos were almost all contributed, even when Greenky did manage to obtain the Quark files, she didn't have the rights to use most of the content. HFNM did have a stockpile of fashion pictures, thanks to a famous in-house fashion photographer named Gilles Bensimon. But it didn't own the rights to a single picture of *George* magazine's John F. Kennedy, Jr., and had to buy one from a stock house.

At Hachette, as at other magazine companies, editors generally resented the apparently effortless success that new media was enjoying, fearing it would take circulation away from the core magazine. Worse, they tended to look at people like Jim Docherty as interlopers who expected the free use of all their content. The somewhat self-important editors of the big consumer magazines like *Premiere* and *Elle* almost never journeyed down to the floor housing new media, which it shared with one of the least sexy HFM titles, *Boating* magazine. In fact, one onlooker who worked in the new-media department for almost two years saw only a single editor make the pilgrimage, and that was JFK, Jr., who was there to complain about something.

In reality, the Hachette editor who related to the online effort the least was Kennedy, the essentially shy but determined son of the late president. There is no question that JFK, Jr., was one of the most mediagenic males of his time. Even if he hadn't been the son of our most charismatic leader, even if he hadn't given that famous salute at his father's funeral, people would still have stared, for he was so physically attractive.

Kennedy had backed into the magazine business. Although he had passed the bar (after several much-publicized failed attempts) and had worked briefly as an assistant district attorney in New York, the law held little appeal to him. He and his initial partner in *George,* Michael Berman, had originally wanted to go into the sea kayak business, but by happenstance, or perhaps because he was curious, JFK, Jr., wandered into a seminar on how to launch your own magazine, at the 1995 annual *Folio:* magazine convention, and the rest was history. Kennedy had been searching for a career that was anything but the two routes often most prophesied for him—politics and acting. Even though he did a little acting in a college and had had dozens of approaches from Hollywood, Kennedy believed that publishing, a business in which his mother had worked, was better suited to his interests and talents. Moreover, his *George* idea allowed him to participate in politics from a remove, a tactic that must have been tempting. He approached Time Inc. for financing first, but Time already had politics (*Time*) and celebrities (*People, Entertainment Weekly*) covered, so they passed.

HFM's David Pecker happened to see a newsletter mention of Kennedy's interest, however, and immediately responded. Pecker called a contact at the talent agency ICM, which he had retained to get the company into TV projects, and obtained JFK's home phone number. "You don't know me from Adam, but I think we're after the same goal," Pecker told Kennedy in a sincere phone pitch. The relationship took off from there. The launch of *George* in October 1995 was a huge success, with the first issue containing hundreds of pages of advertising.

The *George* web site followed shortly afterward, in 1996, created by Radical Media, the same company that had helped Hachette get into the CD-ROM business. Unfortunately, www.georgemag.com was a mess for a variety of reasons, foremost among them that it was badly designed—"an absolute spaghetti factory," in Jim Docherty's words. Part of the problem was that neither Kennedy, Berman, nor any of the other *George* editors had had anything to do with it, pleading their duties at the magazine.

This is a typical phenomenon, and one of which few outside the magazine industry are fully aware. Many magazine web sites—even those large, big-circulation periodicals—were produced with absolutely no input from the top editors of the print product. George Online was a classic example of a web site's failing because of the lack of editorial input. There were no interactive features, no up-to-the-minute news updates. Given the long lead times of monthly magazine publishing, that meant that the articles posted on the site were two to three months out of date, deadly for politics in general and online politics specifically. Despite a generous amount of promotion, George Online was attracting only a paltry 64,000 page views a month three or four months after launch, compared to 8 million for the *Car and Driver* web site.

The blunt-speaking Docherty claims that George Online was so poor an effort because of the "complete ignorance" of the magazine's staff. When Docherty tried to improve the web site, he got no cooperation from the editors, including Kennedy. "They didn't understand it, they didn't know it," Docherty says of the editors' attitude toward the Internet. "They thought it was just kind of nice to have. And then the Internet became bigger and bigger, and in September of that year, I shut the site down."

Actually, closing the *George* web site (without notifying anyone at the magazine) was a calculated risk, given Kennedy's power at the time. Under the terms of Docherty's contract with AOL, he had the right to a certain number of web sites that could co-exist along with AOL areas, while other titles had to remain exclusive on AOL. The major auto magazine *Road & Track* was an AOL exclusive, to Docherty's chagrin, as he was confident it would do well as a free-standing web site, and certainly far better than *George* was doing. When Docherty looked at his lineup of web sites and AOL areas, he saw an imbalance. *Road & Track* was exclusive to AOL, but Doc was convinced it would do very well as a web site, partly because *Car and Driver* was the most popular destination Hachette had on the Web. It was within his power, he thought, to tell AOL that he was changing the rules, and that *George's* Web operation could be shut down, allowing Hachette to put up a *Road & Track* site. Two car URLs would be better than one plus a half-baked political magazine site that no one cared about. He made a preemptive move, one day simply making George Online go away on the Web and planning his own *Road & Track* project. He gambled that JFK, Jr., just wouldn't care that much. He was almost right.

"They didn't even discover it for a month," Docherty remembers. "That was the kind of participation they had." The web site simply disappeared and in its stead appeared a placeholder directing surfers to the *George* area on AOL, keyword Georgemag. Although this was seemingly a bad deal for AOL, since *Road & Track* was far more popular with their users than *George* would be, Hachette insiders think AOL accepted the switch because they saw it as a way to get closer to Kennedy. (Ironically, the terms of Kennedy's contract with Hachette would probably have backed him up had he wanted to challenge Docherty legally, but he doesn't appear to have realized this.)

When the disappearance of the *George* site was finally noticed, Kennedy immediately complained to Pecker, who called for an explanation. This was a month before the Presidential election, which would witness the convincing reelection of Bill Clinton, and Kennedy was a major backer of the President, but the web site had been almost completely divorced from the election maelstrom.

Docherty sums up the denouement: "So Pecker calls me and says, 'Doc, where's his web site?' I said that the *George* AOL area is still up, but the numbers on the web site were terrible. . . . David placed a lot of emphasis on the image of our company. I said, 'These traffic numbers are now being publicly reported, whether we like it or not. The entire company is showing a big traffic jump, except for *George.* It's making us look bad, number one, and number two, it's visible to the same advertisers that are in the magazine. If they see a dramatic indifference to the Web property, how is this going to look to them?'

"David gets it right away but he says, 'Doc, what am I going to say to John?'"

That unpleasant task was left to Docherty and Greenky. Perhaps because he shared Kennedy's Irish temper, perhaps because he had spent enough time with overpaid movie stars when he was young that he was no longer impressed by celebrity, Docherty didn't give Kennedy the same degree of deference everyone else around him did.

"Pecker passed John on to me," Doc remembers, "so I sat in very painful meetings with him, screaming at each other." "How dare you?" Kennedy shouted at Docherty during one meeting and accused Docherty of being "jealous" of him. "Honest to God, it was like sibling rivalry. I would scream until I was hoarse, and then he would run up to David and tell Dad," Docherty says. "We were great partners in that respect. I'm the only guy who was disinvited to his funeral."

Making Docherty's job even more difficult was Kennedy's assistant, Rose-Marie Terenzio, who, as he recalls, "was truthfully less than kind to anyone but John Kennedy. She had John believing that she knew everything there was to know about new media." In fact Terenzio had little knowledge of the subject but didn't let that stop her from asserting herself. During one particularly unpleasant 1996 meeting between Terenzio and Jocelyn Greenky, the two differed sharply over access to *George* material, and what was appropriate to do on the AOL area. A shouting match ensued, and after gallantly coming to Rose's rescue, Kennedy demanded that Greenky be banned from having any further responsibility for the *George* AOL area. Kennedy went to address the problem directly with Pecker, who in turn conferred with the French owners of Hachette. The editorial director of the company, Jean-Louis Ginibre, was a French-born former art director at the *Hollywood Reporter,* and he often served as the liaison back to the Paris headquarters. By 1996, the French had already sunk tens of millions of dollars into *George* and were understandably more likely to side with Kennedy in any dispute. Moreover, Berman, who had been a tempering influence, had already departed *George,* after a violent fist fight with Kennedy, in which shirts were torn and epithets were exchanged. The result of all this conflict was that HFNM, the new media division, became largely isolated and on its own. Editors waited for their opportunity to strike back, resentful of the unit's existence. As the '90s progressed, the tension remained a constant irritant.

The situation confronting Hachette Filipacchi New Media in 1996 and 1997 was typical of the troubled relationship that existed between magazines and their online counterparts. While online heavyweights like Yahoo! and Excite were conscientiously interacting with their users and trying to perfect software that would maximize page views and profits, new-media heads at the large media companies were struggling with major disconnects, personnel conflicts, and culture shock.

David Churbuck remembers this period well. A former news editor at the computer magazine *PC Week,* he was one of the early adopters of the Internet, setting up his own saltwater fishing site in 1994, coding it himself from his bedroom in Cotuit, Massachusetts. Churbuck, famous for his bow ties and droll post-preppie demeanor, had had the foresight to register the domain name Forbes.com in 1994, and wrote a letter to *Forbes* magazine chairman Steve Forbes suggesting that Churbuck helm a Forbes Web project. The letter went unanswered; Forbes was too busy running the magazine and contemplating running for President.

But in 1996, during the all-important New Hampshire primary, Steve Forbes gave a speech to Silicon Valley's Churchill Club that contained many paeans to the innovations of technology. Inspired by some of Forbes contributor George Gilder's loftier predictions, Forbes thought depicting himself as a high-tech visionary was good for his image as a different sort of Republican, although his magazine's forays into cyberspace had been limited to hosting a forum on CompuServe.

In the winter of 1996, columnist Stewart Alsop launched an attack on the supposedly technically savvy candidate and called Forbes a hypocrite because his magazine lacked a web site. Stung by the criticism, Forbes recalled the tech geek named Churbuck who had been babbling about the World Wide Web back in 1994. "He remembered the letter, and I got a phone call," Churbuck explains. "Forbes asked, 'How soon can you set up a web site?'" By May 1, 1996, Churbuck had put *Forbes* on the Internet. It was pretty much a one-man operation—Churbuck created the first *Forbes* Web product out of the same Cotuit bedroom from which his saltwater fishing domain had been launched, and Forbes.com appeared exactly two years to the day after the fishing site debuted.

If a leading magazine like *Forbes* could trust its web site to a complete outsider, an intellectual and computer geek who had little in common with the ambitious Forbes family, then all bets were off when it came to figuring out what media web sites were about. This was disconnect at the most basic level. Churbuck and his counterparts would attend occasional Web-vision meetings with the executive hierarchy, but these sessions were painful for all concerned, and most of the advice doled out by the top echelon was useless and uninformed. The Web was a very demanding medium, asking its practitioners to constantly become immersed in the latest capabilities and buzzwords. When a new technology like Flash, which allowed cartoon-style animation and moving parts, would debut, Web programmers would fall all over themselves making their domains Flash-enabled to keep up with their counterparts elsewhere. TV and print don't do that, and executives from these media didn't have to contend with the bone-shattering paradigm shifts faced daily during the period by Web programmers. After a while, this became apparent even to people like Steve Forbes, even as he was gaining points on the political circuit with a lot of speeches about high-tech wizardry.

Thus a pattern began to emerge all over New York and other media centers. Workers on the Web side of a media outlet would work in what became splendid isolation, basically autonomous, as those picked to oversee them slowly began to realize that they never would figure out exactly what the Internet guys were doing in their cubicles. This eventuality was exactly what the Web side wanted, as they frequently took the position that the "suits" upstairs didn't understand the medium and never would. But the long-term effect of this isolation was highly problematic. It meant that the Web operation, as an expensive and money-draining separate line item in budgets, was often resented and barely tolerated. As long as *Forbes, Fortune,* and *Business Week* were still running cover stories proclaiming the Web as the next Nirvana, these operations were condoned. But as soon as that paradigm changed, the Web operations began to seem like useless and costly appendages. For the David Churbucks of the media world, the future was less than assured. And who wants to work in an environment where you are alternately admired, feared, resented, and, finally, viewed with contempt?

CHAPTER 7

Dispatches from Reuters Online

As the Web took hold, and media chieftains surveyed what their "killer applications" were, the so-called killer apps that would lead them to dominance over the fledgling medium, most saw news as the best vehicle for their online jihad. Weekly or biweekly magazines like *Forbes* had their own issues to deal with, primarily providing business analysis and features in a medium seemingly tailor-made for daily updates. The immediacy of daily news, it was clear, matched the quotidian nature of the Web. If consumers were going to go online every day, or every hour, the best way to hook them in was with constantly refreshed news stories. And daily news was a medium self-satisfied companies like the Washington Post and the New York Times thought they owned. But as certain patterns began to emerge with Web usage, it became quickly apparent that the Web wasn't a daily news vehicle, it was an hourly one. Early on in the medium's life, online computer news competitors ZDNet and CNET began to compete for scoops, and they proved their bona fides by showing that their version of a given story was posted at 4:24 p.m., while their rival's was posted at 4:25. As absurd as this may seem, it matched television news, where bragging rights to scoops could be measured out in seconds. As with TV, once a story was out there, all your competitors could see it and immediately post their rival versions. But to be able to do that, a Web news operation needed an army of online journalists constantly updating and refreshing their content, a costly and unwieldy endeavor.

And there were lots of protocol questions. If during the workday something major happened with the Supreme Court, did the *New York Times*'s online operation wait for correspondent Linda Greenhouse to weigh in with her version (which might not be ready until later that evening), or did they quickly post something by an online staffer? To do that risked diluting the brand-name recognition of authorities like Greenhouse. The alternative was to post a wire-service story from AP or Reuters (UPI was all but irrelevant by the mid-'90s).

AP and Reuters had the right news configuration for the Web. Wire services are, like CNN and MSNBC, minute-by-minute operations. They're staffed with people who can churn out a quick dispatch while news is breaking, without all the preparation and sourcing required of daily newspaper journalists. In theory, they're ecumenical, selling their news product to newspapers, broadcasters, and whoever wants to pay for the service. But the reality is a bit more complicated and can be traced to the origins of these two institutions, both beginning approximately 150 years ago, when instead of Osama bin Laden, newshounds were trying to figure out the meaning of the Monroe Doctrine and its implications to European and American world dominance.

The Associated Press has its origins way back in 1848, when 10 men representing the main daily newspapers in the city had gotten together around an office table at the venerable *New York Sun*. The telegraph had just been invented, making news far more immediate, but also making preparation of the news much more costly for individual papers. The purpose of the meeting was to figure out how telegraph-delivered news could be made affordable. Finally David Hale of the *Journal of Commerce* made a breakthrough suggestion—what if they all worked together, pooling telegraphed news through a central source? The idea seemed a capital one, and a six-newspaper cooperative was born, the Associated Press (AP). The AP grew to a giant serving 1,500 newspapers and 5,000 broadcast outlets in the United States and a total of 15,000 clients worldwide, but it remained a noncommercial entity, to prevent its becoming a news giant that would overwhelm its members. In 1943, the distinguished Judge Learned Hand ruled that AP had to be available to all qualified U.S. news outlets, not just its cooperative members, saying that "AP is a vast, intricately reticulated organization, the largest of its kind, gathering news from all over the world, the chief single source of news from all over the world, the chief single source of news for the American press, universally agreed to be of prime consequence." This wasn't hyperbole of any kind. AP totally dominated how most people got their news in 1943, the same way it does today.

Reuters was quite another story, even though it debuted only three years after the AP. It was founded in London in 1851 by Paul Julius Reuter, memorably portrayed by Edward G. Robinson in the movie *Dispatch from Reuters*. The company employed a nest of 45 pigeons in its early days, plucky British birds that could make the journey between Brussels and Aachen, Germany, in two hours, six hours faster than the railroad. One of its biggest scoops came in 1859, when Reuters reported that the King of Sardinia had given a speech indicating war was imminent between France and Austria. Punch wrote of Reuter in 1869,

> England believes his telegrams,
> Whether they please or fright her:
> Other electric sparks are right,
> But he is always *right-er.*

Reuters, unlike the AP, was a for-profit institution, quickly moving into an emphasis on financial news and information, eventually outstripping the AP in this regard, even in America. Now billing itself as "the world's leading news and financial information organization," it has certainly profited handsomely from that status. In contrast to AP's nonprofit position, Reuters brings in about £3.59 billion a year, with profits of £657 million, and employs 20,700 people in 210 cities and 99 countries.

Reuters is nimble and forward-seeking. If pigeons delivered the news fastest, it maintained an aviary. But if the Web could deliver news faster than newspapers, Reuters wanted in. Unlike the AP, Reuters didn't have to be overly concerned with the worries of its print and broadcast members, who might object to Reuters supplying the new competition. Reuters was ubiquitous in the newsrooms of major papers like the *New York Times* and the *Wall Street Journal,* but it was less of a presence in regional America, where it found it hard to compete with AP's local wires. Thus it had fewer American media clients and was hungry for more. The Web could do the job nicely. The steep slide to irrelevance of big-media online properties owes a lot to a friendly fellow at Reuters, named Andy Nibley, who more than anyone else was directly responsible for helping make news a commodity on the Internet.

Starting in 1993, as the driving force behind Reuters New Media, Nibley had pioneered the concept of news services or "wires" selling their product to portals like Yahoo! and AOL. He got there through a circuitous route, but by the time he was finished, the news business would never be the same again.

Despite his long association with British-based parent Reuters Group PLC, Andy Nibley is an American who had worked his way up as a reporter at the ill-fated United Press International and the now-defunct *Washington Star,* where he was a part-time sportswriter. He joined Reuters in 1980 as a Treasury correspondent and gradually rose to better and better positions—news editor in

Washington, news editor in Europe, editor for North and Latin America, and then senior vice president for news and television. By fall 1993, Nibley was "kind of getting bored." Buford Smith, the American-born head of global technology at Reuters and later CEO, approached him and asked, "If I can get Reuters to fund it, do you want to start a new-media company?" Nibley was tapped to head the unit because back in 1991 he had been the driving force behind selling news to Prodigy, CompuServe, and Apple's eWorld, the leading online services then. By 1993 the revenue from online sales was almost 10 percent of the total for the American operation, a significant figure.

Smith and Nibley were the two senior Americans at Reuters then, and both had a feeling that they were being left on a rickety limb that could easily be sawed off if they failed. "We were as surprised as [Reuters's British managers] were when we came back a few years later and said, 'Hey look, guys—gold, silver, spices.' Most of them had thought that we would drown at sea or something."

The first meeting of Reuters New Media involved about eight people and took place just before Thanksgiving 1993, at the Hyatt hotel in Old Greenwich, Connecticut. (The Hyatt is a former factory—ironically, the former printing plant of Condé Nast. A stone pillar outside the building still lists the Condé Nast magazines from the 1920s, including *Vanity Fair*.) Smith proclaimed himself president of the division, while Nibley was made executive vice president. The group agreed to form a company starting January 1, 1994.

Smith and Nibley had trouble communicating at first, because the former was a technology type and the latter had been a journalist almost all his career. Nibley recalls, "I thought a hack was a guy who writes badly, and he knew a hacker was a guy who can do amazing things with computers. I was essentially a technophobe. If I could learn this stuff, I could essentially give myself a merit badge. Every time I've jumped off a cliff, things have worked out—maybe it's my '60s upbringing." Reuters New Media in 1994 could be compared to John Madden's Oakland Raiders, he adds, "when he went out and got the parolees and the ne'er do wells, the guys no one else wanted, the troubled kids. He pulled the team together and they won the Super Bowl."

Reuters's overall goal had been to push UPI out of its perennial number-two wire-service spot behind the Associated Press, a goal that the company was starting to achieve in the early '90s. A dispute between UPI and the *New York Times* had led the Gray Lady to drop UPI over Reuters, which increased the strength of the British-based news service greatly. A huge presence in England, Reuters had not really had a major presence in America before achieving this coup.

A newspaper can pay AP as much as $1 million for the news service a year.

In an attempt to protect that revenue, AP didn't start selling news to web sites until 1996, and even then sales of its limited feed, the Wire, were restricted to AP members. Among its competitors, Dow Jones had likewise resisted selling to online entities and UPI was in constant turmoil, its very existence questioned on a daily basis. The field was thus clear for Nibley, and he knew it. "I think back to that famous Nietzsche quote, so memorably cited by G. Gordon Liddy: 'That which doesn't destroy me makes me stronger,'" Nibley quips. "We had a Robin Hood mentality. And we knew that the Internet was made for the wire services. I saw this hole, and we ran right through it."

Working out of a floor at a Reuters building at 1700 Broadway in Manhattan, the new-media operation began in earnest by dispatching a British emissary named John Taysom to Palo Alto, to act as liaison with the members of the small but growing "portal" community, including Yahoo!, the fledgling Architext (which later changed its name to Excite), MSN, and Infoseek. Taysom was soon reporting back to Nibley that Yahoo!, which was then little more than a couple of wacky guys in Silicon Valley, was looking for capital. "Taysom brought Yahoo! in, and I have to say this was one of the great sales jobs of all time. For whatever reason the English are constitutionally incapable of saying 'Yah-hoo'; they say 'Ya-hoooo.' Which is extremely funny when you're asking for money to buy a piece of this. I liked it because I thought it gave us a great outlet online for our news, where we could actually get by the AP. Yahoo! [then] had no source for news.

"So John goes to London, and they're saying, 'What is this Ya-hoooo?' We said, 'It's five guys, and they're dropping out of business school at Stanford, and see, there's this thing called the Internet, and there's going to be a need for a lot of white pages and yellow pages.' The more we tried to explain it, the more ridiculous it sounded, especially when someone in London said, 'Can we meet the CEO?' And we had to reply, 'Actually, it's not the CEO, it's the Chief Yahoo!' I think in their minds, London gave us the money because they thought that this would be how we would hang ourselves."

Before then there had been great resistance from London about the Internet sales because Reuters had such a brisk business with stock brokerages and other financial institutions, who paid large sums for Reuters's detailed financial wires. The approach of companies like Yahoo!, which involved giving content away for free, was a major challenge to that model. But the new-media contingent was able to argue this hesitation away by pointing out the enormous brand-building strength that the new-media outlets would give Reuters. And further, they pointed out, for the first time news wires like Reuters wouldn't have to use newspapers and broadcasters as go-betweens to reach the huge American market—they could go directly to the end user with their product.

The stake Reuters bought in Yahoo! was small—$3 million, which represented about 4 percent of the company. But Reuters ultimately made a huge profit out of the investment and got a lot of free publicity for it later, when Yahoo! became better known. But more important, Reuters New Media was able to build its entire subsequent business out of that initial Yahoo! deal, because once its news began appearing on Yahoo!, all the other portals wanted it as well. In addition Reuters not only was Yahoo!'s default news provider, but it received an ad split that awarded it half the ad revenue generated from the news areas.

In 1994 Reuters New Media concluded news deals with AOL and MSN. When Nibley would appear on panels at media conferences during this period, he would be attacked ferociously by his colleagues at AP, Dow Jones, UPI, and other news services, who as much as told him that he was out of his mind. Nibley's wife actually worked for AP, and he heard through her that AP had set its sights on his thinning scalp.

Undaunted, Reuters New Media forged ahead, buying other new-media-oriented companies, including Reality Technologies, which focused on personal finance. (This was the very company that Jonathan Bulkeley had nearly joined back in 1993.) Sources familiar with Reuters and its investment in Reality say that the deal immediately piqued the interest of Steve Case, who wanted to broaden AOL's reach into personal finance.

In 1994, these sources say, Case put a proposition in front of Reuters CEO Peter Job. As a source familiar with the talks recalled, "[Case] said, 'If you give me Reality'—which was losing about $8 million a year then—'and $10 million, I will give you ten percent of AOL.'"

Job's response was straightforward: "I don't like the name, and I think it's an American fad." Nibley and Taysom were crushed. Whether it was due to British jingoism, sheer ignorance, or just resistance to change, they felt that Job had missed out on the deal of the century.

Reuters, a thoroughly British company, ended up as one of the major corporate beneficiaries of the rise of America Online and its counterparts, and it was success of the most unequivocal kind. Undaunted by London's unwillingness to invest in AOL, Reuters New Media took stakes in a plethora of new-media players, including Infoseek, Verisign, SportsLine (later CBS SportsLine), Digimark, US Web, and Firefly (later sold to Microsoft). "John was a phenomenal stock-picker," Nibley says. Some of these companies, including Infoseek, got sweetheart rates from Reuters, which helped them grow quickly and further swelled Reuters's portfolio.

Apart from the investments, what Reuters New Media did so successfully was to establish a novel news paradigm on the Internet, which stymied all the large news-oriented media companies, including big newspapers like the *New York Times,* the *Washington Post,* and the *Los Angeles Times,* and the network news departments at CBS, Fox, ABC, and NBC. Reuters news was integrated into the main news areas of AOL and other portals, especially Yahoo!

If you needed to know what was going on in Bosnia or in Afghanistan, you no longer had to go to a dedicated news company web site. You could get your information on the fly in the normal course of surfing your favorite site. In truth, most users didn't care or even notice where the news came from; many probably assumed Yahoo! had a news department. News was no longer owned by any of the big American news companies, but by the portals. Suddenly a small cadre of media elite in the Time-Life Building in New York or at Ben Bradlee's old stomping grounds at the *Washington Post* were not what the news business was all about.

Reuters also benefited greatly from the huge proliferation of online operations in the late '90s, most of whom opted to get their news from Reuters. The decision to go with Reuters wasn't overly complicated, as AP was a disaster to deal with for online concerns. The conflict it embodied as a nonprofit cooperative of newspapers and broadcasters was apparent in all dealings and all levels. One online company business-development functionary recalls a series of frustrating meetings with AP as late as 1999, in which employees of the wire service struggled—openly—with crafting an agreement to provide news to web sites that wouldn't alienate their bosses. A deal to provide news to this operation took six months to negotiate. While AP did eventually sell news to Excite and other Web portals, the process was difficult and draining, and most portals opted to simply not deal with the organization.

Meanwhile, as AP mostly balked at selling to online competitors, Reuters was cleaning up. The British company ended up with a huge office tower in the newly rehabilitated Times Square, a building that had been at least partially financed by its relationship with AOL and other portals. The *Wall Street Journal* reported that by August 2000, some 60 percent of the revenue to the American media unit of Reuters was coming from more than 900 Web clients.

"Between John [Taysom] and Andy Nibley, Reuters could not have had two better guys steering them into new media," observes former Infoseek CEO Harry Motro, who worked closely with the pair after Taysom steered Reuters into an investment in Infoseek.

Reuters's growth closely paralleled a seeming complete volte-face in the news business as it was understood in the late '90s. Suddenly no one was sure how all this was going to play out. In the boardrooms of large media conglomerates like GE's NBC News, this was of major concern. Was it worthwhile to potentially spend hundreds of millions of dollars online if upstarts like Yahoo!, fueled by Reuters's commoditized news, would dominate anyway? This was a huge concern on the part of media's top rank of executives. For years, the Washington Post Co., for example, had dined out on its reputation as a news leader, dating back to its aggressive coverage of Watergate. By this point, the romantic paradigm of *All the President's Men* had ceased to be the model for how the news business really worked.

Ultimately, the rise of news as a commodity was a critical factor that led the big news providers, including the TV networks, to conclude there was no money to be made in offering news online. One of the watershed events in the online world of the early '90s was GE and NBC's decision to exit the online business, eliminating the competition they had once offered AOL.

Although it has been largely forgotten today, GE operated for several years an online service called GENIE, which, properly managed, could have been a contender. Like News Corp.'s Delphi, it was text-based and didn't offer a graphic interface or Web browser. In 1995, it had 500,000 subscribers, who were supposed to be paying a fairly exorbitant $3.95 per hour of connection time, plus a sizable monthly fee. The acronym GENIE stood for General Electric Network for Information Exchange, a ponderous title for a service that nonetheless was fairly innovative.

Mark Walsh, who served as president of GENIE from 1994 to 1995, recalls that few GENIE subscribers were ever disconnected, whether they paid their fees or not. One of the things that GENIE did right was "community." As a direct antecedent to Scott Kurnit's About.com, GENIE had hundreds of what were then called SIGs, or Special Interest Group discussion boards, operated by expert sysops, or system operators. Topics ranged from the Civil War to hunting and fishing. In later years, Walsh would often remind Scott Kurnit that GENIE had pioneered everything About.com did. "Don't tell anybody," Kurnit would laugh in response.

Even as late as 1995 GENIE would still have been salvageable if GE had put money into it for a major graphics upgrade, gotten a commitment of cooperation from NBC News, and provided a renewed interface with the Web. Like other then-extant services, including Delphi, GENIE had gained some credibility by being early to the online party, but also, like Delphi, it had been slow in integrating an acceptable graphical user interface (GUI), which by 1995 customers were beginning to demand as a standard feature of their online experience.

Walsh remembers making an impassioned presentation to Jack Welch in late 1994, arguing that GENIE should be upgraded to make it competitive with AOL and Prodigy, and moved to a closer affiliation with NBC. "We were in the boardroom in Fairfield, Connecticut, at GE's headquarters. It was the annual GE budget presentation," Walsh says. "I suggested that we put more money into GENIE. I said, 'Imagine [NBC News anchor] Tom Brokaw finishing the news, and then pressing a button on the air and saying, "I just downloaded a transcript of tonight's news to GENIE." ' I was right, but GE wasn't prepared for it."

Later Walsh tried a similar pitch to NBC CEO Bob Wright and his cable guru, Tom Rogers. NBC, of course, was owned by GE, and if NBC had backed the expansion of GENIE, Walsh might have had a shot. Unfortunately, he made his arguments on the same day that Ted Turner was visiting Wright and didn't get too far in his argument. "It was a weird juxtaposition of Ted walking in just as I was there to see Rogers and Wright," Walsh recalls. "Tom was good, but what could he say to me? It was something like, 'You're a good guy. I wish you well, but you missed the window of opportunity by something like fifteen months.' They were already committed to MSNBC."

MSNBC, the joint venture between Microsoft and NBC, which would launch in 1995, was considered a far safer bet than devoting any further resources to GENIE, because Microsoft's Bill Gates had committed to underwrite the hugely expensive overhead cost of an online news operation. Had NBC committed to GENIE, it would have borne the entire financial burden alone.

But GE wasn't prepared to give up completely on GENIE quite yet, at least not publicly. Walsh notes that, in the press release announcing MSNBC, lip service was still being paid to supporting GENIE. But, in the end, that's all it was, for GE was never convinced that it knew enough about the online business to compete with AOL and its fully committed and ferociously aggressive staff.

Later, while an AOL executive, Walsh would put together a presentation arguing that the only online service that could succeed would be AOL, because it was the only service that was 100 percent focused on winning the online battle. The others, with their corporate ownership, were too distracted by other business, a fact he knew from personal experience. "I left because I knew that GENIE would never get real backing from GE," Walsh says today.

Although not a news-oriented company, Bertelsmann, the German media conglomerate, like Reuters was a European company that benefited hugely from the rise of America Online and other portals. In fact, Reuters and Bertelsmann were probably the greatest beneficiaries, if only because of some shrewd deal-making and the circumstances they happened to find themselves in.

Bertelsmann had acquired its 5 percent stake in AOL as part of the launch of AOL Europe, which was briefly headed by Jonathan Bulkeley. Bertelsmann's German-born CEO Thomas Middlehoff had won a seat on the AOL board. Perhaps because he was an outsider, Middlehoff never approached new media as cautiously as did his American counterparts, and he has been praised by the top AOL echelon as one of the few media figures who understood the implications of the Internet early on.

According to former Bertelsmann spokesperson Liz Young, Middlehoff, aged 47 in 2002, had always been fascinated with new media, even writing his Ph.D. thesis on a German online service called T-Online. "When Thomas met Steve Case in Dulles [Virginia] in 1985, he quickly realized that this was a guy like him," Young says. Middlehoff, only 30 at the time, recognized in Case another digital dreamer. Ultimately that realization led to an investment that, combined with other Internet-related equity, added up to an astonishing $11 billion when it was ultimately cashed out at the end of the millennium. "Bertelsmann made the most money in the Internet of all the media companies," Young asserts, without much fear of contradiction.

The Bertelsmann executive who spearheaded much of the company's Internet activity in the music sphere in the United States was Kevin Conroy, who was at the company from 1995 to 2001, having joined from the CBS/Fox home video operation. As the head of marketing at BMG Entertainment, the music group that included the labels RCA and Arista, the pugnacious Conroy, with close-cropped blond hair and a somewhat combative manner, was one of the few top music executives to fully embrace the Web—so much so that he later landed a job heading AOL's music operations.

Conroy immediately saw the Internet as a more efficient and far cheaper way to promote music than the music videos that had launched MTV. The record business had been hugely disappointed with MTV when it abandoned videos in the second half of the '90s, in favor of game shows and features like *The Real World*. Label executives felt that MTV had used and abused their product as the foundation for a successful lifestyle channel, only to turn away from videos when it found it could get better ratings with series television. Although the labels had been barred from starting a music television channel of their own, no such restrictions existed online, and BMG, with its presence on the AOL board and its multinational clout, was an attractive partner for AOL.

Conroy coined a term, "marketing convergence," to describe the myriad ways in which the company planned to use the Web in its music promotion, maintaining it as an integral unit of BMG Entertainment. "We were one of the few companies to resist the temptation to treat our Internet efforts as separate and distinct from everything else," he says.

BMG's Web efforts were much more focused than those of other media companies, which helped limit the confusion experienced elsewhere. Instead of dozens of people working separately, BMG's Web nexis was basically Conroy and his direct reports. "There has been only one person responsible for Internet activities for BMG since 1995. It was relatively simple, the buck stopped here," he says.

Conroy first pitched the idea of an active collaboration between BMG and AOL in February 1996, meeting with AOL development executive David Colburn and basically explaining what a fully committed record conglomerate could do for the service. "My pitch to them was, 'Let me be your program partner,'" Conroy recalls, and that pitch fell on receptive ears. One top AOL executive approached Conroy during this period, admitted he knew nothing about the music business, and asked for a tutorial. Since this individual later rose to a key position in the company, it can be legitimately argued that much of what AOL now knows about music, it first learned from Conroy.

By spring 1997, after the two companies had established a major marketing partnership, BMG was bundling AOL software onto the CDs of some of its hottest acts, a strategy that helped the service reach the youth market. "We put their software on more than one hundred major releases," Conroy estimates. "AOL covered the cost of putting the software on the CD. They paid us for having the software on the CDs and a further bounty for the CD buyers who became AOL subscribers."

For BMG, the relationship was about more than just the money, however, because the company was determined to establish itself at the cutting edge of all that was hip and happening in entertainment. BMG's Strauss Zelnick had come out of the video game business, and he appreciated the value of corporate identification with go-go technology: "We wanted to be the vehicle to launch onto the Web from, via our CDs," he says. There is irony in the fact that two *European* companies ended up reaping the most profit from the rise of *America* Online, but it is nonetheless true.

CHAPTER 8

Time Warner's Black Hole

T he beginning of the end for Time Inc. New Media can be dated back as early as October 1995, when CEO Don Logan made official what many in the business had already been whispering about for months—the magazine company was concerned, *deeply* concerned, about how much the division was costing. Street gossip had Pathfinder losing as much as $15 to $20 million a year, and while company spokespeople would grow visibly flustered when the figure was quoted, they didn't exactly deny its veracity at the time.

Only five years later, a major Internet conglomerate like CMGI would be admitting that its burn rate was as much as $64 million a *month*. But to Logan and his profit-minded Time Inc. of 1995, losing $20 million was a catastrophe and could spell the difference between big and small bonuses, and a contented or an angry boss in Jerry Levin. However much Levin continued to do the visionary thing, extolling the many splendors of new media, he still expected his division chiefs to bring in ever-bigger profits, and Pathfinder was dragging the whole division down.

The undercurrent of discontent at the company finally became public when, speaking at the American Magazine Conference, hosted by the Magazine Publishers of America, Logan had blurted out that Pathfinder "gives a whole new meaning to the scientific term 'black hole.'" The "black hole" remark, unfortunately, stuck with Pathfinder, despite the best efforts of the Time public relations office to explain that Logan's comments were taken out of context, that he was joking, etc. Everyone at Pathfinder, however, knew that Logan had meant every word of it.

Don Logan is, in many ways, a typical traditional media CEO. From tiny

Hartselle, Alabama, he has spent his entire career working his way up the Time Inc. corporate ladder. After joining Southern Progress, later a Time Inc. subsidiary, in 1970 he was named president of Oxmoor House, Southern Progress's book publishing unit, in 1984, and CEO of Southern Progress itself in 1986. He replaced Reg Brack as CEO of Time Inc. in August 1994 and was promoted to chairman in July 1997. At the time of Brack's replacement, Levin was careful to note that Brack had taken Time Inc. from annual revenue of $2.1 billion in 1986, when he had taken over, to $3.3 billion in 1993, the last full year of his stewardship, and had increased the number of Time Inc. magazines from 8 to 24. Brack's launch of *Entertainment Weekly* was the first successful debut of a weekly magazine in 20 years, Levin noted. The Time Warner CEO then went on to introduce Logan this way: "A mathematician by training, the burly, soft-spoken Logan quickly proved a decisive and imaginative partner as the two men together [Brack and Logan] set about positioning Time Inc. for future growth in both print and multimedia in the electronic age."

"Logan is an incredibly smart, perceptive, perspicacious person," says one top Time Inc. executive. "He sees the future pretty well, but he doesn't think the future is here. And his job is the near future. He's under horrible pressure every year for double-digit profit growth. He's taken the profits of this company from $300 million a year to over $800 million a year during his tenure. This is incredibly difficult—*People* can't make any more money. *Sports Illustrated* has matured—how do you grow? He's going to invest a lot of money in something the return on which he's not going to see during his professional lifetime? Or is he going to buy lots of magazines that have lots of earnings, and invest in the properties that he has? He can't afford to be a visionary. This is the whole problem. Media companies in the mid to late '90s were confronted with the decision that to make the conversion they needed to make, they would have to sacrifice current-year and coming-year cash flow. None of the media companies have done that, nor can they do it."

But Logan wasn't supposed to be a tech visionary; he was supposed to make double-digit profits. Walter Isaacson was supposed to be the guy who knew how it all worked and what the acronyms all stood for. He was the person whose minions had done the AOL deal and shepherded *Time* magazine online, bringing in the first actual revenue to the company's fledgling online operation. The problem was that Isaacson, being a quick study, began to see in 1996 that perhaps AOL was not such a great partner after all, that perhaps AOL was getting a lot more out of the relationship than Time was. Isaacson was hardly alone among AOL media partners as he came to that conclusion, but he was the most scrutinized. So when he began to question the AOL relationship and began to think he might do better at CompuServe, it got lots of tongues wagging in the media business.

Isaacson himself recalls the moment: "When we moved from AOL to CompuServe for a large sum of money, I called Steve Case and I said, 'I'm sure you can't possibly match this. This is an offer that came in that was breathtakingly high just for this one magazine.' Case said, 'Walter, I'm sorry, but I understand why you have to do it. I'm sorry because we have such a [good] relationship and loyalty on your bulletin boards and community rooms on AOL, and you're going to lose that, but I can understand that some day I might have to buy CompuServe to get you back.' We laughed, and a few years later he bought CompuServe."

Ted Leonsis remembers the details of the negotiation. "I said to Walter, 'Don't go to CompuServe, they're not going to win.' He said, 'They will pay us more money.' So they got $400,000 more. They wanted an upfront guarantee of $1 million, and we offered $600,000. We modeled a news area without Time magazine, [projected how it would] do, and we were confident. We had to do a gut check. But we still had news, and we plugged in Newsweek afterward. We paid Newsweek $400,000."

For Leonsis, standing up to Time was a bellwether event, because it was he who, along with Jonathan Bulkeley, had constantly reinforced to Steve Case just how crucial the big-media brands were to AOL's early growth. But by 1996, he sensed that there was a new era coming.

"There were signposts that it was our brand that was becoming important, and we learned a lot about what we were permitted to do," he recalls. "In 1996, on April Fool's Day, in the news area we did a spoof about life being discovered on Mars. It was clever and it was well done and it was funny, but our members got mad at us. We didn't fully realize that people were coming to AOL for news." The contretemps helped AOL understand that people took news seriously on AOL, no matter who presented it. It was one of the factors that reinforced the idea that AOL could live without Time. And if it could live without a big brand like Time, it might be able to live without a lot of other media content.

Time magazine's defection to CompuServe received a lot of attention in the media when the story leaked out. While Time had been slipping somewhat in circulation, it was still a premier news outlet, and no major media company had switched online services before. The decision presented some issues a business like Time Inc. would not normally have to deal with. Even if a magazine company changes distributors, everyone still has access to its product. Online, however, that was not the case, because for the most part AOL and CompuServe subscriptions didn't overlap; you had either one or the other.

The CompuServe leak happened in a humorous way. AOL's Mark Walsh and Ted Leonsis were doing a financial presentation about AOL before a business group in 1996 when a reporter came up to the two and asked, "I hear that *Time* magazine is quitting AOL." Leonsis, always quick with a retort, replied, "That's a leak, and we don't comment on leaks." The reporter put two and two together, figured that was a back-handed confirmation, and went with the story. "And that's how it got out," laughs Walsh.

While Isaacson's choice looks odd today, especially in the light of future events, it has to be judged in its proper context. The prevailing wisdom at the time was that the online services would eventually disappear anyway, in favor of the Web. New-media executives at big-media companies were therefore concentrating on short-term gains. A $500,000 difference was significant and could pay for a lot of Web producers and engineers. Even if CompuServe didn't have as sophisticated an understanding of news as AOL, over the long term it wasn't really a critical consideration.

A few blocks away on Broadway, Hachette Filipacchi New Media had remained with AOL, which was still paying it millions of dollars a year. This was wholly the decision of Jim Docherty, who was still under intense pressure from David Pecker to produce profits and would have faced stiff opposition had he wanted to cut the relationship off. Time Inc. New Media managers like Isaacson had a lot more autonomy, primarily because of lack of interference from the 34th floor.

As it happened, after only a few months of Time-CompuServe harmony, CompuServe dropped the magazine, complaining that it wasn't generating enough traffic, and that *Time* was simply using the funds it got from CompuServe to fund its rival web site, Pathfinder. Despite the fact that this claim had some merit, Time Inc. initiated a lawsuit against CompuServe that was finally dropped.

The CompuServe mess was one of the factors prompting Walter Isaacson's departure for the friendlier embrace of *Time* magazine's managing editor job, where all he had to worry about was more straightforward problems like the Middle East. It was easier, and more prestigious work than attempting to figure out the Web and all its contradictions. Editor in chief Norman Pearlstine's 1996 announcement that Isaacson would move to *Time* magazine described him as a "Renaissance man." Steve Case's tossed off comment two years earlier, about Isaacson's becoming the managing editor of *Time,* had proved to be correct.

Outgoing *Time* managing editor Jim Gaines, a former *People* top editor, had had a tepid reign at the newsweekly, a period marked by controversy over an artificially darkened O.J. Simpson cover photo that had angered many black readers, and other missteps. But he, too, waxed poetic about Isaacson. At a staff party to mark the changing of the guard, he had gushed, "I envy Walter this day, and I envy you the chance to work with Walter, who is exceedingly well prepared for this job and will do brilliantly. Walter's magazine will be better than mine was, and I will be rooting for it to be, if perhaps in that bittersweet way that fathers root for their sons to better them." This sort of rhetoric was typical of Time Inc., where a self-congratulatory, tight-knit little clique ruled, and new blood was unwelcome.

Isaacson's defection was even more of a blow to the struggling digital workers at Pathfinder than Logan's dismissive remarks a year earlier. "That was the real damage," recalls Pathfinder features editor Chris Peacock. "Walter was the kind of guy who, wherever he is, he's going to make something big happen." Without Isaacson, they feared, the project would lose its corporate imprimatur.

Shortly thereafter, on November 12, 1996, the staff of Time Inc. was informed in a memo from Norman Pearlstine that Dan Okrent, who had been the managing editor of *Life* since 1992, would become the editor of new media. Pearlstine's memo is typical of big-media company thinking at the time. "Dan brings an exceptional portfolio of skills to this position," he told the staff. "As a writer, editor and on-air personality who has excelled in book publishing, magazines and television, Dan is—as they say—a real triple threat. What's more, his considerable talent, energy, enthusiasm and insight make him the ideal person for this new assignment."

Pearlstine, of course, made no mention of the one kind of experience Okrent lacked—new-media skills. But in 1996, not many people had had that kind of training, and Time was following its long-established (if not proven) tradition of promoting from within. *Life* magazine was largely irrelevant by 1996, and many in the company assumed that if the name hadn't been on the building, *Life* would have long since been put out of its misery. In a world where television and online were the dominant media forms, a sentimental, family-oriented, general-interest magazine had all the relevance of the *Saturday Evening Post,* despite heroic efforts by Okrent to change that fact. *Life*'s publishing frequency had consequently changed several times, as had the focus of the magazine, but the truth was that by the time Okrent left, nobody was sure what the magazine was really about.

Okrent was a talented guy, a former book editor at Knopf, Viking, and Harcourt Brace Jovanovich whose *New England Monthly*, which he'd started in 1983, had been a truly impressive visual project, more a work of art than a commercial magazine. A national authority on baseball who was a featured commentator on Ken Burns's PBS series, he had gained renown in certain circles as the founder of the Rotisserie League. A somewhat rumpled figure, Okrent would never be mistaken for the society-conscious Isaacson.

For Okrent, new media was a consolation prize. Because of his fascination with baseball, he had tried mightily for the managing editor title at *Sports Illustrated* but had lost out in one of those brutal Time Inc. "bake-offs," much as Craig Bromberg had. Paul Sagan, who had been subordinate to Isaacson on the New Media masthead, had been elevated to the title Isaacson had briefly held, president of Time Inc. New Media. The company was trying to figure out what to do with Okrent, so Pearlstine recommended him to Sagan.

A recalcitrant Sagan, however, perhaps convinced that editors had the real power at Time Inc., wanted to retain both of Isaacson's titles, president and editor in chief of new media. Okrent balked, afraid he couldn't work with Sagan, who had earlier conscientiously tried to avoid butting heads directly with the all-powerful managing editors.

An account of a pitched battle between Sagan and the magazine side is illustrative of just how tense the relationship had actually become between Sagan's new-media group and the print editors. In the early summer of 1996, the *New York Times* came out with a preview, a best-of piece on Atlanta Olympics web sites. Pathfinder, with its sports coverage from *Sports Illustrated*, was not included in the article, and Norm Pearlstine was furious.

"The *Sports Illustrated* site was arguably the best Olympics site," recalled Stefanie Scheer, the magazine's senior editor of new media at the time. "There was a deal with IBM to provide the live stats. That meant that you could actually look up results in real time, which was not available to the other sites. *Sports Illustrated* was also publishing a daily magazine for the Atlanta Olympics, and there was a special Olympics commemorative issue. There had been planning for all this for a year. It was a huge publishing endeavor. We had some of the best sportswriters in the country covering these events. And the web site had all the content from the daily magazine, as well as the live stats from IBM."

Pearlstine was justifiably proud of this effort and quickly contacted *SI* editor

Bill Colson, the man who won the "bake-off" with Okrent, demanding to know what had gone wrong. Colson called in Stefanie Scheer, who wrote a long e-mail defending herself. An attractive woman with bobbed brown hair who appeared meek and unflappable, Scheer could be feisty when provoked. She pointed out to Colson that if there had been a failure anywhere, it was with public relations, and not her.

"It showed what a p.r. disaster Pathfinder was," Scheer noted. "There was always a battle between the individual [magazine] titles and Pathfinder, and who had power, and how much they were supposed to do for you." While the Olympics sites were an *SI* project, "We were the sports channel on Pathfinder," so it was up to Pathfinder to publicize the project, "and it never got on the radar."

Scheer further noted in her e-mail that Pathfinder public relations spokesperson Nancy Maloney had also done a poor job of getting the all-important *SI* swimsuit issue site listed on Yahoo! because she had put her own name first in the listing document, rather than the appropriate keyword, so the site would come up first if "Maloney" was used as a keyword, but not if "Swimsuit issue" was entered. That meant that the many cheap Web knockoffs of the expensive Pathfinder swimsuit site were getting the majority of traffic from Yahoo!

Not surprisingly Scheer's e-mail got Maloney into trouble with Pearlstine. It was later forwarded to Sagan, who was incensed—not at Maloney, but at Scheer.

"Pearlstine yelled at Sagan, and Sagan yelled back," Scheer continues. "So Sagan called me and 'invited' me up to his office on the 34th floor, which he had never done before." Sagan, like other top 34th-floor Time Inc-ers, had a massive office, with an outer reception area, an inner reception area where his assistant toiled, and then finally his own palatial space. Scheer entered this privileged sanctum with some trepidation, knowing of Sagan's penchant for tirades of abuse. She wasn't disappointed.

"He just yelled at me for quite a long time," Scheer said. "'Who do you think you are?' Sagan screamed. 'You're just a peon. How dare you blame these innocent people? You shouldn't write things in an e-mail you wouldn't want pasted on a bathroom wall.'"

Scheer wasn't fazed: "I just sat there and didn't say anything, because he didn't really want to hear it, and he had no real authority over me. I wasn't in the least bit worried about it, because I reported to the editor of the magazine, and he [Colson] was a prince." Scheer's comment underscores one of Sagan's great frustrations—he wasn't involved in a creative collaboration with the magazines, which thought of him as the "enemy."

Scheer adds that the Olympics incident "did illustrate the fact that the magazine editors controlled the brands and the content, and they held sway with Norm. Whatever Sagan did, he could never get things done his way. He didn't really have power. The magazines came up in a direct line of reporting to Norm, and Paul was over there. He lurked in the shadow of Walter Isaacson. Paul would come to meetings with his suspenders on, and he looked like a number-cruncher. He thought he was this boy genius, and he looked at us like, 'You're all shit, and I'm a cool guy with suspenders.'"

This incident was typical of the dysfunctional relationship between the magazines and the Pathfinder bureaucracy, she explained. "The Pathfinder people were always trying to take over what you were doing, and you were always staying in your magazine basket because it was safer and you had more power over there anyway."

Despite the hundreds of employees on staff, virtually nobody was around on the weekends. This meant that all-important sports scores from weekend games weren't posted until Monday, giving a huge lead to rivals like ESPNet SportsZone and CBS SportsLine. It was because of this nonfunctional relationship that *SI* chieftains pushed for an alliance with CNN, which was seen as more in touch with daily sports content. That alliance became CNN/SI on the Web and on cable, which was at least partly conceived as a way around the Pathfinder debacle.

While it was obvious to most observers that Sagan's position was becoming untenable, few were prepared for what would come next. First, Sagan got a chance to deal with Kinsella, whom he loathed by this point. There was, by this time, a coruscating personality clash between the two men, a power struggle essentially. At the beginning of 1996, Kinsella had submitted a detailed plan to Sagan called "The Time Warner Gateway," which had proposed a major alliance with an independent ISP, such as UUNet or PSINet, companies that served mainly businesses and might want to conquer the consumer world with Time. AOL had bought its own Internet dial-up network in 1994, ANS, for only about $45 million, the basis for Ted Leonsis's proposed joint venture, and Kinsella was arguing that Time Inc. could make a similar move and beat AOL at its own game.

When Sagan hesitated, Kinsella took the plan directly to Jerry Levin, so convinced was he of its merits. It has always been, however, a major faux pas at Time Inc. to circumvent your direct supervisor. It isn't acceptable other than in the case of extreme personality clashes, and even when it is done, a black mark is placed against your name, and your tenure at the company will almost certainly be short. Levin was puzzled and aggrieved by Kinsella's proposal. Insiders claim he was particularly irked because he simply lacked the knowledge to understand it, and hated being put on the spot about it. Levin finally told Kinsella, his annoyance all too clear, "Our business is run by the individual managers."

For reasons of his own, Kinsella then told Sagan that he'd met with Levin. "It drove Paul batshit," Kinsella admits.

Sagan had also clashed with Kinsella over the Internet Content Coalition (ICC), which had held its first meeting at the Time & Life Building under Kinsella's stewardship. "ICC was trying to prevent the government from enjoining the freedom to publish on the Internet," Kinsella says, but Sagan took the position that Time Inc. should not be an advocacy group. And the two fought about a friend of Kinsella's whom Kinsella had brought in as a consultant to work with the financial structure of the new-media group, an area Sagan thought was properly his domain.

The end came suddenly. Former Pathfinder executives who were present say that Kinsella was in meetings one minute and being escorted from the Time & Life Building the next. Kinsella insists it wasn't quite that abrupt. "I was not escorted out of the building, but if I had, it would be a badge of honor," he laughs.

Sagan's turn came soon afterward. Each year Time Inc. holds an annual retreat, where editors and business-side people can mingle and exchange ideas. Because the company was so rigidly stratified, this occasion was usually the only opportunity people actually had to meet, other than to say hello in the cafeteria or the hallway. During the 1996 World Series in October, the retreat was held at plush Amelia Island, off the coast at the northern end of Florida.

The meeting featured a major speech from Sagan on the status of Pathfinder and the new-media division. "Paul makes a dazzling presentation," Okrent recalls, "he's fast-paced, and his paragraphs make sense. I would say those of us in the audience understood about a third of what he was talking about. He finishes the presentation and says he has to get back to New York for a meeting. Turns off his projector, gets up and leaves the room, and twenty minutes later, Norm gets up and says that Paul is leaving the company."

Insiders say that Sagan had been promised a major job in Atlanta, heading CNN's domestic operations, by the network's CEO Tom Johnson. The talks had gone so far that Sagan had already begun house-hunting in Atlanta. He underestimated, however, how bad a breach in form it would appear for the point person representing Time Inc. in the hotly contested new-media space to be considering a jump to CNN.

Sagan refuses to talk about this period, and it's difficult to ascertain why he ultimately didn't land at CNN. Okrent says his departure was an official recognition that "Paul and Time Inc. were a bad fit." Indeed, unlike virtually everyone else at Time Inc. and Time Inc. New Media, Sagan did not rise up the ranks in print, having established his bona fides instead at NY 1, the Manhattan-based news channel offered through Time Warner Cable.

"Norm was very pissed off about the fact that he took forever to hire an editor [from within the company] for Time Inc. New Media. He didn't have faith in the editors of the magazines, and he was completely frustrated by the decision-making process here, convinced that there was no fucking way that this company would ever get its act together online," says a top Time Inc. executive. Sagan's departure remained a curiosity to the outside world, because those journalists who made inquiries were told he had gone to Switzerland to become a new-media consultant and to spend time with his family—never a convincing explanation, in corporate terms. He later emerged as the CEO of Akamai Technologies and became extremely wealthy, at least on paper.

By the time Okrent stepped into the new-media job, vultures were already circling Pathfinder. The blunt-speaking Okrent acknowledges that new media has really been a disaster for Time Inc. and other media companies, and that it was becoming apparent even when he got the job in late 1996. "Particularly for the larger media companies, which have stable or growing market share, it's much easier to manage stability than change. The change in this context from the old to the new is a change of such enormity and complexity that it's inherently destablizing," he says. "It destablized the business that we believe we know."

Broadly considered, the business that Time Inc. thought it knew at the time of Okrent's ascension was consumer content, news, sports, business, entertainment, and celebrities. *Time* was the flagship, the news vehicle, the magazine started on March 3, 1923, by Henry Luce because he knew that people wanted some analysis with their news, a thoughtful take on the week's events for thoughtful readers. Pathfinder wanted to be different, all things to all people, with the entirety filtered through Time Inc. content. It was an impossible task to create something coherent and Web-friendly out of so much information, and it was perhaps inevitable that the result simply didn't work.

In 1996 and 1997, a glance at Pathfinder's home page would have revealed a hodgepodge of logos and conflicting fiefdoms: news from *Time* magazine, sports from *Sports Illustrated*, CDs from Columbia House, books from Book-of-the-Month Club, celebrity fodder from *Entertainment Weekly* and *People,* financial tips from *Money.* There was also an irreverent webzine called the Netly News, and some daily news content reprocessed from the wires with *Time* magazine's logo slapped on it.

One iteration of the Pathfinder home page around this time was a blue screen with dozens of Time Inc. logo links on it, as if that in itself was sufficient to create a viable web site. Time Inc. seemed to think its brands spoke for themselves, but in trying to say so much, they ended up saying nothing. There was no way to summarize Pathfinder easily, in high-concept terms. Yahoo! was a Web directory. AltaVista was a "search engine." MSN was a "portal." MSNBC.com was a news site. What was Pathfinder, other than an uneasy mix of content that Time Inc. happened to own? Instead of acting as a Pathfinder through the vast Internet, which had grown by that time to millions of sites, Time Inc.'s Web properties led nowhere.

After Pathfinder's launch in October 1994 and until at least April 1995, it remained a tiny project, with fewer than 15 people on board. It later ballooned to about 200 people and a huge array of Web servers and other Internet equipment, filling immense hardware rooms and causing more headaches to Don Logan. Editor Chris Peacock recalls a feverish atmosphere, with pressure constantly building to put different segments of the huge, sprawling company on Pathfinder: "We've got to get *This Old House* online, we've got to get *Southern Living* online, a big push to bring each magazine online to establish a presence for each of them, going through the whole Time Inc. roster. Ultimately the hardest part was putting all that under some kind of Pathfinder umbrella."

While this was the basis for a coherent product, in Time Inc.'s view, in that it carefully balanced repurposed content from each of the company's magazines, it completely ignored the online user paradigms that Ted Leonsis had clearly outlined more than a year earlier. People weren't looking for repurposed content, he'd warned; they wanted a *user experience.* But even if the Pathfinder group had adopted all the right concepts, they would have faced the challenge of competing against the 3,000 driven AOL employees in Virginia, each of them holding enough stock options to make retirement in a few years a distinct possibility.

Prominently placed within Time Warner's 1994 annual report, with its epitaph for the FSN, is a photograph of senior management, all poised for greatness. Standing directly behind Levin, peering over his right shoulder, in fact, is Bob Pittman, who then ran the Six Flags theme parks.

Bob Pittman's odyssey through the media world is a fascinating one, full of contradictions. More than any other media executive, he embraced the rapid technological change of the 1990s and 2000s, presiding almost his entire career over media in transition. He deserves a great deal of credit for introducing new ideas and concepts into the world of big media, which is often resistant to change. Because of his impatience and tendency to grab the spotlight, he's often been sidelined at key moments in his career, but his willingness to break down barriers has to be acknowledged. And his timing has been uncanny; his trajectory to ultimate success at Time Warner is not an accident.

At the time the 1994 annual report photo was taken, however, Pittman's career wasn't burning as brightly as it had in previous years. Born in December 1953 in Jackson, Mississippi, Robert Warren Pittman was a very unlikely candidate to have a place in a lineup of senior executives at the world's largest media company. The son of a Methodist minister, he grew up in small-town Mississippi, landing a job at a small radio station in Brookhaven, WCHJ–AM, before he had even graduated from high school, thus discovering a vocation at the age of 15. After graduation, and before he was 25, Pittman managed to put in mike time at 13 different radio stations.

Pittman DJ'ed at stations in Chicago, Detroit, and Pittsburgh before landing in New York at WNBC–AM, the same high-profile flagship outlet that once showcased Howard Stern. Pittman became the station's program director in 1976, moving into one of the most visible jobs in radio. WNBC, immortalized in Howard Stern's *Private Parts,* was in the midst of format confusion, somewhat uncomfortably poised between talk and top-40, and Don Imus was in and out. Pittman hired a young DJ named Lee Masters, who later worked in executive positions at MTV Networks, E!, and Liberty Digital. Pittman brought Masters to WNBC in 1977 for afternoons, later switching him to mornings, in what became the Howard Stern slot shortly thereafter.

"Pittman and I have known each other since we were teenagers," Masters says, "when he was a disk jockey in Mississippi and I was a disk jockey in Kentucky. We met through a mutual friend in the radio business, and remained friends all through this period."

Pittman's first TV opportunity came in 1979 when Warner AmEx Satellite Entertainment Co., an awkward joint venture between American Express and Warner Communications, was established to enter the cable programming business. Pittman was part of a group that launched MTV there, eventually becoming CEO. It was at MTV that Pittman's relentless drive first became apparent to the media world at large. Although he is often cited as the "founder" of MTV, to the endless irritation of other early MTV executives, in reality, for much of his tenure he was executive vice president and COO. Pittman wasn't named CEO of MTV until December 1985, and he was gone by August of the following year.

Through most of his seven-year tenure at MTV, Pittman worked as part of a close-knit team, although it was clearly his own passion for the concept that was a key influence in convincing late Warner chairman Steve Ross to go ahead with the idea.

In a lengthy Q&A with the *Los Angeles Times*'s Robert Hilburn in September 1986, Pittman attributed the MTV inspiration to a kind of intuition. "I am not sure you ever know exactly what you are doing in this business. It's always a certain balance between logic and intuition that goes into any decision. This was just something I felt strongly about, and I couldn't understand why everyone didn't see it. I told them that people had made the same argument— about not watching music on television—about television when it came to soap operas. Those shows were supposed to be the 'theater of the mind' and they would never work on television. I told them they were underestimating the power of the television set with the young generation."

The young TV viewers of the '80s, Pittman argued, "grew up with television. Radio is a habit of people's lives, but nothing works on radio now except music because my generation really can't hear words on the radio. Talk doesn't work with this generation. It only works with a 34- or 40-plus audience. No one has been able to get successful talk for a young generation. My generation has to see it, to experience it." Pittman's sense that media had to be interactive and tactile to be relevant was a prescient observation, one not immediately connectable to the Internet revolution, but not so far from it.

TV, Pittman argued, "is the one thing that has had the most profound effect on shaping this generation. It's a generation that does not listen to words specifically, doesn't read words. Instead it develops a sense impression of the situation and draws a conclusion from that sense impression, which means that mood plays a very big part, visual image plays a big part."

Even before MTV, he said, young viewers had looked at TV differently. During the Vietnam War, "When my parents sat down and watched the evening news at night, they listened to the words being said and formed their impression strictly from the words. My generation looked at the pictures, and the pictures were telling a different message from the words. . . . 'This is wrong, we shouldn't be there, we are not going anywhere; we are not winning anything.'"

It would be easy to dismiss it all as so much pop psychology, but it can't be denied that Pittman thought about what he was doing a little more deeply than most TV executives, who are not, as a rule, an especially introspective group.

This notion that young people were ready to be informed and entertained in completely revolutionary ways was a theme Pittman would return to again and again, and would expand upon in an op-ed article he wrote for the *Los Angeles Times* on July 28, 1991.

He argued in that piece that the MTV generation had had it with linear information and entertainment. Music videos didn't really tell a story; they threw a lot of images at their audience and demanded that it interpret what those images might mean. Understanding the way young people now process information was key to reaching the all-important youth audience, he stressed. Although his revelations were not specifically about computer-based programming, they presaged that concept by insisting that programming would have to change in order to reach young people.

Pittman went on to make large claims for the influence of MTV. "We were building more than just a channel; we were building a culture," he argued. "MTV had an even wider impact on our culture—in music, fashion, politics, art, advertising, television, and movies. . . . The look and feel of music videos were quickly adopted into television series, motion pictures, even political advertising. Candidates began to sell themselves with an attitude and an image."

It sounds like hyperbole, but it really wasn't. Pittman describes it to Hilburn as TV programmed like music. "We realized that almost all TV was narrative in form—after the structure of beginning, middle, and end. The appeal of music, however, has nothing to do with that structure. Music is about emotion and attitude—it makes you feel. It moves you. With the creation of MTV, we changed the form of TV to fit the form of music, as opposed to trying to fit music into a narrative structure." Many of these ideas would stand Pittman in good stead later, when the first concepts of interactivity began to be articulated.

In 1985, in a shortsighted move, Warner decided to sell its two-thirds interest in MTV Networks (the other third was publicly held), and Pittman became part of a leveraged-buyout effort with other senior management of the channel to take control of the business. Enlisting the help of Forstmann Little & Co. in August 1985, the group offered $31 a share for MTV, a figure that valued the company at $471 million. Later the LBO group upped the ante to $33 a share, but Viacom ultimately outbid Forstmann.

The LBO attempt was an effective public showcase for Pittman's ambition as an executive and a canny dealmaker. After MTV's sale, he received $2.3 million, a fortune then, based on stock options he'd negotiated with Warner. Sumner Redstone, the new owner of MTV Networks, proved that he recognized ability by naming Pittman CEO on December 19, 1985. In his biography *A Passion to Win,* Redstone tells how Pittman engineered a surreptitious tour of MTV Networks for him even as the company management, led by Terry Elkes, was fighting for control of the company with Redstone. He later claimed that he considered Pittman for the CEO spot at Viacom itself as soon as he took control.

In spring 1986, after Redstone appointed Frank Biondi as CEO of Viacom, Pittman left MTV and launched his own TV production company, Quantum Media, in partnership with the entertainment conglomerate MCA, which was stronger on the syndication side than Viacom. Pittman was close to diminutive MCA mogul Irving Azoff, who brokered the deal.

At the time, Pittman proved his agility in reinventing himself. Fresh from failing in his attempt to buy MTV, he began to tell people that schlepping music videos was getting old anyway. "I don't want to turn sixty and still be known as Mr. MTV," he said at one point. At another, he quipped that he wanted to avoid "becoming the Dick Clark of the eighties." It was a clever tactic.

Quantum set up a record label that didn't create any stars, released a few videos, including one for a 1987 prizefight between Marvin Hagler and Sugar Ray Leonard, and produced several quickly forgotten TV series: a reality-based cop show called *The Street,* which anticipated *Cops,* and an '80s phenomenon, *The Morton Downey Show,* mostly recalled today for the Jerry Springer–style fist fights that occurred with increasing regularity on the set.

A perhaps apocryphal story has the chain-smoking Downey approaching Pittman, asking to be allowed to tone down his stridently right-wing, combative image, only to be told to keep the act going. Whether the story is true or not, Downey himself repeated it often. The *Wall Street Journal* noted in July 1989, "Even Mr. Downey conceded he overplayed his hand, but said the producer of the show [Pittman] pushed him to be outrageous." By then, Downey himself was disavowing the genre he and Pittman had helped create. "I don't want anything to do with trash television," he said. That summer, Downey claimed to have been abducted and assaulted by a trio of Nazi skinheads in a men's restroom in San Francisco, which helped demolish any remaining credibility he'd enjoyed. The show was canceled in July.

Quantum was an anomaly in the TV business for a number of reasons. It was small and independent, and the executives owned a piece of the action. "Key executives all have equity, so they're motivated," Pittman told *Forbes* in

June 1987. This concept would later become a key tenet of the Internet culture. Further, he added, "We have no bureaucracy. We write copy, produce it and get it out fast. We know the overnight printer, the 12-hour duplicator."

TV syndication is a notoriously difficult business to succeed in, with the same few shows—King World's *Jeopardy, Wheel of Fortune,* and *Oprah*—dominating the field year after year, and Quantum, more successful than most, still encountered pushback. Pittman tried to diversify by buying a 4.7 percent stake in JWT Group (formed from J. Walter Thompson), a big ad agency that was facing a takeover proposal from Britain's WPP Group. Pittman clearly believed that the ideas he'd developed on how to reach young people through television would be invaluable at an ad agency, especially one as traditional as JWT. But Quantum never acquired a major interest, and Pittman as adman was a concept that never directly became reality. Quantum did, however, make a nice profit when WPP Group went ahead with the acquisition.

Pittman soon gave up entrepreneurship, returning to Time Warner and his Warner AmEx mentor, Steve Ross, in March 1989. At the time the photo was taken for the 1994 annual report in 1993, Pittman was helping the Six Flags theme parks become profitable, a feat he pulled off with a lot of aplomb. Bob Pittman left Time Warner after Six Flags was sold the following year, just missing the Internet boomlet at the company. Despite his truly prophetic writings and musings about new forms of media, and his genuine innovations at MTV, Pittman couldn't be considered an early adopter of the World Wide Web.

His tenure at Century 21 was just an interlude for Pittman before the main event—AOL. This company in 1996 was tailor-made for Pittman's skills. It needed big-media savvy, and it needed an executive who wasn't shy about changing the business culture if it wasn't getting the job done. Pittman was ready, and he had something to prove.

AOL dropped a big bomb in December 1996 at another of its semi-annual partners conferences in Virginia. The company had recovered from a terrible beating it had taken from a recent prolonged service outage, during which the stock price had hit new lows. By December 1996, its stock was valued at almost $40, the service had 7 million subscribers and was now number-one online, and the new leadership of Bob Pittman was giving the company major traction, enough clout for Pittman to tell the partners at the conference a lot of things they didn't want to hear. By that time, AOL had a huge and unwieldy

1,600 content providers, including media companies Hearst, Viacom (MTV), Rodale Press, Hachette, and others.

The service had decided to switch to a flat monthly fee, in the process eliminating the content partner compensation formula, which typically awarded 20 percent of all revenue to the partners based on the amount of time users spent in their particular areas. Bob Pittman was the major catalyst for the change, and he also announced at the conference that he was instituting a 90-day evaluation period, in which as many as 1,000 partners would be eliminated as unnecessary to the future growth of AOL.

Suddenly all the patronizing of the big-media companies, which had led to AOL's being so cavalierly dismissed by people like Walter Isaacson, vanished, almost overnight. With CompuServe a less than credible alternative, how could big-media make money online now? From the Web, which just seemed to drain money? From Prodigy, which was losing market share?

In the winter of 1996, AOL began renegotiating contracts with those partners it did want to keep. When key content players like MTV insisted they should be compensated based on distribution, as cable networks are, AOL firmly rejected the idea.

"The catalyst of these changes was that we went to unlimited pricing," recalls Ted Leonsis, "and so we couldn't afford to pay media prices. And we knew that our traffic would go up like crazy [because users weren't worried about time constraints any more] and people would have to pay *us* to get the traffic; that would be our new business." The change, Leonsis adds, also meant that AOL now functioned much more like a traditional media company, benefiting from higher usage only if ads paid the freight. "Once you did that, you were a media company. Up until then, you could be partners, but once you went into that, our business became monetizing our real estate. It became, 'If you're going to be on our real estate, you are going to pay us.'"

Barry Schuler, then the president of creative development at AOL, noted that *Wired* magazine's site would be among the first that AOL would jettison. Schuler had grown annoyed that some AOL partners had created companion web sites and were using their AOL areas to attract Web traffic. *Wired* was a principal offender. "If people are putting up areas on the Web that anyone can just point to for free, why should we pay for that?" he asked. "No logical business is going to pay these people [to develop content for AOL] that they're giving away free."

Instead AOL pressed its advantage, launching a concept it called "anchor tenancy," in which content partners were expected to pay for key positioning within their channels. Shortly after announcing this policy, AOL had succeeded in convincing some of its content partners—reportedly including CBS SportsLine—to pay huge compensation figures of as much as $2 million annually, thus completely reversing its previous model.

Two months earlier, AOL and CBS SportsLine had announced a partnership giving the sports web site a "continuous presence" on the main screen of the AOL Sports Channel. Andrew Sturner, then vice president of business development for CBS SportsLine, said then that his company had "not disclosed that information." But Bob Pittman wasn't quite so reticent, and in an interview with this writer, he all but spelled out the bottom line: "The AOL channel front screens offer the most valuable promotional real estate in cyberspace. CBS SportsLine recognizes that this placement gives them an unmatched opportunity to capture tremendous market share in one place."

Pittman explained that he had become convinced that AOL had so successfully established its brand name that no one content partner was any longer of paramount importance. "For us, no one piece of content is 'killer' content," he said, adding that he told some AOL partners, "We have to be very honest with you. Your area is not doing very much traffic, and we're just not going to pay you to produce it any more."

One of the first things he did after becoming CEO, Pittman said, was to commission a huge amount of research about brand awareness, the extent to which the public can identify a particular trade name, like Jell-O or Cadillac. AOL's research indicated that at least 40 percent of the people surveyed professed knowledge of the AOL brand, against 10 percent apiece for CompuServe, Microsoft Network, and Prodigy. "What AOL has is critical mass," Pittman asserted. When he made that statement, AOL had 8 million subscribers. The march to the top had really only just begun.

Demanding that AOL partners pay their way was one thing, while actually getting them to do so was quite another. Randy Coppersmith, the longtime aide to Ted Leonsis who joined AOL at the same time as Ted, was the AOL emissary to the service's sports partners at the crucial juncture when the compensation paradigm shifted.

"I survived that time period," Coppersmith laughs. His had to have been one of the most difficult jobs in media—almost unprecedented, really. For hundreds of years, the main business models in media had remained pretty much the same. Newspapers sold ads, and charged their advertisers. Paper companies billed magazines. TV sold commercials. There was a bit of jockeying to deter-

mine the exact business model that would work for cable, briefly the new media frontier in the '80s, but it was sorted out quickly. AOL was in uncharted
territory.

"Everyone in the media community is suddenly told that what had been a
revenue source will now turn into an expense," Coppersmith recalls, somewhat
ruefully. "My fun job was to walk into the ABC office tower at West 67th Street
in New York and tell the ABC guys that all this time we've been paying you,
and now it's going to change and you have to start paying us."

Asked how ABC took the news, Coppersmith replies, "They didn't. Most of
them told me to go fuck myself. One of these guys is a person I consider a
friend, Jonathan Leese, who became a legend in the sports business in the
United States with ABC Sports. He worked for Roone Arledge for twenty
years. Jon was the guy who was tapped by ABC Sports to go and deal with
AOL. And Jon is a character, I don't know how else to say it. His main method
of communication is screaming and yelling. And it kind of goes downhill from
there. I had my turn in the barrel, during which I was proclaimed a fucking idiot like everyone else. We had had a series of people assigned from the AOL
Sports channel to work with Jon, and he burned up something like seven account executives in thirteen months."

Newsweek was an AOL content provider for two years, from 1996 to 1998,
spanning the period when AOL decided to stop paying its partners. "When we
first did our AOL contract, there was concern about making it a two-year deal
because we asked, 'Would they still be around in two years?' " recalls *Newsweek*'s
Michael Rogers.

Newsweek put a lot of time and effort into its AOL area, reflecting the fact
that the magazine had been one of the first media companies to embrace interactive media. Rogers, a six-time novelist and sometime science fiction writer,
got started in the business very early, developing a computer game for Lucas-
film in 1986. A Stanford physics and creative writing graduate, he started at
Newsweek as a tech writer. In 1986 he wrote a piece on CD-ROMs that questioned whether the little disks would become a viable business much before
1991. Rogers received a call from an irate Bill Gates after the piece ran.
"Michael," Gates exclaimed, "I thought you were smart. CD-ROMs are going
to be huge by 1988." That didn't happen, but *Newsweek* did develop a series of
six CD-ROMs in partnership with Sony and Apple, starting in 1993. They
sold about 45,000 copies total, not enough to turn a profit, but a sufficient
amount to convince *Newsweek* and its parent, the Washington Post Company,
that interactive media had a future. It was the unit set up to create CD-ROMs,

Newsweek Interactive, that transported the magazine to Prodigy in 1994. Working with Prodigy's creative staff, Newsweek put up an area that featured the same type fonts the magazine used, which represented a revolutionary breakthrough. "Prodigy was quite sophisticated then in terms of graphics, and they supported sound files," Rogers says.

When *Newsweek* signed with AOL in 1996, the online team of editors Peter McGrath and Rogers put together their own proprietary interface called The Widget to customize their site, in an effort to make it look less like the cookie-cutter media sites cluttering AOL. Still, even they were expendable when the dictate came down in late 1997 to cut off the payment spigot. "It was never made explicit; it was just something that one understood," McGrath recalls.

The two-year contract *Newsweek* had signed with AOL in June 1996, which guaranteed *Newsweek* more than $1 million a year, was now obsolete. "It was pretty clear by the end of 1997 that re-upping would be very difficult," McGrath says. The relationship between the two companies had grown extremely tense by that point. *Newsweek* had been told by AOL executives in 1996 that it had the best-looking area on the service. Now, just a few months later, nobody cared about *Newsweek*. "AOL is not a company where courtesy is given a high priority," McGrath quips.

The online services couldn't have picked a more awkward time to decide they weren't going to pay content partners. (Prodigy and CompuServe also eventually heavily reduced their content payments.) It created a huge dilemma within media companies because many top executives had successfully made a case that online businesses would become a major new revenue source, based almost entirely on the money that AOL, CompuServe, and Prodigy had been paying them. What would they do now? The media had spent their formative years online being dependent on someone else's software, production capability, and personnel; they were woefully short on trained people who knew how to do the jobs necessary to produce a competitive Web operation. Producing an AOL area had little to do with creating a web site, a fact that most media companies didn't even fully understand until AOL's cutoff forced them to consider actually producing web pages.

The departure of Kinsella and Sagan had sent Time Inc. New Media into a management tailspin, in which the top job at the unit began to look hugely problematic. The savvier talent at the company had learned to watch Isaacson closely and take cues from him. As jumping from new media back to print began to be perceived as the smart move, replacing the two men became a difficult, drawn-out process. When Okrent first got the job, he simply combined editorial and business duties, which ran against the grain at the heavily church/state Time Inc. So another "bake-off" was held, this time for the top business job at Time Inc. New Media, again with Pearlstine playing referee.

The two contenders were Bruce Judson and Linda McCutcheon, a dark-haired, forty-ish former advertising and marketing executive who had worked her way up through the ranks of the company and was a much more deeply rooted Time Inc-er than Judson. McCutcheon had been on staff since fall 1989, hired from *The Economist* as director of marketing at *Money* magazine. (When in 1991 she was named director of marketing at *Time* magazine, it was Jonathan Bulkeley who took her place at *Money*.)

A year later, McCutcheon became involved in the first negotiation with AOL on behalf of Time. "On the business side, it was pretty much me," McCutcheon says of the AOL/Time talks. "I started mucking around with digital stuff then. I used to go down to Vienna and sit in Jonathan's little office on the AOL campus, and watch the Stratus mainframes being rolled in. I said to myself, 'Something's going on here.'"

Shortly after the conclusion of the AOL/Time deal, McCutcheon departed for a maternity leave and had her second child. She kept in touch with cyberspace through an AOL subscription, and when she returned in September 1994, she says she was "determined" to become involved with the new-media group. Walter Isaacson had just received funding for the unit and was aware of her role in closing the deal with AOL. He named McCutcheon the first ad sales director, reporting to general manager Bruce Judson.

McCutcheon later won the bake-off with Judson and was named president of Time Inc. New Media in April 1997. Although she, in common with virtually all other top executives involved in the Internet side of Time Warner, had no independent Internet experience, she was a well-respected team player. "And Bruce's manner was all wrong," says a top Time Inc. executive.

Later that year McCutcheon granted an interview to *Adweek,* where she claimed, a few years before some of her competitors, to be on the path to profitability. "On the average, it takes five to seven years for a magazine to see a profit," she said in the November 3, 1997 issue. "At Time Inc., *People* did it within eighteen months, but far more typical was *Sports Illustrated*—it took eleven years to move into the black. I'm determined that we will become profitable sooner than the average magazine and sooner than our competitors." (A little later, when informed that Hachette Filipacchi New Media was already turning a handsome profit, she dismissed the claim as "Hollywood accounting.")

The delineation between roles at Time Inc. New Media was always uneasy. Okrent says he could have assumed the title of president of new media when he first arrived but chose not to, in agreement with Pearlstine, because "A, I didn't know if I was qualified. And B, there was no fucking way I would be able to spend enough time becoming serious about content if I was as obsessed about the deals as everyone else is in this business. Get someone else to do the deals."

Even after McCutcheon's appointment, Okrent says his views often prevailed. "It would be fair to say—and Linda most likely would agree—that in a managerial sense, I probably had more authority, but she was the deal person and the revenue person." Okrent explains his power as a function of his history within the company. "Because I had been one of the princes at the table, the others all trusted me. The first thing I did was reverse Sagan's efforts to create the Pathfinder brand [separate from the magazines]. I said, 'We've got these brands. Let's move the brands up, and we will cooperate with the magazines.'" (McCutcheon extends the chivalric metaphor by calling the managing editors "Prince Valiants.")

Time Inc. did, of course, have huge brands, and dictates about deemphasizing them in favor of the Pathfinder umbrella, which had come from both Sagan and Kinsella, had caused huge problems within the magazines. Each Time Inc. magazine had a person assigned to new media, who reported up through the magazine structure, and not to the management of Pathfinder. That meant that the person in charge of new media at *People*, arguably Time's biggest and most profitable brand, had no loyalty whatsoever to Pathfinder. In 1996 and 1997, the *People* new-media staffer was the independent-minded Hala Makowska, a tough blond woman who was well aware of the power of the *People* brand and often spoke out in meetings about the folly of not allowing the magazine's Web property to use www.people.com as its URL. The *People* group balked at promoting Sagan's favored URL, www.pathfinder.com/people, insisting that it was cumbersome, and ridiculous. That meant that throughout 1995 and 1996, *People* had refused to print the official URL in the magazine, losing the Web property millions of dollars worth of free promotion. When Makowska spoke out against this policy to a columnist at the *New York Post,* it made a ludicrous situation starkly obvious to the rest of the New York media community, and Sagan had been furious.

Now Okrent was proposing to undo all the animosity Sagan had fostered: "Among my many failures, one of my few successes doing new media here was I never had any content problems with any of the editors of the magazines. They gave me absolute authority to do anything I wished with their content." Okrent also moved to centralize the business side. Previously the magazines had been shouldering some of the cost of running the ad operations for their areas of Pathfinder, a source of continuing friction because ad people did not earn out their salaries. Okrent changed the structure so Pathfinder could hire its own ad people and absorb the cost of the operation directly. For the first time, Pathfinder had its own "P&L" line on the Time Inc. budget. ("Believe me, it was all 'L,'" Okrent quips.)

The changes played well both within Time Inc. and with the trade media, which dutifully ran stories about how Okrent and McCutcheon were transforming Pathfinder into a real business. The two initiated one of the first Time online deals with an outside content provider, the Web property operated by the popular media physician and author Dr. Andrew Weil, which immediately obtained a $3 million sponsorship from The Vitamin Shoppe. But even attractive deals like this didn't address the central problem: Pathfinder was losing out to the "portals." Pathfinder had long refused to consider Yahoo! as competition, because it wasn't deemed to be a valid publishing model, and Time Inc. was still clinging to the "content is king" myth, which held that highly paid editors and writers in New York could create higher-quality content than a bunch of khaki-clad kids in Silicon Valley.

Time Inc. was not a significant AOL partner in late 1996. Pittman's new diktat about paying for content seemed to eliminate a big AOL deal as a safety valve for the money-losing Pathfinder. Time was not making significant money from any online service deals, and it was losing up to $20 million a year from Pathfinder, a clearly unacceptable sum to Don Logan. Time Inc. was much too proud to pay AOL for an anchor tenancy, when it had been getting paid just a year before.

Neither Prodigy nor CompuServe were options by this time. A doomed effort to turn Prodigy into a zippy entertainment-oriented service under former Viacom executive Ed Bennett had been a dismal failure, and in July 1996 it had been sold to International Wireless, a telephone company partly owned by Mexico's Grupo Carso, after which virtually all the "creative" staff was fired. Prodigy's days of developing and paying for content were over. CompuServe had stumbled in an ill-considered effort to get web sites to pay for positioning on a planned CompuServe Web guide. While this wasn't too different from what AOL was doing, CompuServe lacked the clout to pull it off, and the service was soon sold to AOL.

The options for Time Inc. New Media were becoming far more narrow. Linda McCutcheon had seen a dramatic downturn in Pathfinder's fortunes in the three years between her ad-selling job and taking the title of president. In 1994, when few competitive web sites existed, McCutcheon virtually "lived in Detroit," where auto advertisers were lining up to place their ads in what was then the leading web site. Ad mavens would adopt a quizzical look back then when Yahoo!'s name was mentioned, preferring to deal with Time Inc., a company with which they were very comfortable.

The primacy didn't last long. By 1997, dominating cyberspace was a much more difficult proposition. Before getting the president's job, McCutcheon would sit in on some Pathfinder management meetings and was surprised by the amount of vacant philosophizing going on, as if Time had all the time in the world, and portals like Yahoo! and Excite didn't exist. "It was torture for me, because they would sit around for three hours talking about paradigms, and I was sort of like, 'Hello, life is changing.'"

McCutcheon began her tenure as president with a Jerry Levin encounter, a somewhat nonsubstantial one. Soon after the appointment was made, McCutcheon got a call from Levin. The CEO gave her a kind of generic pep talk, with few specifics. "He called me. I said, 'What do you want me to do?' He said, 'Keep doing what you're doing, we think you're wonderful, blah blah blah.' He gave me The Vision. Brand primacy, etc. It wasn't very practicable." She had few other meetings with Levin.

Viable paths to profitability would be up to her to find. She began by asserting to the media that Pathfinder would soon be bringing in significant revenue from syndicating its content to Web properties like AT&T Network and Microsoft Network, and would also soon see income from e-commerce deals with Barnes & Noble and online music retailer CDNow, and from merchandise sales.

Before his departure, Judson had championed a subscription plan called Pathfinder Personal Edition, which was subscriber-based, with users expected to pay $4.95 a month for customized content. A further subscription model Judson favored was called Power Pathfinder, with "deep" areas of content that were supposed to be available online, including Time Inc.'s extraordinary picture library. None of these schemes ever led to anything approaching profitability, much to Logan's chagrin.

The Time Inc. New Media unit Okrent and McCutcheon inherited from

Isaacson, Sagan, Judson, and Kinsella was problematic in many ways. It had grown mightily in traffic, now totaling as many as 17 million page views per week. But by 1997, that wasn't good enough. (By January 1997, when Okrent's reign started, Pathfinder had been edged out by the portals, including MSN, AOL, Yahoo!, Excite, Infoseek, AltaVista, and Lycos.) "We had been number one, and we were sliding to number five and then number ten. It was death by a thousand cuts," recalls McCutcheon.

Media companies like Dow Jones's *Wall Street Journal* seemed to have created better business models, and the online subscription fee the *Journal* was charging allowed it to claim significant revenue, even if the online operation wasn't profitable yet. But neither *Fortune* nor *Money* was as vital to America's business leaders as was the *Journal.*

Time Warner likes to win, and it wasn't winning online. Category by category, virtually all of Time Inc.'s magazines were print category leaders, including *Time, Money, Sports Illustrated, Entertainment Weekly,* and, of course, *People.* The only one that was a perennial laggard was *Fortune,* which was a constant ad-page loser to *Forbes,* a much livelier magazine editorially at that stage.

McCutcheon says, "Dan and I often said that it was far easier to do deals with people outside the building than inside it. We were trying to do a big deal for financial information, and we found it impossible to cut across the brands—*Fortune, Money,* and so on—because everyone was feeling very parochial." The animosity between print and new media reached almost comic proportions. "We were sitting on the greatest advertising vehicle in the world with all the Time Inc. and Time Warner properties, and no one would let us run an ad," McCutcheon laments.

The managing editors of the magazines didn't want to promote what they saw as a rival, and they also complained frequently to Logan that new media was undermining them, and that new-media executives didn't play by the rules. But whose rules should they play by?

The brand-new equation for online news that Reuters New Media had handed to Time Inc. and other big-media companies had countless repercussions, and was the direct cause of a big power struggle at the beginning of 1997 between Okrent and Harry Motro, later CEO of Infoseek but then head of CNN's online group.

Within Time Warner, there was a major internal battle between Time and CNN over which of them should host the company's digital news efforts. Would the news operation be run out of New York and *Time* magazine, or Atlanta and CNN? While CNN is by far the bigger news name, it was a fairly re-

cent addition to Time Warner, and battle lines had gone up early when it came
to who had the most muscle corporately. As long as Walter Isaacson was in
place, *Time*'s position at the top of the firmament was fairly secure. But absent
Walter, the field appeared open.

"When Harry was still here, Harry was a pipsqueak, relatively speaking,"
Okrent contends. "Harry clashed with a lot of people, and Harry wanted to be
the digital Time Warner guy, which caused some opposition within CNN, and
an awful lot of opposition outside of CNN. He tried very, very hard to get Jerry
and Ted [Turner] to say, 'Here's digital across the corporate culture, it's yours.'
I remember saying to Harry, 'This is Time Warner. Nothing happens cross-
corporately. Forget it, pal.'"

Motro says this kind of dysfunction was what was wrong with Time
Warner's online effort. "Dan is an editorial person. I liked him; he was compe-
tent. But he wasn't a businessman. When Paul left, there was a huge vacuum."

Working in new media at CNN was always frustrating, in part because Ted
Turner, who had emerged as vice chairman of Time Warner after Levin had
bought his company, never got excited about the Web. Turner was a techno-
pioneer, in that he and Levin had been the first TV executives to put a TV
signal on a satellite, and the stories of Turner's struggle to get on the bird are
legendary. But that didn't make him receptive to personal computers.

Motro himself presented CNN's first Web version in 1994 to Turner in
Turner's huge office at the CNN Center, which is decorated with dozens of
magazine covers Turner has graced. And Turner wasn't thrilled. Motro remembers him looking bored and distracted. "He said that he thought it was too
slow," Motro recalls. A natural enough reaction for a TV executive, but still, it
was demoralizing.

Turner rarely if ever used a computer, and Motro thinks he understands that
too. "Why would you ever send or receive e-mail when you have five secre-
taries, and virtually anybody you call, including world leaders, will drop everything the instant you're on the phone?" he asks.

Ultimately Motro realized that there were simply too many contradictions
within Time Warner for anything coherent to emerge beyond the company's
core competency. The corporate infighting that Okrent alluded to was, in
Motro's words, his way of asking, "Hey, guys, what are we doing here?" Motro
decided that Time Warner would never get its new-media act together, and he
left for Infoseek in May 1997.

Okrent may have won the battle with Motro at the time, but that victory
wasn't very triumphant. Linda McCutcheon observes, "With all due respect to

Dan, whom I love, Harry was right. Harry looked across the warring units and asked, 'Do you think that the people who are building Microsoft's online platform are worrying about what the other divisions are doing? They're focused on the outside world and so should we be.' "

Okrent readily concedes that the separate news fiefdoms within Time Warner made little sense, that Time's news-oriented AOL site should have been combined with CNN's operation from the start. But there was too much power at stake for any easy transition.

McCutcheon, meanwhile, had developed an edgy relationship with AOL's David Colburn, the chief dealmaker at the company. The perennially unshaven Colburn joined AOL in 1996 and quickly achieved prominence with a brash style that left little doubt about his conviction that AOL was destined to rule cyberspace. Colburn would chide McCutcheon about Time Warner's clumsy efforts to keep up with the portals. "What were you guys smoking?" he would ask her, to which she would reply, "I don't know, David, but maybe you could get me some." She adds, "David often says things that are not rooted in actual fact but have high entertainment value. It's David's world; we just live in it."

While he maintained a bantering relationship with McCutcheon, Colburn openly disdained most of the Time Inc. executives. At one meeting involving the Time Inc. New Media group of the McCutcheon years, former Pathfinder GM Oliver Knowlton was present. When the polite, courtly Knowlton entered the room, Colburn blurted, "Who the fuck are you and why are you here?"

But it was Colburn who first approached McCutcheon and Okrent in September 1997 with an olive branch. After the abrogation of the Time/AOL deal a few years earlier, the two companies had done no substantial business together. But Colburn realized that a historic opportunity existed for a further partnership. Media Metrix reports, which rank web sites the way Nielsen ranks TV shows, now had Pathfinder declining to an embarrassing "Top 50" position, when it had been in the top 10 early on.

Pathfinder was getting beaten on the Web by tiny little start-ups that had been in business for seven months, compared to the more than 70 years that Time Inc. had existed on the planet. Worse, Time Inc. New Media's losses were wiping out much of Don Logan's profit margin. The Pathfinder slogan—"The World's Best Web Site"—was clearly not only inaccurate but downright embarrassing. Colburn, however, had a plan to change the red ink to black.

In conversation with McCutcheon and Okrent, Colburn proposed a radical concept: *People,* the print company's profit leader, would jump to AOL, exclusively. Time Inc. would abandon the web site at People.com, much as Hachette had done with *George* magazine early on. This was, in a sense, a return to AOL's previous model, of paying for content, but it was undertaken as only a step in a larger plan to engage Time Warner. It didn't amount to a change in AOL's content strategy. A small, health-related site that Time Warner had invested in was also "thrown in." In return for the *People* asset, AOL would pay Time Inc. an astonishing $16 million for an 18-month license. It's hard to reconcile that sum with the frugal AOL that had emerged in 1996 and 1997, but there was an ulterior motive. The figure wasn't chosen randomly: $16 million is just about the amount that Time Inc. New Media was slated to lose in 1997 and 1998.

In one stroke, Colburn was offering to make the beleaguered unit profitable for the first time. At that point, People.com was attracting some 3 million page views a week—not a shabby showing, but not all that impressive in the AOL context. Time Inc. wasn't likely to mourn the loss of the page views because the traffic wasn't being sold to advertisers anyway. By 1997, the big ad machine that McCutcheon had headed had all but dried up, especially where *People* was concerned. The magazine's heavily female, lower-income demographic was not hugely attractive to online advertisers.

The amount of money involved was staggering, although it wasn't reported at the time. "Maybe I was a good negotiator," McCutcheon says. But there's equally strong evidence that AOL was buying a lot more than just the light celebrity features and Ordinary-Joe-Thrust-into-the-Limelight pieces that make up the unique editorial mix of *People*. If AOL could succeed in making Time Warner dependent on it for online revenue once again, it would clearly lead inexorably to a bigger relationship. A top AOL executive has confirmed that AOL was well aware of where the *People* deal would lead and was willing to pay top dollar for it, like a chess player planning eight or nine moves ahead.

The Okrent/McCutcheon duo was suddenly attaining heroic proportions internally because they brought back real revenue to the online effort. But once that deal was consummated, the dream of building an online empire at Time Inc. would clearly be in jeapordy, for in effect, the company would be returning to the same model for online content that it had started with: licensing to AOL.

The delivery of online content had everyone baffled, not just media people. A few weeks after Dan Okrent got his new-media assignment, *Forbes* magazine held a forum on new media in Seattle. George Gilder, the futurist and newsletter guru, was a featured speaker, and Gilder wanted to talk about online content. Gilder made a number of sweeping predictions and pronouncements, as is his wont, including the statement that Microsoft's decision to team with NBC to create MSNBC had been "dumb," because newspapers, not television, would win the online news war.

Gilder, president of the Gilder Technology Group as well as a consultant to Forbes, dismissed surveys showing young people reading newspapers less and watching TV more. Gilder saw a different future in which liquid crystal video displays will become "competitive with paper in resolution and freedom from flicker" and Americans will go to a newspaper vending machine only to download that day's paper onto their own display unit.

"TV news is not news," he stated. "CNN is dreadful. Newspapers will be able to blow away TV news." Gilder said that he had talked to Nathan Myhrvold, chief technology officer at Microsoft Corp. the preceding week and that during this conversation, Myhrvold talked about Microsoft's decision to form a partnership with NBC. "We were talking about Microsoft's decision to partner with NBC News [to create MSNBC]. He said they had tried to collaborate with the *New York Times* and other newspapers, but they weren't ready to do a deal. I think Microsoft made a terrible mistake; they're collaborating with a dying entity."

Of course, like any prognosticator, Gilder has often been wrong. When grilled during the conference by the merciless *Forbes* editor Bill Baldwin, Gilder admitted being wrong with his 1989 prediction that in the next 15 years (that is, by 2004), "the only keyboards will be on music synthesizers." He had been wrong about voice recognition software, he conceded, but not because the technology developed by companies such as IBM and Microsoft is faulty, but for the "unexpected reason" that people who use their voices all day soon develop hoarseness and have to stop talking. "Vocal tunnel syndrome," quipped Baldwin.

If supposed digital seers like Gilder didn't know what they were talking about in 1996, who did?

CHAPTER 9

Magazines Miss the Web

I n June 1997, the magazine industry attempted to take control of the Web. It ended up looking slightly ridiculous, or at least seriously out of touch. During that month, an industry group known as the American Society of Magazine Editors (ASME), headed by *Money* magazine managing editor Frank Lalli (later editor of the ill-fated *George* at Hachette) issued "guidelines" for "online publications." ASME tries to enforce editorial standards in the magazine industry and sponsors annual awards. It is an advocacy group for magazines in general.

The guidelines called for the same separation of advertising and content that magazines were supposed to honor. ASME wanted all banner ads clearly marked as advertising, and they wanted online "editors" to have control of all "links that appear within the editorial portion of a site. . . ." Lalli commented, "We believe the new-media publications that put their users' interests first by following our sensible guidelines will be rewarded with increased consumer loyalty, now and always publishing's most valuable asset."

But putting up a web site wasn't necessarily the same thing as "publishing" a magazine, and the sites were mostly not created by "editors," a distinction that seemed to have escaped ASME. Within its own world of magazines, ASME's editorial phalanx could punish offenders that didn't follow its dictates by denying them the chance to compete for the coveted awards that the Magazine Publishers of America gives out each year. But what hold did it have over the Web, and, for that matter, who appointed ASME as overseer of the new medium? Even within the small world of online magazines, the ASME's proposed guidelines were widely mocked and ignored. But they did reflect a continuing belief, held by some at Time Inc. and other big companies, that the traditional magazine world could still dominate cyberspace.

By the late '90s, however, magazines were not only not ruling online, they were clearly failing. A little-known fact about magazines is that most of their readers are women—fully 70 percent, by most estimates. But magazine web sites weren't attracting women users. *Advertising Age* reported in April 1998 that CondeNet, the online arm of Condé Nast begun in mid-1995, and Hearst's HomeArts, which aggregated content from various Hearst magazines, were still "trying to gain a foothold," and that magazine sites "languish in the shadows of their often well-known, offline brand parents." As a trade publication, *Advertising Age* risked alienating its important magazine advertisers by printing the truth about their web sites, but the facts could not be ignored by an objective journalist.

The failures of the magazine world were not limited to large-scale missteps. The mere process of getting a site online became an irritant. Magazines were so late to the party in registering their domain names for the Internet that many lost their eponymous URL and had to settle for a compromise like a "mag" suffix, as in Ellemag.com. An especially egregious example of that problem came in 1996, when the racy *Cosmopolitan* magazine, owned by Hearst, tried to register www.Cosmo.com with InterNIC, the domain registration firm, only to find that it had already been registered by a shadowy Hong Kong outfit called Domain Dealer. "There is a problem," *Cosmo*'s then editor, the celebrated Bonnie Fuller, admitted in a November 1996 interview. "We are considering legal action. They have no right to that address." But Domain Dealer had gotten there first, and Cosmo had to settle for the clumsy Cosmomag.com.

Such intricacies of the Internet were hard for media people to absorb. AOL never believed that the ideal programmer was a former journalist anyway, because there were too many ingrained paradigms to overcome. "I used to joke when we were a young company that the ideal AOL programmer was a bartender," recalls Ted Leonsis. "They knew how to get people in and get them to stay at the bar, and the more they talked to one another, the more they drank. That's what an AOL programmer did; that's the taxonomy that we were trying to create."

When it came, the shift in strategy from trying to dominate the Web to abandoning it was shockingly swift. Hearst would soon give up entirely the administration of its own web sites, licensing the right to do so to a California-based Web start-up called Women.com, in return for about half the equity in that company. As part of that measure, Hearst also fired the New York–based staff of HomeArts, ceding all editorial control to Women.com. It was a harbinger of things to come. Hearst was, in effect, the first media company to admit that it was clueless about running Internet properties. More would quickly follow.

Considering that women were half the population, and that American women's magazines had had more than 160 years of publishing experience to figure out what women wanted, it was particularly embarrassing that the print-media companies that catered to women—Condé Nast, Meredith Magazines, Hearst Magazines, Hachette Filipacchi Magazines, and Bertelsmann's Gruner + Jahr—had failed to be competitive online, at least in traffic, with pure-play Web properties like iVillage and Women.com. At the beginning of the Web revolution, these companies had virtually assumed they could transmute their subscriber and newsstand popularity into Web success, but that didn't happen.

Jackie Leo, the talented former editor of *Family Circle,* one of the women's service magazines, and a veteran of ABC News and the *Consumer Reports* online unit, later became head of Meredith Magazines' online efforts. Leo has been active in ASME for years and is one of the more articulate, thoughtful editors in mainstream magazine publishing. She believes that magazine companies were bound to stumble somewhat, given how new the technology was. When interviewed in March 2001, she noted that the Internet was still only about "1,700 days old." That might be mature for a fast-paced industry like the Web, but it's a nanosecond to media companies, where many people typically spend decades in one job.

"We've made a lot of mistakes, because it's all a training ground right now," she says. "Is it good or bad to have things flashing at you and dancing all around a page? Is it good or bad to have the same message delivered in a similar sort of print way on the Internet, as you might in a magazine?"

Ted Leonsis explains that early on AOL had made a serious effort to establish ties with the women's magazines. "Bertelsmann became our partner [when it wound up with a 5 percent equity stake in AOL itself through the AOL Europe project], and I had an idea that as more women came online, we needed to have a moms' area." This was in 1995, when most of the people online were men, but women were making more and more inroads, and it was clearly time to cater to their needs and interests.

Leonsis continues: "So we had made a little investment in a company called Moms Online, which was getting unbelievable traffic. It was [administered by] a mother working out of her house. Bertelsmann and Gruner + Jahr own *Parents,* so I went to Procter & Gamble and I pitched them a three-way deal, a new channel one-third owned by AOL, one-third owned by *Parents* magazine, and a third owned by Procter & Gamble. It would be the Parenting channel, and we would blow it out and let everyone in and sell ads to everybody. Procter &

Gamble said it was very interested. We go to *Parents* magazine, and they listen, and they say, 'We'd rather you [continue to] pay us the $200,000 that you're paying us now for *Parents* content.'" But I still have this plan, and Candace Carpenter was doing some consulting for us. I told her, 'Candace, look at this. You should do this. We will invest in your business.'

"Her first proposal was called Contentland. We said, 'No, this should be named after parenting and women.' Then they came back with Family Soup, she and [early partner] Tina Nederlander. They programmed it, and then they repositioned it for women in general, renamed it iVillage, and they went public and raised tons of money. Candace programmed with community in mind. It wasn't an editorial enterprise; it was a community-building enterprise." IVillage quickly became the number-one women's site, demolishing competition from venerable magazines like *Better Homes and Gardens* and *McCall's*.

In retrospect a lot of the credit—or blame—for the magazine companies' failure to attract women users has to be assigned to the formidable Candace Carpenter. Despite her reputation of being somewhat less than a model executive, Carpenter and her company did more to discombobulate magazine publishers than any other business on the Web.

Carpenter is in many ways representative of the kind of new-media executive who thrived in the go-go years of the late '90s. In her forties when iVillage was conceived, Carpenter had had her start at the Time-Life division of Time Inc., which sold books and music through direct mail, and at Barry Diller's failed Q2 shopping channel, an offshoot of QVC. (Q2 had been touted as a hipper version of home shopping, where cubic zirconia would not be sold. But it failed anyway, because online shoppers happened to *like* cubic zirconia.) When Carpenter and her partner Nancy Evans, a refugee from Wenner Media and Doubleday, started iVillage, they were determined to break most of the media rules—which meant, primarily, grabbing the online spotlight from women's magazine companies.

Robert Levitan, one of the co-founders of iVillage, worked with Carpenter closely during this period. A diminutive former video producer from North Carolina, Levitan had met Carpenter through mutual friends; on his return to New York in 1995, he was introduced by her to various people in the media business. Levitan called Carpenter regarding his possible availability on a date he still recalls with particular clarity, February 25, 1995, "a fateful day. I said, 'Candace, thanks a lot, I really appreciate your help. I'm just chilling out for a few months.' She says to me, and this was on a Wednesday, 'Robert, what are you doing Friday?' I said, 'I could be available, why?' She says, 'I'm working on a project at a company called America Online down in Virginia, and I think I might need help. Would you sit in on a meeting? I'd be happy to hear your thoughts.' I said I would be happy to sit in on the meeting, but there was only one problem. 'I haven't been online.' This is where Candace is so great; she said, 'Oh, that's all right, come in anyway.'"

At this stage, relatively few people *had* been online, and not having done so wasn't a big impediment. "I went online at a friend's house who had a CompuServe account on Thursday. The next day I'm sitting in a meeting in Virginia, and they're talking about the design of the shopping screen of AOL. After the meeting Candace said, 'All right, I want to hire you. Three days a week you're going to have an office next to Ted Leonsis in Virginia, and we're going to develop new business models for AOL. You'll have one day to help me start a new-media company in New York. A day a week in New York.' She handed me an Apple PowerBook, said, 'You now have an online account.' This was Friday; I was to start Monday.

"Candace and I were sitting in an office right next door to Ted, between February and July 1995. [We] had a pretty broad mission—to help AOL develop new business models, period," Levitan continues. "We looked at shopping, whether AOL should develop a credit card. After four or five months, we made a presentation: Here's some things you guys should do. While we were there, we could see what was happening at AOL—where the usage was. We plotted a graph on the amount of times people logged on per month, and the hours they spent per month. What we saw at the very bottom of the graph, with the least amount of traffic, was *Time* magazine and ABC News. At the very top right of the graph, with the highest number of visits and traffic, was the gay and lesbian forum and the Motley Fool [two areas started by AOL itself]. What we saw was that online community was driving AOL usage. At the same time, AOL was beginning its Greenhouse project [under Ted Leonsis], to start its own projects."

This was a key finding, and the group really earned its stripes as consultants by convincing AOL that it could create its own sites that would be just as popular as content from big-media brands. "Leonsis and Candace were talking, and she said, 'It's great you have these Greenhouse things, but what you need is a unit to develop your own programs, the way Liberty Media functioned for TCI,'" Levitan recalls.

"The bottom line was that Candace had come from the cable business, and we had seen what had happened at TCI and Liberty and what was beginning to happen at AOL. Ted said, 'Yeah, why don't you go out and develop some things?' Nancy Evans had joined us for part of our consulting assignment, and one of the things we had recommended was that AOL put out a magazine pushing online shopping. They ended up doing one that was more technology-based. We suggested a magazine that was for new members, how to shop online, how to use the service."

At this fork in the road, it was beginning to look as if Candace Carpenter and Nancy Evans were fated to lead AOL's content push, at least the part of it that catered to women. But reality diverged slightly.

Ted Leonsis, true to his penchant for goading people to do better work, soon confided in Carpenter that he thought she and Evans, then in their forties, were "too old" to lead this effort. Issuing such a provocation was bound to either turn both off or push them into proving him wrong. "Ted knew it; he's a smart guy. . . . [He] loves goading people, and he thinks it's a young people's medium. Candace said, 'Fine, we'll do it, but you have to give us $2 million.' From the get-go, the idea was to build communities around the things that baby boomers care the most about." Thus iVillage was born.

Carpenter became CEO, while Nancy Evans, with her publishing experience, became editor in chief. This left Levitan to become senior vice president of market development—in effect, iVillage's first head of advertising, even though he'd never sold an ad before. "I had no idea of advertising at all. I didn't know any better."

Levitan continues, "Candace had this vision that we would get six- to twelve-month commitments from advertisers, six figures. We hadn't launched a program yet, nobody knew who we were. Nobody would take the job of selling the ads. She had the vision that we could get four brand-name advertisers who would make a commitment to give us $100,000 each. It had to be at least a $40 CPM [cost per thousand], which was twice the price Yahoo! was charging then, and Yahoo! was one of the only other online companies selling ads."

The small sector of the media community that was actually aware of what iVillage was doing simply laughed its efforts off. But Levitan went on 60 sales calls between November 1995 and February 1996, and managed to sign five national sponsors—MGM Home Video, Toyota, Polaroid, Starbucks, and Nissan. The Web was so new at this point that the advertisers had no Web ad banners, and iVillage had to create them. It was so new, in fact, that Polaroid, MGM, and Starbucks didn't have web sites at all, and iVillage built those as well.

This frenzy of selling—in conjunction with a healthy infusion of venture capital from AOL and other investors, including Liberty Media—enabled iVillage to compete head-on with the established women's media, a feat that seems almost shocking, given its shaky beginnings.

David Rheins, who had been president of *Spin* magazine in 1995, became senior vice president of advertising at iVillage in 1996. He soon found the fledgling operation to be somewhat loose in terms of traditional business practices. When he was hired, he found that Levitan was still under the impression that *he* was running advertising there.

"I was hired to be the head of advertising, but the first conundrum was who was going to tell Robert Levitan, who had been overseeing advertising, that I was now his boss. Rather than make that declaration, rather than bringing us together and giving us a plan as to how Candace envisioned us working together, to delineate responsibilities, she just obfuscated my position. Neither Robert nor I were ever officially resolved. So we always had a bump-against relationship. She did that because he was a founder and had been given guarantees that she was now unwilling to officially revoke, but she was clearly unwilling to live up to those promises. She also wanted to motivate me and I felt that veracity played little or no role in governing her behavior."

This kind of uneasy, off-balance management style was typical of new-media companies, where few employees were ever sure of what their exact title or job function was. At one conference in the late '90s, a show of hands was asked for from those who knew their job title. A handful of hands out of more than 100 participants went up.

It wasn't just job functions, but job standards, that also changed. Rheins recalls that it was typical of iVillage to book revenue that wasn't really revenue. "There were all these shell games that iVillage would play. Deals would be announced. We would have negotiations on how some company was going to buy $6 million of advertising. We were going to build 'bridge' sites [a connecting site between iVillage and an advertiser, linked from iVillage], we were going to promote them, build a community, and do some direct marketing. We would book it as a $6 million deal, even if it cost us $7 million to build their sites." Sometimes these deals would fall apart, while the "revenue" remained on the books. This type of practice, originated at Internet companies, soon spread, culminating in the Enron and Global accounting disasters of 2002. An embittered iVillage financial executive later accused iVillage of fraudulent accounting practices, but by then the battle was virtually over. No matter how dysfunctional and unprofitable iVillage was as a company, it had more traffic than most of the web sites from magazine companies *combined*. Whatever the special DNA that was required to build popular web sites for women, iVillage had it, and Meredith, Hachette, Condé Nast, and Hearst didn't.

CHAPTER 10

TV Fails to Master Its Domains

MTV Networks chairman and CEO Tom Freston, a very down-to-earth nonpretentious fellow who has managed to survive almost 20 years at the music network despite being old enough to be the grandfather of many of his VJs, appeared at a conference sponsored by *Forbes* magazine in Palm Beach, Florida, in March 1997, and basically lamented the fact that the Internet and AOL were ever invented. "No one's figured out how to fulfill the promise of the Internet," he told the well-heeled audience. "A lot of people's dreams are going to be dashed."

If print was facing daunting problems with the online medium, TV was encountering even bigger ones.

Freston's pessimism was particularly interesting because, as he noted, MTV was then operating the number-one entertainment site on America Online. Freston didn't reveal how much he was getting paid by AOL, or if he still was getting paid at all, but he dismissed even the AOL income as consistent with "a good hobby," contrasting that with the hundreds of millions in revenue generated by the range of cable channels in the portfolio of MTV's parent company, Viacom—including MTV, VH1, TV Land, and Nickelodeon. Freston concluded, "The gold rush is still a long way off."

The always outspoken Freston wasn't a Luddite. He acknowledged that in 1997, some 41 percent of MTV's TV audience had PCs: "For the MTV audience and the older end of the Nickelodeon audience this medium is real." It just wasn't a real *business* yet, and Freston was in business to make money.

A few months later, Freston addressed another conference, this one Jupiter Communication's Plug In '97, which dealt with online music, and he sounded a more optimistic note: "There's no doubt that a whole new world is opening up on the Web. There's some financial discomfort in the short run, but there will be profitable enterprises in the long run." Freston added, "I'm really glad that MTV is in the Internet business. We'll be doing things five years from now that we haven't even thought of yet."

What happened between the two meetings to change his mind? "That conference back in March was for *Forbes;* it was about making money," Freston quips.

Part of his volte-face also had to do with digital dreams that had suddenly emerged at MTV Networks, dreams far more ambitious than mere AOL licensing. For a time, MTV was confident it could rule the online world. It had the perfect demographic profile, reaching the same teenage audience that was the most frequent user of online chat rooms and e-mail. And it was cool. Cool ruled online, right? MTV *had* to win.

During the early spring and summer of 1997, a key catalyst had appeared at MTV in the form of an unlikely consultant, one who seemed to hold the answers on how to guide the network into the digital promised land. Through him, MTV began to develop a serious Jones for the concept of presenting a live concert venue online.

Andrew Rasiej was a darkly handsome, George Clooney look-alike who had pioneered an online business called the Digital Club Network. DCN focused on live music, an outgrowth of Rasiej's day job running Irving Plaza, a Manhattan rock club. In 1997, as Rasiej recalls it, MTV was still relying on AOL revenue for its digital profits and had a fairly minimal web site that had been up a year. A fledgling rock site called SonicNet was "kicking MTV's ass," as Rasiej delicately puts it. Matt Farber, later to emerge at Tonos and iCast, was in charge of MTV Online. Farber, who liked to call himself an "intrapreneur," had little cooperation from the network early on and had to fight to simply get the MTV cable channel to even mention it had a web site and AOL area.

Farber hired Rasiej in 1997 as a consultant, for a total of $225,000, to help build a live MTV Web channel that would offer big-time acts. A promotional video developed internally showed VJs introducing the Rolling Stones on the Web, in several languages. The software displayed in the video wasn't Internet-based software, of course, because Web video looked terrible in 1997, and MTV executives knew that Freston would hardly be impressed with it. Instead MTV minions created the prototype in Director, the CD-ROM–producing tool. When presented to Freston and MTV's Judy McGrath, the concept looked very cool, and a person who was at the viewing says there was applause as it ended, with both McGrath and Freston saying they were overwhelmed. It's a safe bet that neither Freston nor McGrath had much appreciation for the difficulty of delivering live video to users' homes via the Web circa 1997, with a thicket of competing formats and video quality that at best offered a tiny, jerky picture that was often out of sync with the soundtrack. And it was expensive to produce. Who was going to pay for all this?

To that end, Rasiej organized a summit meeting in Santa Clara, California, between Intel and MTV. The idea was that Intel, which was already giving Rasiej money for his live music events, would be the top sponsor of and possible investor in MTV's live Web channel. Intel had become interested in promoting practical applications as a way of getting users to upgrade to faster chips. Music seemed a likely area, but Intel, like other high-tech companies, had an investment strategy that was based on a fast turnaround.

One of the Intel executives asked Farber, "What's the exit strategy?" Farber was indignant. "Exit strategy?" he queried. "We don't build media companies to sell them. We build media companies to *own* them." The meeting ended on a sour note.

Why should Intel offer money for a project in which it wouldn't have a major stake? In that particular detail, one of the major disconnects between the media business and the digital world was on stark display. MTV was used to dealing with "sponsors" who put up money for programming but didn't ultimately own anything. And Intel was accustomed to seeding fledgling digital projects by receiving equity stakes. That may have been the way it was done in Silicon Valley, but not in New York; the two sides weren't even talking the same language. Intel's passing on participation didn't end the live Web channel project immediately, and it dragged on for months afterward.

When Rasiej describes the MTV Internet effort circa 1997, it sounds like chaos: "MTV, as far as I was concerned, had their heads up their ass." Those running the project were hesitant to tell Freston that it simply wasn't feasible for the $400,000 that had been budgeted for it, and the executives who had shown him the phony Director preview were certainly reluctant to tell him a few months later that Web video didn't really look like that. MTV's top layer went on in blissful ignorance, believing it could be done.

Had Freston been interviewed later, in 1998, he would again have sounded cynical about the Internet, because the MTV project had become mired in a corporate morass. A business plan had been drawn up, which used a pay-per-view model: In other words, consumers would pay for each concert on the Web individually. Rasiej was in charge of signing up music clubs across the country.

"We started realizing that [the MTV] people just didn't get it. The point when we realized that the relationship was going to be over was when we suggested signing up venues that were like the Mercury Lounge, and other little places here and there, where we thought that the up-and-coming artists were going to play," Rasiej recalls.

Rasiej was taking this approach because he knew how difficult it would be to secure electronic rights for bigger acts, the kind MTV liked. "Once a band is signed to a major label, that's it, the rights are now owned by the label," he observes. Once MTV realized this, the notion of a live concert channel was doomed. MTV was right back where it started, and Freston's remarks about hopes being dashed seemed weirdly prophetic.

MTV's experience, while typical, translated differently elsewhere in the TV world. The major broadcast TV networks were in an even more difficult position. Just how big a problem the advent of online was for the major networks was painfully evident in NBC's failure to gain any online momentum from its biggest hit of the mid to late '90s, the great sitcom *Seinfeld*. The show, which virtually defined an urban type who had problems with commitment, dating, and life in general, ended its NBC run in 1998 as one of the biggest hits the network had had in years. It also appealed strongly to the demographic that was online the most, white urban upscale professionals. Yet the network's NBC.com had never done much for the show other than to post its stars' bios online. Why wasn't NBC the master of the *Seinfeld* domain? It wasn't for lack of trying. Actually no less than three entertainment companies attempted to create the ultimate online *Seinfeld* experience, and they all failed.

In February 1997 Castle Rock Entertainment, the company that produced *Seinfeld,* started work on an official *Seinfeld* web site. (Unusually, the company had already had the foresight to purchase the URL www.seinfeld.com.) Jean Wells, vice president of information technology at Castle Rock, was assigned to meet with Jerry Seinfeld and other principals behind the show to iron out creative details for the Web property.

"I've been developing movie web sites for Castle Rock for a year," Wells said in a 1997 interview. "Once our TV department saw the success of their movie sites, they decided to go ahead with a television presence on the Internet." Wells added, "The site will be an extension of the show, a way to broaden the *Seinfeld* experience." Since the show was obsessed with the perils of dating, it seemed natural that it contain a lot of related interactive material on it, such as a *Seinfeld* guide to dating do's and don'ts. On the show, Jerry always had an Apple computer in his apartment, although no one ever saw him turn it on.

Still, everyone was confident that the demographic of *Seinfeld* was right for the online world.

But when soon afterward Wells showed the site to Jerry Seinfeld, he is said to have hated it. It seems likely that because the material would have run counter to his own hands-on approach to his show, it would be seen as missing the mark. Wells quit Castle Rock, and the *Seinfeld* Web project died at the company.

Soon afterward, Castle Rock was sold to Warner Bros., making the *Seinfeld* Web operation at least partly a Pathfinder property. But as it happened, *Seinfeld* was being distributed in syndication by Columbia TriStar, owned by Sony, which meant there was yet another possible "owner" of the online rights. That didn't stop Warner Bros. from wanting to cut itself into the action, and with its purchase of Castle Rock it had at least gained access to the URL that Jean Wells had registered.

As the May 14, 1998, *Seinfeld* finale episode approached on NBC, Warner Bros. TV executives were feverishly at work on a last-minute web site at the Seinfeld.com domain. Chuck Ross, then the media editor for the trade magazine *Advertising Age,* talked about the effort to advertisers, who were stunned at what the studio was attempting to pull off. Ross said Warner Bros. had asked advertisers to put up $1 million in sponsorship money behind the web site before they would commit to develop it. This for a show that was already leaving NBC and would be seen only in syndicated reruns.

The sales pitch for the Warner *Seinfeld* site was described by one agency executive as "heavy on chat and trivia games and polls and that sort of thing." Proposed areas of the site included The Cooler (a chat room), Remember the One . . . (an episode guide), Genius Envy (trivia games), Nice Moves (featuring some of Kramer's trademark entrances), and Sein Your Desktop (which features a download of the Soup Nazi character). This pallid lineup hardly seemed worth $1 million, especially since there were already 161 unofficial *Seinfeld* sites, most of which had better features than this. Jim Moloshok, then senior vice president of Warner Bros. Online, noted at the time, "We have officially refused to comment on the site." No wonder—advertisers balked, and, appropriately enough for a show allegedly about nothing, nothing ever appeared at Seinfeld.com.

NBC's most positive experience online was with a fairly respectable news site, MSNBC.com, launched as a joint venture with Microsoft and edited by the capable former *Washington Post* reporter Merrill Brown. MSNBC, the first cable network to consciously try to integrate with the Internet, had come together in 1995 as the result of a joint pitch that former NBC executive Tom Rogers, NBC CEO Bob Wright, and NBC News president Andrew Lack had made to Microsoft's Bill Gates.

"We created a very smart hybrid," Rogers says now. "There was use of a traditional base [NBC News], and it was put together in an integrated form, with a common assignment desk between TV and Internet. Today it's the number-one general news site on the Internet." When the channel and the web site were first conceived in 1995, Microsoft had fought Rogers on his choice of Brown, a journalist and non-Microsoft guy, as editor. "They really resisted my putting Merrill in there at first," Rogers recalls. "They also resisted setting up a newsroom. Finally I told Peter Neupert, who was the partner in the venture, my counterpart at Microsoft, 'You've got to have Merrill in there. Merrill will make this thing happen.' They thought they needed somebody of and for the Internet, as opposed to someone who understood traditional media and how it was going to be driven into the Internet space. They didn't understand that distinction."

The resulting entity was clearly a triumph for NBC. With $500 million of Gates's money, the network got to operate its own cable channel, which quickly became a profit center; Microsoft ended up with a joint operating position on the MSNBC web site, which didn't make money and is unlikely to soon. Says one former NBC executive, "[GE CEO] Jack Welch was always thrilled that somebody finally had taken Microsoft in a negotiation."

CBS was not as fortunate in its online configuration.

Leslie Moonves, the network's president and CEO, acknowledged much later, in 2001, that his network had suffered pangs of anxiety over the Web business. "People used to tell us, 'But you don't have a portal.' The pundits thought you had to have a portal. It was like being out in the Hamptons without a Beemer. We had a bad case of Portal Envy," he confessed at a conference sponsored by Jupiter Media Metrix in March 2001. In fact, what CBS *did* have was even more dysfunctional than the lack of a portal.

On February 2, 1998, the network launched something it called CBS Now, a co-branded web site that linked the network with its 155 affiliates. At least it was supposed to do that. CBS New Media (the division of CBS responsible for launching CBS.com) called it "a revolutionary online system" designed to "generate and host CBS affiliate content and CBS News, making its online debut on CBS.com."

The idea, CBS explained, was to move "the best of the broadcast network affiliate model" to the Web, and the project seemed designed to compete with

NBC's local news site, Interactive Neighborhood, which also used content from local affiliates. When new users logged onto the CBS.com site, they were prompted for their zip codes. Then Oracle database software would personalize the experience users would have, depending on which affiliate served their area.

This project was far harder to implement than it appeared, with complicated station contour maps matched with software that never worked properly. When one user in Connecticut, whose local affiliate was WCBS–TV in New York, tried to use the service, a "server busy, please try again" message appeared. On a second attempt, the user was prompted for a password and user name, which was impossible because the system had never assigned one.

A beleaguered Dean Daniels, vice president and general manager of CBS New Media, explained that the site had been "hammered by a wave of traffic" on its first day. "Clearly, it was an inauspicious morning," he added. But he stressed that much of the problem had been cleared up by day's end.

But to embarrassed CBS executives, this sort of "dead air" is a catastrophe, especially because the network looked bad in front of its affiliates, the TV stations that it depends on to carry its programming. Most CBS affiliates, like those at other networks, are independently owned, and they were angry at CBS following this fiasco.

CBS, true to its heritage, which had involved ignoring most innovations in rival media, had always been leery about the online business. It became the only network news operation that ultimately chose not to compete in either cable or Web-based news, opting instead for a policy, spearheaded by CFO Fred Reynolds, to take passive investments in an array of web sites, including SportsLine and MarketWatch. The local news fiasco had a lot to do with that decision.

A key CBS executive, who chooses to remain anonymous, explains that this philosophy was a result of CBS CEO Mel Karmazin's insistence that the network not invest any cash in Internet projects. Because of his long-standing admonition, "Don't bring me any deal that doesn't have ROI [return on investment] attached," Reynolds had devised what seemed on its surface to be a clever strategy of offering no cash, just promotion, to acquire a portfolio of a dozen or so Internet-based companies, including CBS MarketWatch, Steve Brill's Contentville, ThirdAge, CBS SportsLine, OfficeRunner, Webvan, and a bizarre contest-related "portal" called Iwon.com. While Internet stocks still had huge valuations, this strategy made Reynolds look like a genius. Later these investments became a drag on earnings as online companies slumped.

In his 1991 book, *Three Blind Mice: How the TV Networks Lost Their Way* (Random House), Ken Auletta showed how the big networks had been ineffective in dealing with the huge threat posed by cable in the 1980s. They watched helplessly as their dominance of TV viewing was eaten away by ESPN, MTV, A&E, Discovery, and TBS, among other popular networks. The feeling was strong in the late 1990s that the big four, including Fox, were about to lose out in another technological revolution, the Internet.

Their problem, fundamentally, was determining what a broadcast network really *was*. Was it an entertainment entity or a news-based entity? It was especially difficult to define exactly what a big network like NBC actually was when expressed as a web site. To make matters more confusing, most of the applications that seemed to work best for sites like AOL and Yahoo! weren't either entertainment *or* news but software-based tools like e-mail and chat. Such applications were beyond even the most savvy engineers at 30 Rockefeller Plaza, NBC's towering headquarters. Suddenly companies that had been so cutting-edge in the 1960s and 1970s were looking positively quaint, and people like Bob Pittman kept gleefully pointing out their newfound irrelevance.

Another problem the networks faced was that they didn't own most of the shows they broadcast and hence didn't automatically have the rights to build web sites around them. At NBC in 1997, only a handful of shows, such as *Homicide,* were actually produced by the network. Edmond Sanctis, then in charge of NBC.com and later an executive at Snap.com, NBC's beleaguered portal play, complained to reporters that he had very little to work with.

This was hardly an isolated incident. When Time Warner had decided to launch its cable modem service, a bright light at the cable company immediately decided that Road Runner would be the perfect name. But Road Runner was the property of Warner Bros., a completely separate unit of the company, and it took months and months of wrangling before the name could be secured. Meanwhile the service debuted as Line Runner, a ludicrous substitute.

TV networks were all feeling a sense of "disorientation," according to Whitney Goit, the long-serving executive vice president of A&E TV Networks, which includes the History Channel. A&E is partly owned by Disney, NBC, and Hearst, and Goit watched each of the parent companies struggle with the new Web paradigm. "It was a distortion for everybody," he says. Like other media companies, A&E experimented with an e-commerce application, in their case focusing on Heritage Tourism packages offered through the History Channel web site. But like most such efforts, in which the host had no experience in retail or selling this sort of package to consumers, the venture failed.

It wasn't just business initiatives that went awry, but the very corporate cultures that undertook them. At A&E, "normally conservative businesspeople became unnaturally aggressive," Goit says. Web employees often worked until late at night—a practice generally frowned upon at the company—and they petitioned for a new dress code, refusing to wear the suits and ties that were a requirement at the buttoned-down network. A&E dealt with the malcontents by housing the Web operation, headed by Todd Tarpley, in a separate building, and by devising an incentive program that, while hardly competitive with Web-company stock options, was considered a radical step at A&E.

There was turmoil even in the narrow confines of licensing TV content to the existing "online services." With AOL now charging media companies for carriage on its site, a lot of media outlets turned instead to the Microsoft Network, which was promising to be an entertainment-oriented alternative to AOL.

In 1996, MSN had paid Viacom Inc.'s Paramount and its Paramount Digital Entertainment unit an absurdly high fee for two properties—one informed source puts the sum at $8 million for a one-year license for *Star Trek* material, and at least $3 million more for Paramount's *Entertainment Tonight,* which translated poorly to the online medium. MSN had spent hugely on entertainment-related projects like *Mungo Park,* a travel adventure webzine that sponsored such "expeditions" as sending Mariel Hemingway, the actress and granddaughter of Ernest Hemingway, to Cuba to visit some of the writer's old haunts. Mariel Hemingway may be many things, including a successful restaurateur, but explorer and travel journalist she is not. The Mungo Park project was hugely expensive, having underwritten trips to seven continents, but it, too, had paltry traffic numbers.

When online companies tried to emulate TV, the results were even more embarrassing. Microsoft had an especially uncomfortable experience in 1997 with one of its program producers, Cobalt Moon, which put on a "show" on MSN called *SC Naked News.* This contribution to society, transmitted via crude video, consisted of a pair of semi-naked "anchors" seated at a desk, reading racy news stories. Matti Leshem, a Cobalt Moon partner, explained that the original idea for the site had been that the anchors would really, *really* be naked, "But there are no breasts allowed on MSN," he added. Part of the humor on the show consisted of making fun of Bill Gates. "I hope he's not logging on," Leshem laughed. MSN also initiated talks with Lorne Michaels, the producer of *Saturday Night Live,* and his Broadway Interactive Group to produce a live comedy show for the service. It finally debuted in 1997 on MSN's "Channel 5," but nobody cared.

As they struggled to translate their own properties to the new medium, the big TV producers simultaneously tried to clamp down on unofficial use of their copyrights online, and the resulting mayhem was particularly comical. In early 1997, Viacom ordered its legal department to shut down unofficial *Star Trek* sites, of which there were (and are) thousands. Viacom counsel Mallory D. Levitt accordingly sent out a threatening letter to many teenaged Web Trekkies, ordering them to take down their homage web pages. "We have recently learned that you have posted various elements of the *Star Trek* properties on your site," the document noted. "Your posting of these items is an infringement of Paramount copyright and trademark rights in the *Star Trek* properties." Fan sites were henceforth prohibited from posting "artistic renditions of *Star Trek* characters or other properties, sound files, video clips, books or excerpts." A Viacom spokeswoman defended the action: "For a company like ours, our copyrights are some of our most valuable possessions."

According to copyright law, Viacom was fully within its rights. But the company clearly didn't appreciate how deeply these kids loved *Star Trek,* how they went to the movies dozens of times, and how they religiously viewed the TV show. Viacom likewise didn't understand that the Web simply couldn't be controlled by the demands of a lawyer in New York. An AltaVista search in January 1997 found more than 100,000 *Trek*-related sites. Even if anyone took the warning seriously, could Levitt send out 100,000 letters?

Some fans started putting up *Trek* sites that violated copyright just to receive the coveted letter from Levitt, which quickly became a hot collectible. One teenaged webmaster came home to discover his mother had opened Levitt's missive and pinned an alarmed note to the refrigerator, informing the Trekkie that lawyers from New York were on their way to shut him down.

The young fans eventually fought back, and a group of *Trek* zealots, led by Luca Sambucci, banded together to form the Online Freedom Federation. Their goal, explained OFF chairman Sambucci, was to reach a "compromise" with Viacom over "fair use" of *Star Trek* copyrights, according to a doctrine spelled out in the copyright act. The OFF web site issued an "Open Response" to Viacom and asked visitors to sign a petition supporting their efforts, which collected more than 1,000 signatures within 10 days. The site, reproduced in Italian, French, German, and Spanish, revealed how international a phenomenon Trekdom had become by the late '90s.

Dean Bender, a spokesperson for Paramount Digital Entertainment, said that the original legal action had been taken, at least in part, because MSN had insisted the copyright be enforced, to protect its investment in *Star Trek.* This was the kind of publicity that made entertainment companies look like ogres.

Ultimately Viacom allowed *Trek* to be exploited online regardless of copyright. A Google search in March 2002 resulted in 1.3 million Trek sites, indicative of just how big a Web phenomenon the series had become, and how impossible it had been to control.

Microsoft had good reason to be concerned about its investments, for its own efforts to produce TV on the Web were running into serious trouble. During the summer of 1997, reports kept spilling out of Redmond, Washington, Microsoft's headquarters, that Bill Gates was livid over the losses and red ink flowing out of MSN.

John Neilson, then a vice president of Microsoft's Interactive Service Media Division, was forced to deny premature reports of his unit's demise: "We are alive and well; we have a lot of contractors, some of whose contracts are not being renewed. . . . It's a normal ebb and flow. . . . We have variable staff." At a conference on online advertising sponsored by Jupiter Communications in August 1997, Neilson announced that Microsoft had recently been wrestling with a big question—is content a "software business," or not? This might seem to be a ridiculous and irrelevant consideration, but it was all-important in Redmond. Microsoft is a software company, and if it had decided that "content" wasn't software, it would have gotten out sooner. Microsoft understood software. And as Neilson indicated, "In software, one or two players always do extremely well."

Neilson may have convinced Bill Gates that the online business was something it could deal with, but that didn't make it any easier to actually dominate. None of the advantages that Microsoft enjoys in operating software—lack of a strong competitor, a superior product—was in evidence for the company in the online world. It was the same disconnect shared by the TV networks, who were also used to being in a strong competitive position.

CHAPTER 11

Portal Envy

All revolutions start with an apparently innocuous catalyst, an event that seems to have little resonance when it initially takes place but later expands to have enormous significance. For much of the media world, the potential bonanza of the Internet business wasn't really evident until a man named Tom Evans hit the Internet lottery in a way that was so overwhelming that the whole media industry developed instant respect, fear, and loathing for the Internet world, and AOL and Yahoo! in particular.

One major cornerstone of this change in the media zeitgeist was laid in November 1997, when Evans received a call from Eric Hippeau. Evans was at the time the New York–based publisher of the weekly newsmagazine *U.S. News & World Report,* owned by Mort Zuckerman, whose fledgling media empire also included the New York *Daily News* and a brand-new "rocket ship" of a publication called *Fast Company,* launched in Boston by a bunch of Harvard Business School grads, which had taken the magazine world of 1997 by storm.

Evans, a ruggedly handsome guy, who looks a bit like a younger version of Senator John Kerry of Massachusetts, knew Hippeau well. The French-born Hippeau, as CEO of Ziff-Davis, the computer magazine publisher, had managed to steer his company into a hugely profitable takeover by the Japanese-based Softbank investment conglomerate, while still retaining his job—a neat trick. Hippeau had also tried to buy or partner with *Fast Company,* and Evans was the point man for those talks.

Softbank had recently invested in a Santa Monica–based consumer web-page builder called GeoCities, founded by David Bohnet. Hippeau was representing Softbank's 29 percent interest in the start-up, and he invited Evans to move out to Santa Monica and become the company's CEO. Evans had been through this "join-our-new-business" drill many times before, and had in fact already been approached for the GeoCities position by a team of headhunters at Russell Reynolds. He had told the recruiting firm he wasn't that interested, but he paid attention to Hippeau's proposal. "Eric's a very smart guy, and he sees a lot of trends before others do," Evans says. In the heretofore staid milieu of magazine publishing, Eric Hippeau had something of a reputation as a tech genius. This was not because Ziff had had any notable successes in the field. The company had actually supported a rival technology to HTML called SGML and in the early '90s had tried to launch its own SGML-based online service, Interchange, which was later bought by AT&T and quickly aborted. Despite this failure, because Hippeau was ensconced at the world's foremost publisher of computer magazines, he was regarded by the magazine world as understanding the Internet at a time when few others did.

Leaving *U.S. News,* however, wouldn't be a simple decision. Evans had taken the perennial number-three newsweekly to an unheard-of number one in advertising, selling 2,300 ad pages and grabbing a 35 percent market share before he left, something no predecessor had ever managed to do. The feat was all the more impressive because *U.S. News* was still a fairly colorless magazine, avoiding the celebrity profiles choking *Time* and *Newsweek* in favor of "News You Can Use," a somewhat bland but effective concoction that for a time marketed itself as a clear alternative to the big-league competition. Being Mort Zuckerman's factotum also had a lot of associated perks, including presiding over Washington parties attended by all the top dignitaries in the capital. Moreover, Evans had three kids in high school in New Canaan, Connecticut, a New York suburb, and was not inclined to uproot them with a move west. But Evans is a bit of a maverick, and a risk-taker. He knew Zuckerman was never going to give him any sort of equity position, which was a routine part of employment-packages in dot-comland. And Mort's number two was the combative Fred Drasner, who liked to appear in tough-guy ads for the *Daily News,* which made the most out of his outer-borough demeanor. It didn't look as if Drasner had any intention of leaving that post, so if Evans wanted to move up to a CEO spot, it was clear he'd have to do it elsewhere.

Evans accordingly flew up to Andover, Massachusetts, to meet with David Wetherell, the chairman of CMGI, the Internet incubator that owned 30 percent of GeoCities. During the week of President's Day, Evans flew to Los Angeles for discussions with Bohnet and board member Peter Mills, Wetherell's partner at CMGI. GeoCities and its partners wanted Evans so badly that they agreed to let him work out of New York, at least part of the time. Evans officially joined GeoCities in April 1998. The event wasn't considered particularly newsworthy in the media world; that would come later.

Considering its unprepossessing nature, it's somewhat startling to consider the array of Internet and New Economy talent that sprang from *U.S. News & World Report*. The magazine, at one time or another, has nurtured Jake Winebaum, who went on to run Disney's online operations; Pat Hagerty, an executive at CMGI and Primedia; Robin Johnson, the first CEO of Infoseek; Bill Harris, the CEO of Intuit; Karl Spangenberg, the CEO of AtPlan; and Kathy Bushkin, who became senior vice president of communications at America Online.

Evans surmises that one reason the magazine served as such a strong nurturer of talent was that, as a perennial underdog, it had been forced to behave more like a start-up than an established media property. Its executives consequently worked harder and were less complacent than those at Time Inc. They were also much more accustomed to working without a net.

"Because I was at *U.S. News,* and wasn't at Time Inc., I had to do a lot of things myself," Evans explains. "There wasn't a huge infrastructure at *U.S. News.* We wrote the business plan for *Fast Company*—we conceptualized how it was going to be positioned, marketed, distributed, sold, who was going to do it, and how it was going to be done. It was like building a small business."

Evans, who had worked at trade publisher Penton Publishing before going to *U.S. News,* had first been exposed to the online world in 1993, when the magazine made its CompuServe deal. (CompuServe had paid a significant sum for its college guide, later called .edu, which enabled the magazine to make a profit.) He had found the experience interesting, if not completely revolutionary. "My theory is that all media is additive," he says. "TV didn't replace radio, radio didn't replace newspapers. Traditional media doesn't just go away. Video stores didn't replace the movie business. I didn't leave [the magazine world] for another four years [after working with CompuServe]. I had watched the development of online and the Internet, to see if there was a role in it for someone with my skill set." In 1998 online companies were actively looking for talent who knew the media business, he explains, "who had relationships in the media business, who understood marketing and branding. And people who could cobble together a media company or a staff of people who could move an online company toward (a) being a business and (b) being a media company."

GeoCities looked like a real business in the late 1990s. Because so many Internet users immediately took to web sites as a powerful and widely visible means of self-expression, allowing them to "publish" in a more accessible way than print ever had, GeoCities was a hugely attractive concept. It was "personal publishing," one of the ingredients Ted Leonsis had identified a few years earlier as key to online success. Without containing any generic "content," but merely all the tools that people needed to create their own sites, GeoCities quickly became a top-10 web site, soaring past Pathfinder and other media properties.

"When you really drilled down, it was the perfect web story," Evans says. "It was all about people sharing content, sharing it with other people. People would be allowed to see it and use it and engage with it—it was everything that the web was supposed to represent. It was generating a tremendous groundswell on a daily basis; the company was growing at a pace of 18,000 new users a day. I could see that there were many things you could do to make it more user-friendly, easier to navigate. And it was clear that you needed to put some business discipline into the company and that it could be a major success. It had been run by a bright, entrepreneurial guy, and it wasn't intended to be a business; it was intended to be a soapbox for people to express their personal views and lives. If you knew baseball or Palm Pilots or rose gardening, you could converse with those people through GeoCities."

Although there were dozens of projects vying for attention when Evans arrived at GeoCities, he quickly identified the top 15 that needed immediate action. Well aware that digit-heads at new-media companies sometimes resented CEOs from big-media backgrounds who came in without a granular knowledge of technology—a problem faced by Scott Kurnit at MCI—Evans told the GeoCities staff, "Hey, I don't know everything about technology, but I do know about managing a business, hiring people, bringing in revenue. I'm not going to tell you how to code for a new HTML editor. I don't even know how that works. But if we learn this together, and focus on what the company needs to do, we will succeed."

Evans also made a crucial decision to not allow a small cadre of engineers run the company, a familiar turn at many unsuccessful Web operations. "You get engineers who can envision the product, but none of them can manage people," he says.

Although Evans took a huge pay cut to go to GeoCities—about 60 percent—the salary was beside the point. What truly turned the media business on its ear was the stock-option package he received, which was revealed when the company filed its S-1 IPO registration with the SEC. Nobody wrote an article about it, but Evans's package was there for all to see, and it became the equivalent of samizdat literature, passed from corporate office to corporate office, where it was used as the basis for many executive packages to come. If GeoCities had an even moderately successful IPO, Evans would be worth more than $50 million. The gasp was heard all over Manhattan. While most observers didn't think he'd pull it off, they did recognize that there was at least the potential to do so, potential that was just not available at traditional media companies, where the best-performing publisher could make up to $1 million a year in bonuses and perks. That was the glass ceiling, and Evans now stood to top that by a mind-boggling factor of 50.

GeoCities had already decided to go public by the time Evans arrived. The company had an enormously successful road show, ending up with an IPO that was 26 times oversubscribed, in a very difficult market—so difficult that there wasn't a single Internet IPO during the week before GeoCities', and there wouldn't be another for 50 more days, until eBay broke the logjam.

"I'd never done a road show, but you know what, it's just like sales," Evans says. "When we launched *Fast Company*, I went to every single ad market, and did eight presentations a day in Detroit, three straight presentations in Chicago, in New York, in Dallas. You make the same pitch over and over again, day after day. I had done this my whole life making sales calls, and the road show was exactly like that." Evans says a successful road show is all about credibility. He recalls going to Detroit during the *Fast Company* launch effort and meeting with the GM ad team, including Phil Guarascio and Karen Ritchie, who was responsible for GM's marketing millions on the ad agency side. "Guarascio said, 'Are you going to be involved?' I said, 'Yeah.' 'Is Mort committed to this thing?' I said, 'Yeah.' He says, 'We're in, period.'" Something similar happened during the GeoCities road show, in which Evans's experience and that of the members of his team got them into places where 23-year-old business neophytes couldn't have entered. And Evans worked unbelievably hard at it, making 59 cross-country trips during his tenure at GeoCities.

GeoCities went public on August 11, 1998, at $17 a share, but it soared to $37 by the end of the first day. The IPO triumphed despite the fact that August 11, 1998, was a nervous day on Wall Street, with the Dow down 230 points. On August 15, the FTC hit GeoCities with one of the first consent orders for privacy violations to plague an Internet company, and the stock plunged to $13, briefly "underwater," meaning that those who had bought at the opening price were now looking at a negative investment. But by the fall, the company announced a major e-commerce deal, and the stock was trading in the $40s. At many media outlets envious onlookers tallied up the net worth of Evans and other media veterans who had taken a chance on the project, and realized that they were now worth millions of dollars, albeit on paper. Though everyone had witnessed the incredible showings of other dot-com companies that had gone public, this was the first time that someone from the big-media world was involved, and it got personal fast.

GeoCities' successful public offering, followed by that of eBay, started a Gold Rush for Internet-related properties that lasted almost two years. During the fall of 1998, publishers and TV executives scrupulously kept track of Evans's options and realized he was worth more money than they'd made in their entire careers. Ron Bernstein, the former publisher at Hachette Filipacchi New Media, who had reported to Jim Docherty, had also joined GeoCities as head of advertising, and his stock option riches were also public knowledge.

Soon a parade of former media wage slaves started to make huge sums by becoming part of Internet IPOs. Former CBS executive Dean Daniels, who had encountered numerous obstacles in getting CBS News on the Web in 1997, had jumped to a GeoCities–style play called TheGlobe.com, which went public a few months after GeoCities. Despite the fact that the company had a very thin management layer, including two founders barely out of their teens, stock in TheGlobe soared to $91 on its first day of trading. This development also had significant impact because Daniels had visibly failed to get CBS convincingly on the Internet but had succeeded in a major way at TheGlobe, despite the fact that the service was little more than a clone of GeoCities. It helped reinforce the notion that you had to leave the media world to hit it big.

In fall 1998, Tom Evans got a call from Jeff Mallet, the president and COO at Yahoo! Prior to GeoCities' IPO, Yahoo! had a nonvoting "observer's" seat on its board; Yahoo! CEO Tim Koogle and Mallet would merely sit in to observe the company at work. The two companies had already begun to establish links to each other in earnest. Yahoo! needed the kind of community features GeoCities offered, because it knew its competitors would soon acquire them, and because GeoCities was an incredible traffic-builder that would allow Yahoo! to quickly take an irrevocable lead over its competitors. Yahoo! had started a Clubs section, which was intended to gather people of like interests, but it was primitive next to GeoCities.

The two companies met formally on Friday January 22, 1999. Evans and CFO Steve Hansen, a former Universal Studios executive, flew up to Silicon Valley to meet with Yahoo! Facing them across a long conference table were Koogle, known as "TK" to his buddies; Jeff Mallet; Jerry Yang; J.J. Healey, the head of business development; general counsel John Place; CFO Jerry Valenzuela; and Elizabeth Blair from business development.

"They were there to talk about an acquisition," Evans says. The meetings extended to Sunday. GeoCities was not formally for sale but couldn't deny that Yahoo! was an exciting company to sell to.

Yahoo!'s final offer of $4.6 billion, or $117 a share, was not based on the paltry $20 million in revenue GeoCities had generated the year before; it was, rather, a preemptive bid designed to keep the company from being put in play, with such a huge premium over the stock price that no one else would be tempted to enter into a bidding war. The premium was staggering. GeoCities' IPO had been only five months earlier, and the company's market cap then was $520 million. Now it was judged to be worth almost ten times more. It was hard to argue with the logic of the deal. "It was pretty compelling," Evans concludes. The portal that acquired GeoCities was bound to become the number-one Web property overnight. At the time of the Yahoo! deal, GeoCities was getting 55 million page views a day, and it was the number-three site, according to Media Metrix. Yahoo! was number one, and AOL was number two. GeoCities called the final sale price a "kingmaker premium."

The Yahoo! offer had a number of contingencies attached, including unanimous board approval, which had to be reached within the next 24 hours. When the offer was tendered on that Sunday, January 24, GeoCities was also informed that Yahoo! wanted contracts signed and an announcement made by that Wednesday, January 27, again fearing the terms of the deal might leak and trigger a counterbid. GeoCities signed in time.

Exactly how much money Evans made from the sale is difficult to calculate, but it was tens of millions of dollars. He suddenly became a hot property and received more than 90 jobs offers, from companies like the Motley Fool, Akamai Technologies, and others. Instead he took the summer off. Evans, who abhors conspicous consumption, kept the same New Canaan house that he'd bought ten years earlier, and just sat back and pondered his next move.

Yahoo! offered Evans a job as some sort of Washington lobbyist, a somewhat ridiculous concept that he quickly dismissed. Years later, in 2001, when Yahoo!'s problems became apparent, the *Wall Street Journal* ran a front-page piece on the "Gang of Six" who founded the company. "Yahoo! acquired lots of other Internet companies, but it became apparent to executives at these companies that their input wasn't welcome in the inner circle," the *Journal* wrote on March 9. "The result was that Yahoo! lost some of the sort of talent that it badly needs today, now that Old Economy realities are hitting the young company."

One GeoCities veteran says the aftermath of the Yahoo! takeover was brutal. Ad staffers in New York were instructed not to go on sales calls, because they weren't capable of presenting with the panache that Yahoo! thought it specialized in. Yahoo! executives made it clear that the kind of old-media skills that Tom Evans and Ron Bernstein represented were not valued at the company, which believed it could transcend media tradition. Evans, in fact, has a lot of the same skills as AOL Time Warner's Bob Pittman and could have proved invaluable had he stayed at Yahoo! But most observers concur that if Pittman himself had showed up looking for a job at Yahoo! in 1996, the same year he joined AOL, he would have been quickly dismissed as an old-media has-been and shown the door.

It was this mind-set that also prevented Yahoo! from acquiring or partnering with a major media company. Yahoo had a number of small media projects in the late '90s, such as a short-lived joint venture to create a music directory with MTV and a more lasting magazine effort with Ziff-Davis called *Yahoo! Internet Life*. According to insiders at Viacom, the MTV project, awkwardly called UnfURLed, was a disaster, with Yahoo! doing next to nothing to maintain the site, which was quickly abandoned. "They simply wanted to do a deal with MTV, but they didn't know what to do with it," a former Viacom executive says.

James Spanfeller, who was the group publisher of *Yahoo! Internet Life* and other Ziff-Davis magazines in the late '90s before emerging as CEO of Forbes.com, recalls that Yahoo! co-founder Jerry Yang took a special interest in the magazine and was readily available for consultation. Yahoo! never tried to influence the content of the magazine, beyond the general diktat that they wanted it to be a directory, without a heavily critical focus. While many subscribers thought that Yahoo! was actually producing the magazine, given its name, the portal company actually had little involvement in putting it out, with editorial offices remaining in New York under editor in chief Barry Golson.

The *Wall Street Journal*'s Kara Swisher diagnosed the company's shortsightedness astutely when she argued, on March 9, 2001, "Most agree that Yahoo! could have spent its stock more wisely and bought a more traditional media company to give a solid foundation to its impressive distribution network. . . . Yahoo! should have been furiously knocking on the doors of then-scared media partners like Rupert Murdoch and Michael Eisner of Walt Disney Co."

Despite Yahoo!'s contradictions, at this juncture, the so-called "portals" looked like the long-term winners online. There were many other factors related to the sudden belief, in late 1997 and early 1998, that companies like AOL and Yahoo! had won the online race, and that the major media companies had failed. That had initially been a hard concept to grasp in New York, always the center of media power, where so many tech developments had seemed remote and not all that relevant to big media. Ever since the late 1870s, when New York had won out over Boston as the principal publishing mecca, Gotham had gotten used to considering itself the content capital of the world. But rude, jarring messages kept disrupting that complacency in 1998. On March 31, Bob Pittman gave a speech at the Big Picture conference in New York, sponsored by *Variety* and Schroders bank, that opened a lot of eyes across the media spectrum. In his talk, Pittman proclaimed that AOL had all but destroyed its rivals. By the time of his appearance, AOL had 22 million households subscribing. Its nearest "competitor," CompuServe, had 2 million, but it had already been bought by AOL. AOL users then spent an average of 50 minutes with the service a day, up from 14 minutes in August 1996.

And Pittman went well beyond a declaration of victory online: His explicit message was that AOL had triumphed over big media as well, and that eyeballs that were now glued to Instant Messages and AOL mail were no longer as interested in TV and magazines. "That extra time has to come from the TV set," Pittman told the group, many of whom were network TV executives. AOL had "paid all our attention to the mass market," he said, and it had paid off handsomely. Even more impressive was the manner in which AOL had become an e-commerce juggernaut with its pop-up screens, which appeared on the user's screen directly after sign-on. Forty-two percent of then current AOL users had bought something from the service, many from pop-ups. AOL had sold 20,000 copies of the *Titanic* soundtrack in one hour through a pop-up. AOL had already sold as much J.Crew merchandise as the chain's second-largest store, he boasted.

Pittman wasn't the only person touting the scary notion of AOL über alles in 1998. In October of that year, Tom Wolzien, a key analyst at Sanford C. Bernstein & Co., Inc., issued a report called "America Online: The Next, Best Network," which turned a lot of media heads. Wolzien wasn't a faceless analyst. In the late '80s and early '90s, perennially rumpled and his thick, black hair always in a formidable tangle, he had been a key executive at NBC, and had been behind some of the network's earliest investments in digital technology, including Interactive Network, an attempt at two-way TV in the early '90s.

"AOL," Wolzien proclaimed in his report, "is poised to become one of the most powerful media companies. It represents the logical evolution of the network [TV] model: better targeting; more valuable consumers; higher growth;

and lower cost structure. This model wins: EBITDA [before-tax earnings] in five years will exceed CBS, NBC, ABC, Fox, or Viacom without Blockbuster." He predicted a possible merger with Time Warner, noting that the "fit with Time Warner's cable, advertising and direct-marketing operations is unique, but likely dilutive to Time Warner for more than five years." Of course, that assumed Time Warner was the surviving entity. Wolzien noted that among big-media companies, only AOL had three revenue streams—from advertising, subscriber fees, and "transaction" fees.

"What's funny about it is the major companies, Time Warner included, made the same mistake they made with music, with MTV. They let somebody else build a network on the back of their brands," says Jim Banister, a former Warner Bros. executive. And the irony was that the traps that MTV and AOL laid for companies like Warner Bros. were both set up by the same man—Bob Pittman. MTV had thrived in the '80s by programming free music videos the network got from the record labels. As soon as MTV became fully established, it began to switch away from music videos to game shows and reality-based gimmicks like *The Real World,* which got higher ratings. The record companies, including Warner Bros., felt betrayed.

Wolzien's report had a bitter aftertaste at the media companies, many of which, like Time Warner, had had numerous chances to buy AOL in the early days. For the four TV networks, many of which were represented by top executives at the Big Picture conference, AOL's ascendancy was particularly galling. The Walt Disney Co., which owns ABC, wouldn't accept AOL's strong new position without a fight. Ultimately the Mouse fought AOL as hard and as long as Time Warner did, out of a combination of ambition, pride, and sheer competitiveness. There were times when those gloves that Mickey always wears began to look like boxing attire.

It was hardly a surprise that the Walt Disney Company made a major play at Internet supremacy in the late 1990s. Ever since Walt Disney himself had flown over Orlando and scoped out the property that would become Disney World, with its pavilions devoted to the technology of tomorrow, the company had liked to think of itself as ahead of the curve. CEO Michael Eisner, well known for his huge, overweening ego, was very unlikely to simply cede the online business to arch-rival Time Warner, and he didn't. The problem for Eisner, however, was that even he had to admit that he knew virtually nothing about technology.

He was fond of giving speeches in which he portrayed himself as an uninformed Luddite. Eisner needed an online lieutenant, and he found one in a savvy magazine entrepreneur and former marketing executive, Jake Winebaum.

During this period, no one in charge of new media at an Old Economy media outlet worked harder to gain dominance than Winebaum. If Disney didn't ultimately end up with a winning hand, it certainly wasn't a result of any half-hearted efforts by its new-media team.

While not a tall man, Winebaum can fill a room with his energy and low-key self-confidence. He's handsome in a boyish kind of way, with dark brown hair generally kept close-cropped and well-tailored casual clothes. He can be charming, though when you deal with him personally, he's all business.

For Jake, it all started with a magazine idea. He had been a senior vice president of marketing at *U.S. News,* but, like Tom Evans, he chafed at the lack of entrepreneurial opportunities within Mort Zuckerman's empire. Unlike Evans, however, he went off to do his own project from 1991 to 1993, a magazine called *FamilyFun.* It's here that the careers of Dan Okrent and Jake Winebaum intersect, in a way. Okrent's *New England Monthly,* as noted, had been a commendable project, but its beautiful photography and elegant writing proved not to be specific enough for New Englanders, who would rather have read about goings-on in their town than somewhere in Maine. So in 1991, when Jake was looking to launch his own magazine, he ended up grabbing most of the staff of Okrent's recently shuttered publication. That meant that the New York–based Winebaum would have to commute each week to Northampton, Massachusetts, where the staff was located.

"Jake had the idea of what the basic editorial feel should be and what the basic marketing position was, but he needed someone to make a magazine, to connect the dots and fill in the color," Okrent recalls. "So he hired me to do the first two issues. I brought in some people who had worked for me at *New England Monthly.* I was a schmuck, having told Jake, 'No I don't want to be paid in equity for this, I want to be paid in cash.'" Okrent left after helping with the launch, landing at Time Inc. in New York, although he kept in touch with Winebaum.

FamilyFun was the product of Winebaum's experiences with his own family, in that he had been frustrated by the lack of a central source for things that families could do together. The magazine directly answers the questions of how and where to have fun with your family. Given the subject matter, it was inevitable that it would end up owned by Disney, because the company would see it as the perfect vehicle to promote its theme parks in a way that catalogs or brochures never could. Disney is not a company that makes a lot of acquisitions, or it hadn't historically up to that point, and Jake likes to recall the 75 meetings that he'd attended as Disney considered purchasing his magazine.

The final meeting was with Disney CEO Michael Eisner himself. As Winebaum tells the story, he was ushered in to see Eisner, who almost immediately acted as if he'd never heard of Winebaum or *FamilyFun*. "Who the fuck are you?" was the friendly greeting he got from the head of America's family entertainment empire. But Disney eventually did buy the magazine, and began to see Winebaum as a strong addition to its executive ranks.

Winebaum started on his new-media adventure in 1993 when he was watching his 2-year-old daughter play with a computer and read a book at the same time. The revelation that kids were far more computer-savvy than most adults then led to the idea of a brand extension, *FamilyPC*, which ended up as a joint venture between Disney and Ziff-Davis, the computer publisher. Winebaum had been named president of Walt Disney Magazine Publishing in 1992, while still serving as both editor and publisher of *FamilyFun*.

"During the period when I was editing *FamilyPC*, I met with a large group of PC-oriented executives. I was watching families and real consumers and seeing how the Internet was becoming part of people's lives," Winebaum remembers.

A shrewd negotiator, Winebaum had secured a long-term contract with Disney as part of the *FamilyFun* buyout agreement. That meant that if he was going to get into the Internet business, "I knew I had to do it at Disney." So in April 1994, Winebaum presented a proposal to Disney executives for forming an Internet group called Disney Online in Burbank, where Team Disney toils. This initial business plan was based on an ambitious goal—that Disney would launch its own dial-up, family-friendly online service to compete with AOL and Prodigy. "At the time, no one was working on going after the family market," Winebaum explains.

The ultimate business plan was presented to senior management in Burbank in late 1994, and in early 1995 Winebaum was officially named president of Disney Online and then the Buena Vista Internet Group. At the time, whenever Eisner attended media conferences and the subject of new media came up, he acted as if he were the number-one technophobe. Fond of assuming the role of a street-savvy tough guy when he's among peers, Eisner told audiences at many speaking engagements during this period that he really didn't understand new media.

Still, he approved Winebaum's project, which called for a variety of different approaches. The most ambitious was the dial-up online service, called the

Daily Blast, which would run on proprietary software. This was designed explicitly for kids and promised to be kid-friendly. With more than 90 million households in America, many of them with children, Disney saw a potentially vast market, one that the company could steamroll over. AOL was squarely in Disney's sights.

Besides the dial-up service, Winebaum was insistent that Disney take a major position on the Web. In 1995 Winebaum bought the URL Family.com from a woman named Alison Garber, who later became a Disney employee. Family.com was aimed at parents, and a former editor of *Martha Stewart Living*, Susan Wyland, was brought in to oversee editorial development. Disney.com, also on the Web, became the showplace for Disney products and content aimed at kids. David Vogler was brought in from Nickelodeon to develop that project.

Craig Bromberg, who had exited Time Inc. after his bruising battle with Jim Kinsella, signed on with Winebaum as an editorial consultant in late 1995. The Bromberg/Winebaum connection was a happy accident, or collision, depending on your point of view. As he was preparing to exit Time Warner in July 1995, Bromberg was doing some last-minute liaison work with Warner Bros. He had worked on Warner's *Batman Forever* web site and had gotten friendly with some of the West Coast Warner Bros. executives. On a plane out to L.A. that July, Bromberg spotted an intense-looking passenger preparing a Power-Point presentation, which he couldn't help but notice was showcasing web pages. He struck up a conversation, and the man turned out to be Jake Winebaum.

"I see you're preparing a presentation for Disney Online," Bromberg noted to Winebaum, who instantly turned suspicious. "Who told you about Disney Online?" Winebaum queried. "There hasn't been anything in the press." Bromberg quashed his fears about a press leak and by the end of the plane ride had talked Winebaum into hiring him as a consultant. Bromberg worked for Jake for about seven months, starting in September 1995. At the time, Disney had a handful of magazines, including *Disney Adventures, Discover, FamilyFun,* and *FamilyPC*. (The company would later start *ESPN* magazine, and Dan Okrent would be asked by Winebaum to be the launch editor. Okrent decided to stay put at Time Inc., where he had assumed a variety of editorial positions.) Bromberg's assignment was to get all of the magazines online, with a tiny budget of $100,000 for each. "Jake knew how to use the politics of decentralization," Bromberg says. "Eventually the magazines realized that $100,000 in the Web context was nothing." But by that time Winebaum had been able to focus his attention on his primary interest—the online service.

The Daily Blast, amusingly code-named Net Funicello while it was in development in tribute to the ailing former Mouseketeer, was programmed with the belief that Disney characters still ruled with the under-eight set. (The idea had originally been planned as a Sunday newspaper supplement. Although that idea was ultimately abandoned in favor of the Web, a group of consultants who claimed to have originated the Daily Blast concept later sued Disney and were paid off with a major settlement, Bromberg recalls.) In the Daily Blast Web prototype, cartoon characters greeted kid subscribers by name, and many of the games and activities featured famous Disney icons like Mickey Mouse, Goofy, and Dumbo. The company was hoping for about 1 million subscribers its first year.

Although the Disney.com free web site quickly became a popular destination on the Internet for kids, the Daily Blast, launched in 1997, was not a success. After a somewhat rocky start, the product improved. Disney added a proprietary e-mail system called D-Mail, and the service was heavily featured with animation, sound, and music. Plans were also announced by Richard Wolpert, executive vice president of Disney Online, to launch a Best of the Web feature within the Daily Blast that would link to other kid-oriented brands, not just those from Disney.

This was a belated acknowledgment that services like Yahoo! Kids had proved effective on the Internet, and an especially big step for Disney to take because it would mean directing customers away from the sacrosanct brand–including, for example, a link to the web site just launched by arch-competitor Nickelodeon, owned by Viacom. The sites pointed to from the Daily Blast would be those considered "kids-safe," Wolpert explained. Nickelodeon's Alex Maghen, vice president of production at Nick Online, said that his service was considering doing the same thing.

A number of factors intervened, however. Winebaum chose to offer the service through the Microsoft Network, which failed early as an online service with proprietary software. And a company called Humongous presented competition with a line of interactive CD-ROMs featuring characters like Putt-Putt and Blue's Clues that were easier to use and more fun than the Daily Blast. In the final reckoning, it may have been simply too late to launch an online service with proprietary software, and it may have been that kids found enough to keep them occupied on AOL and Prodigy. Or they might not have wanted to be torn away from endless repeat viewings of *The Lion King* video.

Disney boasted at one point that it was adding 500 new subscribers a day, but the company never released formal subscription totals on the Daily Blast.

They certainly weren't significant enough for AOL to worry about—which didn't mean that AOL didn't worry about them anyway.

Ted Leonsis claims that if Disney had not been distracted, it could have beaten AOL. "I have often said, if Bill Gates and Steve Ballmer [of Microsoft] did nothing but online services, they would have won. If Michael Eisner and Jeffrey Katzenberg did nothing but online services, they would have won. They had their core businesses, and [only] an eye on what we were doing. We had nothing else to do but twenty-four hours a day focus on online. We were adding people. You start to get so focused and build up so much momentum. When Kurnit went to MCI, I said to him, 'Scott, by the time you're able to schedule your next three-way board meeting, we'll add a million subscribers.'"

Disney's position as the number-one kids brand would not inevitably translate into online kids hegemony, some at AOL believed. "Just because Disney is hugely successful elsewhere, that doesn't mean that their brand extends into this arena," a top AOL executive said in December 1996. "Microsoft has a big brand name, but the Microsoft Network and MSNBC are by no means leaders in the online world."

A more direct AOL broadside against Disney was fired some months later. In late June 1997, Leonsis spoke at an Internet conference sponsored by the fledgling magazine the *Silicon Alley Reporter* and the International Radio and Television Society Foundation, or IRTS. He chose to talk about how Disney had missed the market with the Daily Blast. "You need 16 megs [megabytes] of RAM to run that service. But what kind of computers do parents actually have?" Leonsis asked an audience of about 150, mostly from the Internet content community. "Macs, Presarios, and 14.4 [band] modems," he said.

Earlier in his presentation, Leonsis urged his listeners not to be intimidated by Disney's push into cyberspace. In a foreshadowing of his later theme, he told the group, "If Michael Eisner just focused on interactive, he'd kick our butts," Leonsis said. "But there are more people in this room than Disney has employed in new media."

Disney Online spokesperson Rebecca Buxton told a reporter it was odd that Leonsis was getting nasty with Disney, because there were several ongoing relationships between the two companies, including a Disney site in AOL's marketplace and collaboration between ABC News and AOL. "I don't know how this is strategic for them at all," she commented.

As far as hardware was concerned, Buxton argued that Leonsis should have paid more attention to "what's been sold at CompUSA for the past two seasons. By next Christmas, this won't be an issue at all. CompuServe got hammered when Wow! [a youth-oriented CompuServe subsidiary] came out only available for Windows 95, but it wouldn't be a big deal now." She added, "Parents expect a certain quality level from Disney. You can't create and market something that's not quite rich enough."

Perhaps the competitiveness with Disney was also related to a series of discussions between the two companies in 1996 that included the possibility of Disney's taking a stake in AOL. Randy Coppersmith opines, "I don't know that Disney was all that interested in buying AOL. I think they were more interested in sucking AOL's brain. There was a discussion about some kind of investment in AOL; there was a discussion about a joint venture; there certainly was a lot of discussion between the two companies in 1996. Disney invested a lot of money in the Internet. Eisner signed off on it, and Jake Winebaum was driving a lot of it. Disney's history of Imagineering has always pushed them to look at new technology, and their history of innovative motion pictures has always helped them to look into special effects and other high-tech gear. The extension of that franchise to Disney was logical. They spent a lot of time looking for possible partners."

Winebaum says the talks with AOL foundered for the usual reasons: "Given what Disney wanted to accomplish from a long-term control point of view, we were not able to agree." In other words, AOL had no intention of selling out to Disney. Others would be more accommodating.

Disney's online approach had been influenced by its sprawling empire and the sometimes conflicting needs of the various units. In June 1995 Disney had acquired the ABC Network, which changed the situation dramatically. ABC News had not even launched a web site yet, as had CBS and the MSNBC partnership, but ESPN, majority-owned by ABC, had already started its popular ESPNet SportsZone, which had been built by a Seattle company called Starwave. The ESPNet project had been spearheaded by a tall, thin, athletic New Yorker named Tom Phillips, who had been the publisher of the irreverent *Spy* magazine for six years. Phillips had gone to Starwave in 1993, after selling the money-losing *Spy* in 1991 and dumping a short-lived attempt at launching a toy catalog. Phillips met Starwave CEO Mike Slade through a friend he and his family were visiting in Seattle in 1993. By the end of the visit, Phillips agreed to move to Seattle and figure out what Starwave should be doing.

Phillips relocated in Seattle at about the same time as Michael Kinsley, the former *New Republic* editor and CNN *Crossfire* host, who had left Washington, D.C., to launch the Slate.com web site. Kinsley, after epic agonizing, had turned down the job as editor of *New York* magazine, later taken by Kurt Andersen, *Spy*'s high-profile editor in chief. Friends of both Phillips and Kinsley—and the media community in general—questioned their sanity for choosing to work for outfits like Slate and Starwave, which no one in New York cared about in 1993. When Phillips got to Starwave in August 1993, the eight-person company was experimenting with video games and CD-ROMs. It ultimately produced five CD-ROMs, all of which lost a lot of money. Microsoft co-founder Paul Allen was a major investor in Starwave and had given the company "an open checkbook," Phillips recalls, and a large amount of Allen's money financed CD-ROMs featuring Sting, Peter Gabriel, the Muppets, and Clint Eastwood.

Starwave had divided the content world into various "verticals," and Phillips, who was made a senior vice president, was told to investigate sports. He quickly decided that timely sports scores were a very hot killer app to pursue. Since Starwave had Paul Allen behind it and it seemed to be a zippy new-media company, it quickly acquired a higher profile than most start-ups, and Phillips, who isn't a rabid sports fan by any means, held his first meeting with ESPN in January 1994, a meeting requested by an ESPN executive named Tom Hagopian.

ESPN asked Starwave point blank if it could build an ESPN Web operation. ESPN had gone up on Prodigy, but the deal was due to expire in March 1995. By August 1994, however, Starwave still hadn't figured out which online platform to work with, and Phillips was kicking the tires of Ziff-Davis's ill-fated Interchange online service, and examining an affiliation with Microsoft Network, code-named Marvel.

Phillips recalls that a chance conversation in September 1994 with a Starwave engineer radicalized his thinking. "We had the infrastructure in place, and the guy said, 'All we have to do is just publish it to a server and put it out there on the Internet.' This was one of the engineers, it wasn't a high-level conversation. I remember him telling me there was this thing called the World Wide Web that people were starting." That offhand remark resulted in Starwave's embracing Web publishing in a major way. (Oddly, several top executives in the new-media business, including Time Inc.'s Paul Sagan, also first heard about the Web from a similar encounter with an engineer or "techie.")

Before a deal had been struck with ESPN, Starwave created its own site in October called Satchel Sports, after famed baseball player Satchel Paige. This took place just before Pathfinder went up, and Phillips maintains that Satchel was one of the first nonpornographic general-interest web sites. Interestingly, when Starwave finally launched ESPNet SportsZone ("a negotiated name that we all hated") on April 1, 1995, it wasn't really all that interested in ESPN's vast resources as a source of content.

"The content didn't matter a bit, especially the first year," Phillips says. "But the name and the promotion mattered a whole lot." A network of stringers created the web site, he explains, "and ESPN doesn't have stringers; ESPN has TV reporters. They had no usable content. They used to give us video feeds. Video feeds, excuse me, on the '95 version of the Web? No one cared." If ESPN had tried to create the web site itself at its headquarters in Bristol, Connecticut, "it never would have happened," Phillips maintains. "There was no buy-in from the top."

However much Michael Eisner enjoyed playing at being a Luddite, Disney was seriously committed to getting somewhere online. Through the ABC acquisition, the company was soon very involved with Starwave, and liking what it saw. "We had the goods; we had the tech stuff and the culture to make things happen," Phillips says.

Besides ESPNet, Starwave had launched a site called Family Planet that Winebaum coveted. Disney invested in Starwave in stages, until on April 30, 1995, Starwave employees in Seattle were startled to get an e-mail message from top executive Patrick Naughton. "Please clear your calendars for an 'All Starwave' company meeting May 1. This is the presentation that you've all been waiting for." The announcement that quickly followed confirmed the memo's import—Disney would buy the company from Allen for a total of $350 million. The negotiation had been protracted, partly due to management rivalries. "The Disney negotiation went on forever," Phillips says. When asked about his relationship with Winebaum, Phillips pauses for a lengthy period and then explains, "We had a very fundamental disagreement with what to do with Disney on the Internet, basically."

Winebaum, never someone who brooks opposition easily, forced out Tom Phillips, who was soon exiled to New York for thwarting what Phillips calls Jake's "Master Plan" for Internet dominance. ABC News belatedly got a web site in 1997, built by Starwave, and Phillips was briefly put in charge of that effort before his eventual departure. Richard LeFurgy, executive vice president of ad sales for ESPN/ABC's ad efforts, was also soon gone. Starwave's web site Family Planet had been named the best family-oriented site by *USA Today* in August 1996, but soon after Disney's takeover, it was folded into Family.com. Disneyfication was soon steamrolling over the rest of Starwave.

A determined empire-builder, Winebaum had a vision for Disney's online future that would not only establish the Magic Kingdom as the number-one Internet player, it would make him rich in the bargain. Clearly, since AOL was unlikely to hand the keys of its Dulles headquarters to Jake, the only way for him to achieve his goals in 1998 was for Disney to acquire a portal, one of the top-10 Internet sites, and that's just what he determined to do after the Starwave deal closed. It was Winebaum's dreams of expansion, in fact, that helped set off a flurry of major deals in 1998, involving media companies trying to become online powers.

In fact, for a short while, in the summer of 1998 and early 1999, it was possible to believe that the media companies would succeed in taking over the Internet. There had been many missteps, but at the beginning of 1999 they all still claimed to be fully committed to building a winning Internet strategy. It is astonishing how quickly that mind-set would change.

CHAPTER 12

The Great Portal Grab

Disney wasn't the only media power shopping for a Web empire at the end of the decade. On Thursday, February 4, 1999, a frigid day in Manhattan, an NBC executive named Tom Rogers received a call from Bob Davis, the CEO of Lycos, one of the top portals on the Internet. Unbeknown to the rest of the business world, Lycos and NBC had been negotiating for months, and a deal was set to be announced the following Monday. NBC would be buying Lycos and with that purchase taking a foremost position on the Internet.

It was all part of Rogers's overall plan. He had earlier served as counsel for the House committee on telecommunications and was the actual author of what became the Cable Act of the 1980s, which freed cable operators from many constraints. NBC CEO Bob Wright, himself a former cable operator at Cox Cable, recruited Rogers to NBC in the 1980s to help the network get a foothold in cable. In his later years at NBC, with CNBC in capable hands, he had turned his attention to the Internet and building a major and lasting edifice in that sphere.

"What I've done my whole career is build new franchises and new businesses where they didn't exist before," Rogers asserts. He had created CNBC despite opposition from within NBC from executives who argued that, since the Financial News Network already existed, what need was there for another cable business channel? Cable became a major revenue stream for NBC and its parent company, GE, which was very much appreciated by GE's do-no-wrong CEO, Jack Welch. The Internet looked almost as promising to Rogers, and the Lycos deal was the centerpiece of a strategy that involved growing large fast.

The contract was almost completed, and the exclusive negotiating period was ending on the following day, Friday.

The final round of negotiations between Lycos and NBC had been scheduled for that day, but in his call Davis told Rogers he had a personal problem and would have to postpone the session. He spoke as if it would be only a minor delay, nothing disastrous. "I'll be back in town next week and we can resume then," Davis told his NBC counterpart. Fine, Rogers said. But Rogers's capable factotum, Penny Bushell, happened to have noticed the number Davis was calling from.

NBC had just installed a digital phone system that featured caller ID, and the phone number that was displayed for Davis's call had a 212 area code, which meant it had been placed in Manhattan. And Davis was claiming he couldn't make it to New York . . . Having experienced too many corporate shenanigans in his time, Rogers dialed the number Bushell had seen on the digital readout after Davis hung up. A female voice chirped, "Mr. Diller's office," and that's how NBC discovered it wasn't going to be acquiring Lycos after all.

When he thinks about that day, Tom Rogers still manages a rueful laugh. He recalls the scenario: "Bob and I ended up having a little discussion on why [his talks with Diller] hadn't been disclosed. I guess caller ID was something that wasn't top of mind when Bob made the call. My advice [to him], for what it was worth at the time, was that the markets weren't going to accept [the Diller] deal. I didn't see how it was going to work."

The ill-fated attempt by Barry Diller's USA Networks to purchase Lycos was announced the following Monday, February 8. It would be dead by May, after a large drop in the Lycos share price, and after large Lycos shareholder David Wetherell, CEO of CMGI, who had at first welcomed the deal, decided he didn't like Diller as a partner after all. Wetherell blocked the deal, telling intimates that Diller knew little about the online world. Davis, who was furious with Wetherell, had outsmarted himself.

Barry Diller is notorious for making his deal partners question their sanity, and he's also widely regarded as a control freak who has little tolerance for anyone else's input. Despite the fact that he needs big-money men to help him make his deals, he inevitably ends up squeezing them out and publicly belittling them. Diller partner Edgar Bronfman, whose Seagram's fortune had bankrolled Diller's buyout of USA Networks, was constantly being mocked in the entertainment press, with much of the material provided by Diller cronies.

Wetherell had no intention of suffering the same fate, and he frequently insisted to insiders that, in a meeting he had with Diller, the media mogul had demonstrated that his actual knowledge of the Internet was minimal, certainly not sufficient to impress a guy with a software background like Wetherell. To Wetherell, Diller was an arrogant braggart and Hollywood type who had no business taking control of a major piece of the World Wide Web, and Davis could never convince him otherwise.

For its part, NBC soldiered on without Lycos, convinced there were other opportunities. CNBC had been built piecemeal by Rogers from the ashes of two failed cable networks: Tempo, owned by TeleCommunications, Inc., and the Financial News Network, which had been put up for sale in the early '90s after having been accused of various improprieties. FNN was co-owned by Data Broadcasting Corp., a Midwestern-based financial data company whose decision to get into the Internet would cause yet another headache for NBC's Bob Wright.

The Lycos/NBC conundrum was accompanied by other possible deals. Before Davis had come calling, Data Broadcasting had approached NBC to request a meeting with CNBC CEO (later chairman) Bill Bolster, with a proposal to join with the cable network to create a web site about investing and the stock market. Bolster refused the invitation, complaining it wasn't worth his time. ("Bolster didn't understand the Internet," says a former NBC executive.) Data Broadcasting made a deal with CBS's Mel Karmazin instead, and the resulting Web property, co-owned by the two companies, became CBS MarketWatch. That business went public in spring 1999 and quickly soared to more than $100 a share. Soon Bob Wright was screaming that his minions had mishandled a huge opportunity; CBS MarketWatch was the logical extension on the Web of what CNBC was doing on television. At this point an onlooker might have asked: Why didn't NBC simply create its own MarketWatch–type service at CNBC.com?

CNBC's web site had been largely a promotional tool for the cable network for much of the late 1990s—the result of a little-known term of the deal between Microsoft and NBC that had created MSNBC. When that agreement had been made in 1996, NBC took responsibility for running the cable channel, while Microsoft took charge of the web site, MSNBC.com. But because Microsoft had been concerned that NBC was planning to double-cross Redmond by turning CNBC.com into a competitor on the Web, as part of the deal it included a $27 million payment to NBC that came with the stipulation that the network would not launch any competitive news web sites in the areas in which MSNBC.com specialized, including general and business news and sports. That left little role for CNBC.com, and as the Internet boomed in the late '90s, NBC's Bob Wright began to see that concession as a costly mistake. "CNBC was crippled on the Internet," the former NBC executive says. By 1999 Bob Wright and his chief dealmaker, Tom Rogers, were determined not to get sandbagged again.

For Rogers, whose subsequent Internet deal-making would be the occasion for major headlines, media companies had consistently stumbled in their Internet efforts because they didn't know how to integrate new media with old. Many such businesses made new media a part-time hobby, he charged. "Even if they did do it full-time, it was still a function of [a lack of] integration. What Time Warner did with Pathfinder is not terribly different from what most traditional media companies have done on the Internet and continue to do. They set up separate operations, staffed by a separate group. There may be some soft linkages between what they're doing on the traditional side and their new-media efforts, but they basically report to different people. The incentives are different. They created all kinds of boundaries that had people negotiating almost at arms' length, which creates turf and ownership issues of who has what, and why. It creates a lot of internal conflicts among people who aren't really focused on extending the franchise beyond that, and it's really not doing what you need to do. The core of the operation isn't thought of as having at its heart the need to drive to its existing cost structure the success of the new offering. As a result it becomes separated and distant, and boundary and turf issues surface, [as well as] compensation jealousies, and all those other things develop."

This observation was clearly not informing the portal race that had developed in the summer of 1998 and culminated with NBC's failed attempt at Lycos. In June 1998 Disney announced it would buy 43 percent of Infoseek, the Silicon Valley search engine and portal, for $70 million in cash and its ownership in Starwave. At around the same time, it had been reported in the *Financial Times* that AT&T had tried to buy AOL and had been rebuffed. The previous week NBC had announced plans to pay $26.2 million for a majority stake in CNET Inc.'s Snap! Web portal service. All of this frenzied activity took place within a two-week period. All the big-media companies and telecommunications giants had become convinced by this point that the Internet business was going to be huge; in fact, it might just replace everything they owned. If they didn't establish themselves online now, they might wind up being viewed the way IBM was in the '90s, as the company that let Bill Gates develop Windows because they didn't think software had a consumer marketplace.

NBC's Snap! announcement, in particular, was a revelatory moment for the

Time Warner group, who, only six weeks earlier, had had an opportunity for a deal with Snap! According to Linda McCutcheon, CNET founder Halsey Minor had offered them a major stake in the just-launching portal for only about $10 million in TV and print promotion and some nominal stock outlay. This potential deal had collapsed after Jerry Levin met Halsey Minor and disapproved of the attitude of the slick CNET representative. "Halsey was seen as a young whippersnapper, and I was like, 'So what?'" McCutcheon remembers.

"I haven't met an Internet company that wasn't arrogant, to some extent," Rogers says. "There's also a degree of entrepreneurial success that allows these people to talk with a degree of authority that most of the people you deal with in the traditional media worlds don't have. The media guys are generally not the guys who created those businesses or franchises."

By the late '90s, cable empires were already maturing businesses. If you had a big job at a cable or broadcast network, chances were that it was just a job; you weren't an entrepreneur with that "vision thing" that drives self-made men and women. The Internet CEOs were largely the people who had built their own businesses, and consequently their entire outlook was more fervent, more evangelistic. While media companies like Time, CBS, and NBC liked to celebrate their heritage with reference to legendary figures like Edward R. Murrow and Henry Luce, Internet executives tended to dismiss anything that happened before the Internet as essentially irrelevant. They had all the moral fervor of the French revolutionaries or the Khmer Rouge, whose key minions actually introduced new calendars starting at Year One. It was a crucial difference in outlook, and it produced a major disconnect between the two sides.

However cocksure Halsey Minor might have seemed to media people, his Snap! was one of the only up-and-coming portals that was a feasible target for NBC control. Rogers had always been hemmed in by the fact that big acquisitions were frowned upon within the GE family, because such deals would be reflected negatively on the all-important bottom line. GE favored buying smaller companies and growing them.

That's what Rogers had done in cable, and it was the approach he preferred with the Internet: "We decided that rather than pay a lot of money for something that even then we realized we weren't sure which way it would go, we would focus on something that had smart people who looked like they'd created some value on the Internet," he says. "CNET by that time was already a player in that regard. Something that was small enough that we could do the kind of deal where we weren't risking anything upfront, and it was all a function of what we created out of it. The issue with Snap! was to begin to get us into a position where we had some kind of general offering, like a television network, that we could use as a vehicle, to tie to NBC."

But investing in Snap! and integrating it with NBC, and the network's later Internet acquisition, a community site called Xoom, proved a daunting task. How could a TV network create a differentiated online product? A TV network represents many different things to its large and heterogenous audience. It doesn't have a single face it shows the public. In the afternoons NBC is *Days of Our Lives*. At 6:30 p.m. NBC is Tom Brokaw. At 8 p.m. on Thursdays it's *Friends,* and at 10 p.m. that same night it's *E.R.* These programs aren't necessarily related to one another, nor do they have to be. The people who produce *Days* have no connection whatsoever to the people who produce *E.R.*—they both just happen to sell their product to the same network. But portals don't work this way. They have to have a thematically coherent home page, and the question of what that home page should contain would bedevil NBC and the other networks.

A former NBC executive puts it this way: "The single biggest impediment to the growth of Snap! was the tie to the traditional broadcast affiliate distribution. That was a limitation that came up in almost everything that we've done. NBC is not a pure content-marketing company. It is heavily tethered to distribution channels, which can be enormously valuable but also have enormous problems."

In other words, because NBC was so dependent on its TV stations to broadcast its signal, it would be difficult for the network to make any move that didn't feature its stations front and center. And what kind of web site could accomplish that? CBS had already failed spectacularly with its effort to integrate its local stations into its local news Web play. NBC has never resolved that question; in the end, it may simply not be resolvable. Snap! quickly evolved into a fairly standard portal and never caught up with bigger rivals like Yahoo!

Jake Winebaum's ambitions were equal to those of Tom Rogers. Spurred on by Starwave's Mike Slade, Disney had started discussions with a host of portals, including Excite and Lycos. An Excite agreement was ultimately stymied by a previous deal that Excite had done with Netscape, which blocked a partnership with a player like Disney. (Excite was later bought by AT&T.) And talks with AOL got under way again in 1997 and 1998, represented on the AOL side by Ted Leonsis and David Colburn, and on the Disney side by Stephen

Wadsworth and Jake Winebaum, among others. The Disney people felt almost patronized by AOL, which clearly believed it had no compelling reason to sell out to the Mouse. The same divergence existed as in earlier talks—AOL wanted Disney to cede its brands in exchange for a cash payment, and Disney wanted to control its brands through some kind of joint venture. AOL didn't wish to establish that kind of precedent with media companies, and didn't think it had to. Disney finally agreed to license ABC News to AOL, one of the last cash-payment deals AOL made for such a property. But anything beyond that was looking problematic.

Winebaum found Infoseek the most accommodating of the available alternatives, partly because he was dealing with CEO Harry Motro, who knew how big media worked and wanted a Disney deal. Motro, 38 at the time, with a B.S. from the University of Virginia, had gotten his start at Coopers & Lybrand, where he spent six years, focusing on telecommunications clients. He graduated to CNN, where he was first involved with mergers and acquisitions and in 1994 founded CNN Interactive. With that background, he was far more receptive to the old-media world than many other Internet executives of the late '90s, many of whom assumed that it would simply fade away into oblivion.

It was Motro who initiated the conversation, having already met Starwave's Mike Slade when Starwave had approached CNN about a news and sports deal before it was purchased by Disney. So he called Slade and made a request: "Introduce me to Jake Winebaum." The three—Slade, Motro, and Winebaum—met for the first time in the summer of 1997, but Winebaum wasn't ready to commit at that time. A protracted series of discussions followed, with Disney still talking to Excite.

A big incentive for Infoseek to form an alliance with Disney was the flood of promotion, from ABC and other Disney properties, that was built into the deal. The exposure Disney guaranteed was valued at about $165 million, which meant that it would promote Infoseek properties with "interstitial" ads and features. Each TV network has two kinds of ad space—that which is allocated to the network for program promotion, and that which is sold to advertisers. For ABC, it wasn't an overly costly proposition to hand some of its program promotion time over to Infoseek.

As we have seen, Winebaum's strategy from the start was to mount a credible challenge to AOL and Yahoo! To accomplish that, he needed a publicly traded stock like Infoseek to use as collateral to build a significant online company. Infoseek had gone public in 1996 with a somewhat premature IPO, because the company peaked before the huge run-up in Internet stocks. From its initial price of $12, it had slumped to $4 by the early summer of 1997, when Motro finally joined with Disney, alleviating some of the pressure on its equity. With the deal done, Disney was now armed with 25.8 million shares of Infoseek and a further $139 million worth of stock warrants that would allow Burbank ultimately to take a majority stake in the company. Few at the time knew just how expensive it would be to exercise those warrants, and from the perspective of June 1998 Winebaum looked like a genius.

In public, Motro was effusive about the deal. "It changes everybody's view on who's going to be a player in this industry," Motro told *Interactive Week*. "I've got the biggest and best partner. Now we're just going to let the chips fall where they may." Privately, however, he was soon telling confidants that relations were less than smooth between the new partners, though he had a massive trump card with the warrants that Disney held. If Eisner or Winebaum wanted to force him out and take control, it would cost well over $1 billion. Winebaum and Eisner would eventually have to exercise their warrants, for they wouldn't be able to tolerate a maverick like him operating independently. Indeed, the fissures in the personal relationships of the top executives at the two companies quickly began to be obvious. While Motro says that Eisner is "brilliant, a great leader, a very human person," like other observers of the Magic Kingdom he feels that Disney's leader became too grandiose and remote after the death of his number-two, Frank Wells, in a helicopter accident.

Motro says Team Disney had become somewhat formulaic by the time of the Infoseek acquisition, with every major venture subject to stringent financial analysis by an all-powerful corporate finance group, a system that proved confining given the lightning-fast pace of the Internet. Winebaum found a way of working with the number-crunchers, but Motro observes that he never "sucked up" to Eisner the way many junior Disney-ites do: "Jake had enough confidence that he didn't need to do that."

Although the Disney Internet Group was housed in a different building than the Team Disney headquarters in Burbank, lending a certain independence to the operation—or as much independence as any Disney-owned business was likely to get—the corporate style remained overbearing and stifling, and most of the Infoseek cadre fled. Of the original Infoseek team when Disney was bought in, virtually 90 percent left the company soon thereafter, Motro estimates, unwilling to accommodate themselves to the Disney regimen, sometimes pointedly referred to as "Mauschwitz."

But all that came later. In 1998 it still looked as if Winebaum had succeeded in monetizing Starwave greatly in a very short time, and had made a great leap forward toward Internet domination, with the first media-owned portal.

"It's very simple," Chris Dixon, head of the communications group at PaineWebber, said at the time. "It was not about just doing a portal deal. It was about getting a market value for Starwave"—to turn it into a valuable asset and hence to use other people's money to go out and make a much bigger deal. Analysts like Dixon were impressed with the transaction at the time because it seemed to have allowed Disney to operate on the same playing field, with the same assets—principally stock—as AOL and Yahoo! No media company had done that yet.

By combining Starwave with Disney's online assets, Winebaum had quickly built up a business with a $300 million evaluation, a feat Time Inc. wasn't close to achieving. When confronted with this fact, Pathfinder spokesperson Graham Cannon quoted Don Logan's comments in the company's latest annual report: "Using comparable multiples of publicly traded Internet companies, Pathfinder is already a very valuable business."

At Time Inc., Dan Okrent was watching the debacle with growing dismay. Clearly Pathfinder wasn't worth $300 million, and it was hard to determine what its true worth was. Okrent says that the Time Inc. discussions with Snap! were propelled by the same logic that had motivated Disney, and that Time Warner CFO Richard Bressler, who had taken a special interest in new media, was "really pissed off" when NBC grabbed Snap! "He felt we could have done that," Okrent recalls.

With Snap!, Infoseek, and Excite all out of the picture, another major portal player and search engine, AltaVista, began to look attractive to Time. What ensued was perhaps Time Warner's most painful, protracted, and unsuccessful negotiation yet. It was also the deal through which many Time Warner executives hoped to get rich. By 1999, increasing numbers of former media players had already done so.

Alan Meckler, rebuffed by virtually every magazine player in the business, ended up selling MecklerMedia and his Internet World tradeshow, by the late '90s an international extravaganza, for $274 million to Penton Publishing. Meckler took the approximately $90 million he personally made on that deal and plowed some of it back into the Web company he'd started called Internet.com. The public company had a valuation in the hundreds of millions during the Web boom.

Paul Sagan, after a lengthy sabbatical in Europe, reemerged as CEO of a publicly traded Boston-area online video-distribution company with the un-likely name of Akamai that soared in value in 1999, making his stock worth hundreds of millions of dollars. Walter Isaacson is fond of saying that two people who worked for him at Pathfinder ended up being worth $500 million each, at least on paper: Sagan and Jim Kinsella. The latter had left MSNBC, where he ran the business side of the Redmond-based MSNBC.com, and had become CEO of a Dutch-based ISP called World Online. After World Online was acquired by Italy's Tiscali SpA, Kinsella's paper worth soon matched Sagan's. (Kinsella won't comment when asked if he was ever worth $500 mil-lion, but he laughs when told that Isaacson had said he was.)

Harry Motro, as CEO of Infoseek, ultimately reaped a huge reward when Disney bought the company out. He declines to say just how much, but the wealth was substantial and real, so much so that he hasn't had to work full-time since, although he did start his own venture fund, Motro Ventures. He joined other media refugees—like Forbes's Jeff Cunningham (who quickly made mil-lions in CMGI stock before that company's crash); MTV's Doug Greenlaw, who became CEO of Switchboard.com; Tom Phillips, who became CEO of Deja.com; and Excite CEO George Bell, a former Times Mirror executive—in gaining some measure of stock-option wealth by riding the market wave before the downturn.

It's fair to say that, as the decade ended, most media executives were think-ing about cashing in on the dot-com explosion. They thought that Meckler and Evans were no smarter than they—so why were those two swimming in stock riches while they were still salary men? The situation was bound to pro-voke some excessive and regrettable business decisions. And it did.

AltaVista in Play

As the Web began to develop into an increasingly valuable commodity during 1998 and 1999, it became clear that Time Warner had to become involved with it at a corporate level. No longer could new media be allowed to be merely a quarreling fiefdom run out of the magazine company. Dan Okrent and colleagues across the Time Warner spectrum accordingly formed a small, informal new-media oversight group that, for the first time, involved the other Time divisions on an ongoing basis. The group included Linda McCutcheon, Warner Bros. Online executives Jim Moloshok and Jim Banister, and CNN's Lou Dobbs.

Dobbs and Moloshok may have arrived a little late to the new-media party, but they were in their own way far more ambitious than either Okrent or Isaacson, who were, after all, Time Inc-ers who simply wanted to find a comfortable berth within their home port.

Dobbs, who has a legendary temper and is prone to volcanic eruptions over minutiae, was the longstanding host of the hugely popular *Moneyline,* on CNN. While this alone would have made him powerful at Time Warner, he had also been instrumental in developing one of Ted Turner's pet projects, the CNNfn cable channel. (Dobbs was a close confidant of the maverick Turner, who had been given a somewhat powerless role as vice chairman after Time Warner bought his company in 1996.) Although Dobbs clearly wanted a big role in new media, he was too busy producing a daily show during this period to have any lasting impact on what the company actually did online.

The Warner part of Time Warner, headquartered on the West Coast, had entered the online fray later than the Time side in New York. Craig Bromberg lays claim to having built one of the first movie web sites, for one of Warner's *Batman* movies, at a time when there was no new-media activity worthy of the name from the Left Coast. Later, as Internet movie promotion proliferated, Warner Bros. produced its movie sites in New York, with a small team headed by Don Buckley, domiciled in a big office tower on Sixth Avenue. The West Coast team, headed by Jim Moloshok, eventually turned their attention to new media, and when they did, they started eclipsing what was left of Pathfinder.

Jim Moloshok's whole previous career had been in the TV business. Soon after college, he went to work for a local station, and then clawed his way up to a job as senior vice president of marketing and advertising at programmer Lorimar-Telepictures, which had been affiliated with producer Aaron Spelling. That company was bought by Warner shortly before the Time Warner merger. "The first thing I worked on at Telepictures was a package of Bruce Lee movies," he recalls. (The movies didn't actually have Bruce Lee in them, but that was another story.) The first big series Moloshok was involved with was the syndicated *People's Court,* followed by *Here's Lucy, Real People,* and *The Love Connection.* After Warner and Time merged in 1989, he had responsibility for the syndication of such off-network Warner hits as *Friends* and *E.R.*

Before being swallowed by Warner, Lorimar-Telepictures had prided itself as being smaller and more nimble than the syndication giants like Disney and Paramount. By 1994 Moloshok and his crew in Burbank were watching what was going on in New York with Time Inc. New Media with some dismay, and notions that they could do better.

"At Warner Bros., no one really embraced the Internet in the beginning," says Moloshok. "It percolated up. Don Buckley in New York was doing things with E-Drive on CompuServe [an early entertainment venue] in 1993 and 1994. On the West Coast, we were launching *Extra.*"

Extra was Warner's fairly successful effort to create a "hipper" version of Paramount's *Entertainment Tonight* for the much-coveted prime access time slot for TV syndication. When it was first conceived, Time Warner had announced the celebrity-heavy show as a showcase for corporate "synergy," to be produced with much input from *People* and *Entertainment Weekly* magazines in New York and Los Angeles. It didn't really turn out that way, because television and print are not necessarily compatible media. (One hapless scribe, *EW*'s Alan Carter, did try a stint as a correspondent on *Extra* only to find that he was asking questions that were far too provocative. He was quickly dropped.)

Though the print relationship was unsuccessful, *Extra*'s producers decided some interactive elements might give the show a little extra zip. Moloshok says that his first exposure to Web production came when Warner teamed up with Hollywood.com, an entertainment-oriented company, to produce a site called @Extra on AOL, an adjunct to the TV show. "We were making money," Moloshok recalls; Warner Bros. Online received some advertising support from clients like McDonald's early on.

In September 1994 an intense young man named Jeff Weiner joined Warner Bros. Weiner had been a highly paid consultant for a number of major companies and was soon assigned the task of developing ideas for new-media extensions for the company. Weiner came up with a business plan for a unit to be based in Burbank called Warner Bros. Interactive Entertainment. According to former Warner Bros. executive Jim Banister, who worked closely with Moloshok and Weiner, the original WBIE plan had four components—CD-ROM publishing, licensing, location-based entertainment, and online. Weiner was aware that the interactive group would have to move cautiously, given Warner Bros.' history with new technology. Under Steve Ross, who had died in December 1992, it had acquired Atari, the games manufacturer that had seemed to be the interactive future but turned into an expensive disaster.

"The company had gotten terribly traumatized by Atari. It almost brought all of Warner Communications down," Weiner explains, "and there was enormous reluctance to get back into any inventory-based business." The vision of all those unsold Atari units piled up in warehouses was still haunting Warner. Because online wasn't an "inventory-based" operation, however, it looked to be a less risky proposition, and, as Weiner says, "the company approved the online portion of the plan. The mandate was to break even."

In December 1994 WBIE issued an in-house invitation: "What we did was put out the word throughout the company—anyone who is interested in online, please come and see us," Moloshok says. About 60 people throughout the creative and business divisions of Warner responded, and Steve Koltai, who was in charge of strategic planning at Warner, was impressed. "He saw that there seemed to be something here. The CD-ROMs went by the wayside."

The interactive division at first reported to the Consumer Products group, which wasn't totally supportive of its efforts. "When we started, the company to a great extent was looking at everything as cash flow, like they would for a syndicated show. They didn't look at it as asset appreciation. They didn't see it as an asset play. Had they gotten into some of the initial projects that we proposed internally, they would have had really good assets. But they didn't understand it. They didn't use it; they didn't consume it. You could probably figure out how to launch a television show if you're in the movie business;

maybe you would have to shoot a little closer up because it's a smaller screen, but you could generally figure out how to get in there. If you're not an online user, it's very difficult to understand the medium," Moloshok continues.

Entertainment conglomerates had a history of being slow to embrace new technologies. In the 1980s, a Connecticut-based company called Vestron Video had been able to build a business by licensing movies for home video release, because the studios had no interest in entering that business. Only later, after having left a huge amount of money on the table, did the studios launch their own home video divisions. (Vestron tried to get into movie production and distribution itself when the studio product dried up, finding early success with *Dirty Dancing* but flopping with all subsequent releases.)

Jim Banister observes that, even when entertainment companies did begin to get serious about going online, they tended to approach it with tunnel vision. He cites an original *Star Trek* episode, in which a salt-sucking monster was able to project wish-fulfillment fantasies onto the crew of the *Enterprise.* (When Doctor "Bones" McCoy looked at the creature, for example, he saw his lost girlfriend.) In the same way, Banister explains, "TV guys look at online and see it as a TV outlet. The home video people see it as a pay-per-view outlet. The consumer product and retail guys look at it as a new store. That pervaded all aspects at Warner."

Despite the static from corporate, the WBIE team moved ahead with a varied menu on AOL. Besides @Extra, the Warner Bros. AOL areas soon included interactive hubs for *Babylon 5,* a sci-fi series; Warner Bros. Records; and *Insomniacs Asylum,* for late-night users. Warner Bros., which also owned the syndicated, popular *Rosie O'Donnell Show,* received good promotion from the AOL areas. But the promotion it offered AOL was more valuable.

Moloshok notes, "What AOL was paying for was the marketing exposure. Rosie would mention something [about AOL]; it would be in the promos. To this day, AOL still doesn't understand the value of the content behind the brand, as much as the marketing value. It's not really *People* content they care about; it's having the *People* logo there and a statement that you can only get *People* on AOL."

Even as early as 1995 there had been concerns expressed at Warner about AOL's ultimate intentions as a partner. In June 1995, after the WB interactive group had made a major presentation, Warner Bros. chairman Terry Semel, who co-chaired with Robert Daly, warned, "This is rhetorical, you don't have to answer right now. But we need to figure out a way to stop other people from building a network based on our content. That was what happened in the forties and fifties with broadcast television and again in the seventies and eighties with basic cable."

To protect their brands and to present them online apart from AOL, the WB group eventually created Web content that first found its way onto Path-finder. The WBIE unit soon took the more suitable name Warner Bros. On-line, which quickly began to take a far more active role in online affairs than anyone from the Left Coast had previously done. A "skunk works" Web proj-ect called Entertaindom from Warner Bros. Online appeared on the Web in spring 1998, the beginnings of an entertainment hub.

Because Moloshok was overseeing a production group based partly in New York, he set up an office in Manhattan and began spending much time there. He began reporting back to Burbank that the new-media operation at Time Warner had devolved into infighting and chaos, and that Pathfinder wasn't go-ing to succeed on its own. The Burbank group decided that they had to get more proactive and not wait for Time Inc. New Media to produce anything co-herent.

There had been sporadic attempts by Warner executives to escape the Pathfinder orbit. In one of the few recorded moments of actual "synergy" across divisional lines at the sprawling Time Warner, CNNfn's Rich Zahradnik, who was based in New York, and WB's Jim Banister, based in Burbank, collab-orated during 1997 on a plan they called GoTo. This was a portal play, with a deep Web directory in such categories as sports, finance, entertainment, and kids. Zahradnik, who ran the web site for CNNfn, was a former trade maga-zine scribe at media publications like *The Hollywood Reporter,* and he had a good sense of what was going on in the industry. He had been particularly in-sistent on a heavy directory component for the new web site. Instead of the Pathfinder straitjacket, tied as it was to the print side, GoTo would be run by a new unit, Time Warner Online (TWO).

Jeff Weiner wrote the business plan for the GoTo venture, and it was sub-mitted to the corporate side, where it wound up on the desk of a little-known Time Warner business functionary named Terry Hershey. A blond, thin, per-petually nervous-looking woman of around 50, Hershey was notorious within the company for not "getting" the online thing; new-media types complained that she didn't even have a Web connection on her desk. "Terry didn't under-stand it at first, so we went through God knows how many meetings, with thirty people at a conference table, from all around the company, most of them trying to kill it," Banister recalls. "[But] they couldn't find any real reason to kill it. Terry Hershey took a perfectly good business model, before the portal stocks went crazy, and repackaged it, put her little stamp on it, put her little memo under her name. It had never gotten to Jerry Levin before. And she killed it."

The final meeting evaluating the GoTo plan was held in fall 1997 and had dozens of people in attendance, including Lou Dobbs, Richard Bressler, and other Time Warner executives. The company had "low-level" analysts give a PowerPoint presentation to the group, few of whom were Web-savvy. (Moloshok later did an evaluation of what the meeting cost, factoring in the time of all the high-level suits involved, and arrived at a figure of $50,000.) Banister and Zahradnik realized fairly quickly that the gathering wouldn't go their way, because the phalanx of corporate bean counters was unlikely to embrace anything as out of the ordinary as a Web-style business plan.

As the meeting ended Hershey approached Banister and admonished him. "Why are you so negative?" she asked. Banister replied, "I'm not negative. I'm the most optimistic person out there. I believe this is what we should be doing, but this isn't the way to do business. You can't manage and make decisions by committee."

In the end, the group behind the GoTo plan, including Weiner, Banister, Moloshok, and Zahradnik, was told that the "numbers didn't work." Weiner says Levin "didn't think advertising would reach the critical mass to support the economics." Levin was advocating more of an alternative plan, something involving e-commerce.

Time Warner could have done well with the GoTo project if it had been introduced in the period when Internet evaluations were skyrocketing. Weiner estimates that building the directory would have cost about $75 million, which would have put the company in an excellent position when the portal stocks began their run-up in January 1998. Needless to say, this was a bitter pill to swallow in Burbank, where the trio of Moloshok, Banister, and Weiner had to watch the phenomenal success of companies like AltaVista, Lycos, Excite, and Yahoo! They, too, could have been portal contenders: Maybe they still *could* be.

As Weiner tells the story, portal fever finally did manage to reach Levin, and even if he wasn't about to build one, he did become interested for the first time in buying one: "Now that it bubbled up to Jerry, they wanted to pursue alternative strategies. And AltaVista then came into the picture."

The first major contact with AltaVista from Time had come through Linda McCutcheon, who had pursued a search-engine deal in 1998 with the company, trying to replace a "lame" Web search product called Verity, one of the many weaknesses inherent in Pathfinder. AltaVista agreed to pay Pathfinder

$250,000 for the traffic it would get replacing Verity on the Pathfinder home page.

Time Inc.'s editor in chief, Norm Pearlstine, McCutcheon's boss, liked to proclaim that search was the "spell-check of the '90s," and he proved highly receptive when McCutcheon began to champion the idea that Time Warner could buy AltaVista. Under the somewhat byzantine reporting structure in place then, McCutcheon had very little contact with Jerry Levin himself. "I had Norm's ear, and Norm had Levin's ear," is the way McCutcheon describes the relationship.

The Burbank group also started championing the AltaVista connection soon after the GoTo project tanked. Still another advocate who had Levin's ear on AltaVista was Steve Newhouse, who ran the Newhouse family's cable systems and had collaborated with Time Warner on many key projects, such as the Road Runner cable modem.

Weiner recalls being told by corporate, "'The other guys are talking to Alta-Vista, you guys should all get together,' so Terry Hershey became the central point of communications at first, and then CFO Rich [Bressler] got involved." McCutcheon recalls taking to AltaVista a Time delegation that included Hershey, Moloshok, and a CNN representative. "For about twenty minutes, I was driving the deal," McCutcheon says, "and then I woke up one day, and Terry Hershey was driving the deal."

According to Moloshok, Bressler later confided to him that Hershey wouldn't be the point person on the deal. Moloshok was told that he would have that responsibility, but that Hershey would still be involved to avoid creating corporate ill will. "Bressler said he didn't want her feelings to get hurt, which is typical Rich, always skirting the line, never saying yes or no. He said, 'Keep her up to date,'" Moloshok recalls.

AltaVista, which sometimes seems to have been born under a bad sign, appeared in California in 1995, at Digital Equipment Corporation's Research Lab in Palo Alto. The company says that it evolved from a chance lunch encounter. During the spring of 1995, three scientists at DEC in Palo Alto were discussing the latest line of Digital's Alpha 8400 computers. The 8400 was much faster than its rivals and could run database software at about 100 times the speed of any other available computer. One of the scientists—no one seems to recall which one—suggested that it would be fun to store every word on the Internet in a searchable database, and use the higher processing speed of the Alpha 8400 to deploy a "search engine" that could provide relevant information from that database.

The name came from a laboratory white board that had been partially erased but still bore the words "Alto," from Palo Alto, and "Vista." During a meeting someone called out, "How about Alto Vista" as a name? That name evolved into AltaVista, which means "high view," or the "view from above" in Spanish.

Despite its brilliance in engineering, DEC had no idea how to properly exploit AltaVista, and certainly didn't have any portal-building dreams. Instead of creating its own directory and competing against Yahoo!, DEC chose to license its search software to Yahoo!, which certainly made it money but made a lot more for Yahoo! AltaVista started a web site of its own after leasing its service to Yahoo!, but this operation got off to a shaky start.

In the mid-'90s, when URLs were available for a $50 license fee, DEC had not even bothered to wrest the www.altavista.com domain name from the tiny company, AltaVista Technology Inc. of Campbell, California, that had already registered it. DEC officials preferred the cumbersome designation, www. altavista.digital.com, a simple mistake that cost AltaVista millions of page views, because Web surfers entering the expected URL were directed to a California marketing site that bore no relation to what they were seeking. Much later, when the decision was finally made to purchase altavista.com, it ended up costing a painful $3.3 million. This was just one blunder in a string of bizarre moves from DEC officials.

Although the company lost much of its early-mover advantage, it still managed to be a top-10 site because its search engine was such a good one. And AltaVista stayed popular almost despite itself. Reporters who tried to communicate with the company were often directed to a low-level DEC manager who knew nothing about media, marketing, or what the potential of AltaVista could be. Indeed it was difficult to get anyone at the company to say anything about the web site that made much sense.

When Compaq Computer Corp. bought DEC in 1998, AltaVista came with it as part of the package. In a possibly apocryphal story repeated by top AltaVista executives, Compaq CEO Eckhard Pfeiffer is said to have been asked about AltaVista during the 1998 press conference announcing the DEC deal. The first question was about AltaVista, and Pfeiffer turned to a minion and asked, "What's AltaVista?"

Pfeiffer learned fairly quickly about the search site, and Compaq went through an elaborate search, run by Compaq executive Rod Shrock, for an AltaVista CEO. But Shrock would often not even call back high-level candidates sent to his office. Ultimately Shrock decided that no one measured up to the job, and he appointed himself CEO of AltaVista in January 1999, announcing plans to spin the company off from Compaq with an IPO that many valued at up to $5 billion. Eckhard Pfeiffer, now converted to a portal advocate, was enthusiastic about the idea. "We see this as a significant opportunity for Compaq to expand its share of the rapidly growing Internet market for content and services. It also enables us to unlock the tremendous value of AltaVista for our shareholders."

Despite the public show of support, observers felt that Compaq wasn't that much more savvy about tending to AltaVista than DEC had been. "They were a computer manufacturer who had no idea what AltaVista was," Dan Okrent says of Compaq. "It came in another deal. They had no idea what they had."

Throughout this process, the talks between AltaVista and Time Warner still continued, stretching on for almost seven torturous months at the end of 1998 and the beginning of 1999. "The original AltaVista deal was for us to take control of the asset, roughly half of it," says Weiner. "We were going to contribute marketing considerations and content and no cash, Jerry was adamant that it not be cash. We initially spoke to them about it, and they were very open to the idea."

Early on during these talks, Moloshok had been summoned to New York for a meeting with Norm Pearlstine, who grilled him about how the deal might work. His answers seemed satisfactory, and he was officially given Pearlstine's imprimatur. This was, in fact, something of a Rubicon, because it represented the first acknowledgment from Time Inc. that it was no longer taking primary responsibility for new media. The Pathfinder era was definitively over. Shortly after, Time Inc. announced that Pathfinder was officially dead and that the individual magazines and media properties would assume responsibility for their own web sites and AOL relationships. It was a legitimization of a situation that had been de facto for more than a year.

By the time the online group began its meetings with newly appointed AltaVista CEO Rod Shrock at the end of 1998, however, the situation had grown more complicated. Compaq was going through a difficult period, and Shrock's big plans clashed with the bottom-line realities.

Events quickly bore out Dan Okrent's assertion that Compaq didn't know how to deal with the Internet industry. After the January announcement that AltaVista would be spun off from Compaq with an IPO, Shrock made a series of acquisitions costing about $500 million, including the e-commerce destination Shopping.com for more than $200 million, and Zip2.com, which built portal sites for newspapers, for an outsized $300 million.

Insiders say that Shrock never really understood what Zip2 did and was shocked to discover that it was actually a much more mature company than he realized, and thus didn't have as much room to grow as he had assumed. In one meeting, Shrock waxed effusive about the tens of thousands of newspapers that Zip2 would cobble together into a network that would beat Microsoft's Sidewalk and AOL's Digital City at their own game. When an underling noted that most of the papers he had in mind had tiny circulations and wouldn't be worth working with, Shrock's enthusiasm for Zip2 cooled quickly.

Nevertheless, in early 1999 Shrock was still full of plans to conquer the Web world. In one meeting with Time Warner reps, he told the group that he was thinking about buying Amazon, the top e-commerce player, which had a market cap in the billions, far more money than AltaVista had available. "We're going to play in e-commerce, we're going to play really big," Shrock told the group. The Amazon purchase didn't happen, but Shopping.com did, a deal that stunned the Time Warner group, which was still forced to play at least nominally by the old rules, where P/E ratios mattered and acquisitions were expected to have positive cash flow attached. "Shopping.com [was] easily the biggest piece-of-shit deal I've seen in six years in the industry," Weiner says.

Time Warner became convinced, because of the Shopping.com debacle, that Shrock could not remain in place under any circumstances if they were to buy into AltaVista. "We were adamant that we would have to control the asset," Weiner says. "We would not do a deal where he was controlling this thing." Despite their differences over Shrock's leadership, a deal was cobbled together during a series of marathon sessions headed by a Time Warner team consisting of Bressler, Moloshok, and Weiner, backed up by Okrent and Hershey in New York. It was never set exactly who would lead AltaVista under Time Warner, nor was it clear how exactly an IPO would be mounted.

By this time, Banister had become a skeptic, convinced that between Time Warner's corporate straitjacket and the woes befalling Compaq, "it would never happen." Part of the problem was that Moloshok and Weiner were getting conflicting input from various divisions of Time Warner. The period during which Time Inc.'s Isaacson, Kinsella, and Judson had been three musketeers, exploring the world of online on their own, without interference from any other part of the company, was long over.

Among the kibbitzers in the AltaVista negotiations were CNN's advertising guru, Steve Hyer, and Turner Broadcasting's CEO, Terence McGuirk, who both demanded various deal concessions. Moloshok would return to his hotel during the negotiations and immediately have to jump onto a series of conference calls from various division heads asking for details on how the advertising would be sold, how the business would be structured, and other key points. Moloshok was told that CNN would have to have responsibility for selling all advertising appearing opposite any news on AltaVista, which would have been a major blow to AltaVista's existing sales force.

An even more vexing issue was that of Time Warner's content, and how that content would be "boxed" into a digital asset that AltaVista and Time Warner would share. Under Levin, Time Warner had essentially accepted the idea that ultimately all the assets would become digital assets, that ultimately the main product of what today is a magazine or TV show would be online. So-called "electronic rights," covered in the little contract clause that had wreaked such havoc at Hachette Filipacchi New Media, were ultimately to become the key to the future development of all the brands at Time Warner, from Looney Tunes to *People* magazine. Giving up half those rights to a company as apparently unstable as AltaVista seemed almost inconceivable.

Before long, the deal began to teeter under its own weight, as more and more "bricks" were added to a structure that had been at least nominally structurally sound. Some sessions ran until 1 in the morning, and during one protracted stay at AltaVista's Massachusetts headquarters, Moloshok and Weiner had to have clothes flown to them from Los Angeles. Negotiations went down to the wire. Both Dan Okrent and Linda McCutcheon recall being told the week of Martin Luther King Day that the deal was a definite go. Okrent remembers leaving the Time & Life Building that Friday expecting a formal announcement the following Monday.

But in the end, the control issue became paramount, and the various claims couldn't be reconciled. "That's ultimately how it fell apart," Weiner recalls. "AltaVista started by being willing to cede control, but by the end they would retain a majority, and Shrock would run it and would retain control." Bressler, who was in the final negotiation with Shrock, had the responsibility for reporting back that Time Warner was giving up.

A few months after the collapse of the AltaVista deal in early 1999, Moloshok flew to Atlanta to take part in a cross-company meeting about a planned new cable channel and Internet site pitched to women, a favorite project of Ted Turner's. Terry McGuirk made his entrance and announced, much to the chagrin of both Moloshok and Newhouse, "I want to congratulate everyone in the room. This is the group that killed the AltaVista deal."

The Warner contingent was incredulous, because they remained convinced that Turner Broadcasting had prevented the deal, as CNN purposely inserted demands that undermined the negotiations. CNN didn't think Time Warner needed a portal; CNN.com should serve in that capacity. Further, CNN didn't want to find itself buried under layers of Internet management that would ultimately have included Moloshok, Weiner, and others. It was another example of pure rivalry across Time Warner divisions, a factor that had killed so many initiatives at the company.

As it happened, one reason for Shrock's reluctance to cede control was that several other suitors were already courting AltaVista in early 1999, including CMGI. That company's chairman, David Wetherell, had always chafed at having to deal with Lycos CEO Bob Davis. Wetherell was the largest single shareholder and a board member, but Davis often insisted on operating independently. Indeed Wetherell often acted as if all the heads of companies in which he had a stake were just so many chess pieces to be moved around on a board.

After the collapse of the Lycos/USA Networks merger, there were bad feelings between Davis and Wetherell. While the two maintained an outward impression of comity, insiders knew there was no love lost. An urban legend even circulated that Davis, frustrated with Wetherell's blocking his plans, had once driven his SUV across Wetherell's carefully tended lawn in Andover. As apocryphal as this story surely is, it illustrated the animosity people assume existed between the two men.

On the other hand, AltaVista looked like an asset that CMGI could own outright. And Wetherell was much more comfortable with Shrock than with Davis and didn't mind leaving him in place. CMGI would announce its majority purchase of AltaVista, in August 1999, with Shrock still in place as CEO. Shrock had gotten what he wanted, but Time Warner executives looked on in frustration. They felt that they had missed one of the last available portal plays. Time Warner bureaucracy seemed to be getting in the way of making what appeared in 1999 to be an all-important online deal. It left some in the Time Warner ranks more determined to ultimately succeed with a new partner.

CHAPTER 14

Hub Caps Unite, You Have Nothing to Lose but Your Jobs

With the collapse of the AltaVista deal, Time Warner was effectively without an Internet strategy, a dangerous position for America's largest media conglomerate to be in during early 1999, when Internet stocks were reaching unheard-of levels. Around that time a trio of Virginia college students sold a tiny stock-discussion web site they'd built, Raging Bull, to CMGI for a few million dollars, making more money from digital media than Time Warner had seen.

Pathfinder was dead, the AltaVista lifeline was dead, and the Time Warner web sites had slid far down the Media Metrix totem pole. Time Warner thought of itself as a perennial winner, but how to explain that it had no Web assets worthy of its name? Analyst Tom Wolzien described its position succinctly: "They set themselves up to fail. I think Levin has really tried to promote the company through grand visions and schemes, like the FSN and Pathfinder. These things could just as easily have been rationally presented as not being the future of the universe." If Levin didn't come up with a solution soon, he was going to look like a "clueless" Luddite, an image that he'd spent much of his career disproving.

His salvation came riding out of the West, once again in the form of Jim Moloshok and Jim Banister. After the failure of his GoTo plan, Banister had kept clear of Time Warner's corporate mess and had remained in Burbank, working to create an entertainment powerhouse on the World Wide Web.

It had been widely believed in Los Angeles, and prophesied many times from the podium at Digital Hollywood and the Jupiter Entertainment summit in Los Angeles, that it would be the entertainment industry that would ultimately rule online. Powerful people with huge assets believed that, including Steven Spielberg, Ron Howard, and others who had invested in an entertainment portal called Pop.com. AOL's Ted Leonsis had spent a fortune a few years earlier trying to build a big entertainment destination on AOL and the Web called Entertainment Boulevard, initially in partnership with the late Brandon Tartikoff, former president of NBC Entertainment. In early 1999, despite many efforts to do so, no one company seemed to rule online entertainment. Warner Bros. Online thought the relative emptiness of the playing field could give it a shot, and so Moloshok and Weiner returned to the fold and began to concentrate "under the radar" on the Entertaindom site, which had been set up the previous year.

In February 1999, Jerry Levin was in Los Angeles to attend an annual meeting of Time Warner West Coast–based divisions. Sandy Reisenbach, head of marketing at Warner Bros., had been placed in charge of squiring the CEO around Burbank, with a group that also included Time Warner President Richard Parsons and CFO Richard Bressler. One morning the group unexpectedly found itself with a few hours to kill, because its meeting didn't start until 11.

"Sandy, who's always been a major supporter of our efforts, said, 'Let's go over to Warner Bros. Online and see what those guys are doing,'" Moloshok recalls. The WB trio did an impromptu presentation for the visiting executives of Entertaindom, which by now had a lot of bells and whistles, including material from several animated series, many created especially for the online medium. The site had a cutting-edge youth appeal that was unmistakable. Moloshok had struck a deal with a community-style Web service called FortuneCity, taking an equity stake in the company in exchange for promotion. The FortuneCity software enabled Entertaindom to offer features like build-your-own fan sites, message boards, chat, and other "community" features. This represented a complete reversal of the position that, for example, Viacom had taken only a few years earlier, with its threatening letters to college-kid webmasters. Now Entertaindom was actually *encouraging* fans to use its content.

Suddenly, viewed through the prism of Entertaindom, Time Warner looked hip and cool, something Pathfinder had never achieved. Levin, who was due to appear the following day at the Big Picture conference sponsored by *Variety* and Schroders bank—the very same conference that Bob Pittman had torn up a few years before—was by now fairly desperate to have something to announce there that made it seem as if the company had a vision of its role in the Internet.

As the demo ended, something clearly clicked in Levin's mind. Throughout the presentation, he'd been argumentative and skeptical, disputing the budget numbers WB Online was proposing. But somehow it all suddenly added up, and Levin expressed his relief to the assembled trio. "Thank you very much. You've helped me crystallize Time Warner's Internet strategy." For the guys at Warner Bros. Online, it was a career highlight.

"These guys could see that Entertaindom was almost done, that it was pretty robust," Moloshok recalls. "They were saying, 'This could be the thing that jump-starts us, because we could lift this out of Warner Bros. and make it a Time Warner entity. We could say that it was the first of our 'vertical hubs.'"

The "hub" paradigm was accordingly articulated at the Big Picture gathering, and received wide play in the media, for it seemed to indicate that Time Warner had finally formulated some sort of strategy. The idea was that Time Warner content could be grouped into themes—news, sports, entertainment, and business and finance. With that speech Levin had bought some breathing room for what was still a highly chaotic, unsettled situation. In the next six or seven months, a series of Internet-related announcements, many of them contradictory or confusing, poured forth from Time Warner. For anyone attempting to follow the company's new-media moves closely over much of the first three quarters of 1999, the only common themes discernible were the by now familiar ones of corporate power plays, competing fiefdoms, and thwarted ambitions.

Levin was still clinging to the belief that the creativity and inventiveness of Time Warner would decisively triumph over whatever new-media usurpers arose to challenge its hegemony. For many years, there had been an inviolate conviction in New York and Los Angeles that they were the sole capitals of content, that everything else in between was just the Big Flyover.

There was certainly some basis for Levin's optimism. In late 1999, many on the West Coast were betting that Web entertainment operations like Digital Entertainment Network and Pop.com would be the companies that finally fulfilled the long-held dream that Hollywood genius would ultimately conquer the Web. *Variety* proclaimed that notion on the cover of its very first issue of *eV,* its new-media spinoff. Hollywood creative talent agencies like International Creative Management and Creative Artists Agency had been promoting new media incessantly, and an aura of new-media savvy also surrounded former CAA honcho Michael Ovitz that wasn't quite earned, given the agency's somewhat erratic showing in the field.

Errol Gerson, the courtly former head of new media at CAA from 1997 to 1999, remembers this period well. An accountant and MBA, Gerson is a former music management executive, best known for overseeing the careers and fortunes of "self-destructive" heavy metal acts like Megadeth, Slayer, XYZ, and others, before bone cancer left him with severely limited use of his hands and forced him to quit the business. Gerson launched an early California-based Web design shop in the early '90s and attempted to corner the Las Vegas market with a portal called Vegas.com. After CAA launched the Intel/CAA Media Lab, in partnership with the chip company, to serve as a West Coast adjunct to the famous idea factory at M.I.T., Gerson was brought in as the agency's media guru. When Gerson was hired in January 1997, the CAA Lab, which had been announced with much fanfare, was already somewhat moribund. On arriving at CAA, with only a small staff, Gerson met with every one of its agents, told them his ideas, and promised that new media could become a major element of CAA's operations. Gerson defined his mission as helping CAA clients to take their talents to the new-media world, but he quickly realized that the Hollywood community was simply taking for granted that it would be able to transport its culture, with all its excess and extravagant spending, whole onto the Internet, and assuming it would have the support of a mass audience that the Web simply couldn't deliver.

Digital Entertainment Network is a case in point. Designed to function just like a Hollywood production company/TV network, DEN at its height was producing more than a dozen online entertainment programs. It founders, Marc Collins-Rector and Chad Shackley, had an impressive and apparently unimpeachable track record in the online industry, having launched the ISP Concentric Network. The two, who together owned 25 percent of the company, founded DEN in 1996, and it quickly became an industry leader as important investors, ranging from Microsoft to Warner Bros. chairman Terry Semel, signed on.

"When I was first shown the Digital Entertainment Network, I realized the model was flawed from day one because, unfortunately, you could never aggregate a large enough audience," Gerson says. "Some of their work, like *Frat Rats*, . . . [was] very funny and it was clearly something college kids would like. The trouble was there wasn't enough stickiness to keep the kids coming back. And more important, they were not garnering enough eyeballs to make the CPMs [that is, ad dollars] pay for the show."

Gerson knew that the company was bound to fail, but he found himself in an awkward position, for DEN was offering cutting-edge work to CAA clients.

"They wanted to hire our clients to either act or direct or write. . . . Some of the guys from DEN would call and say, 'Listen, we'd like to see if so and so, a stellar name, would like to write an episode of one of our series. We'll pay him $2,000 an episode.' And immediately I would have to say, 'I will take your offer to him, but I have to tell you that as a television writer, this man makes between $400,000 and $700,000 every year, and that's without residuals.' The DEN people would say, 'Yes, but I'm sure he can write this in his spare time, and if he builds enough of a base in this business he can actually make a lot of money.'"

Gerson listened to these arguments with total skepticism, because he knew most screenwriters would opt for a network TV series, and not some web site that few of their peers had ever heard of. Even when DEN did manage to attract aspiring writers to create its shows for a mere $2,000 an episode, its total costs were still far too high to be justified in Web economics.

Lee Masters's experience with DEN was slightly different, because, as CEO of Liberty Digital, he represented a possible cash infusion to the company, which had an enormous burn rate. Masters recalls being half of a two-person delegation visiting DEN's lavish headquarters on 2230 Broadway in Santa Monica, only to be greeted by a phalanx of twelve DEN executives, grouped around an immense conference table laden with a small mountain of sushi. Each of the DEN representatives tried to outdo the others in superlatives about what a major player the company would become. Masters walked out of the boardroom shaking his head, convinced the exorbitant effort would collapse under its own weight.

Even with evidence of its profligacy and mismanagement clearly visible, many money managers in Los Angeles ignored the warning signs, so starry-eyed were they about quick IPO riches. Masters recalls: "One guy called me, a very prominent person from our business. He asked my advice on DEN. I said, 'Don't go near it.' And I told him why. He said, 'Well, I think I'll put some money into it, let it go public, and then I'll flip it.' And I said, 'Good luck.'"

In 1999, shortly after this conversation, Marc Collins-Rector was served with a sexual misconduct lawsuit and had to leave the company. The suit was later settled, but the scandal was damaging. The following year, DEN ran out of money and laid off most of its staff, filing Chapter 11. Top executives like Terry Semel had to endure having their connections with the ill-fated business continually aired in the press.

Even with such spectacular failures, the Internet had clearly opened the floodgates. In 1999 CAA was getting 100 proposals *a day* from would-be entrepreneurs who were proposing ideas for video series on the Web. Investors like Lee Masters, who had built eight businesses in his career and had spent years creating conventional cable networks like E! and VH1, knew immediately that this model couldn't work. "They didn't understand how difficult the TV business really is," Masters explains. "What you have to understand is that what has happened in the last couple of years has badly warped people's perspectives on how the real world operates."

Perhaps the nadir of CAA's new-media involvement came in 1999 when a company called Pixelon, Inc., based in the scenic southern California town of San Juan Capistrano, came to the agency claiming that it had developed a secret technology that could "do broadband video and audio at 28.8" kbps modem speed.

Gerson met with the Pixelon group, which included its founder and chairman, Michael Fenne, and Craig Parrish, CAA's chief technical officer. After listening to some wild claims from Fenne, Parrish remarked, "Do you want to nibble on my ear when you say that, because I like a little passion when I get fucked around. Do you want to show me how you do this?" Pixelon replied that they couldn't demonstrate their system because their patent was still pending. Pixelon was claiming that it had proprietary technology, an encoder, and a playback software suite called the Pixelon Player that offered much higher quality than Microsoft was delivering through its Windows Media Player.

"We use a revolutionary set of capturing techniques that revolve around seven proprietary sampling procedures," Pixelon claimed on its web site in 1999. What many of those who saw the Pixelon Player in investment demonstrations didn't realize, however, was that what they were actually watching *was* the Windows Media Player, because Pixelon's product wasn't ready to be demoed.

Fenne and the Pixelon group told CAA they intended to spend $15 million on a giant Pixelon webcast from the MGM Grand in Las Vegas called iBash '99, with KISS, the Dixie Chicks, Sugar Ray, and the reunited Who as the star attractions. Despite the fact that CAA thought it was probably doomed to fail, Gerson said the agency "was getting its clients working, and as an agent I was required to get them work." A variety of CAA clients appeared in the webcast, including KISS. The event was hosted by David Spade and Internet pinup Cindy Margolis.

Gerson notes, "It was a fiasco; they spent $15 million. I don't know how many people saw it—60,000 or 70,000. It was jerky. At CAA on our T1, it took me fifteen minutes to begin to download it."

Shortly afterward, it emerged that Pixelon founder and chairman Michael

Fenne was really one Paul Stanley, a fixture on Virginia's most-wanted list for several years who had run out on his bail after being convicted for stock swindling. After Stanley was finally jailed, Pixelon was hit with a lawsuit by four creditors who claimed they were never paid for $500,000 worth of services offered, and the company headed for bankruptcy. Gerson notes that the fact that an individual like Stanley could raise money so easily is proof that most of the venture capital firms were simply not doing due diligence, caught up as they were in the frenzy of the Web explosion of 1998 and 1999.

While no one ended up in jail over online TV network Pseudo.com, the debacle was real, sustained, and wildly out of sync with even the lax standards of the Internet content business. Lawrence Lux became CEO of Pseudo at the end of 1999. A former executive at Cincinnati Bell, Lux had worked on online efforts since the late 1980s and had been one of the first customers of the fledgling online consulting firm Jupiter Communications, co-founded by a garrulous, unconventional, out-of-the-box thinker named Josh Harris. Lux was the founding executive of National Geographic Online, which was built from the ground up with about $12 million from the parent company. While at National Geographic, which had missed out on cable TV and was determined not to be a no-show at another media revolution, Lux transformed himself from a guy who looked as if he had indeed worked at Cincinnati Bell to a goateed, tough-talking digital powerhouse who knew what people really wanted online. Although National Geographic Online was a serious travel and exploration site, Lux notes wryly that the most common search term was "naked native" during most of his tenure there.

In late 1999 Lux was recruited to be the first professional CEO of Pseudo.com, which had been started by Josh Harris with the money he had earned from the rapid success of his creation, Jupiter Communications. Pseudo was conceived as a kind of mini-TV network empire, but most of its programs were webcast from Harris's huge loft at 600 Broadway in the SoHo district of New York City, which soon gained a reputation as the site of a 24-hour party of sex, drugs, and rock and roll.

By this time, Lux had abandoned the suits and ties that had once been de rigueur at his previous jobs, but he still found the atmosphere at Pseudo to be insanely chaotic. "Josh believed that you threw the creative people together and got out of the way," Lux recalls, "but you can't just have some guy doing Buddhist chants and playing finger cymbals and have that be your programming."

But in many cases, that *was* Pseudo's programming. And it wasn't being created by just a few crazies at the fringe of the company. One of the more outrageous offerings was hosted by Harris himself. Called "Luvy the Clown," the show featured Harris performing the part of an off-color transvestite clown. The story was that Luvy was a TV junkie when he was growing up, so the clown was named after the nickname of Mrs. Thurston Howell III, a character on *Gilligan's Island*.

The various Pseudo web channels were programmed as if the artists and bohemians of New York's downtown scene were their only audience, and contributors were encouraged to be as unconventional as possible. (This was despite the fact that the most popular channel by far on the network involved a single individual in Toledo, Ohio, who webcast reviews of computer games.)

Luvy wasn't an anomalous feature on Pseudo; it was the norm. "You had this kind of girl sex show, where you had these crazy East Village chicks being very blunt about sex. These girls weren't shy about taking their clothes off, and there would be product demos of sex toys sometimes. Some of that got a little obnoxious."

For Lux, the irony of his position was profound, in that he later landed at Playboy.com. *Playboy* the magazine has long been boycotted by an array of straight-laced advertisers, including car companies and Microsoft, which claim to frown on prurient material. But Microsoft placed ads on Pseudo with few questions asked. "I had to believe they weren't actually watching the shows they sponsored," Lux says. Few of Pseudo's advertisers were actually given reliable audience numbers. "All the channel heads did so much lying about their page views, it was almost impossible to get real numbers," Lux laughs. Pseudo flouted the rules of normal advertising by simply selling sponsorships not tied directly to audience counts. Sponsorships generally came out of sponsors' promotional budgets, and oversight was lax.

During a Pseudo fund-raising round in 2000 that eventually saw $20 million raised from such sources as Intel and the Tribune Company, Lux saw up close just how distorted the venture capitalist world had become. "Josh would show up at these meetings [looking] like he had just rolled out of bed," Lux recalls. "He hadn't shaved, and his hair was sticking straight up. He would be raving about how Pseudo was going to conquer the world, and a lot of [investors] were entertained by that."

Lux recalls taking one investor group on a tour of 600 Broadway. Participants in the bacchanale at the loft recall fondly a "full monty" of drugs, constant and public sex, and an unreal, day-for-night atmosphere where nothing was conventional. As the straight-laced delegation entered the loft, the first sight greeting them was a guy "with his forehead pierced riding a skateboard." Later, as the group ventured further into the loft, they became engulfed in a huge cloud of marijuana smoke. Everyone smiled, as if this sort of dysfunction was an integral part of the New Economy.

Raising the money turned out to be "relatively easy," Lux believes, because so many of the investors were young and had only ever known a bull market and couldn't imagine that Pseudo could fail. And the older, more seasoned professionals involved in these discussions were often so far out of their depth in evaluating companies like Pseudo that they just threw up their hands and committed their money, no matter how many private reservations they might have had. "People thought it was cutting-edge," Lux says. "The people at Tribune and other conservative executives, they just said to themselves, 'This is the Internet and we don't know anything about it. This is cool, hip, edgy content. We just have to let these guys do their thing.'

"Jim Kyles, who ran Intel Ventures, made the decision to invest in Pseudo. He tells the story of presenting the Pseudo investment to the Intel board in June 1999 . . . but chose not to delve into some of the racier content. Jim ends up with [Intel chairman and co-founder] Andy Grove on this conference call . . . He tells the story of an anguished Grove piping up, with his Hungarian accent, 'Jim, vat is dis with Luvy the Clown?' And they're all sitting there thinking, 'Oh my God, how are we going to explain?'" As Lux recalls, the basic pitch that people like Kyles used with CEOs like Grove was: "The kids think this is cool. We have to be here." In the confused world of 1998 and 1999, that argument usually worked, as lacking in substance as it was.

Pseudo was ultimately too bizarre to be able to sustain a market downturn. In late 2000 Lux attended a performance piece that the network was webcasting called "Box Opera." The event, held at a suitable downtown New York location, was a wacky attempt to marry boxing and opera. Afterward Lux returned to his office and wrote Harris a memo that stated, "We're not going to spend another dime on this kind of crap." As reasonable as the memo might have been, it didn't convince the quiescent Pseudo board, which sided with Harris. Lux left the company shortly thereafter for *Playboy*, and what remained of Pseudo was later sold off.

Pop.com wasn't as self-consciously transgressive as Pseudo, but its fate was much the same. The $10 million venture had the backing of prominent Hollywood talent like Steve Martin, Eddie Murphy, Matthew McConaughey, and Drew Barrymore, all of whom submitted work of some kind to the site. (Directors with the stature of Steven Spielberg and Ron Howard were also supposed to provide material, although they never quite got around to it.) Part of the problem with Pop.com was that full-length productions didn't typically work online because of bandwidth limitations. At the time, most people connected at relatively slow modem speeds, on which video is jerky and virtually unwatchable. As a result, the programming that did exist on Pop was short-form, the kind of thing shown at film festivals and in student film classes.

"My concern for Pop.com was the same I had for any short-form entertainment site," Gerson says. Short films are great for showcasing new talent or for interstitial programming on TV, but they're not really a sufficient basis for a business. Gerson also notes that 70 percent of the money that could be considered entertainment revenue on the Web comes from pornography, which doesn't leave a lot of wiggle room for expensive legitimate entertainment productions, no matter how clever. And because the DEN and Pop.com productions tended to be so adamantly ultra-hip and elitist, they almost guaranteed they would attract only a "select" audience, to borrow the words of Spinal Tap's hapless manager.

For Jerry Levin, such distinctions seem to have been overlooked, because, like his innate belief in technology, he also had a bedrock faith in the superior talents of the creative people who made Warner Bros. movies and music. Insiders at Warner Bros. tell the story of auditioning a particularly prickly bit of Entertaindom content for Levin. The online serial story in question was created (or, more accurately, overseen) by Warner's reigning star of the moment, Adam Sandler. But it was so filthy and morally questionable, featuring a Peeping Tom called Mr. Peepers, that the Entertaindom group felt Levin should see it before it went up. Levin viewed the material and asked only one question: "Does Adam really believe in this?" The group answered that he did. "Well, then, it's his vision," Levin responded, giving it the go-ahead.

Levin's response recalled an incident a few years earlier, when he came under attack because one Warner-owned label was releasing music with racist, sexist, violent, and misanthropic rap lyrics. Levin faced the criticism by turning up at a company event wearing a jacket promoting one of the rap stars in question. It was knee-jerk defiance at its worst. Levin seems to have not seriously questioned that his company could put out material that was offensive to many listeners, which is a curious lapse, considering the number of times he has chosen to ascribe high moral values to himself and Time Warner.

/ / /

Corporate executives like to boast about where the buck stops, but figuring out where exactly the Time Warner new-media buck stopped in 1999 was a daunting task, as there was a major struggle going on for control of that portfolio. Moloshok, Banister, and Weiner of Warner Bros. had gotten nice praise from Levin, but that didn't immediately translate to power over any other division. And the situation was made more complicated by the sudden, inexplicable ascension in January 1999 of Michael Pepe to the newly named position of president of Time Warner e-commerce, a title reflecting Levin's increasing focus on applications that had more of a shot at making the company some money. From the perspective of Warner and the West Coast, the appointment looked nonsensical and pointless. What did Michael Pepe know about new media anyway?

Pepe, a somewhat colorless executive, was the epitome of what Levin seemed to value in selecting new-media talent. He had had no new-media experience whatsoever, but he'd been a loyal foot soldier at Time Inc. for thirteen years when he was given the job. Forty-four at the time of his promotion, Pepe had joined the company in 1986 and had quickly landed at *People,* always a quick path to advancement at the print company. Pepe was named general manager of the magazine in 1989 and was next raised up to a corporate post, vice president of marketing for Time Inc., in 1992. He became group publisher for *Fortune, Money,* and *Your Company* the following year, and then president of the Business Information Group in 1998.

Linda McCutcheon resigned as president of Time Inc. New Media in April of that year, having failed to gather any obvious momentum around her revenue-generating ideas. By the time she left, she says it was impossible to have much contact with Levin at all, and the action had shifted to others. The Michael Pepe announcement, as puzzling as it was to many in the company, was the last straw for McCutcheon. "At a certain point, I realized there were better things I could be doing with my life. I had a great time, a great run. I don't have an MBA. I didn't go to Harvard. I didn't go to Haverford. I've had this incredible experience and I've learned a lot; it was time to move on."

For a few months, Pepe seemed to be the executive to talk to if you wanted to pursue a new-media alliance at Time Warner. But the e-commerce designation in his title was ambiguous and was widely derided within the company's various divisions. Pepe told confidants in early 1999 that the company would convert Pathfinder's loose network of web sites into a universal e-commerce user interface. This seemed to mean that the point of Time Warner's Web operation was not interactive content, but generating revenue from relevant commerce opportunities. The e-commerce ventures that already did exist were very limited, and halting. People.com's People Store, launched earlier, specialized in selling books from Barnes & Noble and CDs from Total E, a web site maintained by its Columbia House unit, a joint venture with Sony. Nonetheless, Christin Shanahan, director of commerce at Time Inc. New Media, told News.com's Jim Hu in March, "Michael's tapping into every division and everyone's expertise right now, so a lot of people are wrapping their minds around this."

All those working minds notwithstanding, very little that was useful was ever produced. Time Inc. is one of the world's largest direct marketers of magazine subscriptions and other merchandise, but it isn't much of a retailer. Its book and record clubs relied primarily on a business model in which club "editors" picked out selections for its user base, resulting in far more limited choices than were available at the major online retailers. The Web actually posed a serious threat to Columbia House and Time's Book-of-the-Month Club, which were not seen as competitive. (It was for that reason that the People Store was selling books through Barnes & Noble and not the Book-of-the-Month Club.)

Warner Bros. had studio stores, but what kind of retail establishment could Time Inc. have operated? A big newsstand that sold only Time Inc. magazines and *People* weekly baseball hats?

Despite its lack of a retail knowledge base, the company scrambled to fulfill Levin's vision. Shortly before Pathfinder was closed down, Time Inc. had launched an online shopping guide called Giftfinder. The service featured a shopping "bot" or comparison guide powered by Junglee (later bought by Amazon.com) and offered links to partners including Office Depot, Barnes & Noble, and Cyberian Outpost, as well as a center for subscriptions to Time's magazines. But the site brought in minimal revenue and showed little promise as a new commerce strategy for Time Warner.

Pepe's obvious lack of experience in new media and his firm grounding within the print side led to widespread restiveness at the company. Why should Moloshok and company listen to him? Why should Lou Dobbs, who had Ted Turner's ear, have any dealings with him at all? The latter was a protocol question, in part. Dobbs felt he was senior to Pepe within the Time Warner pecking order, and he knew that Pepe not only had no background in new media, he also had none in television. CNN continued to believe that it rightfully should emerge at the center of Time Warner's web strategy.

In March, the *Wall Street Journal* reported that Time Warner was considering developing a separate public company from its Internet holdings. CFO Bressler didn't exactly deny the rumor, but said that Time wanted to develop its "vertical hubs" first. This caused huge speculation within the various divisions that each of the "hubs" would be spun off independently, and many employees began to have visions of Internet IPO riches.

On April 14, Levin tried to shore up the hub strategy by announcing that Time Warner didn't need a partner. "The necessity to buy something isn't readily apparent to me," he told Bloomberg News. What Levin seemed to mean was that Time Warner could develop its own hydra-headed portal and didn't need to buy one, in contrast to Disney and NBC. While he acknowledged that the company might consider spinning off some Web units, it felt "no compulsion" to do so. Attempting levity, Levin claimed that the digital world had been completely integrated into the company's makeup. Time Warner "doesn't have an Internet strategy," he quipped, in what would seem to have been a Freudian slip.

Shortly after being given the e-commerce title, on April 16, Pepe held a "town-meeting" conference to discuss the hub strategy, which he was struggling to make a reality. He had identified the various "hubs" that could be built out of Time Warner content as news (*Time* and CNN), sports (*Sports Illustrated* and CNN), business and finance (*Fortune, Money,* CNNfn), and entertainment (Warner Bros., *People, Entertainment Weekly,* CNN). But actually defining the organization of each of the hubs would be more daunting, for once again the demands of the various fiefdoms would have to be taken into account.

Who would be responsible for news, *Time* or CNN? Was *Fortune,* a venerable brand that had been a cornerstone of Henry Luce's empire, a more logical "hub" center than the fledgling and struggling CNNfn, which was completely overshadowed by CNBC? Could the competing entertainment kingdoms in New York and Burbank work together? On the latter question, the *Extra* debacle had already cast doubt on the possibility of smooth synergies between *Entertainment Weekly* and Warner Bros. There was every reason to believe that harmony would not prevail in this instance, as well.

Time Warner's belief that it was the center of the content universe also blinded it to what was taking place in the rest of the Internet world. By mid-2000, "hubs" were already in place in each of these categories at corporate entities not quite as Internet-challenged as Time Warner, including Disney and NBC. Time Warner's plans looked a little threadbare.

Although Jake Winebaum eventually left Disney in June 1999 to form an ill-fated Internet incubator called eCompanies, before his departure he oversaw the convergence of the Disney and Infoseek properties into a mélange called the Go Network. Although Go quickly became a top-10 site, its constantly declining valuation made its expense unpalatable for the ever cost-conscious Disney.

The Go Network was launched on January 12, 1999, with a great deal of fanfare, including parties in New York and Los Angeles, both attended by CEO Michael Eisner. At the Manhattan event, held at the trendy terra-cotta Puck Building off Houston Street, Eisner mingled with Harry Motro and Infoseek's 33-year-old chief technical officer and senior vice president, Patrick Naughton. Eisner had come to depend on Naughton as a technical guru, frequently consulting him on infrastructure matters. Beginning his career as a software engineer in 1982, Naughton was the classic tech geek, earning a B.S. in Computer Science from Clarkson University and joining Sun Microsystems' window systems group in 1988.

At the company's SunLabs, Naughton had been involved in a "secret project" called Green, which was "intended to create a completely new platform for software development which would solve many of the problems in existing systems." As a Go company bio stated in 1999, "The most significant technology to come out of the Green project was Java. . . . Naughton was instrumental in the creation and evolution of Java, from its inception through to its revolutionary transition into the language of the Internet." The message wasn't subtle: This guy is a technical genius who will build another AOL. Certainly Eisner seemed to believe it.

When a reporter asked Eisner at the New York Go launch party if the company was looking to emulate AOL and add ISP connectivity to the service, Eisner asserted it was a strong possibility. He then called Naughton over to his side and asked, "Patrick, Web connectivity is a commodity, right? We can do that easily if we want?" Naughton appeared uncomfortable with the question, all too aware that Eisner hates to be told bad news. He mumbled something about it being feasible, although he looked dubious when he said it.

Eisner joked at the party about Disney's challenge from Internet start-ups. "If you put two eighteen-year-old kids in a warehouse in Santa Monica, they could probably make more money off the Internet than we can," he quipped.

Infoseek and Disney were still separate entities at this point, and the network was, to put it mildly, loose. At launch, Disney described Go as "the next-generation Internet destination." The portal had "the easiest URL in the world," Disney proclaimed. "Go Network is more than a loose confederation of content and basic services. It is a true media portal designed to be a destination, not just a point of departure. It blends Infoseek's superior search capabilities with integrated Internet services such as Go News, Go Sports, Go Money and Go Kids and Family, adding up to a total of 18 Go content centers." The Go Network, Disney promised, "will reach beyond the boundaries of the Internet and connect with people in their daily lives in tangible, meaningful ways. The promise of Go Network is to empower people by balancing the freedom of the Web with the power to control it."

It's hard to say why any of this was really distinctive. At its heart, Go was simply a typical Web directory with news from ABC News instead of, say, Reuters, which Yahoo! used. The combined sites would attract 1 million users a day, which was a significant number in 1999, but exactly how Go was supposed to "empower" any of them any more than Yahoo! was already doing was an open question. Infoseek had real revenue—$34.6 million in 1997, the last figure reported before the deal was announced—but an even moderately successful Disney movie would make more.

In the end, the exact purpose of Go was never clear. Few could explain exactly what a "media portal" was. Go was busily trying to submerge the Disney identification by renaming ESPN Sports and ABC News as Go Sports and Go News, respectively, a tactic that seems both bizarre and counterproductive. Why would a company with some semblance of sanity jettison brand names as powerful as ESPN and ABC? The answer lies in the contradictory goals of Disney and Infoseek at this juncture.

Infoseek was still a public company, and the world was still judging Web sites at least in part by how much traffic they received. If Infoseek simply became a conduit for traffic to Disney web sites, it would quickly lose ground to other portals like Yahoo! and Excite. Infoseek therefore insisted that the Disney brands be deemphasized and blended in with the portal concept.

In this spirit, a press release announcing the Go network noted "strategic relationships" with ABC News and ESPN, which made their connection sound like the same type of affiliate deal that AOL might sign with these media powerhouses. This clearly wasn't the case. Go was a Disney operation, masquerading as something else, which is a hard act to pull off in the Internet business. Moreover, as Disney executives later lamented, it took Mouse eyes off the prize of building their own brands at a time when other media companies, particularly MSNBC and CBS SportsLine, were just becoming competitive. Some at Disney now claim that their own web sites would have been profitable today if Go hadn't interfered.

As the first "media portal" Go was bigger than the Web properties of other entertainment/media companies, but it was hardly unique. Under former CEO Lee Masters, E! Entertainment Television had set up a popular Los Angeles–based web site helmed by a former *People* West Coast bureau chief. In news, the list of competitors was long: MSNBC, the *New York Times,* the *Washington Post,* and *USA Today* all had well-established Web brands by this time, and Reuters had spread its headlines across the Web. In sports, CBS SportsLine was competitive with ESPN, and both had completely eclipsed *Sports Illustrated* on the Web. And on the financial side, CBS MarketWatch, TheStreet.com, Bloomberg, Yahoo! Finance (with its popular message boards), and the *New York Times* all had far livelier Web presences.

Time Warner was too inner-directed to be fully aware corporately of all these developments—most of all Jerry Levin, who often seemed to operate within a hermetic seal. And if Time Warner knew the territory it was entering, it would have realized that the hub strategy may have been a logical, if belated way, for the company to organize, but it was at least two years too late.

For the few months after Michael Pepe's town meeting, there was huge confusion at the company as the various divisions vied for supremacy. One directive that was clear from Pepe's presentation was that each of the "hubs" needed a leader, who were quickly dubbed "hub caps," in somewhat derisory fashion. This also caused a great deal of rivalry to spring up *within* the divisions. The "princes" at Time Inc., the managing editors, each assumed they would automatically be granted "hub cap" status. They included such important Time players as John Huey, who had rescued *Fortune* magazine from a serious slump and was a hero within the company. But Lou Dobbs was not someone who could be passed over easily, and had Huey been given the business "hub" job, a huge firestorm would have erupted from the always-volatile Dobbs.

The vying for "hub cap" status wasn't just about consolidating power. Many of the division heads were salivating over the possibility of an IPO strategy that would make them rich. The lesson Tom Evans had taught them was still fresh. But most of the Time Warner division heads were too firmly entrenched at the perk-heavy company to want to leave; moreover, they were all heavily vested with Time Warner stock options. The spin-off idea started to look very attractive, but just who would benefit?

Pepe soon became frustrated at the inertia that resulted from the chronic infighting. "He started asking, 'Where's the business plan? Where are the numbers? We just have to get out there and do something. I'm so sick and tired of not doing anything,'" an executive close to him recalls.

In late April, Time Warner formally announced that it would put an end to the vestiges of the Pathfinder concept, something which had actually happened, de facto, already. Although it wasn't clear at the time, this also sounded the death knell for Pepe's tenure, because it represented a corporate dismantling of the structure that Time Inc. had built, and a corporate recognition that it had failed.

Jeffrey Coomes, vice president of marketing at the then still extant Time Inc. New Media, told CNET's News.com, "We have decided to go to the next step in the brand strategy and pull out Pathfinder and all the URLs. Pathfinder's demise became an ultimate consequence in that strategy. There is more power in the individual brands than the Pathfinder brand. Why bury them under the Pathfinder name? Basically that's what the market told us." Of course, others, including *Vibe*'s Chan Suh and *People*'s Hala Makowska had told the company the very same thing years before, but the 34th floor wasn't listening then.

After McCutcheon's departure, Pepe had said he would find a successor for the Time Inc. New Media president slot. That would have given him a more substantial power base, but in fact it was little more than a fig-leaf, intended to obscure the fact that the once-powerful print division was no longer the center of the new-media universe at Time Warner. Indeed, on June 15 Time Warner corporately announced a completely new Internet group, in which Pepe's e-commerce title had seemingly transmuted into an even grander one, president and chief operating officer of the newly named Time Warner Digital Media. For the first time, Time Warner's name was front and center in a new-media group's division, indicating that this business had become a company-wide effort. Time Inc. New Media didn't immediately go away, but its mission was redirected back to represent the print side only.

Time Warner CFO Richard Bressler, who was 41 at the time, was named chairman of the Digital Media unit. Bressler was another longtime company veteran to whom Levin felt especially close. Bressler had joined Time Inc. in 1988 as an assistant controller, coming on board after making partner at Ernst & Young. He was named executive vice president and CFO of Time Warner in January 1998. Although his official Time Warner biography credits him with leading "a cross-divisional team in developing an Internet strategy for the company," most insiders say Bressler was not very knowledgeable about the Internet or the world of online services that included AOL.

As for Pepe, his grand-sounding title was illusory; he was now reporting to the much more powerful Bressler, a top Levin lieutenant. His power was quickly diluted further when shortly thereafter Olaf Olaffson, president of a Pennsylvania-based financial services company called Advanta Corp., was brought in as vice chairman of the division, supplanting Pepe in authority. Time Warner insiders say this reorganization had its tragic side, because Pepe was intelligent, a quick study, and had actually mastered much of the arcana of the business. "When it came to the end, he was smart enough to get it. He turned around and became more like Moses, the champion of the Egyptian slaves," Banister jokes.

Olaffson's appointment was yet another example of Levin's failure to grasp how actual Internet experience could prove valuable in trying to build digital brands online. Despite an impressive-sounding resume, the handsome blond Icelandic executive, 37 when he got the job at Time Warner, was better known as a novelist than an Internet pioneer. Olaffson had trained as a physicist at Brandeis, joining Sony as a researcher in 1985. His major accomplishment had been serving as founder, president, and chief executive of Sony Interactive Entertainment, Inc., the unit that had developed the immensely popular PlayStation. Olaffson had not participated directly in any Internet company and was derided within Time Warner as yet another Levin hire to whom everyone could feel superior.

Under Bressler, Time Warner Digital Media did start to try to sort out the various factions, and to come up with a plan on how to compensate new-media executives at a level somewhat commensurate with the rest of the industry. The media was then full of stories about Internet geeks in their twenties making millions off stock options. But how could a company like Time Warner reasonably parcel these out? While each of the hubs would be built in part with content that was first originated in print or on television, it was hard to envision that everyone connected with every last byte that would appear on the web site would be entitled to stock. Bressler's appointment had been largely predicated on the concept that only a CFO could figure out how to structure all this.

IPOs were what one former Time Warner executive calls the "common currency" of the Web in 1999; in order to compete, Time Warner would have to exchange its digital assets into that currency. Jake Winebaum had seemingly succeeded in doing so by swapping Disney's online properties into a public stock. Time Warner's own effort to emulate Winebaum with AltaVista had failed, however, and now began the much harder task of building a public company from within.

In the early '90s, according to a former senior-level executive, Warner Bros. had compensated a certain celebrity with Time Warner stock as part of a multi-year pact. Word of this had "rippled through the company," the former executive says, and soon many other of the studio's high-priced talent, including top actors, were demanding equal treatment. In the film world, actors' salaries are supposed to be secret and are zealously guarded by the studios, which fear salary inflation. Chuck Ross, a scribe at *The Hollywood Reporter,* was fired from the paper in the 1980s for writing a story on Sylvester Stallone's $12 million payment for an arm-wrestling bomb called *Over the Top,* which made studio executives look stupid. In this context, Levin knew that if a stock-option plan was announced, all the leading agencies would immediately begin demanding stock for every client of theirs who had ever appeared in a WB film. This nightmare scenario had to be avoided at all costs.

Within the divisions, the problem of stock grants was just as acute. At Warner Bros., for example, Entertaindom could have been spun off, and an IPO would have probably been successful in 1999, when virtually anything could go public, with or without revenue. But key questions were raised at the division. There was the matter of what to do for top executives like Warren Lieberfarb, who headed the home video division of Warner, which generated in the area of $2 billion annually. Lieberfarb couldn't legitimately argue that he was generating intellectual property that was fueling Entertaindom, yet leaving him without any stock perks was unthinkable. Considerations like these made it virtually impossible for the corporate side to structure any public offering that was workable.

Some of the divisions had taken small equity stakes in new-media companies they had done business with. Warner Bros. Online had 15 percent of the community site FortuneCity.com. When that company went public, the WB team was sitting on about $70 million worth of equity. But as long as this stayed the property of the division, not the executives, it was workable.

In May, the long-awaited "hub cap" lineup was announced, and it clearly demonstrated that CNN had fully gained ascendancy over the print side. Lou Dobbs, who was formally president of CNNfn, was tapped to head the business operation. Steve Korn, the vice chairman of CNN, got the news job. Jim Walton, president of CNN Sports/Illustrated, was named to the sports post. The only person from a print division to become a hub cap was Ann Moore, president of the People Group, who got women. Jim Moloshok got entertainment.

"I didn't even know I was a hub cap," Moloshok recalls. "I was on the road, flying to New York for a meeting, and somebody from Warner Music told me that you're now in charge of entertainment programming. It was news to me."

Immediately a feverish round of meetings commenced, presided over by Bressler, in which the hub caps began to try to get the diverse elements of their new empires in line. Bressler briefed the hub caps privately, telling all of them that, despite their new designation, they would still have to work closely with the top executives at each of the traditional content sources—the magazines, television, the movie studio, and the records company. This was in complete contradiction to what had been announced publicly.

To present at least the appearance of credibility, Time had told the press that the hub caps would report directly to a four-person management team—including Bressler, Don Logan, Terry McGuirk of Turner Broadcasting, and Terry Semel, co-chairman of Warner Bros.—which in turn would report to Levin. The difference may seem negligible, but within the company it was significant. The announced structure made it sound as if the hub strategists would have some autonomy from the rigid corporate hierarchy. In reality, they had to work within that structure. If the traditional media and entertainment heads remained in the loop, then very little would be likely to change.

There was a suspicion among some of the hub leaders that the entire hub strategy was in fact serving as a sideshow to what was really the main event—a Time Warner merger with AOL. The fact that Time Warner had been in discussions with AOL was by now an open secret in some higher echelons of the company. Despite claims made later that the merger had happened quickly, insiders have documents dating back to as early as the beginning of 1999 that include references to the talks. Hallway gossip was that Case was "hounding" Levin with a barrage of phone calls, which Levin had initially resisted. Although a Bressler lieutenant named Rob Marcus, listed as the vice president of corporate development at Time Warner Digital Media, had in fact been dispatched to deal with AOL, many of the top executives at the divisions dismissed the rumors. Hadn't the company been talking to every power in the industry for almost ten years without any tangible result?

The hub caps, of course, were resistant to an AOL deal, because it would destroy their power base. In May, while the desultory AOL discussions continued, a group of CNN executives led by hub cap Steve Korn began approaching investment banks asking for advice on setting up a public offering centered around CNN's online holdings. Moloshok made similar inquiries about an Entertaindom IPO. But their dreams would have to be deferred, for shortly after statements from CNNfn's Lou Dobbs surfaced in the press about an IPO for the business hub, official statements were issued from Levin's office cautioning that no IPO would be forthcoming soon.

On June 9 the media world was startled by the sudden announcement that Dobbs would resign from CNN. Dobbs, then 53, had been clashing with CNN's U.S. president Rick Kaplan over an independent role for Dobbs at a web site called Space.com, and serious tension had also arisen over the business hub that Dobbs headed being separate from the news hub centered at CNN. (Dobbs had already made his displeasure with Kaplan public when he had complained on-air about his program's being interrupted by a news conference featuring President Clinton's response to the high school massacre in Littleton, Colorado.) Dobbs told Bloomberg News, "I feel very good about the timing," adding that ratings for his popular CNN *Moneyline* program were up 20 percent in the past year, and that the CNNfn web site was off to a good start. Dobbs had been assumed to be a permanent fixture at CNN, having joined the company as anchor of *Moneyline* in 1980, when CNN was still being widely derided as the "Chicken Noodle Network." That his unquestioned tenure could be interrupted, in part, by the Web was a sign of just how disruptive it could be to traditional media companies.

As it happened, the advent of Time Warner Digital Media was not the final stage of new-media empire-building from the print division. In September, a bizarre announcement came from Time Warner that yet another new-media division would be formed, this one to be called Time Inc. Interactive. Eileen Naughton, like Bressler a former financial executive, was named president of the division, which was intended to replace Time Inc. New Media with a decentralized unit.

Don Logan's internal memo explained the revised system: "Simply put, this means that the responsibility for the various magazine web sites, currently housed at Time New Media, along with their attendant business and editorial functions, will return to the respective magazine divisions. So, for example, Time.com and Time Digital will go to Time, People Online and TeenPeople .com will move to the People Group—and so on." Time Inc. Interactive would also "operate as a clearinghouse for all Time Inc. Internet deals with outside vendors, search engines, technology partners, and others. In addition, Time Inc. Interactive will coordinate with Time Warner Digital Media."

While the confusing move sounded like a significant reorganization, it really represented a circling of the wagons. At the same time as the Time Inc. Interactive announcement, Bill Burke, the president of the Turner Broadcasting

TBS Superstation, was named president and CEO of news and information at Time Warner Digital Media. This added yet another layer of online news responsibility apart from Time Inc. There wasn't much evidence that the print unit was getting its say on any new-media decisions. Okrent had retreated back to a somewhat loosely defined writer's position at the magazine group, and Pearlstine seemed largely invisible.

A further sign of the print unit's diminished status had surfaced with the direction of the women's cable channel, web site, and print magazine that were pet projects of Ted Turner. In June, Turner Broadcasting had said it would work with Condé Nast Publications to help launch the web site, with Pat Mitchell, president of CNN Productions and Time Television, to head the effort. Although Time Inc. did not have a strong roster of women's magazines, it did publish *People, InStyle, Southern Living,* and *Teen People,* all of which were heavily read by women, and it had a long-standing affiliation with *Martha Stewart Living,* which Time Inc. had launched in partnership with the style guru. The decision by a Time Warner unit to work with a rival magazine company was a painful public embarrassment for Time Inc., and especially for *People*'s Ann Moore. Few could conceal their glee when the women's project was shut down only a few months later.

As 1999 progressed, the hub strategy seemed clearly unworkable, and in danger of imminent collapse. Many of the people who had campaigned for an online position were forced out by the end of the year or in 2000. Others saw the writing on the wall. CNNfn's Craig Forman and Helen Whelan, who'd been prominent in the money hub, left to join web site MyPrimeTime, and CNN's top dealmaker, Mark Bernstein, jumped to SpringStreet.com. The new Entertaindom finally launched in late November 1999, but it was already clear that its three creators wouldn't survive the new-media meltdown at Time Warner.

To say that the company was floundering in new media would be an understatement, for by now Levin and company were actually issuing fairly direct messages that something was going on behind the scenes. In late October, the company redesigned its corporate web site, adding video featuring a smiling Levin announcing that, "In the coming months we'll be making other important additions to our online presence."

Acknowledging that its decision to not take a position in new-media companies had been a costly mistake, Bressler announced in December that Time Warner would create a $500 million fund to invest in "digital media." Presumably with a straight face, a Bloomberg reporter wrote that the money was earmarked to give Time Warner "access to technology in areas such as e-commerce and interactive television."

As Bressler explained at the time, "This is an outgrowth of the digital makeover of the company. What is new is the focus and the size of our commitment, and we're going to step up the pace a little bit." Absent from any coverage of this decision was the acknowledgment that Time Warner had in fact already invested almost 10 years and hundreds of millions of dollars in failed attempts to give it "access to technology in areas such as e-commerce and interactive television." Of course, the announcement may well have been a red herring, intended to distract reporters from the AOL talks. But it was also an admission that the company was beginning to despair that it could build anything internally that had any value in the new-media world.

Contrasting Time Warner's digital achievements with those of AOL at the end of 1999 pointed up the striking differences between the companies. Time Warner had virtually no monetizable digital asset, except for a few small investments. In the seven years since the AOL IPO in March 1992, AOL's market cap had soared to more than $120 billion, 20 percent higher than that of Time Warner. Moreover, AOL had beaten the media companies at their own game, bringing in close to $3 billion in annual advertising and commerce revenue by 2000. As Ted Leonsis had noted, when AOL went to unlimited pricing, it became an ad-supported media company, and a phenomenally successful one at that: "It took the *New York Times* one hundred ten years to get to $1 billion [in revenue]. It took us three."

If you believed the "irrationally exuberant" market of 1999, Steve Case, himself worth more than $1 billion, had managed to build an empire that was more valuable and more streamlined than its much bigger rival. What was even more remarkable was that all the trends were in AOL's favor. In 1992, users spent only five minutes a day on AOL; by 1999 that figure had jumped to 54 minutes. Each $100 invested in AOL at its IPO was worth $28,000 by the end of 1999, while Time Warner's stock was higher before the Internet reared its ugly head.

What was particularly impressive to other media companies, even a bottom-line-oriented one like Time Warner, was the fact that AOL had developed three distinct revenue streams—subscriptions, advertising, and e-commerce licensing. That was a very difficult achievement in an area in which two revenue streams were the norm. Broadcasters receive all their revenue from advertising, and they envy cable networks, which get subscription fees from cable subscribers and ad revenue. But now here was a powerful, growing company that had successfully developed a third revenue stream, helping it attain revenue of $4.8 billion in the 1999 fiscal year.

Why *was* AOL so successful? Pavia Rosati, the former News Corp. producer, who, before she resigned in January 2001, ran AOL's Entertainment Channel, and earlier, the Influence Channel, suggests one explanation: "At AOL, there was, at once, incredible arrogance and paranoid scrappiness. AOL has never once said, 'We're the Best! By a factor of twenty! Let's kick back and have a beer!' It was always, 'Who's coming at us? What's next? How do we maintain our competitive edge?' Always, always, always. AOL was never about sitting back and resting on its laurels. It was always about how do we do it better. It's a really scrappy culture, a culture of parvenus and young people who attained great positions of power by working their asses off. And they were very protective of it."

Rosati observes that the go-go culture that was the norm in the New York media scene—dominated by outsized celebrities like Michael Bloomberg, Tina Brown, and Anna Wintour—could not be more different from that of AOL.

"AOL has no scene. It's just work, work, work," she explains. "They all work in the middle of a field [in Virginia], which one of my colleagues used to call Dirt Valley. There's nowhere to go." She mentions a "gross strip mall" in Dulles, Virginia, near AOL, that "serves a really good pizza." However, "you would never leave the office for pizza. You would never leave the office, period. When I would spend time in Virginia, it was a joke trying to leave the office before eight-thirty, because you'd get there at eight in the morning, start working, maybe grab a sandwich for lunch, and back to work." Even after getting home, AOL staffers would log on and work from home, she adds. "If I went for three hours without logging on, that was a lot."

AOL executives and minions were driven by a sense of mission, of belonging to an elite team that was building something new that had the potential to dominate the communications industry. Most other Internet cultures had a comparable drive; the difference between AOL and the rest of the pack was that AOL happened to be right. They *were* on a mission, and that mission was clearly a success. It was heady and it was real. "I loved the work and I wanted to be really good," Rosati says with simple understatement. "I wanted to create an outstanding product."

At Time Warner and other Manhattan-based media businesses, the corporate culture could not have been more dissimilar. If you joined *People* or *Time*, you were taking your place in an organization that had been around for decades, with an established mode of doing things. Moreover, being in New York City, where going to lunch is a big part of most executives' day, meant that your life was rarely just about work.

Yet while Time Warner minions may have worked in a far more glamorous milieu than those at AOL, and Time Warner's revenue dwarfed that of Dulles, the stock market didn't reward it for these things in 1999. Levin, who had for so long isolated himself from the minions he had entrusted with online responsibilities, now talked mainly to a few close aides like Richard Bressler and president Richard Parsons.

Levin had lost confidence in the various new-media gurus who had promised to build him a profitable digital enterprise. Indeed, by their own admission, most of them had given up on the idea that Time Warner could build anything of value in the New Economy. Top executives were increasingly coming around to believing that a combination of some sort with AOL might net them the biggest payout they could imagine. The only money they had ever made in new media came from AOL. By the end of 1999 AOL was the clear winner in the online business. So why not partner with that winner?

Levin himself perceived another benefit from a partnership with AOL, a top Time Warner executive says. When the Time Warner chairman looked around him he saw nothing but chaos and infighting among the six powerful divisions of the company—publishing, music, TBS, HBO, filmed entertainment, and the cable systems. This had resulted in almost complete corporate paralysis, especially where new media was concerned. The theme for the 1996 annual report had been "Even Better Together," referring to the purchase of Turner Broadcasting, but it was clear to everyone that neither the addition of Turner nor of Warner Bros. before it had resulted in the company's functioning as a single operation. The Time Warner of 1999 was a sprawling, warring corporate calamity, with none of the units able to work together on anything. The easiest way to evoke a smile on the face of a Time Warner executive was to say anything about "synergy," a theme championed since the Warner merger that signified failure on every count.

Reg Brack likes to tell the story of the time Warner Bros. arranged a screening of Michael Moore's caustic, coruscating anti–General Motors documentary *Roger and Me,* probably the most anti-corporate (if funny) film any major film corporation has ever put out. Steve Ross arranged a screening for Brack and other top executives at Time Inc. When it was over, the print guys were stunned. The film depicted GM and its CEO, Roger Smith, laying waste to

Moore's hometown of Flint, Michigan, and being as uncaring and greedy as any corporation and CEO could possibly be. Of course, they had to deal with ruffled corporate feathers all the time as the result of *Fortune* or *Time* stories, but this was much, much different. General Motors was one of *Time*'s largest advertisers and had just signed a huge deal with *Time*. And GM was held up for ridicule in the film, which was to be widely shown on television. Ross asked point blank, "Should we release this or not?" Brack, knowing the strong tradition of church/state separation at Time Warner, gulped a few times, and said, "Sure, Steve." The fallout was immediate and precipitous, with GM canceling contracts and revenue lost forever.

Levin had told shareholders in 1996, "Separately, our two companies [TBS and Time Warner] helped shape the global media and entertainment industry. By joining our uniquely complementary assets, talents and cultures, we have created an enterprise without peer." Very few inside the company believed that these assets had been truly joined in 1996, and even fewer believed this at the dawn of the new millennium. Ted Turner spent much of the '90s trying to add to his TV empire, only to be thwarted by Levin, who wouldn't let Turner buy NBC, or CBS, or much of anything, actually.

Time Warner wasn't one company, it was six or even seven, full of disharmony. HBO had long warred with the Warner film studios about license fees. TBS/CNN was in constant combat with Time Inc. over news primacy. All the TV production units, from HBO to Warner's syndication company, simply laughed at the many professed plans by the magazine company to enter the TV sphere. And the biggest management disaster in Time Warner history had occurred when, briefly, Levin had allowed HBO kingpin Michael Fuchs to assert his hegemony over the music division.

A single, dramatic transformative event could change all this, Levin thought. As a top Time Warner executive expressed it, "Jerry saw that the invading force of a merging company would integrate these six divisions that never had anything to do with each other, and, Baby, it's happening."

CHAPTER 15

Time Warner's Surrender

At 7 a.m. on Monday, January 10, 2000, Dan Okrent awoke the way he often does in his Manhattan apartment—to the sounds of Bob Edwards and National Public Radio's *Morning Edition* on WNYC–FM, a show calculated to blend just the right amount of unctuous happy talk with actual news. This morning, however, a particular business story snapped Okrent to attention. "I remember my response exactly," he says. "My wife and I were in bed, the alarm goes off, and a voice says, 'Hello, this is Karl Kassel. America Online is merging with the world's largest media company, Time Warner.' I sat up in bed and said, 'Holy shit!' The first thought was that it was unbelievable. Not good or bad, just unbelievable. It was staggering. Who could possibly have guessed it? I was stunned, stunned, stunned."

In his gravelly tones, NPR's Kassel described what was taking place between the two as a merger, and when he got to work that day, Okrent was still hearing top managers using the same terminology. "It wasn't until Wednesday that everyone really understood that they were buying us," he explains. It was then that they comprehended the true meaning of the fact that Steve Case was now the chairman of AOL Time Warner, the leader to whom they all ultimately reported.

The extraordinary closely held secret wasn't revealed to top executives and even to board members until astonishingly late in the game. Insiders say that Don Logan, whose troops' new-media failures were responsible in part for the deal's becoming reality, wasn't informed until the Saturday before the Monday announcement and was angry that he'd been kept out of the loop. Henry Luce III, the Time Warner board member whose grandfather had founded Time, wasn't notified at all, and he learned about the deal only when a friend called him on his cell phone while he was driving in to Manhattan from his country home.

At AOL, employees were not sure what to think. One top-level manager puts it this way: "I got a call at 6 a.m. the morning that it happened. My first reaction was, Thank God it wasn't CBS/Viacom. That rumor had already been lurking about. The people who had been speculating about such things had been saying, 'Well, CBS/Viacom should be poised to buy AOL soon.' That was a time when AT&T was making bids, and there were a lot of rumors swimming about a merger, and the leading candidate for many people was CBS/Viacom."

This AOL executive, who worked with some Time Warner units, thought that the merger might just work. "I remember thinking at the time, this isn't Prada and Wal-Mart, this is Old Navy and Banana Republic. They're not that different. Time Warner isn't Condé Nast. They're an old company, but they're not that snobby. They're kind of like the nice media company."

One of the reasons for the somewhat slow wakening to the new reality at Time Warner that day was the fact that Time Warner executives were far too busy cashing out on their option packages to really care who would eventually end up in the executive suite. Under the terms of the deal, Time Warner executives, many of whom had spent 20 years or more slowly accumulating stock through the company's TSOP stock plan, could sell their holdings immediately. Time Warner stock, which had been trading in the low $60s, immediately rocketed up that morning to just south of $100 a share. Okrent had an option exercise order with his broker to sell his shares when the stock hit $78. He suffered for some anxious hours when he thought his broker had done as instructed. Not till the next day did he discover that there was such a backlog of sell orders that his broker didn't sell until the stock hit $97.

But leading Time Warner executives had a lot more liquidity than soldiers like Okrent. At the beginning of 1999, Levin had 2,099,994 options that were worth almost $200 million when the deal was announced. Time Warner president Richard Parsons's options were valued at almost as much. Rich Bressler, the CFO and new-media chieftain whose inability to close an Internet deal had been a major factor driving Time Warner into the arms of AOL, had almost $20 million in options.

In the cover piece he would write for the following Monday's *Time* magazine, Okrent made it clear what had really happened: "Time Warner, the immense media conglomerate that had sprung from the loins of the magazine you are now reading—having failed to beat the Internet upstarts with its own efforts—had decided to surrender to them for the best price it could get, about $162 billion in AOL stock. The companies valued the combination at $350 billion."

Levin's decision to embrace AOL had everything to do with his belief that succeeding on the Internet was an all-important goal. In an internal company memo dated December 14, a few weeks before the merger announcement, he asserted that the "superior worth" of Time Warner wasn't being acknowledged by the stock market. "It's not my purpose to compare Time Warner to a dot-com company. By whatever measure you use . . . we're so much more." But as he vacationed in Vermont over the holidays, he came to the erroneous conclusion that the marketplace would never acknowledge the true value of the company until it appeared to be a winner online.

In case anyone had overlooked the fact that the company's new-media projects had been a dismal failure, Okrent referred to "Time Warner's stuttering, stumbling ill-managed efforts to score on the Internet (in which I and several of my Time Inc. bosses have participated)." All these efforts "have foundered on the inability of the various divisions to work collaboratively and on the relentless bottom-line pressure that discouraged investment in the distant future when there was a quarterly target to meet."

The two companies held a press conference on January 10 that was unusual in a number of respects. Levin, who had sported a clipped moustache for thirty-five years, had shaved it off just a few days previous to the event. In addition, no one could remember ever having seen the chairman without a tie (except for the time he'd worn the jacket promoting one of the company's gangsta rap acts, during the period when the company had been under fire for the lyrics on some of its records), but he went tieless on the day of the press conference. Case, who had always worn the casual clothing that was the uniform of Web businessmen, wore a necktie. The obvious message being conveyed was that the distinctions between the two worlds—the "old" traditional media represented by Time Warner, and the New Economy company represented by AOL, would soon disappear. In fact, nothing could have been further from the truth.

As the deal unfolded, it became ever more clear that it was in no respect a merger. AOL was taking over Time Warner, jettisoning many of its key managers and refashioning the company in its own image. Ted Leonsis stated its strategy succinctly: "What Jerry saw was that the Internet is transforming industry by industry and will change the way movies are delivered, the way music is delivered, the way magazines are delivered. With the size and scale that we have, we can transform the Time Warner family of businesses quickly. That's what you're going to see start happening. That's why it's called AOL Time Warner."

Perhaps the most alarming realization for Time Warner managers was that AOL didn't just think, it *knew,* that it had the better business in many respects. When AOL surveys the movie industry, for example, it sees a business that is fundamentally flawed, whose problems will never be as easy to fix as those of AOL itself. Certainly, AOL wants these companies, because of their great cash flow and brands, but that doesn't mean that it admires them uncritically or has its nose pressed up against the glass, envying the corporate jets and movie stars flocking around Warner Bros.

"When we look at the movie business, we go, 'We think we kind of understand it,'" said Ted Leonsis. "You put twenty-five movies out, five aren't any good, ten break even, five make a bit of money, and you hope you have five franchise movies. And you bring in lots of talent, some years you have lots of hits, some years you don't. It's formulaic, but it's still roll of the dice. You can't say why some movies work and some don't. We don't have that problem.

"There's a fundamental difference, a cultural and DNA understanding of the business we're in. I've always said that today's the worst day AOL will ever be. That if something isn't working, that's okay, we'll just fix it tomorrow. But with a movie or TV show or magazine, this isn't true. When we put out something, we can tell immediately if people are having a hard time navigating it, don't get it, or don't like it; in five days we can do it better, it can be right. It's so endemic to the medium itself. And that's such a big advantage."

Despite the hugs and smiles at the press conference, no one viewed this as a marriage of equals. Insiders at Time Warner, who tend to be a bit in awe of AOL, believe that Levin was outmaneuvered, that he too was intimidated by AOL's invincible aura of online success. Notes one top Time Warner executive, "There is that story out there, that Case said to Levin, 'Let's make it friendly, because if we don't make it friendly, I'm going to make it unfriendly.'"

Coming from this particular source, the story has credibility. *Time's* rival *Newsweek* reported on January 24 that "if the accounts of several senior media-industry execs are correct, Case was prepared to make an unfriendly bid for Time Warner. The idea quickly evaporated, these people say, when a major Time Warner shareholder, fund manager Gordon Crawford, supposedly learned of Case's plan and opposed it. An AOL exec vehemently denies this scenario." Levin himself told *Newsweek* that Case wouldn't have considered a hostile bid because "I don't think it was in his constitution to do it."

/ / /

According to insiders, AOL's serious talks with media companies began with Bertelsmann. The huge German-based conglomerate had emerged with a 5 percent stake in AOL (worth $8 billion by the end of 1999) and a board seat in 1995 for Thomas Middlehoff, the German-born head of Bertelsmann's U.S. operations, as a result of Bertelsmann's investment in Jonathan Bulkeley's AOL Europe. Bertelsmann's joint ventures with AOL in Europe included running both AOL and CompuServe services there, as well as operating Netscape On-line, a free British ISP. They also jointly launched an Australian version of AOL.

"Middlehoff timed his AOL investment brilliantly, both going in and going out, and that's remarkable," says Strauss Zelnick, the smooth, well-tailored former CEO of Bertelsmann's primary U.S. investment, BMG North America, which includes the RCA and Arista record labels. "[In] his decision-making and his timing, getting in AOL Europe, getting out of AOL Europe, getting in the stock and then out of the stock, he optimized the investment."

German periodicals, including the highly respected *Der Spiegel,* had reported just before the AOL Time Warner deal was announced that Steve Case had made a formal offer through Middlehoff to buy Bertelsmann that fall. Middlehoff, whom Case would later praise for his "counsel, strategic advice, and for the unique perspective he brings to any challenge," dutifully took the offer to Guetersloh, Germany, where Bertelsmann is headquartered, only to see the Bertelsmann board reject the proposal because of the difficulty of merging a public company (AOL) with a private one (Bertelsmann).

Zelnick confirms that such a discussion took place, although he's not convinced that AOL really had its sights on Bertelsmann, always preferring the well-known media assets grouped under Time Warner's massive corporate umbrella. "I do think it was a possibility and that it was discussed, but I don't think it would have been a good deal for Bertelsmann, any more than it eventually was for Time Warner," Zelnick says. "AOL would have been the buying entity."

Because of the differences between the adventurous Middlehoff and his conservative board, Bertelsmann turned out not to be in line for a deal with AOL, although sources close to the company believe that some sort of agreement between the two companies is perhaps more likely now than ever before. One reason is that Bertelsmann is planning to go public within the next "three to four years," according to spokesperson Liz Young.

But in 1999, with Bertelsmann out of the picture, that left Time Warner. The official version of the deal trajectory was that Case called Levin in mid-October to directly propose a deal. The two knew each other; Case had attended a forum sponsored by *Fortune* magazine in September 1999, where the two CEOs were said to have chatted amiably and somewhat pompously about how their companies stood for more than just corporate profits.

Steve Case can be charming when he wants to be, and when the two finally met for a session at Case's McLean, Virginia, mansion, he went all out. And Levin was impressed. "Nice dinner, good wine, good dessert," he told *Newsweek* for its January 24 issue. "It was a nice environment."

No matter how the offer was initially made, though, the final deal was an acquisition or, as Dan Okrent had put it in *Time* magazine itself, a "surrender." Time Warner executives had dismissed AOL time and time again as a company not to be taken seriously, and certainly not worth investing in. Ted Leonsis recalled the fateful day when his joint-venture proposal was rejected by Walter Isaacson, and he reviews all the attempts to do away with AOL that were launched by Time Warner and other media players. "First newspapers online were going to kill us, then phone companies and AT&T getting online was going to kill us. Then Microsoft and Windows 95 were going to kill us. Then the Web was going to kill us. Then broadband was going to kill us. Then free ISPs were going to kill us. Now wireless. I've had eight boogey men after me."

To really comprehend the magnitude of what took place on January 10, 2000, the complex reality of the evolution of the Internet business in general has to be taken into account. At the beginning of 2000, Internet stocks were still flying high, but there were already warning signs that the madness that had propelled them to such irrational levels was going to come to an end.

AOL knew that the valuations given Internet companies were dangerously out of line with any normal metrics. What had happened in 1999 made little sense from most accepted ways of looking at business. In December 1998, Time Warner had a higher market cap than AOL; a year later, AOL would be worth more than twice the value of Time Warner, despite having the same level of revenue as only one of Time Warner's six divisions. Recognizing that everything that goes up has to come down eventually, AOL and its media-savvy CEO, Bob Pittman, craved solid, real cash flow, the kind that wasn't subject to the wild fluctuations of the Internet economy. While AOL was clearly thinking about aligning Time Warner much earlier, with its rich 1997 *People* deal, it was only during 1999 that it had enough clout to consider actually buying a huge media conglomerate.

While the news had a huge impact in boardrooms around the world, it was particularly sobering for the big-media companies, which suddenly realized that their worlds had been profoundly transformed. "When I heard about the deal, I said 'My life changes today,'" says Tom Ryder, CEO of Reader's Digest Association. "I knew that a new force had been created, a true melding of the old and new economies in the media world. And all the rest of the companies would have to contend with that force. For a medium-size player, there was no question that it would affect my life in profound ways. I just knew that sooner or later we would have to have a way to join ourselves with the world of the Internet in a way that we couldn't do ourselves." This didn't mean that Ryder suddenly sprang into action, offering huge sums to AltaVista or Lycos, but he did have to formulate a response to this cataclysmic event. "The rest of us in the world of publishing and media would be scrambling to try to find connections which would give us some kind of equivalent power."

But where would they find an equivalent power to AOL and Time Warner? The very size of this merger mitigated against any other media company's hoping to duplicate its scope.

Almost immediately after the January 2000 AOL Time Warner deal, both stock prices declined. While both stocks briefly jumped upward after the announcement, AOL stock plunged more than 10 percent, to $64.50, by the day after the deal, in response to fears that AOL was diluting its exalted status. Time Warner stock dropped a little less, about 8 percent. Typical of this reaction was a story by Corey Grice and Scott Ard of CNET's News.com, who wrote on January 11, "As a result of the acquisition, some analysts are expressing concerns that AOL will no longer be a 'pure-play' Internet company, tossing aside the stellar growth and stock gains many Net firms have enjoyed over the past year. Investment banking firm Schroder & Co. downgraded AOL stock and cut its 12-month price target to $85 per share from $105, while removing AOL from its recommended list." The two noted that AOL stock was up more than 1,300 percent from the same period two years before. They also quoted Henry Blodget, the Merrill Lynch analyst, who asked, "The big question for shareholders is whether the market will accord the new entity a traditional valuation or an 'Internet valuation.'"

There's something quite odd about this statement, viewed in hindsight—an analyst at a major Wall Street establishment wonders whether P/E ratios and earnings statements still matter. Within a few months, the answer would be all too obvious. On February 28, more than a month after the press conference announcing the deal, AOL's Ted Leonsis appeared at an industry conference in San Francisco, sponsored by Robertson Stephens, the brokerage firm. By this point, AOL stock had fallen to just over $60. Wall Street, Leonsis lamented, was having trouble comprehending the merger. "It's hard for them to understand the deal right now," he said. Stock analysts were "boogeymen" who were too blind to see that AOL was "uniquely positioned to lead the new Internet revolution." By the following October, the stock price that so chagrined Leonsis would look good indeed, because AOL would then be trading in the low $40s.

Leonsis's complaint notwithstanding, the fall in both companies' stock was not really a reflection of the fact that Wall Street didn't understand the deal or that it had turned with fickleness on AOL Time Warner, but rather of the general crash in technology stocks in March and April of 2000. In April, Sanford C. Bernstein & Co.'s Tom Wolzien issued a report hailing the acquisition, saying it would provide "at least" $1 billion in extra revenue "and perhaps as much as $1.9 billion," announcing a new target price for Time Warner stock of $130 a share and up to $90 a share for AOL. There was a feeling that even if tech stocks fell, AOL Time Warner wasn't really a tech stock anymore, while still benefiting from cutting-edge developments.

Just a few months after News.com was worrying that AOL was abandoning its enviable position as a pure-play Internet company, analysts were praising the fact that it was now a diversified conglomerate. Perceived wisdom changed fast in this era. PaineWebber's Christopher Dixon noted in his June 20 report that "strong second-quarter fundamentals at both America Online and at Time Warner underscore [the] inherent strength of [the] proposed combination. . . . The pending merger of America Online and Time Warner creates a company superbly positioned to benefit from the development of the Internet as the newest mass medium, as well as from the growth of subscription revenue, advertising/e-commerce and content licensing across a broad array of traditional and emerging distribution platforms."

For Time Warner executives involved in the company's various new-media efforts, the aftermath of the deal was uncomfortable, to say the least. It was clear to all of them that they had become redundant, with AOL executives now calling the shots. Some simply left the company or went back to whatever they were doing before their misadventures on the Internet. In March, Michael Pepe, whose reign as chief operating officer of the Time Warner Digital Media division had been a fiasco, jumped to become president and CEO of the magazine company's international division, reporting to Don Logan. Former CNN vice chairman and COO Steve Korn, who had "enjoyed" a brief run as the CNN/News "hub cap," along with his designated successor, Bill Burke, both left the company in February.

Warner Bros. Online's Jim Moloshok, Jim Banister, and Jeff Weiner all departed in April, convinced that there would be no roles for them in the new order. "In light of the pending AOL merger, which brings with it a seismic shift in Time Warner's digital strategy, we certainly understand their desire to move on," commented Barry Meyer, the chief executive at Warner Bros. The three soon reestablished themselves in a new Los Angeles–based investment firm, in partnership with Terry Semel, who also had left Warner Bros. This meant that most of the hub caps were now gone, and in fact, within a few months after the merger announcement, virtually every executive at Time Warner who had had anything to do with the Internet had exited the company.

The sole top-level survivor from Time Warner's foray into new media was Walter Isaacson, who had successfully reinvented himself by simply denying the past. In November it was announced that Isaacson would be moving up to the position of Time Inc. editorial director, a job that involved serving as the liaison with AOL. In commenting on the appointment, he cast aside his credentials as new-media guru, credentials that had enabled him to so easily dismiss AOL's proposed Internet joint venture six years earlier.

Objecting to Norm Pearlstine's characterization of him as a "technologist," Isaacson told the *Washington Post* on November 15, "I think it means that I use a little BlackBerry [a pocket two-way pager] to do my e-mail. I think he's misinformed. I know that I don't know anything [about the Internet], which is why it's going to be fun to learn." With that statement—even if it had been made in jest—he simply erased almost 10 years of Time Warner's struggle to gain a foothold in new media, a struggle with which he was intimately involved. In the new AOL Time Warner, the less a Time Warner executive had had to do with the Internet, the better.

Richard Bressler, the head of Time Warner Digital Media and CFO of Time Warner, was quickly sidelined with a job as head of a questionable new division called Time Warner Investment Corp. Bressler's humiliation was complete when *Industry Standard* magazine published an article on October 30 about the AOL Time Warner deal. The feature recounted a meeting that took place about a week after the announcement, between Bressler and AOL's David Colburn, president of business affairs. Colburn was trying to explain to Time

Warner that it could promote its magazines through the infamous and hugely lucrative "pop-up" messages that appear onscreen to AOL subscribers before they can access the service (unless they're aware that they can be turned off).

"What are these pop-ups? How big are they? Can you send me some information on them?" Bressler is said to have asked. His questions seemed to indicate that he'd barely glanced at AOL itself, even though his company had just been sold to the service. "Rich, why don't you invest $21.95 in an AOL subscription and consider it due diligence?" Colburn responded acidly.

Bressler's Time Warner Digital Media managed to survive, if only in skeletal form. What remained of the unit was placed in charge of overseeing transition matters related to the merger, on a committee that included Bressler, Time Warner president Richard Parsons, AOL's Pittman, and AOL co-chair Ken Novack.

But these reassignments were merely a sideshow. In May, AOL Time Warner announced a new management structure that made it clear that Pittman was running the most desirable units of the company. On the surface, there was at least the appearance of power-sharing, with Pittman and Parsons both named as co-chief operating officers, formally reporting to Jerry Levin. But Pittman's portfolio was far more expansive than that of Parsons: Pittman had been placed in charge of AOL, Time Warner Cable, Time Inc., HBO, Turner Broadcasting System, The WB TV Network, and all business development at the merged company; Parsons had been given Warner Bros., New Line Cinema, Warner Music Group, and Time Warner Trade Publishing.

Consequently there was almost immediate speculation that Parsons would leave the company. Rumors that he would get a Cabinet-level job within the Bush administration were so rampant that top company executives were calling Parsons "Mr. Secretary" while the vote-counting fiasco in Florida was still unfolding. And since Secretary of State Colin Powell had been an AOL director (making out very handsomely with AOL stock), it was not inconceivable that Powell might pull Parsons into the government. (Such an appointment never took place.)

"His job is a pretty shitty job," said one cynical top-level Time Warner executive, speaking of Parsons then. "He has performed his function. He was the front man with the FTC [the Federal Trade Commission would approve the merger in December 2000] and management. His job was to get this thing through." This was a popular view at this juncture.

For his part, Pittman was in control of virtually all the divisions of the company that could be molded into the digital future. For the first time since he had made his prophetic statements about the media future, and written that prescient op-ed piece for the *Los Angeles Times,* Pittman would have an opportunity to take a big traditional media property and shape it along the lines of his own vision.

To fully appreciate what an opportunity and challenge that job represents, consider Pittman's career in the 1980s, when he nearly got to be an owner of MTV Networks. His trajectory after that had been somewhat erratic. His own company, Quantum, eventually folded, leaving little legacy. His subsequent role at Time Warner, where he worked with Quincy Jones and ran the Six Flags theme parks, was largely out of the limelight. And as far as his stint at Century 21 was concerned, that was not a company frequently written about in the more modish business pages. Even at AOL, Pittman had often been overshadowed by Steve Case. But it appeared that AOL Time Warner was clearly Pittman's to run. When *Business Week* did a cover story on the merger, it was Pittman, and not Parsons, Case, or Levin, who was its focus. This was to prove problematic for Pittman later. Levin was said to be furious over the *Business Week* article, thinking it had made him look irrelevant.

Under the new power structure, all the operating power was held by AOL executives, a fact they wasted no time in making clear. Pittman made an early appearance at the Time-Life Building on Sixth Avenue, saying all the right things about separation of "church" and "state," the time-honored tradition that business wouldn't try to control editorial. "Unless we are serving our readers, we're not going to have the most successful magazines in the world," Pittman told top editorial executives. But he also alerted employees to the fact that, if they wanted to undertake any major projects, they would have to go through his office.

The full ramifications of that directive became clear when the *People* magazine group's Ann Moore made a formal presentation in November to a group that included Pittman and Don Logan. The idea was that *People,* through its *InStyle* magazine brand, would launch an e-commerce operation that included handling its own distribution. It was a measure of how insulated Moore was from the reality of the new situation that she would make as naive a proposal as this to Pittman, who could hardly be expected to let the print division, which had failed so miserably at creating online products, have another go at it. Pittman quickly shot the project down, arguing that it would be too expensive. (Moore was later given a promotion, which insured that her job would be safe as long as she left new media alone.) The symbolism of the decision was lost on no one—AOL was in charge, and wasn't interested in new-media ideas from the print side.

On May 18, Levin addressed the 11th and final annual meeting of Time Warner Inc., held at the Apollo Theater in Harlem, in the course of which he tried to summarize the merger for the shareholders. For the first time the gathering was also webcast. Anticipating government and shareholder approval of the deal, he announced, "We'll begin functioning as AOL Time Warner, the world's preeminent Internet-powered media and communications company." He took credit, appropriately, for a 380 percent increase in the stock price over the past decade, which had risen at a compounded annual rate of 17 percent. Levin then summed up his management philosophy: "If there's a single principle underlying what we've done, it's 'form should always follow function.' We've recognized that the future growth of our combined company will be driven by the core functions of content creation, and of subscription services, advertising and commerce."

Levin's dictate that the form of Time Warner had to adapt to the new functions of the Internet was his somewhat elliptical way of acknowledging that in order to do so, the business had to be swallowed up by the company that had had the largest success in that medium.

"Remember," he continued, "no company has ever before been specifically designed to fit the unique paradigm created by the convergence into a single framework of TVs, PCs, telephones and a burgeoning number of wireless devices and music players." Levin insisted that the acquisition—which was listed as such on SEC documents—was in reality a merger. "Steve Case and I agreed that for this to work it can't be a series of half-measures. We intend for each company to embrace and absorb the other, blending our skills, sharing our resources, uniting our strategies until we're a single entity."

Levin went on to introduce a video that featured some interesting echoes. Dick Parsons, speaking of the merger, noted, "Our information and entertainment businesses are powerful engines for the creation of compelling content. And by combining this content with these new digital delivery platforms, we're going to be able to offer more consumers more choice, anywhere around the world." Of course, this was almost precisely the rhetoric used to launch both the FSN and Pathfinder, although the irony seemed lost on Parsons.

Particularly amusing in this context were Don Logan's remarks on the same video: "We have terrific journalists who know their business, who are able to create stories and images that highlight the brands and products of the publishing businesses. The readers and we believe that that's going to have great value as we translate those over into electronic form and distribution."

Terry McGuirk of Turner Broadcasting, who had been influential in killing the AltaVista deal, spoke of the "magic of this merger." And HBO CEO Jeff Bewkes also inadvertently evoked memories of the FSN when he discussed a product called HBO on Demand. "You pick the program, pick the movie, pick the HBO series, and it will be digitally delivered to your home. And that's the essence of the digital revolution."

Richard Bressler, whose exile from the main power structure was announced at the meeting, touted the size of the combined companies: "We're going to touch over two and a half billion people a month. We have over one hundred million subscriptions on a monthly basis, and our combined revenues will start at over forty billion dollars."

The single cautionary note amidst all the hosannas came from the ever-questioning Ted Turner, who was seen in the controlled format of the video, intoning, "The challenge now is to integrate and execute." Indeed.

As far as integration and execution were concerned, the Time Warner staff put the best face possible on the sometimes awkward process. Walter Isaacson, the official liaison with AOL as editorial director, said late in the year that, "So far, there have been a lot of meetings that have been incredibly cordial, with a lot of give and take. I've been meeting with a lot of people at AOL to coordinate what we're going to do online. All the meetings have been fun and friendly, but I've pushed a few notions, knowing that I've made my share of mistakes, and some of them they've argued me out of and some of them they've accepted, and I feel it's really fun to deal with them."

There were many ruffled feathers on Sixth Avenue on May 15, however, when the *New York Times*'s Alex Kuczynski wrote an article implying that AOL might appoint an overall editorial commissar for AOL Time Warner: "Two senior Time Inc. executives said last week that an editorial job might be created above Pearlstine's, a sort of AOL Time Warner super-editor who would oversee—and try to create synergies between—the journalistic activities at Time Warner and America Online. In this scenario, one person would supervise the journalistic work of CNN, Time Inc. and America Online."

Although Isaacson insisted that the story was false and that AOL had never considered such a plan, he did acknowledge that it caused a lot of consternation at Time Inc. "There never was a move that way," he said. "I know a couple of people in this building talked to Alex, who didn't really know. I was not involved with any discussions that would have been about that, and there was no consideration [about] an über-editor who would cross divisional lines."

Isaacson remains convinced that AOL will never take over editorial control of the magazines, though some consider that wishful thinking on his part. "One thing that Logan and Levin and Pearlstine have all believed is that you can't have editorial control over a product that you don't also have financial responsibility for. To have an über-editor responsible for different divisions without their budgets and finances and everything else, that was never in the cards. The only place that ever printed that was the *New York Times*. And no one else picked up on it because it wasn't right. And Levin wrote a letter because it wasn't right. Logan will run Time Inc., and Logan's comfortable with Norm Pearlstine." (Pearlstine's contract *was* renewed for three years in November, but this took place before the merger was consummated, so it's unclear if Logan would have needed AOL's approval for the editor in chief's deal. Moreover, letting Pearlstine go before the acquisition was finalized would have sent exactly the wrong signal to the governmental bodies overseeing the deal.)

But Isaacson will admit that, at least theoretically, AOL could assume editorial control if it wanted to. "It's quite possible that Bob Pittman or Jerry Levin could say we will now put [someone] in to run CNN or for that matter HBO; we will put in our own person to run that. But I have never heard any rumors to that effect. If Pittman decides he wants to make Jesse Kornbluth [the AOL editorial guru] the head of CNN, maybe stranger things have happened, but I think even Jesse would think it was pretty strange."

In September, seeking to shore up his position, Pearlstine gave a somewhat revisionist interview to *Adweek,* in which he claimed that Pathfinder had been the "first portal." "At its worst, it seems to me Pathfinder was a useful, legitimate and appropriate investment," he told the trade magazine, noting that "it never lost an amount of money that to me was inappropriate." He took credit for putting *Time* magazine on AOL when "I think it was the fifth-largest online provider" and proclaimed that he had no worries about AOL's editorial vision, insisting, "There is a comfort level with these people."

Of the integration and execution activities evident in the second half of 2000, most involved AOL's working Time Warner products into its online marketing machine, including the pop-up screens. Virtually none focused on Time Warner integrating AOL into its culture. Time's new magazine, *Real Simple,* was promoted online, generating 35,000 subscribers in six hours. AOL took credit for getting an Atlantic Records release by the group matchbox twenty, *Mad Season,* onto the Billboard Top Internet Album Sales chart, as well as for the 60,000 downloads of CNN Headline News and Hollywood Minute streaming videos through the high-speed AOL Plus service. AOL's inclusion of *Time for Kids* in its Kids Only Channel was responsible for growing traffic of the Time children's site by more than 1,400 percent, and AOL promotion was said to have boosted *Fortune*'s page views by 100 percent, to 2.5 million impressions the first week of the promotion.

It was hard to argue with AOL executives' oft-repeated contention that Time Warner products were burgeoning under AOL guidance—or, for that matter, the underlying message that AOL knew what it was doing in the new digital age, and Time Warner didn't. The implicit characterization of Time Warner executives as hapless bumblers not qualified to deal with the realities of the new millennium was memorably reinforced at the end of May, when Time Warner blundered into one of the most embarrassing corporate confrontations in the history of the television business. At a time when the AOL Time Warner deal was undergoing intense scrutiny by the FTC, Levin and Time Warner Cable CEO Joe Collins chose to pull the ABC signal from 3.5 million subscribers in New York, Los Angeles, and Houston, causing a major outcry from consumers, and even forcing somnolent congresspeople to make disapproving noises.

Disney CEO Michael Eisner, aware of Time Warner's delicate position, had cleverly chosen that moment to demand large price increases for his programming, including the Disney Channel and new services like Toon Disney, Soap-Net, ESPN Classic, and ESPNews. Outraged, Collins and Levin decided to get tough with Disney/ABC at the worst possible juncture, blacking out ABC and its attendant programming, including the then mega-popular *Who Wants to Be a Millionaire?*

Insiders say that, before they made their move, Collins and Levin called Case, rather than Pittman, to tell him of their plans. While this made sense in corporate terms, since Case stood above Pittman in the new power structure, Case is not a trained, experienced traditional media executive and apparently didn't realize the enormous ramifications of what he was agreeing to.

Had Levin consulted with the highly media-savvy Pittman, it is likely that he would have been immediately warned against making such a rash move. There's an old saying in the cable industry, "You don't take anything away from subscribers," and most operators try to abide by it. Subscribers won't complain too vehemently if the cable company removes, say, E! Entertainment Television or Bravo, but consumers were not about to be complacent at the disappearance of ABC. No amount of careful explanation from Time Warner could mollify the public, and the fracas quickly became one of the top stories in the media and remained that way for days, with Time Warner looking worse and worse as coverage continued.

The reaction was so strong and so negative that Dan Okrent, in the piece he did for *Time* on May 15, was again more or less forced to criticize his own company. The story, headlined "A Looney Tunes Cable Clash," called the Disney/Time Warner imbroglio "almost a perfect illustration of how not to run a business," and suggested that Time Warner could now be in the running for the coveted "Worst P.R. Move of the Year" award. Citing two of the company's best-known entertainment figures, Okrent said, "TW displayed the attributes of some of its prize properties: the discretion of Jenny Jones, the gentleness of Tony Soprano."

In a May 29 article, *Fortune* ran the headline "Dumb & Dumber: Who Wants to Be Seen as a Bullying Monopolist?" Writer Marc Gunther quoted a "senior AOL executive" as blaming the blunder squarely on Time Warner's top management. "This could never happen in the new company," the executive asserted, clearly implying that dumb and dumber executives like Collins would no longer be calling the shots. (It was part of the bad timing of the debacle that it occurred the same week that the new power structure was announced, and Collins was ordered to report to Pittman.)

AOL's powerhouse management team prevailed during the 2000 transition period despite the steep drop in its stock price, part of the technology crash that began at tax time and grew worse and worse as the year progressed. AOL shares hit $37 in October, dragging down Time Warner stock to a low of $57.51. The exchange ratio that looked good to analysts and Time Warner shareholders at the time of the merger started to look more problematic toward the end of the year, and people began to wonder if Time Warner had sold itself out at the peak of its acquirer's valuation. By December, analysts were noting that if the deal had been done then, Time Warner shareholders would have ended up with 65 percent of the company. From the period of the merger to December, Time Warner stock fell only about 5 percent, while AOL stock fell 44 percent.

"Short term, anyone objective would say probably Steve [Case] got the better part of the deal," concluded Larry Haverty, senior vice president at State Street Research in Boston, speaking to the *New York Times* on November 2. Sal Muoio, a principal at SM Investors, told the *Wall Street Journal* on December 6 that Levin and Time Warner had "panicked" by agreeing to the terms of the deal when Internet stocks were at a high. "They really blew it," he concluded.

Muoio's criticism wasn't wholly fair, however, because AOL's lowered valuation wasn't really an accurate picture of the company. AOL's stock fall had nothing to do with mistakes made by AOL executives or weaknesses in the merger, but everything to do with the April technology stock crash. Triggered by concerns about e-commerce profits, analysts like Merrill Lynch's Henry Blodget finally decided that P/E ratios *did* matter when evaluating Internet companies. And once you adopted that approach, virtually all Internet companies started looking bad, because even the biggest, like Amazon, were losing lots of money.

By the middle of 2000, it was possible to believe that we were all living in the Bizarro World, the Internet version of a parallel universe, in which everything, everything that was true at the beginning of the year, was reversed. None of the metrics that had been employed to evaluate the confounding Internet business were retained, and in a New York minute, the Internet suddenly became more than a little terrifying.

CHAPTER 16

The Bubble Bursts

D avid Wetherell was grinning broadly as he strode up to the microphone to deliver a pep talk at a former factory building called Brickstone Square, his well-appointed CMGI headquarters in Andover, Massachusetts. It was the beginning of April 2000, and the CMGI chairman was addressing a few hundred beleaguered Andover-based staff members of MyWay.com, a troubled division of his burgeoning empire. MyWay, formerly called Planet Direct, was a direct result of Wetherell's desire to take on America Online. The idea behind it was to provide portal software to a network of independent ISPs (Internet service providers), and to then consolidate their traffic, thus creating a powerful joint attack against AOL's hegemony. It was one of several assaults Wetherell had aimed at AOL, none of which proved to be especially bothersome to AOL. But on that day Wetherell was still the chieftain of what seemed to be an almost invincible business, and he gave a rousing presentation of the company line: Combined in a loose *keiretsu* with other CMGI investments like AltaVista, MyWay would eventually become a billion-dollar addition to the group, which then had a market cap in the tens of billions of dollars.

Wetherell had been the subject of a fawning cover story in *Business Week* the previous October. "Who is David Wetherell? And why is everyone talking about him and his hot company, CMGI?" the magazine had asked. Since then the huge momentum that the article had chronicled, in which investors in the various CMGI investment funds had seen returns as high as 9,000 percent, had only continued. In April CMGI stock was trading at over $150. And if employees listened carefully, it sounded as if it was about to go much higher.

CMGI, Wetherell had told the mesmerized group, was about to enjoy a huge new investment, "our biggest ever." The deal would be announced the following week, he explained, with the full confidence that comes with a stock that is trading at such incredible levels.

After the meeting staffers either rushed to call their brokers or huddled among themselves. Company scuttlebutt was that AT&T or another large conglomerate was prepared to invest over $1 billion in CMGI. On that news, most believed, the company's stock would double again and head for $300 territory. MyWay employees bought all the stock they could, some on margin. Based on the anticipated run-up of the stock price, many executives had already purchased new houses in the Boston area. One had bought two grand colonials, less than 20 miles apart—just because he could. If they were acting on insider information, so what? The SEC didn't seem to be listening.

Only a funny thing happened on the way to collecting on these Internet riches: The deal that Wetherell had promised was all but closed never actually materialized, having become a prisoner of the "collars" in the deal language, a provision that killed the investment if CMGI stock traded below a certain level. The timing was exquisitely brutal for some employees, who began to face not only margin calls but the threat of layoffs, in sharp contrast to some of the top CMGI executives, who had sold enormous blocks of stock at the top of the market a few weeks earlier, apparently not convinced that the future was going to be quite as solid as they were promising.

In fact, the great 2000 technology stock slide began the very week that Wetherell was promising MyWay staffers that their company was headed for prosperity. During the 1990s, the Nasdaq had moved in only one direction, rising a remarkable 795 percent. On March 13, the Nasdaq closed at 5048.62, its all-time peak. Yahoo! was a typical beneficiary of this trend. The stock was trading at $30 in the fall of 1998. By January 2000, its price had risen to $250, giving it a market cap of $133 billion, more than Ford and General Motors combined.

Today, even at so close a remove, this period seems disconnected to reality. Former Merrill Lynch analyst Henry Blodget, a former cheerleader for the Internet, compares the "irrational exuberance" over tech stocks to the enthusiasm that accompanied the rise of such bedrock industries as the telephone (1883), the automobile (1900), TV (1956), and the PC (1984). During the craze for each industry, Blodget explains, "over-capitalization led to silly valuations." In an address to a small group at the 2001 Merrill Lynch Internet conference in New York in March, Blodget spoke of an astonishing $156 billion that had flowed into tech companies between the fourth quarter of 1999 and the first quarter of 2000. "During that period, VCs [venture capitalists] were auditioning to be allowed to invest," he recalls. "We would meet with one of those companies. We would tell them that in our opinion they were worth $1 billion, and we would swallow hard when we said it. They would say, 'We're not a start-up, and CS First Boston just said we're worth $6 billion.'" Blodget believes that this huge influx of capital, spread by Web entrepreneurs throughout the economy—especially since much of this money flowed into advertising and media—created the impression of a robust future. But it was illusory and couldn't possibly last.

On April 4, a few days after Wetherell gave his bullish speech to employees, efforts to solve the government's antitrust dispute with Microsoft collapsed. A defiant Bill Gates was widely perceived as being out of touch with the reality he faced, and tech investors grew nervous. That day the Dow plunged 349.15 points, or 7.64 percent, its biggest-ever point drop. On April 11, as bad earnings reports were released by Microsoft, Hewlett-Packard, Intel, and IBM, the Nasdaq fell 286.27 points, its second-worst showing ever, and it would drop another 355.49 points on April 17.

Analysts suddenly began to apply real-world analytics to dot-coms, and under that harsh light, almost all of them began to look bad. The main coverage of these companies began to shift from IPOs to measuring burn rate and gauging how long they could expect to survive. *Barron's* published a much-noticed article that featured a list of businesses on the "death watch," and reported that public Internet companies had burned up about $2 billion in cash in the third quarter of 2000, with little hope of a turnaround in their fortunes. The question for many of them became what would come first—delisting off the Nasdaq or shutdown.

Over the next several months, pure-play Internet content companies began draconian layoffs and/or simply dropping from sight. Among those that announced staff cutbacks were Jake Winebaum's eCompanies and his personal project, Business.com, DrKoop.com, DrDrew.com, Kibu.com, Quokka Sports, Salon.com, StarMedia (a Spanish-language portal), and TheGlobe.com. Others—including Urban Box Office (which filed for bankruptcy), APB Online (a crime news site), Furniture.com, Pseudo Programs, Pets.com, Toysmart, Living.com, Garden.com, Eve.com, Reel.com, and Worldsport—closed down completely. All of them had been launched as alternatives to content operations from media companies, many with e-commerce components, and all had attracted significant investor capital.

The same venture capitalists who, in investing in dot-com companies had ignored the fundamental rules they'd learned while getting their MBAs, were suddenly reborn as cautious investors. According to Jerry Colonna of Flatiron Partners, a top New York VC firm, his company invested in 17 transactions in the first quarter of 1999, five in the second quarter, two in the third quarter, and two in the fourth quarter. "When the crash hit the public markets, every one of us had to look at our core business," he told the Internet Content conference in October of 2000.

Almost overnight, the media, which had run countless stories about 24-year-old dot-com millionaires, turned on the Internet world. The *New York Post,* which had entered into a news exchange with CNET's News.com, inaugurated a "Dead Dot-com of the Day" feature, and even the fluffy *Entertainment Tonight* syndicated program started covering ailing dot-coms. *Business Week,* which had all but knighted David Wetherell the previous year, now rushed to proclaim his company in deep trouble. Financial columnists like MSNBC's Chris Byron, who had been derided as wrong about dot-com stocks from the start, having warned investors to stay away from companies like Amazon and Yahoo!, loved hearing stories like this. They now proclaimed themselves vindicated because the Internet stocks had finally come down to earth.

Of course, much of this attitude was simply schadenfreude on the part of old-line journalists, who had been too complacent to give up their nice offices for the uncertainty of a tiny cubicle and stock options, who had fretted over the possibility that their more adventurous friends might get rich, and who were now all too smugly noting that those same friends were scrambling to get back to the traditional world they'd left.

Janice Page, an editor at the *Los Angeles Times* who had departed to join Microsoft's local Sidewalk service in Boston in 1997, recalls her colleagues at the newspaper being utterly convinced she would make tons of money just by joining Microsoft. "They all said, 'We'll see you when you're rich.' They thought I was instantaneously a millionaire somehow." In reality, Page had had to take a $10,000 pay cut, and while she did receive 500 stock options in Microsoft, the stock split and skyrocketed during her ride there, she didn't get rich. In the end, after taking into account various bonuses and severance in 1999 when Sidewalk shuttered, Page probably would have made more money had she stayed at the *Los Angeles Times,* because the employee stock options granted to long-term employees instantly vested when Tribune bought the *Times* in 2000.

One particularly vulnerable target of the I-told-you-so crowing in media circles was Kurt Andersen, the former editor of *New York* and *Spy* magazines, who had been perhaps the bravest of the pack of senior-level editors, in that he had started his own web site, Inside.com, at the height of the Internet craze.

A few months later, with the Web business in freefall, Andersen and the high-profile scribes who'd joined him, including former *Spin* editor Michael Hirschorn, provided a convenient object lesson for all those congratulating themselves that they had never chosen that path. In June, Andersen penned a piece for Inside.com titled "Can Online Media *Ever* Be a Good Business?" At the end of the piece, he trotted out the by now familiar mantra of the beleaguered online property: Hadn't it taken 12 years for *Sports Illustrated* to make a profit? *Vanity Fair* needed $200 million and a dozen years to break even. "Give me a break" seemed to be Andersen's subtext.

Andersen commented later, citing the three years that it took his *Spy* magazine to become profitable, "People need in this world to understand that as transformative as the Internet is, it doesn't mean that a media entity has shortened the time it takes to be a profitable business." Of course, *SI* and *Vanity Fair* had been allowed such long gestation periods because their publishers understood their business, saw encouraging signs, and had the finances to back up their convictions. The problem with Web investments, as Andersen discovered to his chagrin, is that the financial backers sometimes have only a hazy comprehension of the Internet, see mostly discouraging results, and don't have either the patience or the commitment to keep funding what they regard as a losing proposition.

In April 2001 Inside.com was folded into Steve Brill's Media Central, itself a partially owned subsidiary of Primedia. The implication was that Andersen and Hirschorn had not cashed out with great Internet cash payouts, which made their rivals in media companies very happy. Brill's tenure over Inside.com was also brief.

Some insiders in the print industry had begun to issue warnings even before magazine refugees like Kurt Andersen began to run into trouble. The magazine industry's trade organization, the Magazine Publishers of America, commissioned a study in early 2000 on magazines and their Web ambitions by noted consultants McKinsey & Company. Despite its vaunted reputation, McKinsey had had a mixed track record with magazines; insiders at Time like to snicker about the firm's disastrous early '90's advice to CEO Reg Brack that Time Inc. adopt a regional selling plan. Despite such missteps, McKinsey was still taken very seriously in magazine circles, and its eventual report carried a lot of weight with magazine company presidents in 2000. The document took a pessimistic tone, as it noted, "Magazines got off to a late start [on the Web]—which may be a good thing in retrospect. Only 27 of the top 100 magazines, defined by revenue, appear on the Media Metrix list of the top 3,000 Web sites, defined by traffic. . . . We are curiously absent from the Media Metrix Top 100. Instead, it is made up of search engines and portals, as well as the largest e-commerce sites and the combined sites of major entertainment companies."

Even more sobering was McKinsey's estimate of the cost of building and maintaining a magazine web site: "Assuming the use of a top-tier Web design shop and purchasing state-of-the-art software licenses, servers and back-office infrastructure, developing a companion Web site should cost about $275,000. This gets you a 'cheap site done right.' Almost half of the costs come from product development. Unfortunately, the annual maintenance costs also need to be factored in on top. Using a bare-bones staff of two full-time employees—grown-ups, not part-time school kids—you can expect maintenance, including personnel, Web hosting and annual upgrades, to cost about $270,000. We made the assumption that you can stretch your Web investments over a three-year period, and then you will have to re-invest. Over this period, development and maintenance expenses sum to a little over a million dollars, not including any marketing expenses to promote your site!"

While there seems to have been an assumption that this was information that was new to its readers, a rather astonishing proposition six years after Pathfinder went online, McKinsey, with its exclamation points, had only just begun to scare the magazine world. "Are you gasping for air?" the report asks, after delivering its cost summary. "If you are, take a breath now, because the revenue side of this model is pretty tough, too. We see four viable revenue streams for magazine Web sites: print subscription generation, advertising, content syndication and affiliate commissions. Adding up all the conditions necessary to break even, subscription generation is responsible for the lion's share of revenue, and most assumptions are tough to believe for the average magazine."

One has to assume that some magazine presidents had stopped reading the report by this point and had already dispatched an underling to fire the vice president of new media. But had they read on, they would have learned that McKinsey concluded that magazines were failing at even the most basic Web goal—selling subscriptions online. Magazines actually generate less than 1 percent of their subscriptions this way, McKinsey noted, a dismal result. But the advertising story was even worse. To make money selling ads online, the consultants concluded, "15 percent of your available banner impressions would have to be sold at a premium $25 CPM rate in our break-even base case. Major Internet ad networks sell only 5 percent to 7.5 percent of the inventory at premium prices, with the remaining inventory selling for slightly more than 'added value.'"

Translating that from consultant-speak, what McKinsey was saying was that the $25 CPM was a ridiculous goal for a magazine to attempt. If ad networks like DoubleClick were basically giving away 95 percent of their banner impressions for "slightly more than 'added value,'" how could magazine companies even hope to get their CPMs out of single digits? The reality, as the readers of this report had to know by the year 2000, was that many advertisers like Procter & Gamble were refusing to pay higher than $2 CPM.

For content syndication to work, McKinsey advised that magazines would need to sell at least 180 articles a year for a $300 monthly license, although it admitted, "We've seen few Web sites able to extract the $300 per article." Outside content syndicators, including iSyndicate and Screaming Media, were actually paying only a tiny fraction of that amount, and some magazine companies, unwilling to assign expensive personnel to the task, were accepting such fees.

McKinsey was equally discouraging about possible revenue from e-commerce affiliate commissions. (These are referrals a company like Hearst might generate by operating an Amazon.com bookstore on its web site.) An affiliate might pay a few pennies for each successful referral, but McKinsey concluded that magazines "must realize an average affiliate purchase of $60 from four out of every one thousand site visitors, with the companion site negotiating a 6 percent commission. Forrester [Research] reports that less than one out of a thousand site visitors buy through affiliate links. You better have really good stuff to sell!!"

For the few unintimidated souls still reading this far into the report, McKinsey concluded that a "full-blown" destination web site would cost the beleaguered executive "about $17.5 million over three years." In order for a site this expensive to break even, it would have to attract 1.9 million unique visitors a month. Given the reality that magazine web sites were completely failing to attract visitors at all, this figure was the coup de grâce. For any magazine executive who took these findings seriously, the only alternative was to simply dump the Internet from his or her agenda. This wasn't too difficult a decision to make, in the end, because virtually all magazine leaders were all too happy to see the Internet in their rearview mirrors after years of disappointment.

Out of a sense of relief that their long nightmare was finally ending, many media companies were hugely enjoying watching the Internet industry fail, however much short-term financial hardship was involved. Perhaps no career better illustrates the confusion and ambivalence that these businesses felt than that of Rupert Murdoch. The Australian mogul had been viscerally angry after being abandoned by MCI and had confined new-media activities at News Corp. to trying to build web sites for its media properties, crowned by an entertainment portal called TV Guide Entertainment Network. Like the other media conglomerates, News Corp. held endless and fruitless talks with a variety of new-media concerns about acquisitions and mergers, none of them leading anywhere because Murdoch ultimately found all these would-be partners too arrogant. TVGEN was abandoned with the sale of *TV Guide,* but even so, Murdoch could hardly continue to ignore the burgeoning Internet business.

In March 2000, right before the bubble burst, Murdoch opened up his new-media operation to *Wired* magazine, which wrote a breathless story, "Rupert Discovers the Internet," proclaiming the venerable Australian to be a converted technophile. The magazine noted that "a little over a year ago," Murdoch had spoken to a forum on 21st-century media in Singapore and had dismissed Internet stocks as far too expensive, cautioning that the Web "will destroy more businesses than it creates."

But "that was then," *Wired* added, and now Murdoch "has got the Internet religion." Murdoch told the magazine, "I was thought to be anti-Internet, which I never was at all. I did say I don't know how you justify the price of some of these stocks, which I still say, but I've been wrong."

He concluded, "I think this is the most complicated, the most fundamental thing we've faced. We've had lots of problems, but not like this. There is some fundamental change going on, and it raises difficult questions. How do we adapt to new media? We're searching, we're experimenting, and we have some fairly strong ideas, but no certainties." Indecision and acknowledgment of weakness were qualities that were uncharacteristic of Murdoch and an indication of just how out of his depth he felt.

Thanks to his epiphany while surfing the wild side of the Web with Scott Kurnit, Murdoch was particularly enthusiastic about page3.com, the web site that featured semi-nude Page Three girls from his tabloid *Sun* newspaper in London. "We had something like twelve million hits in three or four weeks," Murdoch enthused to *Wired,* getting his traffic nomenclature a bit confused. "People sign up for it and want the chance to vote on the prettiest girl of the month. We're getting their names and so on, and we'll get back to them."

After the MCI venture had gone awry, Murdoch had given his errant son, James, then 27, what was left of News Corp.'s online portfolio. James had been initially more interested in rock and roll than the Internet and for years carried a card that proclaimed himself News Corp.'s executive vice president of new media and music, a dubious title given that the company had no music investments. James had dawdled with a short-lived rock label on the side, which quickly fizzled. (In like manner, Michael Eisner's son, Eric, was involved with a Web effort called Romp.com, which the *New York Post* described as a "babes 'n' animation site," offering such fare as animation based on the raunchy film *Booty Call.*)

James was featured front and center in the *Wired* article, modestly refusing to take credit for convincing his father that the Internet had to be taken seriously. The piece failed to note, however, that several years earlier James had tried to get News Corp. to buy PointCast, the champion of so-called "push" technology, which became one of the biggest flameouts in the early Web industry. James's deal to pay more than $300 million for PointCast fell apart only after News Corp. CFO David Devoe allegedly objected to the terms.

By 1999, however, James had brought his father around to Internet religion, and on December 7, 1999, News Corp. agreed to trade $1 billion of its assets for 10.8 percent of WebMD, an online heath-care site. In common with other TV industry deals, this one involved $700 million of promotion on News Corp.–owned channels, and 50 percent of a fledgling cable network called the Health Channel.

At the time, News Corp. indicated it would follow the example of CBS and build a portfolio of Internet investments (although CBS never gave any of its Internet companies equity in its offline assets). A year later, however, when the value of News Corp.'s WebMD stock had plunged from almost $1 billion to just over $100 million, the deal was renegotiated so that News Corp. now had to offer only $205 million in ad time to WebMD, and Murdoch took back the half-stake in the Health Channel that had been ceded to the dot-com company.

After the April slide, the old, skeptical Murdoch returned with a vengeance. It must have become clear to him by now that, had he listened to his younger son and invested in PointCast, his losses in new media would have totaled almost half a billion dollars by the beginning of the new millennium. He was no longer heard waxing poetic about page3.com.

On October 18, 2000, Murdoch appeared at News Corp.'s annual meeting in Adelaide, Australia, and resumed his savaging of the Internet. He was now a "bear on all that pure dot-com business. I think unless you are planning a dot-com [with] large transaction revenues, which is the B-to-B [business to business]—and we even have doubts about that—you are simply relying on putting out information and having it paid for by the advertising community.

I don't think there is a business there, and I think that is what we are seeing now with the collapse. Without a bricks and mortar institution behind you, you are being blown up in 99 or 100 percent of the cases."

A reborn Luddite, Murdoch wanted recognition for his refusal to have been hoodwinked. "We have been criticized for being too slow, very slow, but I don't hear anyone going around praising me, having lost a fraction of what all our competitors lost."

These remarks, which echoed Don Logan's a few years earlier, effectively squelched whatever enthusiasm existed across News Corp.'s sprawling empire for any future new-media projects. The company fired more than 200 of the survivors of its new-media division and announced plans to close down its West 18th Street operation. It was truly the end of an era.

The *New York Post,* always a sure bellwether of prevailing winds at News Corp., turned on the Internet business. The paper's Joe Gallivan, who had been assigned to the dot-com beat, wrote, "Suddenly, the pressure of tracking stocks, runaway valuations, and python-eats-pig scenarios such as AOL buying Time Warner are off." By December 2000, News Corp. CEO Peter Chernin, reporting on his company's fortunes at the UBS Warburg (formerly PaineWebber) media conference, managed to give an entire presentation without even mentioning the Internet. When asked about that afterward, Chernin grinned. "Not a single time," he admitted, adding it had been intentional that he'd avoided talking about "that Internet crap." He intoned, almost like a mantra he'd just learned, "Bricks and mortar, John, bricks and mortar." No wonder. In February, News Corp. reported a net loss for its fiscal second quarter, a loss directly attributable to its new-media problems.

Reader's Digest CEO Tom Ryder, who had been so affected by the AOL Time Warner merger, had a similarly jolting experience with Internet properties. When he became chairman and CEO of the Reader's Digest Association, Inc., in April 1998, he had inherited an investment the company had made in an Australian-spawned Web portal called LookSmart.com. The project had been a pet project of Jim Schadt, a previous CEO, and LookSmart had actually been incubated on the leafy Reader's Digest campus in suburban Pleasantville, New York. It grew quickly, but after Schadt's ouster, successor CEO George Grune reduced Reader's Digest's stake in the site to only about 10 percent, when it had previously been a majority holder. Grune's decision began to look misguided by the end of 1999, when LookSmart's stock peaked. Even with only a 10 percent stake, however, RDA's investment was worth more than $700 million in 1999, an incredible return. "I gave a speech in January 2000 at a CIBC Oppenheimer Internet conference, and I said that as of today, we have over $800 million in Internet assets on our balance sheet," Ryder recalls, including an investment in WebMD, the same company in which News Corp. had invested. "I also had to realize that about a month later those assets were worth $100 million, and a month later they were worth $10 million."

At the height of its run, LookSmart's market cap was over $7 billion, almost twice that of the Reader's Digest Association itself, a venerable company with a massive direct-mail operation and a magazine with a circulation of almost 30 million. How could anyone begin to make sense of these kinds of numbers?

Most media CEOs didn't even try. After March 2000 virtually every other media company was in lockstep with News Corp., scaling back or abandoning joint ventures with new-media concerns and firing many of their own Web staff.

CBS laid off 24 new-media employees in June, out of 100 total. Two months later, NBC Internet laid off 170 people, 20 percent of the total, and in September, MTVi, corporately connected to CBS and under the new leadership of former SonicNet chieftain Nicholas Butterworth, cut 105 jobs, 25 percent of the total. Butterworth's hoped-for IPO was in ashes, along with many, many others. In November Discovery.com, the new-media unit of the Discovery Channel, laid off 45 percent of its staff, abandoning its ambitious content strategy and focusing instead on promoting the cable channels. The same month, the joint venture between the Hearst Corporation and the web site Women.com began to unravel. In March 2001 competitor CondeNet, the online arm of the Condé Nast division of Advance Publications, announced a layoff of 18 people, or 12 percent of its 147 employees. It seemed to herald an almost total capitulation of the women's magazines to their online competition.

Knight Ridder delivered a Christmas layoff message to 68 of its new-media employees in December, 16 percent of the new-media staff. The New York Times Company, which had about 400 people working for the New York Times Digital unit run by Martin Nisenholtz, laid off 69 employees in January 2001 and abandoned plans for a tracking stock. The employees learned they were being fired through an article in the *Times* itself, forcing Nisenholtz to issue an embarrassed memo.

The *New York Times*'s enthusiasm for the Web was dampened by the inarguable logic of statistics, which Nisenholtz called a "dirty little secret," and which revealed that while readers of the newspaper spent 30 minutes a day on average with it, users of the web site were logged on for an average of only 30 minutes a *month*. According to Nisenholtz, even 30 minutes a month is a good number, considering that many top web sites average only 2 minutes per month. For advertisers, numbers like that were problematic, and for executives at the paper they reinforced the suspicion that the Web was not a great business, that people looking for news online only wanted headlines. The *New York Times,* unlike, say, *USA Today,* is not a headlines kind of newspaper but an in-depth read, and it galls the *Times* to realize that institutions like Reuters may be better adapted for the Internet world than it is.

One of the few media Web operations that didn't announce a layoff in early 2001 was the *Wall Street Journal*'s WSJ.com, which was reaching 500,000 paying subscribers by the end of 2000. Peter Kann, chairman of Dow Jones & Co., said in a brief interview at the end of December that WSJ.com wasn't profitable yet because of heavy marketing costs, but "it could be if we slowed the pace of our marketing efforts."

The WSJ.com subscription model is "widely envied," Kann added, "in light of recent developments." WSJ.com is unique partly because many of its subscribers are able to put its subscription costs on their travel and entertainment (T&E) reports, something they couldn't justify for almost any other web site. Tellingly, Kann was one of the few media chieftains to mention his Internet operations in detail at the 2001 UBS Warburg conference. For many onlookers, WSJ.com looked like the media brand with the brightest future on the Internet, because, unlike its competitors, it actually had a subscription model that worked.

Even with layoffs, backing out of new media would prove to be a difficult process for the three broadcast networks conglomerates. Disney/ABC's Go Network and NBCi were now public companies, and no amount of staff reductions could make them go away. By the end of 2000 the Go Network was the sixth-largest web site, with 28 million unique visitors a month, roughly one-fourth of the total traffic. Considering that about 122 million Americans were then using the Internet, that should have been a remarkable accomplishment, but its popularity was ultimately irrelevant.

Wall Street suddenly didn't care how many million people were looking at your web site, but only if they were spending money while doing so. You could certainly make money if you reached one-fourth of the American population with cable TV; the Disney Channel reached fewer than that, and it was highly profitable. But operating the number-six web site held no such guarantees. Keeping up with Yahoo! was hugely expensive, and Disney wasn't gaining ground, it was losing it.

Jake Winebaum's dream had been to conquer cyberspace, and Disney hadn't achieved that. It was dwarfed by America Online, which it had tried to buy, and Yahoo!, which hadn't been interested in an alliance with Disney. Winebaum's departure had left a big hole at the company, and remaining Infoseek executives like Patrick Naughton had taken on an even bigger role. Naughton was consequently an Internet star in Burbank, at least until the unthinkable happened.

On September 16, 1999, Patrick J. Naughton was arrested in Santa Monica and charged with interstate travel with the intent to have sex with a minor, as well as possession of child pornography. He was also charged with using the Internet to force a minor into sexual activity. An FBI agent named Bruce Applin had been in contact with Naughton for seven months, posing as an underage girl. It's impossible to overestimate what a blow this case was to Eisner and Disney in general, a company that makes much of its considerable coin by presenting itself as a morally upright purveyor of wholesome children's content to impressionable young minds.

The company quickly moved to distance itself from the resulting flood of publicity, but the damage had been done. It also cast a pall over the Go project that didn't go away no matter how many restructurings and revampings were announced. For months after Naughton's arrest, details of his actions and of his subsequent trial, which began in December 1999, made headlines.

Even worse for the relentlessly bottom-line Mouse, the Disney Internet Group was trading in the low single digits by the end of 2000, giving it a market cap of only about $600 million, far less than had been invested. In a profile of the company in the July 2000 issue of *Worth* magazine, Linda Keslar and others opine that Disney spent about $500 million on the Go site and had "little to show for it." Keslar asserted that in the 18 months between the writing of the article and the inception of Go.com, it had lost a total of $1.5 billion, mostly related to exercising the warrants to acquire the rest of Infoseek. Eisner himself had purchased 150,000 shares of Go.com stock on the open market. The stock was worth almost $3 million in March 2000 but had dwindled to $825,000 by January 23, 2001, which means that Eisner personally lost more than $2 million on the Go debacle.

A forecast of stagnant first-quarter 2001 earnings, attributable in part to losses from the DIG operations, led to a 15 percent drop in Disney shares on November 9. "The Disney Internet Group hurt Disney's results," Bloomberg reported that day. This trend only got worse. By February 2001, when Disney announced its fiscal first-quarter earnings, Disney's net income had plunged from $356 million for the same quarter the previous year to $63 million, a drop that was a direct result of a $253 million loss at DIG.

The damage from Internet holdings had gotten so bad, according to the *New York Times*'s Geraldine Fabrikant, writing on February 7, that "some analysts [have begun to] use operating income before Internet expenses and one-time charges to evaluate the health of the operating businesses." Setting aside its Internet losses, Disney would have earned 28 cents a share, which was better than analysts had forecast.

Eisner had seen this lamentable result coming, as he had acknowledged to the *New York Times* on August 14: "People told me we had to be like Microsoft and put out version one and two and three, and eventually we would get it right. We did that with Go, then people told us it wasn't as good as Yahoo! or America Online. I've never been involved with anything where I didn't believe what we did wasn't the best. But here we were, experimenting in front of the public." Still reeling from the Naughton imbroglio and unwilling to invest in another dot-com genius, Eisner appointed Steve Bornstein, a trusted manager from ESPN, to try to revive Go.com, but it was clearly too little, too late.

Bornstein tried to refocus Go as an entertainment destination, rather than a broad portal, but the transformation had little effect on traffic or profits, and the first rumblings started to surface that Disney wanted to unload the entire mess. According to the Media Metrix web-site listing for January 2001, the Web properties of the Walt Disney Internet Group attracted more than 21 million unique visitors, a showing that sounds impressive, until it is weighed against AOL's 64 million or against the fact that AOL was collecting money from most of those 64 million visitors (some visited AOL.com for free), while Disney was collecting much less. Disney could no longer conceivably believe it was competing against AOL in any way, shape, or form. To put the situation in perspective, if the ABC network attracted only one-third the audience of NBC, CBS, or Fox, all the people running it would be fired.

Eisner might have gotten some satisfaction in seeing that Jake Winebaum, the mastermind behind the Go strategy, was having troubles of his own. Winebaum's eCompanies, an Internet incubator, had managed to raise $160 million, but much of that evaporated as virtually all the eCompanies investments went south with the technology downturn, and he was refused a second-round capitalization by his primary investors, who had included Eisner. In October, Winebaum merged eCompanies with Evercore Capital Partners, a New York investment firm that had put money into such Old Economy stalwarts as the tabloid newspapers the *National Enquirer* and the *Star*. With most of the companies in his portfolio out of commission because of the tech debacle, Winebaum was left with Business.com, the very expensive URL that he was trying to jump-start into a financial portal. ECompanies partner Sky Dayton, the founder of Earthlink, dismissed eCompanies this way in a March 25, 2002, article in *Forbes ASAP*: "I admit I drank my share of Kool-Aid during the craze." Many of eCompanies' investments "turned out to be lemons," he concluded.

Disney's network rivals weren't faring any better. Snap.com had been transformed into NBCi, but that hadn't helped. NBCi's layoff did little to help NBCi stock, which also plunged to single digits in 2001, from a high of 106. NBCi spokesman Robert Silverman had predicted in mid-2000 that NBCi would turn profitable by 2002, despite a burn rate of $40 million a quarter. He had boasted that Snap! had been the 57th-largest web site as measured by Media Metrix when it was acquired by NBC in July 1998 and had risen to number 12 by mid-2000 as a result of NBC promotion and new leadership from former Fingerhut executive Will Lansing. But with the sudden squeeze on portals, NBC seemed to simply run out of ideas, and NBCi itself seemed to lose its raison d'être altogether. In making the layoff announcement on January 18, the web site reiterated that it "anticipates becoming profitable before non-cash charges and NBC promotion in the fourth quarter of 2001 or the first quarter of 2002." But this sounded more like a rhetorical gesture than anything else, and those predicting doom for NBCi, by now a large contingent, didn't have long to wait.

On April 9, with NBCi shares slumping to $1.50, parent company NBC announced that it would be shutting down NBCi completely and buying back the shares of the public spinoff it didn't own for $2.19 a share. That cost NBC about $138 million, adding to a long list of expenses that the dysfunctional Internet venture had cost the company.

In the end, though, the money was less important than the prestige that NBC and GE were giving up. GE had been one of the first companies in the online space with GENIE, and it had enjoyed for years a reputation under Jack Welch, who was retiring in 2001, as the best-run company in America. GE was supposed to understand technology, but NBCi ended up proving that GE, like all the country's other big corporations, was stymied by the Internet and convinced there was some kind of special mojo zeitgeist Internet know-how out there, if only they could find it. In the end, it was intolerable for GE to be associated with so public an embarrassment, a daily reminder of its failure to lead in the Internet space. Ted Turner used to like to say, "Lead, follow, or get out of the way." GE chose, in the end, the latter solution.

From his vantage point as CEO of the magazine-based media company Primedia, former NBC executive Tom Rogers watched the missteps of NBC and its media rivals. It had been Rogers who had purchased the web sites Xoom and Snap!, but now, as head of the magazine arm of Kohlberg Kravis Roberts, the same company that had taken over Nabisco, he had vowed to turn the company's sprawling trade and consumer magazine empire into a digital powerhouse.

True to his word, on October 30, 2000, Rogers and Scott Kurnit announced the second major old/new media merger, after AOL Time Warner: Primedia would acquire Kurnit's About.com, the seventh-largest web site, which vied with Go in terms of Internet site rankings from Media Metrix, for $690 million in stock. Like other New Economy stocks, About.com shares had had a steep downfall, dropping about 75 percent from the high of March 2000, making the About/Primedia deal far cheaper than it would have been had it been concluded at the height of the market.

Kurnit had launched About.com in February 1997 with virtually no investor capital and had grown the business organically. The novelty of About. com was that the site offered a human face on the same kind of Internet directory that Yahoo! featured. (While Yahoo! also has editors who scour the Web, they remain invisible on the service.) At About.com, outside contractors who are experts in more than 300 categories are paid based on the traffic their area attracts, much in the way that media companies were once compensated by AOL. Their pictures appear on the site, and they are promoted as "guides" to help users surf favorite categories. The formula worked because, like AOL's friendly graphics, it made the Internet seem less imposing, more accessible and human. In the end, About.com had spent a tiny fraction of what Disney had to get virtually the same traffic. Kurnit freely admits that the idea came from concepts bouncing around Prodigy and MCI, but he was the one who actually made them happen.

Kurnit had tried to secure an alliance with a leading media or Internet company earlier in the year, including CMGI before its stock had gone into freefall. (He had since gotten over the fact that he had brought his concept, then called the Mining Company, to Wetherell before it had launched. CMGI had passed but shortly afterward launched a site called ZineZone that Kurnit thought was imitative.) Kurnit talks ruefully about having called Time Warner's Richard

Bressler before the AOL deal was announced, only to be told, bizarrely, that Bressler would respond only to faxes, which he decided just wasn't worth the trouble.

The About deal didn't happen overnight. Kurnit and Rogers had started their discussions, significantly, in February 2000, directly after the AOL Time Warner deal was announced. The two had known each other from the cable business, where Rogers had gained a large measure of respect for steering NBC into the creation of CNBC and MSNBC. "Tom was a major, major part of my doing this deal. I knew him for a long time, I knew his accomplishments. We initially thought that there might be a joint venture in the business space," Kurnit recalled. The conversation started with Primedia's expressing its need to get its hundreds of trade magazines online, to create so-called B-to-B online hubs out of the magazines.

"Scott came by here, paid me a visit, in terms of what they were planning to do in the trade area; basically that they were going to put all the trade magazines out of business," Rogers jokes, "and that they didn't think most of the trade guys got it. But based on what we were doing, he thought that we might be a good match. And we talked about it some. I said that's a great theory, but I don't understand how we're not going to end up maximizing your value without hurting our own. It wasn't clear to me that we could get a tremendous amount of integration out of the deal. He said, 'Maybe we put all our business stuff together.' I toyed with it; I wasn't taken by it."

In early spring, About and Primedia reconvened, talking about video joint ventures this time. Rogers was convinced that the problem the dot-com world was having was that it had created far too much broad-based ad inventory that it could never sell efficiently. Essentially the difference between the Web and other media forms came down to the amount of ad space available. The situation was comparable to that of the money supply: If money is too easy to get, there is inflation. Similarly, in media, if there is too much ad supply in a given medium, it becomes "commoditized" and loses value. In other media forms, such as TV, the powers that be were always careful to limit the amount of ad inventory. But on the Web, that sort of control wasn't possible. Whenever the big Internet portals expanded their traffic, they created more and more inventory, because it was traffic, not "space" per se, that they were selling. The very success of the Internet was proving to be its own undoing, because as usage went up, more and more unsold ad inventory went begging. Rogers realized that targeted ad inventory, which could still be sold at a premium, was by far the best asset to take hold of in the recession-spooked economy of 2001.

Rogers continues, "The only way a model is going to work here is for it to be a way to get the cost structure totally different than that of Internet stand-alones. You had to get a revenue approach that was packaged using people that had the sales relationships, the sales contacts, the real understanding of the marketing needs of clients, and have a single sales approach driving revenue. The more I got focused on that being the central theme to the execution of a successful strategy, the more I thought the ultimate integration was putting the two companies together. The match seemed to make enormous sense on the B-to-B side, where the discussion had started. It had moved to the video discussion, but the place where we both knew we had circled each other, where we knew we were going to end up being enormous competitors, was the consumer enthusiast area."

Primedia owns a large number of targeted consumer magazines, on subjects ranging from fishing and hunting to Vietnam and the Civil War. The real breakthrough on the acquisition came when Rogers and Kurnit realized that this would be just as fruitful an area in which to combine forces as the business space.

Although both Primedia and About.com had more than 700 brands, the two CEOs were well aware that not everything would easily mesh. Kurnit estimates that 25 percent of the Primedia brands would be comfortable within the About.com framework. The major appeal of About.com, Kurnit said, was that it offered online economies of scale to Primedia, which would have had to spend tens of millions of dollars to place all its magazines into convincing online hubs. "There will be a tight integration with About," Kurnit said. "We can do it more efficiently, with efficient production and a network effect."

The deal didn't happen without a lot of stock-related pain on both sides. True to the new market reality, which considered any Internet investment to be a mistake, Wall Street quickly turned negative on the merger, sending Primedia shares plummeting from $15 to as low as $3. By the end of October, its value had fallen to about $500 million, despite the fact that About.com's numbers were closer to those of the media mainstream than many other dot-com businesses. Kurnit was projecting $170 million in sales and a black-ink balance sheet by 2001, but skeptical investors, who had become jaded from hearing virtually all Internet companies claim to be on the "path to profitability," simply didn't believe him.

As for About, the trade monthly *Silicon Alley Reporter,* which illustrated the depths of the Internet stock crash by placing a picture of the 1937 crash of the zeppelin *Hindenberg* on its cover, noted in the same issue that About.com "was virtually alone in avoiding the management turmoil, vast layoffs, and outright collapses that plagued its content-focused brethren." Kurnit kept his sanity through this turbulent time by continually putting everything in perspective. "Looking out my office window [then on 42d Street in Manhattan], I could see the former Pan Am Building and the former Wang Building. I could get a daily reminder that, however strong you get, you can still be dead."

Kurnit likes to talk about "long-term shareholder value," and the fact that, given the turmoil in the pure dot-com field, there may not be a lot of well-financed Internet hubs left long-term. He likes to contrast the approximately $80 million that About.com spent to get to the merger deal with the more than $1 billion that Disney spent. "We had a very different business model than Disney did," he said, "an aggressive business model versus that of a large corporation. They did a poor job of integrating Infoseek into their existing structure."

Yahoo!, of course, was accused of having the same failings as Primedia. By March 2001 the company's very future was called into question when it announced it was missing its financial projections, and the company's chairman and CEO, Tim Koogle, revealed he was stepping down. In a wrenching conference call on March 7, Koogle said the "macroeconomic climate has weakened drastically," although he still managed to boast that Yahoo! had $2 billion in cash and no debt, with 185 million people worldwide using the service. But Yahoo!, unlike AOL, had not figured out how to make enough money from its users. Company insiders said in early 2001 that Yahoo! had spent more than a year searching for a top ad salesman, to no avail. Its top echelon was still wary of bringing in talent from outside, fearing such recruits would not understand their unique culture.

Yahoo! also consistently had trouble recruiting top ad talent because its homegrown sales chief, Anil Singh, had demanded complete power over any new hire. Singh had been trained in the software business, and he rejected old-media modes of doing business; consequently top media sales executives wanted no part of the company. "He's a software sales guy," said a former Yahoo! executive, speaking of Singh. When Singh finally announced he would step down in May 2001, it was too late to stem the erosion in confidence in Yahoo! When the company finally brought in Terry Semel as the new CEO in early 2001, many people assumed that his appointment was a calculated risk—that the former Warner Bros. chairman, who had already had such a difficult time with the Internet, would simply try to sell the company to a multinational media conglomerate. Focus shifted to potential European acquirers like Bertelsmann or Vivendi, both of which claimed they were not interested, at least initially. Should Semel succeed, he stands to make hundreds of millions of dollars. In late May 2001, Yahoo! announced that it had awarded him a stock-option package worth just under 2 percent of the company—this equaled the almost 2 percent owned by Tim Koogle—with a $310,000 base salary that was beside the point. Another hire from old-media company Reader's Digest, Gregory Coleman, was paid a base salary of $750,000, a signing bonus of $1.25 million, and 300,000 stock options. Both men would have to work hard to make those stock options truly pay off.

AT&T's commitment to Excite@Home was questioned, after widespread criticism in 2000 and 2001 of CEO Michael Armstrong's failed digital strategy. Excite@Home has always promised to be an excellent service when broadband becomes a reality, but waiting for that to happen had already proved troublesome for Time Warner. A joint study on broadband conducted by McKinsey & Company and Sanford C. Bernstein & Co., Inc., and issued in 2000 concluded, "It is now clear that broadband deployment will create enormous value for the industry, but will also put even greater total value at risk for a wide range of companies."

This isn't the kind of conclusion nervous investors like to hear when they're long on a stock like AT&T. The report noted that "the market remains in its infancy" and that "fewer than 2 million households and far fewer small businesses" were wired to broadband connections. For AT&T, getting a large enough broadband customer base was proving a far more elusive goal than Armstrong had predicted, due to the huge cost of rebuilding its TCI cable plant, a task John Malone had long neglected. Worse, the report noted, "AT&T does not at this time appear to be integrating its various broadband offerings. Different installers and customer service reps handle each service." This was enough to insure customer confusion and disarray for years to come.

CHAPTER 17

AOL Everywhere

As 2001 began, AOL Time Warner, with government approval from both the FCC and the FTC, hit the ground running. There had been little doubt that the Clinton administration would allow the deal to go through; it was hard for anyone to think of an acquisition it *had* blocked. While FCC approval in January came with some minor stipulations about instant messaging, AOL knew it had triumphed in every respect.

The unpredictable Jim Cramer, known for his somewhat erratic behavior as a founder of TheStreet.com, was often a savvy stock-picker, and he was unrelentingly bullish about the new AOL in his column "Wrong" on January 22. AOL was supposed to have lost subscribers because of the rise of broadband, and that hadn't happened, he noted. AOL was supposed to have had to cut prices, and that hadn't happened. Instant messaging was supposed to have been supplanted by better systems, Microsoft was supposed to have given AOL increasingly fierce competition, and "by this point, someone, some media company, was supposed to be offering a complete suite of advertising products, Web to magazines to television. But rather than Disney or Viacom or General Electric, it will be AOL-Time Warner across AOL, Time–People–Fortune–Money and CNN," Cramer wrote. "And now the easy part begins. The expenses, which have been out of control for years at Time Warner, will become history. The costly Web initiatives from all the disparate arms of Time Warner will go away." They did, but not all of Cramer's optimism proved prescient.

By the time Cramer's article appeared, those costly Web initiatives had, of course, already been disposed of. With the exception of Walter Isaacson, still insisting that he knew nothing about the Internet, there was literally no one at

Time Warner now in charge of any major Web initiatives, all of which were un-der AOL control. Ironically, the major Web effort involving the magazines, ac-cording to various insiders, was to integrate their digital content within Netscape's NetCenter, in the same kind of AOL/Web alliance that Ted Leonsis and Steve Case had proposed to Walter Isaacson and Curt Viebranz almost seven years earlier.

Dissension over this project was already evident as the new year dawned, as *Time* magazine, in its December 25/January 1 issue, questioned the basic Net-Center approach. "That's not prime real estate," grumbled Time's Frank Gigney, Jr., "and there are some murmurs within Time Warner that AOL's quest for its own content is exceeded by its lust for rent-paying deals. Don't ex-pect Time Inc.'s *Money* to replace CBS MarketWatch on AOL anytime soon."

Time and its 39 other magazine siblings within Time Inc. weren't used to be-ing treated as second-class citizens, and suddenly, they found themselves vulner-able second-class citizens indeed. On January 12, AOL Time Warner announced a new 16-person board, including such luminaries as former Netscape executive James L. Barksdale, Ted Turner, Michael A. Miles, former chairman of Philip Morris, and former Disney and Hilton executive Stephen F. Bollenbach. Except for the maverick Turner, it was considered a very Case/Pittman–friendly board, not one likely to revere the traditions established in 1923 by Henry Luce.

On January 19, AOL also promoted a key group of executives who had built the service to its preeminent position, including Jan Brandt, the marketing whiz who had distributed tens of millions of AOL disks, to vice chair and chief marketing officer; Ted Leonsis, from president of the Interactive Properties Group to vice chair and new product officer; Audrey Weil, a leading AOL ex-ecutive in the early days, to president of CompuServe; and Jonathan Sacks, the former New Line executive who had developed the content side of AOL, to president of the AOL service.

Bob Pittman had promised that the merger would result in $1 billion in cost savings and new revenues within the very first year of his reign, and that rev-enue for the combined company would increase by 15 percent during 2001. But those projections were made when AOL was experiencing 37 percent rev-enue growth and Time Warner was growing 6 percent annually. With the threat of a recession looming, many questioned how Pittman could achieve these aims, among them *Business Week* in a January 15 cover story.

Firing 400 people at CNN before January was out should have been an in-dication that none of the powerful fiefdoms at Time Warner was sacrosanct, but people at the magazine company persisted in believing that AOL would leave them largely alone. This was the most wishful of thinking, because a quick glance at the masthead of any Time Inc. publication revealed layers and layers of editors, far more than at any other comparable magazine company. Many observers feel that severe cuts will eventually be made in the editorial ranks, but that such a move was too politically volatile to tackle immediately.

The attrition at Disney was both more extensive, and more severe. By January 2001 Michael Eisner's discomfiture over the losses at the Disney Internet Group (renamed from Go.com in August 2000) was increasingly evident. In an interview with the *Financial Times* in late January he complained, "The advertising community has abandoned the Internet," and then added, "If a portal becomes only a search engine and a directory, then a portal may not be what we want." Since he did own a portal, it wasn't hard to see what was coming.

On January 30 Disney announced that it was closing Go.com, firing 400 employees of the 2,100 in the Disney Internet Group and taking a fiscal second-quarter charge of $790 million, or 37 cents a share. Shortly afterward, Disney let go another 135 employees. "These layoffs will help enable us to operate in a more efficient and streamlined manner as we drive toward becoming a profitable business," said Steve Bornstein, the chairman of Walt Disney Internet Group, in what had by now become a predictable mantra for leaders of Internet companies.

By this time, the stock, now trading under the symbol DIG, had sunk to low single digits, and Disney announced it would buy back the DIG securities and convert them to Disney stock at an exchange ratio of 0.19353 Disney shares for each DIG share. This set the value of DIG to its shareholders at a dismal $5.77, when it had sold for as high as $84. No one believed Disney could find a lucrative buyer for what was left of Go, including the domain name.

In an e-mail message to Disney employees, Eisner justified the move: "Like the two skiers who are crossing Antarctica, we have to keep adjusting our strategies as conditions keep changing so that we can reach our ultimate goal of success and profitability in this extraordinary new electronic space."

On January 30 Eisner told the *New York Times*'s Saul Hansell, "We were waiting for something at the end of the rainbow that was looking less and less worth waiting for." He predicted that advertising would eventually rebound on the Web, but Go wouldn't have benefited. "Seventy percent of the advertising for portals is going to the top three players," Eisner said. "The ten second-tier portals are left picking up the scraps." He stressed that Disney would continue to support its prominent web sites, such as those for ESPN and ABC News:

"Times have changed, but our enthusiasm for the Internet has not waned. The future of the Internet is content and interactive television and pay-per-view."

Eisner was again trying to put the Internet into a context that Disney could understand, but the truth was, it still bedeviled him. He knew he had almost no opportunity to build a combination like AOL Time Warner, and he certainly wasn't about to give up control of Disney to do so. In February 2001 he appeared at an analysts' forum and was asked if Disney and Yahoo! might get together. This union might be the only one that could conceivably attempt to compete with AOL Time Warner, but Eisner turned the notion into a joke.

According to Dick Glover, the executive vice president of the Walt Disney Internet Group, who was present, "The first question to Michael Eisner was 'Are you buying Yahoo!? If so, as a shareholder, I hope you reconsider.' And his response was, 'We try to buy where we think there is good value, and while Yahoo! is a terrific, terrific company, I don't think that anyone thinks that at its current valuation it is necessarily a good value to acquire.' He then went on to say that that is something he learned from Walt [Disney], and if he went to the crypt and unfroze Walt [who is said to be cryogenically frozen], once he explained what a portal was to Walt, Walt would then kill him for having gone out and bought it."

But speculation about a possible combination between Yahoo! and Disney misses a critical point. As Dick Glover notes, "Traditionally, Disney doesn't like to take minority stakes in major businesses. In fact, I don't think I know of any examples where we have." To pull off an unlikely pairing like this, Eisner would have to accept a minority position or, worse, agree to be acquired. Since his desire to control the interactive media business was never remotely as strong as that of Jerry Levin, it seemed improbable that such a deal could take place, unless the Internet business simply fell apart, in which case Disney would no longer find Yahoo! an attractive partner. Moreover, the incompatibility between Disney and Yahoo! cultures made such a combination almost inconceivable.

All in all, it's unclear exactly what Disney learned institutionally from the Go Network debacle. In Dick Glover's explanation, the lessons are mostly negative. Disney learned what not to do, but it's unclear if it discovered what it *could* do. "We learned, stick to your knitting. We learned that integrating companies is not easy," he says.

Glover explains that those lessons were different than Time Warner's because Go was "a different play" than Pathfinder. "From our perspective, as we looked at the world unfolding, we said that we inherently believe that our content and the strength of our brands will always drive through any barriers. We believe we have the most powerful brands in the world and the best content in the world. However, the fewer barriers there are, the better. And clearly, we thought that portals had a potential to drive through barriers. They became the entry point for consumers."

He continues, "We said, 'There are going to be three or four portals, and we would like to be one of them.' We did the Infoseek acquisition, but we never looked at the portal play as an aggregation of our content. We said, 'Look, we think this is a business. The portal business. Let's build a really good portal, and then let's have the advantage of knowing that that portal is not going to provide a barrier to our brands; in fact it's going to enhance our brands and the distribution of our brands.' So it was really looked at as a two-pronged attack. It wasn't Pathfinder. They just thought that the best way to go on the Internet was to aggregate all their brands in one place. That didn't work."

Of course, in avoiding one failed paradigm, Disney headed directly into another. As calamitous as Pathfinder was, it didn't cost a fraction of what Disney ultimately spent.

At CBS, now a subsidiary of Viacom Inc., there was also Internet-related *agita*. The network had kept its Web investments to provide equity for promotion deals, under the watchful eye of executive vice president and CFO Fred Reynolds, a bottom-line executive who could be almost Dickensian in his vigilance on keeping the corporation from spending any cash on Internet frivolity. (In these arrangements, a media company would acquire a minority stake in an Internet concern in exchange for free media promotion and ads.) But by 2001 even that strategy didn't look especially productive.

CBS Network president and CEO Leslie Moonves delivered a speech in March 2001 that tried to put the best face forward about the company's Internet investments. He noted Disney's almost $800 million charge against operations to end the Go debacle and boasted that, on the same day that Eisner was announcing the distressing truth about Disney's Internet failure, CBS was airing the Super Bowl, with an audience of 131 million, and hosting a web site for its ongoing *Survivor* series that had attracted 160 million cumulative page views. Traffic to its CBS SportsLine site had increased greatly after the Super Bowl, he noted, with on-air promotion driving viewers to the Web. After its bout of suffering "portal envy" in 1998, CBS had dodged that particular bullet and now was moving confidently ahead.

"We stayed away from the big money investments no matter how tempting they were," Moonves said. "What we did invest in, we paid for in airtime, something that we have a lot of. It was like the Saudis paying for beachfront property with oil." Moonves admitted that many of the investments CBS had made had "flopped," but he put those misjudgments in a familiar context: "Mark McGwire hit 70 home runs, but he struck out a few times also."

CBS spokesperson Dana McClintock later added some perspective, noting that losses from the public companies that CBS had invested in were now showing up on "Viacom's bottom line." But he quickly added that CBS has "a lot of off-ramps on this. Most of the companies that have failed we can get out of quite easily. And the amount that we've made on the ones that were successful outweighed the losses. A lot of [media] companies are regretting the decisions they made about the Internet. We regret ours less, and we're still excited about most of them." In 2001 that was about the best explanation anyone who was a spokesperson for a major media company could offer.

In fact, the network's commitment to the Internet was not quite as risk-averse as McClintock and Moonves's characterization had implied. According to CBS's SEC filings, in order to acquire equity stakes in 21 Internet companies, the network had committed a total of $836 million in 1999, the year the Web exploded for most media businesses. Of that amount, $604 million was earmarked for promotional and/or ad time, while $45 million in cash was spent. The strategy looked shrewd when the stock market was riding high and CBS's equity value was ballooning, and with it the network acquired significant stakes in Switchboard.com, MarketWatch, SportsLine, Hollywood.com, Loudeye Technologies, Medscape, Rx.com, Jobs.com, StoreRunner.com, the Webvan Group, Wrenchhead.com, the sweepstakes-oriented site Iwon.com, and nine others.

The impact on the bottom line was immediate: According to CBS's 2000 10-K filing, operating losses in the Internet Group were $35 million in 1999, with a negative EBITDA of $37 million. As long as the value of CBS's equity stakes was many times the amount of the losses, however, the tactic still seemed to be sound. But in 1999 alone, CBS had to give these companies $19 million in promotional airtime and ad spots. And the report warned, "Future losses in these 21 companies are expected to increase dramatically due to their recognizing marketing and promotional expenses as we deliver our advertising and promotion time. Additionally, our losses will increase as the number of such investments expand and as full-year results are recognized. We expect future non-cash equity losses and amortization to be material to our consolidated results of operations."

That was an understatement. With the stock market heading heavily into negative territory, the equity in these companies became a drag on CBS and its parent, Viacom, so much so that executive vice president and CFO Fred Reynolds, the author of the investing strategy who had been in place since 1994, left the job in March 2001 for a position with CBS's station group. Viacom chairman Sumner Redstone, never a big fan of the Internet, was dismayed with the results of the new-media investments.

The numbers again tell the story. According to a Viacom SEC filing, "Principally as a result of significantly higher amortization of goodwill resulting from the merger with CBS, the non-cash pre-tax charge of $99 million attributable to the decline in market value of several Internet investments and increased income taxes for the fourth quarter of 2000, Viacom reported net earnings of $30 million, or $.02 per share, for the fourth quarter of 2000. These results compare with net earnings of $133 million, or $.19 per share, in the same year-earlier period." All the promotional time and effort that had been committed to the Web companies was a matter of additional concern, as it was promotion that could have been used in support of Viacom's own units. Viacom began a series of confusing shuffles of its Internet groups, eventually dumping most of the responsibility for the web sites back in the hands of the individual units, such as the CBS network (CBS.com) and the CBS news division (CBSNews.com). In an attempt to reduce their expenditures across the board in a tough ad climate, these divisions were much more focused on cutting back during 2001 than on expansion.

By 2001 Viacom's interest in making any further commitment to the Internet had all but vanished. That was abundantly clear when Sumner Redstone published his memoir, *A Passion to Win,* that year, and in it did not mention the Internet at all, not even in a footnote.

With the demise of Go, and the further news that AT&T's Excite@Home would release 250 employees and write off a gigantic $4.8 billion, the portal race was all but over. It was an almost total rout.

That left AOL Time Warner, and its relatively young leader, Bob Pittman, in what seemed like a pre-eminent position. It was an eerie déjà-vu, in that Time Warner, under Levin's leadership, had been the company that most fully embraced the digital future early in the '90s. In the first years of the new millennium, Time Warner was still out there on its own. Levin was clearly basking in the glow, even as his power was being chipped away.

In a presentation to analysts on January 31 about fourth-quarter results,

Levin crowed that AOL Time Warner was "in a different zone" than other media companies because of its ability to grow while others shrank. In fact, AOL Time Warner wasn't even a media company, he asserted, much to the surprise of reporters who'd covered it for years. "We are not a media company and we are not an Internet company," Levin claimed. "We are a large-cap global company that happens to be in both of those businesses." This was a transparent attempt to minimize the travails of the media and dot-com industries, and simply proclaim global victory.

AOL had added 2.1 million subscribers in the fourth quarter of 2000, for a total of 26.7 million, at a time when other portals, like Go.com, were readying an exit from the business, and the new Terra/Lycos combination was running into trouble. The additional subscribers enabled AOL to grow its revenue by 27 percent, to $2.1 billion. Pittman went so far as to claim during the presentation that AOL Time Warner was immune to the normal business cycle, a topic that had become of growing concern as the first signs of recession hit the business community. "One advantage [we have] that many companies don't have is that if things slow down, we can open up inventory" from around the conglomerate, he explained.

Merrill Lynch analyst Henry Blodget, speaking on March 8, 2001, at his company's annual Internet conference, when Web stocks—particularly that of Yahoo!—were again taking a beating, talked about the "Big Three" companies that often dominate any one business, such as the auto industry. But in the case of the Internet, he added, "maybe it's the Big One," referring to AOL Time Warner.

By the time Blodget had made this observation, AOL's dominance was virtually unprecedented. In February 2001 the company's products were responsible for one-third of all time spent online in the United States. This represented an "at-home penetration" of 72.3 percent, according to the measurement firm Jupiter Media Metrix, and the AOL service and web site were responsible for most of that, with Time Warner properties attracting only 15.7 percent of the total.

In June 2001 Jupiter Media Metrix released figures revealing that, if anything, AOL's lead is continuing to grow. According to the report, a total of 110 companies had controlled 60 percent of Internet usage and American eyeballs in 1999. Two years later, that number had shrunk to just 14 companies. But the position of AOL Time Warner was very telling. The top four businesses— AOL Time Warner, Microsoft, Yahoo!, and Napster—controlled fully half of the time Americans spent on the Internet in March 2001. And AOL Time

Warner had almost five times the traffic of its nearest rival, Microsoft. Two-thirds of AOL's traffic was coming from applications like e-mail and instant messaging, a field that AOL has completely cornered and against which no other media company could hope to compete.

Almost 59 million people visited AOL or its web site in January 2001. AOL visitors spent an average of 436 minutes on the service that month and a piti-ful 12 minutes in Time Warner properties. Ironically AOL's achievement was similar to the dominance that Time Warner magazines have traditionally en-joyed in their marketplace. Time publications have typically been awarded al-most one-third of all magazine advertising, a position that was threatened, however, when *Time* magazine lost ground in the tough ad recession of early 2001. With a big downturn in advertising in 2001, it became increasingly evi-dent that the company was going to seize an even larger piece of a shrinking pie.

Bob Pittman views this phenomenal success as an outgrowth of the sub-scription model to which AOL has remained committed. "If someone's paying for a relationship, it's a lot more loyal relationship," he says. "If you're in the business of building consumer relationships, the best indication that you're succeeding is that people will pay. It's not reach; it's not necessarily circulation." He cites the Media Metrix numbers to make this point that online the play isn't about the traditional yardsticks of reach and frequency as it is in, say, print. It's about something else.

"Other companies have, what, eighty or ninety percent of our reach?" he asks. "But when you look at time spent, people actually using it, AOL Time Warner accounted for about a third of all usage on the Internet, and I think the closest competitor was in the single digits. That's the difference between pay-ing relationships and free relationships. It's harder to build that kind of rela-tionship, but once you've gained an online subscriber or a cable subscriber, that sticks, and you can do much more with it. People think that consumers buy on price—they don't, they buy on value."

When AOL lowered its monthly fee to $19.95 in 1996, many pundits pre-dicted it would go under, Pittman noted in early 2001. "Our competitors low-ered their prices thinking they'd win, but they didn't, AOL subscriptions kept growing. Free ISPs happened. MSN started paying people $400 to switch to MSN—I think they stopped about a week or two ago. All of these things that were supposed to break this subscription relationship haven't. Why? Because subscription relationships are hard to break."

AOL Time Warner now has the top online subscription service by an unimaginable order of magnitude, as well as the top pay-TV subscription service (HBO), also far ahead of its closest rival, Showtime. The company is also selling the most magazine subscriptions of any publisher, with AOL now helping in that effort.

"We are selling magazine subscriptions for Time Inc. using AOL," Pittman continues. "We're on a run rate of over one million subscriptions a year, generated out of AOL, probably one of the most important subscriber acquisition tools a magazine company has. If you're in the magazine business, you know the tough part is to try and get a renewal. The minute you get a subscriber you start trying to get them to renew; you bombard them with subscription cards, you send out notices. It costs you a boat-load of money. The best solution is to go on an evergreen subscription, that you keep giving it to the consumer until they ask you to stop."

Also key is the entertainment center in the home, Pittman insists. Pittman breaks down the home communications/entertainment business into the "four boxes that we love": the mailbox, the TV, the computer, and the home entertainment center or stereo. AOL and its instant messaging have gradually eroded the amount of time spent at the mailbox.

But Pittman cautions that the belief that the online experience would replace the home stereo or the TV is where many top executives, including those at the company he now controls, have made their mistakes.

The computer connected to the Internet, he says, is "the manage-my-life box, it's not the entertainment box. It's not the TV set. It is doing something very important for consumers, something they would [otherwise] waste a lot of time doing. It is easier with the PC, and that's why they're not going to give up. I can plan my vacation in two hours online. My son [Bo Pittman, his son with former wife, Sandy] can do his term papers online. He never goes to a library. He's probably never even seen the inside of a public library, and he's a senior in high school. That box, the stuff that works there, is the stuff that helps you manage your life. And the folks who have tried to turn it into a TV set haven't met with much success because it's there for a different purpose."

Whether he truly believes AOL Time Warner is no longer subject to normal business cycles, Bob Pittman knew a great thing when he saw it. In February 2001 he sold about 1 million shares of AOL, taking advantage of a short window of opportunity, netting him about $50 million. He retains about 15 million shares.

There are many, many barriers to making AOL Time Warner a success, especially justifying the huge cost of the deal in a recession-plagued era. Pittman stayed on at MTV after leading a failed buyout, becoming CEO in the bargain. He noted in March 2001 that when he joined Warner Amex and its fledgling cable programming business, the whole cable industry was serving only about 12 million homes, "and it looked like a terrible business to be in. Fortunately I got in at the right moment." At the beginning of 2001, it looked as if he had made another canny choice, arriving at just the right moment once again, when he became the heir apparent of the company to beat in the new millennium. But the triumph was by no means guaranteed.

EPILOGUE

As 2001 progressed, a few paradigms of the new world of media became evident:

- Web content is dead as an independent business.
- The remaining Internet businesses will undergo rapid consolidation.
- Digital dreams have been deferred for "broadband."
- AOL Time Warner will dominate.

Taken together, the lessons of 2001 were remarkably similar to those of 1994–1995, when the telephone and cable companies, led by Time Warner and Bell Atlantic, promised an information superhighway that would be a license to print money for the companies that would build it, and consumer Nirvana for the customers who would use it.

The dream of an information superhighway was abandoned by 1996 because it proved too technically complicated to build and too expensive to deliver. But the ramifications of this experience were largely ignored in the rising euphoria over the new business of the Internet. Moreover, many of the same conglomerates that had a stake in new communications systems, including Time Warner, were publishers of key business outlets like *Time* and *Fortune* magazines, which had a vested interest in supporting novel technology, whatever form it took, and so weren't about to draw any lasting conclusions from the failures of the RBOCs. Time Warner's Jerry Levin in particular had a stake in the concept that technology could be harnessed to deliver a shining new future. When that didn't happen in 1994 with his Full Service Network, he simply papered that failure over with a new vision for the Internet, and the corporation simply went along with him without question.

The Internet promised the moon and ultimately delivered much, much less. While it revolutionized communications in many ways, it had no such dramatic effect on business. There are many reasons for that.

When the Internet started taking off in the latter half of the '90s, it was in large part controlled by an elite of high-powered executives who were convinced that they were completely changing the rules of corporate behavior. They had reason to believe in their new ethic. David Wetherell, Halsey Minor, Jeff Bezos, Candace Carpenter, Bill Gates, Steve Case, Jerry Yang, and David Filo had all broken rules and ignored conventional wisdom to achieve their success.

Mainstream business had not understood them, and they saw the absolute failure of the media companies to capture the public's attention with their own Internet products. Not surprisingly, they came to believe that they were invincible, beyond the laws of traditional business cycles. *Wired* magazine was the bible for many of them, because it and its founders articulated the credo that Silicon Valley and its values and innovations would completely change the face of the American economy.

The nexus of this almost cultish fervor was the Internet World conference, held at the Javits convention center in Manhattan. The annual show came to be dominated by hordes of tech minions, each tight-knit team dressed identically in Polo shirts emblazoned with the witty moniker of their company, each counting the hours until they could cash out with option riches.

During my time at CMGI, one of my most surreal experiences was being assigned to interview a managing director of Bear, Stearns who had applied to our unit for a job. The man told me that he was being paid $1 million a year; our top salary was then about $200,000, and that's what the CEO made. He knew absolutely nothing about the Internet, and it was impossible to imagine him even lasting a day at CMGI. But the fervor that brought him from Bear's posh Park Avenue headquarters to a brick former factory building in chilly Andover, Massachusetts, was real. He was so starstruck from hearing tales of overnight fortunes that he was willing to chuck it all for a laptop and a dream.

This new mind-set reached its zenith at the end of 1999, when Jerry Levin began his courtship with AOL. What was clear to Levin and other media chieftains by then was that, try as hard as they could, they simply couldn't duplicate the elements that led to dot-com success in 1999. They could remove their ties, or shave their moustaches, or pride themselves on their e-mail adeptness, but none of it worked. It was humiliating, and it was unconscionable, because in 1999 winning online became paramount. For a CEO like Levin, it was everything. It was in part his need to prove that he'd been right all along—that his dream of a digital future could and would happen, courtesy of AOL—that led him to the epochal decision to sell his company.

At the time, there was a unanimous belief that the Internet business had triumphed. In fact, this triumph took place in only one arena, the stock market, but it was such a prolonged and convincing victory that finally, reluctantly, even the most hidebound holdouts began to succumb. Rupert Murdoch was one of the most poignant cases of all. After the ugly shenanigans of the MCI/News Corp. joint venture, he had tried to sit out the Internet revolution, complaining repeatedly that the valuations of these companies were unacceptable to the conventional business mind. Finally, in late 1999, when interviewed by *Wired,* he had done a volte-face, gushing once again about the same kind of online T&A that had captured his attention when he surfed the Web in 1995 with Scott Kurnit.

As soon as the market correction began in April 2000, the newfound enthusiasm for the Internet disappeared, almost overnight, in the corridors of the communications industry. All the big-media companies pulled back completely, with the exception of AOL Time Warner. As 2001 progressed, it was clear that in one respect, at least, Levin had emerged victorious. He was now nominally in charge of a monolithic company that was so far ahead of the rest of the pack, with so many advantages, both wired and unwired, as to seem almost unfair. That dominance was a significant factor in the total new-media capitulations of 2001 at NBC, CBS/Viacom, Disney, and AT&T. They recognized they couldn't compete with AOL Time Warner, and the vehicles they had assembled to that end—Disney's Go Network, NBCi, MTV Online, AT&T's WorldNet—were simply too flimsy and too expensive to maintain.

As always in business, the future is going to resemble the past. Stripped of all the glitz and glory, the Internet looks all too much like the cable network industry.

When cable started in the early '80s, it was a multichannel dream. Visionaries touted public access as if it were a complete communications revolution. For the first time, the people would create their own programming, out of the reach of corporate greed and manipulation. But as the cable industry matured, public access became the domain of right-wing cranks and religious programming. In more than 20 years of public access broadcasts, not one of these programs ever captured the public interest in a major way or migrated into the mainstream. Literally, they didn't matter. Meanwhile, the independent cable networks, such as Discovery Channel and CNN, were gradually brought into the major networks' fold, and the business consolidated down to a handful of corporate owners: Liberty Media, CBS/Viacom, Time Warner, News Corp., Disney.

Substitute "the Internet" for "public access," and you will have a rough equivalent. There are billions of web sites, but how many of them matter? Meanwhile, the business is rapidly consolidating down to a few providers. The corporate lineup is slightly different, but the end result will be the same. Eventually, if *Newsweek*'s Michael Rogers is right in his prediction, Web news and content will become a viable business around 2006, and the media conglomerates will be there to pick up where they left off.

When AOL Time Warner's Levin and Pittman sketched out their vision for the future, they emphasized the streamlined nature of it all. They shrug off concerns about one company owning too many assets; in fact, AOL reveled in the prospect. Pittman is much too careful to reveal his hand, but AOL Time Warner will likely embark on a major acquisition campaign when the dust settles. "We wouldn't announce anything, but a company our size always looks at acquisitions," Pittman says. With a compliant Justice Department under the conservative John Ashcroft unlikely to be overzealous in its antitrust actions, and former AOL director Colin Powell as a key member of George Bush's cabinet, AOL Time Warner would seem free to expand in any direction it chooses.

Hearkening back to the relationship that existed between AOL and its partners in 1993, when the first partnerships occurred, Bob Pittman urged media companies at the 2001 Jupiter Media Forum to join with AOL, rather than attempt to build anything themselves. "Do you want to try and build the business from scratch, or would you rather be in business with someone who already has an infrastructure and you can leverage off of that?" he asked. It was the same question that Jonathan Bulkeley had posed in 1993.

At a presentation in New York in January 2001, AOL's CEO Barry Schuler envisioned a future where AOL Time Warner literally dominates all entertainment and communications needs. At present, Time Warner owns Maverick, the label that releases Madonna's albums. When her *Music* CD launched, it was featured on the AOL welcome screen. Madonna was named Artist of the Month in the AOL music area and got big plugs from AOL's online radio channel Spinner.com, AOL-owned Netscape.com, and CompuServe. AOL is planning a download subscription service, and when that launches, "we would promote it there as well, where you could buy it as a CD or buy it as a digital download." Madonna was also promoted corporately, on Time Warner's *Rosie* show, and she made an appearance on the broadband service AOL TV. "If you really love Madonna," Schuler continued, "we will send you pages, instant messages, and provide you a listing for it on the calendar embedded in the service. And if you're on AOL TV and you were at work when Madonna was on *Rosie,* you could tell AOL TV to record it for you. If [consumers] really love this stuff, we can make it more convenient for them."

This is a new world where "convenience" is just another euphemism for consolidation and dominance. Wal-Mart has a business model that Pittman has cited approvingly. In small-town America, traditional downtowns evolved in the 18th and 19th centuries around a central square, with small businesses arrayed around it—the tailor, barber, butcher, blacksmith. Buildings were multistory, because people lived in a compact area.

Then the auto came along, and with it the rise of the shopping center and its big parking lot. These businesses impacted traditional downtowns negatively, but did not destroy them; they held their own, at least until the 1970s. But as Wal-Mart grew to massive size in the '70s and '80s, it evolved an inviolate model: Build a huge store on the outskirts of the downtown, with an enormous parking lot. Offer virtually everything available from downtown merchants at cut-rate prices, which you obtain through your ruthlessly efficient central purchasing arm. Eventually the downtown will shrivel and die, as townspeople all flock to Wal-Mart for "convenience." With 4,000 stores worldwide employing over one million people, Wal-Mart is providing unparalleled "convenience" today.

This is the essence of the AOL Time Warner dream. If you picture all those iconoclastic web sites as forlorn businesses in a fading downtown, you have an image of the future as AOL Time Warner sees it. Eventually AOL Time Warner will so dominate communications that it will alter America permanently, in ways that can't even be forseen today. This may not please everyone, but it's a solid blueprint for the future.

We have come a long way from the digital dreams of the '90s. What we face is not a world of limitless choice that the Internet promised, but something smaller and more controlled than that. A lot of dreams died as AOL Time Warner was born, and it will be fascinating to see if their sacrifice was worthwhile. There's every reason to believe that the cultures of AOL and Time Warner will clash and collide, and that many top managers of Time Warner, already enriched by stock payouts, will simply depart, letting AOL bring in its own people. In a worst-case scenario, Time Warner's culture may simply disappear.

Dan Okrent, who retired from AOL Time Warner in the summer of 2001 after twelve years with the company, believes that the culture that Henry Luce founded in the 1920s, which may have had its flaws but possessed its own kind of editorial integrity, will be safe as long as there remains continuity from the past, as long as executives like Norm Pearlstine and Don Logan, and editorial director John Huey are still around. "Are these magazines in good hands?" Okrent asks. "Yes, because whenever anyone at AOL [proposes a violation of editorial integrity], Norm, if it ever gets to Norm, says, 'Fuck you.' And often it wouldn't get to Norm because we're all big boys—my successors and my colleagues—and we could all say, 'Fuck you.' The question is, who succeeds them? Don Logan's replacement will be picked, presumably, by Bob Pittman."

In July 2001 Pittman gave his blessing to Walter Isaacson's leaving the editorial director job for the top news position at CNN in Atlanta. This was a symbolic move that seemed to strengthen AOL Time Warner's editorial commitment, while concomitantly moving Isaacson out of the New York headquarters at a time when Norm Pearlstine's contract would be soon up for renewal. The deck seemed to be cleared for a sweeping change at the top of the editorial heap.

And with that change, and the eventual move into an opulent new headquarters on Columbus Circle, the Luce legacy may be left behind for good.

The same week that Okrent retired, in June 2001, a potent indication of what that may portend took place a world away from Manhattan. AOL Time Warner owns a magazine called *Asiaweek,* based in Hong Kong, that publishes an annual list of the most powerful people on the continent. In a provocative move, given that Hong Kong is now officially part of China again, the magazine named the spiritual leader of the cult-like group Falun Gong, which the Chinese government is waging war against, to the top of the list. Every year previously, a CNN special had aired profiling the people who made the list. In 2001, however, CNN balked. "They said we can't do that, because we're doing deals with the Chinese," Dan Okrent observes. The incident attracted little of the outcry that Rupert Murdoch was subjected to when he canceled a Harper-Collins book by the former British governor of Hong Kong and also banned the BBC from his Star TV, also as a way to curry favor with the Chinese government, but it was just as significant. In December 2001, AOL Time Warner closed *Asiaweek* down, ending a magazine that was both unprofitable and a political irritant.

Big media is just going to get bigger, and big companies have increasingly complicated interests to protect.

With the almost total meltdown of the Internet industry in 2001, it also became clear that even with all the cutbacks at the media companies' online efforts, they would remain the likely heirs to whatever part of the Internet content business that survived. If an Internet content business model is virtually impossible to devise, then what will remain of Internet content will be that spun off from media operations.

At the same time that the punditocracy was pronouncing Web content "dead," and virtually all the pure-play Internet content sites were giving up, there were many still viable content sites maintained by media companies, such as that operated by *Forbes* magazine. From the point of view of Jim Spanfeller, CEO of Forbes.com, media companies will eventually have to compete aggressively on the Internet because of simple advertising demographics. "As an advertiser looks at this space, they see that more and more people are spending more and more time on the Web," he says. "Now, today, people spend more time with the Web than they do with magazines."

While that is perhaps an unusual observation from an executive who is ultimately the employee of a magazine company, he raises an undeniable fact that big media can't ignore. The trends favor the Web, or at least electronic distribution, and the business favors those who will be well-funded and supported to meet those trends. And for the media companies, the current zeitgeist feels more recognizable and comfortable than the frightening months of 1999 and early 2000. It's now a world playing by the rules big media has always played by. "So now we're back to, 'Oh yeah, I know this world. In this world, you have to have a business plan that shows you go from here to here and at some point in time you're profitable,'" *Forbes*'s Spanfeller observes.

The logic of the marketplace dictates that a huge amount of merger and acquisition will take place in the communications business. That logic also dictates that new media forms will arise, perhaps trumping the Internet entirely. Dan Okrent likes to talk about future products that "will feel like magazines, fold like magazines, smell like a magazine, but will be digital. They've got a long way to go, but it is going to happen."

One person who certainly won't be around to see what happens next for media and technology at AOL Time Warner is Jerry Levin, who surprised many by announcing on December 5, 2001, that after more than nine years as CEO he would be retiring the following May, and that COO Richard Parsons, not Pittman, would become the new CEO. Insiders say that Pittman's transparent push for the job, a key element of which was that bothersome *Business Week* cover story that belittled Levin and Parsons, had been instrumental in turning the board and Levin against the ambitious Mississippian.

Levin was leaving on a high note, AOL Time Warner trumpeted, and in fact, he was walking away with a huge package worth hundreds of millions of dollars. He had been paid $357.7 million for the first eight years of that tenure, and the total in stock and pay for the rest of his time as CEO could push the total to over $500 million. Although many in the somewhat sycophantic press corps were quick to agree that Levin was leaving on his own terms, with the big tasks already behind him, others were more dubious. Jon Friedman of CBS Market-Watch was one of the most prominent critics in the immediate wake of Levin's stepping down, noting on December 7 that "Levin, 62, is leaving at a time when AOL Time Warner shareholders desperately want to hear some good news. Since January, the company's shares are down some 24 percent, approximately double the size of the decline of the benchmark Standard & Poor's 500 Index. Levin is handing off a host of headaches—I mean challenges—to Parsons."

On February 4, a sudden bolt from the unlikeliest of sources—AOL's own *Fortune* magazine—shattered the reassuring spin from AOL Time Warner's p.r. department with a piece called "Is There More to the Story?" by Carol J. Loomis. Challenging Levin's legacy, Loomis noted, "You can't look at AOL Time Warner's brief stock market history—a decline in value over two years of more than $155 billion—and find much to cheer about." Moreover, she added, "AOL Time Warner director Francis 'Fay' Vincent . . . told at least one person, 'Jerry was forced from the company.'"

The 63-year-old Vincent, a respected veteran of the Coca-Cola Co., was a "close friend" of Levin's, Loomis continued, and was thus an unimpeachable source. For Levin to have been forced out, at least 12 members of the 16-member board would have had to vote against him, or he would have had to have stepped down knowing the vote would go against him. Loomis asserts there never was a formal vote on the matter, but Levin must have been convinced it might not go his way. The apparent compromise ended with Levin's retiring, but having a say in appointing Parsons, not Pittman, in his stead, a kind of last revenge for the way he believed Pittman had slighted him in his final years.

Many outside AOL Time Warner said privately that passing over Pittman for the CEO job was a mistake, though few would acknowledge as much publicly. One advantage of being CEO of a big conglomerate like AOL Time Warner is that your landing is sure to be relatively soft, as the power that comes with the job tends to continue even after retirement. But those who criticized Levin's tenure deserved to be heard, because in many ways he was the ultimate dupe of technology; it had crippled his career and left problems behind that would take years to sort out. During the 1990s, even as he disseminated the dubious notion that technology would solve all of Time Warner's problems, he maintained a somewhat awkward relationship to new media itself. Levin was unnerved by AOL and its tech-savvy executives, including Pittman, even as he rushed to publicly embrace the company and to make many optimistic revenue forecasts related to it.

Wall Street Journal reporter Kara Swisher came up with a telling anecdote on December 10. "When Gerald Levin hosted the launch party for Time Inc.'s digerati magazine, then called eCompany Now, in the spring of 2000, it was clear even then that he was a bit uncomfortable with the whole dot-com thing. He wore the outfit (casual khakis and a sports coat). And he spent the bucks (a boat cruise around San Francisco Bay, renting the new Pacific Bell baseball park, and a private concert featuring the Barenaked Ladies). And, of course, he talked the talk about the importance of the Web and its interactive services to the future of all media. But there was also a whiff of discomfort in his manner even then, and his words sounded scripted, rather than from the passion of a true believer. That is, until the topic of cable came up."

And this was after Levin had already agreed to merge his company with AOL.

Why would an executive so nervous about even discussing the online world want to sell out to a company that epitomized the most aggressive aspects of that milieu? The answer has to do with the profound disruption that the Internet revolution caused. At the end of 1999, when the decision to go ahead with AOL was made, Levin could not simply walk away from the Brave New World of the Web. His ego told him Time Warner had to win in this all-important new arena, and joining forces with AOL, the biggest player, would be the only way for proud Time Warner to pull it off. "This really completes the digital transformation of Time Warner," Levin had said when the merger with AOL was announced, and he clearly wanted to appear to be leaving as his crowning achievement—setting Time Warner on its future digital course—was finally realized.

But one had to ask if the digital transformation of Time Warner was, finally, such a signal achievement. The somewhat uneasy rapprochement between the AOL and Time Warner cultures that prevailed at the merged conglomerate as 2002 got under way was hardly an advertisement for the smooth integration of two disparate worlds. And Levin took pains, in a December 11, 2001, speech at the Beverly Hilton, to paper over the many large claims made for the deal, and the failure to even realize half of the savings promised. "We indicated that a lot of what we projected would depend on what went on with the overall market," he asserted. "As it turned out, advertising continued to worsen."

In covering this speech, the trade paper *Variety* noted on December 12 that Levin "said the large array of [cable] systems already in the AOL TW fold eventually will prove invaluable as a platform for broadband content distribution and e-commerce." Levin told his audience, "Cable is emerging as the broadband platform of choice, at least in this country." Reading that statement makes one wonder about whether anything was learned since 1993. The following month, Levin reiterated, on a company conference call to announce disappointing fourth-quarter earnings, that, "While I mentioned the advertising recession, the expansion of broadband will have a profound impact on the advertising industry," a dubious assertion given Time Warner's history with interactive advertising.

Levin's claim about a new cable-based platform for "broadband content distribution and e-commerce" was exactly the same one he had made in 1993 and 1994 for the FSN. His speech came the same month as the great broadband hope of the 1990s, Excite@Home, collapsed in a welter of recriminations and bankruptcy. Excite@Home, created in 1999, was the unwieldy amalgamation of the Internet portal Excite with the @Home cable modem service, which was started by cable operators and eventually acquired by AT&T. In an article about the fall of the service in its December 17 issue, headlined "Excite@Home: A Saga of Tears, Greed, and Ego," *Business Week* noted, "Its fall may well be a cautionary tale for the future of broadband." AT&T had paid $3.5 billion for the company. At one time, Excite@Home's market cap had shot up to $35 billion, but by the time it fell apart in December 2001 it was worth less than $40 million, and its stock was selling at 3 cents a share. The service ultimately failed through a combination of missteps by AT&T, poor service, badly mistimed service upgrades, and the fickle stock market, which had driven the stock up to almost $100 as recently as April 1999.

The end of Excite@Home caused many to question the future of broadband as the panacea people like Levin still claimed it was. "If the No. 1 broadband player, with so much money and corporate support behind it, cannot survive, which broadband player can?" *Business Week* asked. Only 10 percent of U.S. homes were broadband-enabled at the beginning of 2002, this after the 10 largest cable companies had spent a staggering $46 billion on upgrading their systems, according to estimates from the Yankee Group. There are estimates out there that 30 percent of American homes will have broadband access by 2004, but such figures seem highly optimistic. In the tough times of the recession of 2001, it was hard to see how a luxury service that costs $50 a month or so would grow at so healthy a rate, especially when Excite@Home simply cut off the 850,000 customers it had with AT&T cable subscribers. What company would take up the slack now?

Moreover, it is also questionable that any truly compelling applications will ever be found for broadband, beyond the faster Internet access it primarily delivers now. In any case, AOL Time Warner doesn't have until 2004, and Levin's successors seem to belatedly realize that. According to an April 21, 2002, *New York Times* piece, Pittman told AOL employees that the company had been "distracted from its core mission by overemphasizing new technologies like interactive television," and that this view reflected "a deep strategic difference with Mr. Case," not to mention Jerry Levin himself. Pittman was reacting to the company's stock slide: in the latter half of April, it had at times dipped below $20. The stock collapse led the *Wall Street Journal*'s Kara Swisher to declare in an April 15 piece that Pittman should consider "spinning off the AOL unit." A week later, on April 22, Reuters was taking the idea seriously, quoting Vick Khoboyan, an analyst at Financial Management Advisors, that the spinoff talk "is the nail in the coffin (proving that the deal has failed)."

By the time all this had happened, the company's market cap had dipped below the value of Time Warner itself at the time the merger was done, meaning that AOL had not only added nothing to the new conglomerate's net worth, it had actually contributed to its decline. "Shares of the world's largest Internet and media company have fallen 70 percent since its $106.2 billion deal to buy Time Warner, bringing it to a level that many analysts said values the AOL Internet unit at almost zero," Reuters reported on April 22. The company had said in March that it would take a staggering $54 billion charge to reflect just how much the value of the combined company had been reduced since the deal was announced more than two years before.

There was little doubt by this point that, indeed, the deal had been a disaster. Moreover, Levin's dream of a hyper-connected, *Jetsons*-style AOL Time Warner, full of synergies and explosive growth, had failed as well, the product of a short-lived era when it looked like technology could solve everything. The long-term engineering of his departure insured that Levin wouldn't have to deal with the fallout, however, and other people, Pittman included, would have to figure out what to do with the company.

INDEX